Potent Brews

D1554248

East African Studies

Potent Brews

A Social History of Alcohol in East Africa
1850–1999

Justin Willis

Senior Research & Development Associate
History Department
University of Durham

The British Institute in Eastern Africa

in association with

James Currey
OXFORD

Ohio University Press
ATHENS

E.A.E.P.
NAIROBI

Fountain Publishers
KAMPALA

Mkuki na Nyota
DAR ES SALAAM

The British Institute in Eastern Africa
10 Carlton House Terrace
London SW2Y 5AH
& P.O. Box 30710
Nairobi

in association with

James Currey Ltd
73 Botley Road
Oxford
OX2 0BS

Ohio University Press
Scott Quadrangle
Athens, Ohio 45701

East African Educational Publishers
Mpaka Road/Woodvale Grove
P.O. Box 45314
Nairobi

Fountain Publishers
P.O. Box 488
Kampala

Mkuki na Nyota
P.O. Box 4205
Dar es Salaam

1 2 3 4 5 06 05 04 03 02

British Library Cataloguing in Publication Data
Willis, Justin
  Potent Brews: a social history of alcohol in East Africa, 1850-1999. - (Eastern
  African Studies)
  1. Drinking of alcoholic beverages - Africa, East - History - 19th century 2.
  Drinking of alcoholic beverages - Africa, East - History - 20th century 3.
  Alcoholic beverages - Social aspects - Africa, East 4. Africa, East - Social
  conditions - 19th century 5. Africa, East - Social conditions - 20th century
  I. Title
  394.1'3'09676'0904

ISBN 0-85255-471-0 (James Currey Cloth)
      0-85255-470-2 (James Currey Paper)

Library of Congress Cataloging-in-Publication Data
Willis, Justin
  Potent brews: a social history of alcohol in East Africa, 1850-1999/ Justin Willis.
    p. cm. -- (Eastern African stusdies)
  Includes bibliographical references and index.
  ISBN 0-8214-1475-5 (cl : alk. paper) -- ISBN 0-8214-1476-3 (pbk. : alk. paper)
    1. Alcoholism--Africa, East--History. 2. Drinking of alcoholic beverages--
  Africa, East--History. 3. Alcohol industry--Africa, East--History. I. Title. II.
  Eastern African Studies (London, England)

HV5646 .W55 2002
394.1'3'09676--dc21   2002075510

ISBN 9970-02-298-9 (Fountain Publishers Paper)

Typeset in 9/11pt Baskerville
by the British Institute in Eastern Africa
Printed and bound in Great Britain
by Woolnough, Irthlingborough

Contents

v

Abbreviations

AG	Attorney-General
BEA	British East Africa Protectorate
CNC	Chief Native Commissioner
CS	Chief Secretary
DC	District Commissioner
DO	District Officer
EABL	East African Breweries Limited
HDA	Hoima District Archives
IJAHS	*International Journal of African Historical Studies*
JAH	*Journal of African History*
KANU	Kenyan African National Union
KBL	Kenya Breweries Limited
KNA	Kenya National Archives
LNC	Local Native Council
MP	Member of Parliament
OiC	Officer in Charge
PC	Provincial Commissioner
PRO	Public Record Office
RHO	Rhodes House Library
SAB	South African Breweries
SHP	Southern Highlands Province
SNA	Secretary for Native Affairs
SoS	Secretary of State for the Colonies
TANU	Tanganyika African National Union
TBL	Tanganyika/Tanzania Breweries Limited
TNA	Tanzania National Archives
UNA	Uganda National Archives

Note on Political & Administrative Terminology

At the end of the nineteenth century, East Africa was divided into three administrative portions. The area which is now (more or less) modern Uganda became the Uganda Protectorate; the area of modern Kenya became the British East Africa Protectorate, which was retitled Kenya Colony in 1920; and the area of modern Tanzania became German East Africa, being restyled Tanganyika Territory in 1920. In 1965, following the formal unification of Tanganyika and Zanzibar the previous year, the new state adopted the name Tanzania. In this text I have tried so far as possible to avoid anachronisms in the use of these terms.

Through the colonial period, district administration was in the hands of district officers and district commissioners, who were usually subordinate to provincial commissioners. In Kenya these titles were retained at independence (after the brief experiment with regional government in 1964).

Glossary

busaa	grain beer (Kenya)
chang'aa	locally-distilled liquor (Kenya)
ebihotoole	part of a batch of liquor reserved for the chief or king (Uganda)
enguli	locally-distilled liquor (Uganda)
fumu (pl. *mafumu*)	(in Rungwe) adviser or counsellor to the chief
gongo	locally-distilled liquor (Tanzania)
haragi	locally-distilled liquor (Uganda)
kangara	a strong grain beer (often with sugar added)
kibuga	the royal capital in Buganda
kikao (pl. *vikao*)	drinking gathering (Tanganyika/Tanzania)
kilabu (pl. *vilabu*)	club, a drinking place (Tanganyika/Tanzania)
kimpumu	millet beer
ekirabo (pl. *ebirabo*)	club, drinking place (Uganda)
Katikiro	senior minister of Bunyoro Kingdom
komoni	maize beer (Tanganyika/Tanzania)
kwe[e]te	maize beer (Uganda)
malwa/marwa	term used of various fermented liquors, usually grain-based (Uganda)
masaza	county chiefs (Uganda)
mlafyale (pl. *balafyale*)	chief (Rungwe)
Mukama	(as title) King of Bunyoro
mnazi	palm wine
moshi	locally-distilled liquor (Tanganyika)
pombe	grain beer (used as generic term for all kinds)
tembo	palm wine
wananchi	citizens
waragi	locally-distilled liquor

List of Maps, Tables, Figures & Illustrations

Acknowledgements

This research and writing of this book were made possible through the help and kindness of many people – so many, in fact, that in retrospect it seems extraordinary that the project was ever completed. In trying to list all I may neglect some, but some attempt must be made. So, with apologies to all not mentioned by name: I must express my gratitude first of all to John Sutton, Keith Hart and John Lonsdale, without whose initial support and interest this research would never have begun; and to Charles Ambler, whose advice and encouragement helped create the project. For their work in the field, I must thank Rahab Nyangena, Daniel Lekanaiya, Jonathan Ololoso and Jacob Mayiani in Kajiado; Charles Asumwisye, Anthony Ntupwa and Sunday Tuntufya in Tukuyu; and Solomon, Joseph and Enid Turumanya, Margaret Rwabugahya, Rogers Musinguuzi and Sarah Kyalisiima in Hoima. Mark Bearn, Naomi Mason and Felicitas Becker all gave willingly of their time and energy.

The research was conducted with the permission of the National Council for Science and Technology in Tanzania; the Uganda Council for Science and Technology; and the Office of the President in Kenya, and I should like to thank Professor Henry Mutoro, Dr Ephraim Kamuhangire, Dr Paul Msemwa, Dr Nestor Luanda and Professor Isaria Kimambo for lending their support and encouragement to the project. The assistance of the staff of the national archives in Kenya, Tanzania and Uganda is gratefully acknowledged, as is that of the administration of Rungwe, Kyela, Kajiado and Hoima districts. A number of people in the formal drink industry were kind enough to share their knowledge and advice: thanks to Charles Rasugu and Chris Ondito of KBL; Daniel Niemandt and Wilfred Mwingiza of TBL; Henry Rudd of Nile Breweries and Mr Sentamu of Uganda Distillers. Many academics also shared knowledge, and offered advice and encouragement along the way: thanks to Nici Nelson, Rosemary McNairn and Nite Baza Tanzarn.

A great many kind people extended hospitality during the research: the Fathers at Lenkisem Mission; Sandy Baldwin and Melvin Woodhouse; Charles and Lucy Asiimwe; Rev. and Mrs George Kasangaki; Bishop Wilson Turumanya and his family; Mrs Freda Katuramu; Roo and Simon Woods; John de Coninck and Grace Natoolo; Frank and Chrissie Atherton; Paul Lane and Skye Hughes; the Family Health Project in Mbeya District; the Diocese of Bunyoro-Kitara; David Schoenbrun and Kearsley Stewart; David Edgar; Jenni and Mike Russell; and Joe Cockerill.

In trying to turn inchoate thoughts into writing, I have been grateful (as always) for the comments of John Iliffe and Andrew Roberts, and also at various times to David Anderson, Deborah Bryceson, Richard Waller, Shane

Doyle and Paul Lane, as well as various anonymous reviewers; and most of all to Margo Russell, who helpfully crossed out much of an early draft. In Nairobi, Innocent and Jane Mwangi played a crucial role in processing data and in the technical work on the book; Gilbert Oteyo produced the maps. At the African Studies Centre in Cambridge and at the Department of History in Durham I have been fortunate enough to find myself amid supportive colleagues; I should like to thank all at both institutions. This research was funded by a grant from the Economic and Social Research Council (ref R 000 23 7019); their support is gratefully acknowledged. So too is the support of the British Institute in Eastern Africa, without which this work would have been impossible.

And thanks most of all to Susan, Morris, Vuli and Malia, for coming along with me.

Durham

Introduction

Ambiguous power

Drink, drunkenness & society

Today the changes in beer parties are very many and generally they
are cause for anxiety. All sorts of strong drinks are made for sale. Most
men and women, boys and girls, drink anything any day at any time
and anywhere. The consequences are clear to everyone.
M.B. Nsimbi, 'Village Life and Customs in Buganda', *Uganda Journal*,
201(1956), 27-36

I think everyone will agree that it is most degrading to the whole
community for a white man to be unable to control his consumption of
liquor in front of the natives.
L. Lea-Wilson, letter to the *Uganda Herald*, 2 March 1917

[the] consumption of illicit liquor [is] a major cause of poverty, mental
instability, ill health, irresponsibility and immorality in society . . . people
who take [illicit liquor] fall prey to immoral practices and forget about
their families.
T. Misoi, Kenyan Member of Parliament, quoted in the *Daily Nation*, 1
September 1989

When you get drunk, you do bad things.
Ernest Bandaro, Kasasa, Hoima

When they talk about alcoholic beverages, people talk about proper
behaviour, and about the well-being of society as a whole. In the practice of
drinking, the unspoken rules of behaviour – who may drink with whom,
and when – reflect and reproduce a whole set of assumptions about status
and propriety. It has been said that alcohol is the dye of the social sciences,
for it reveals patterns of behaviour, authority and interaction.[1] Yet alcohol
is more than dye; for it participates in the very processes which it helps to
reveal. And, as Akyeampong has pointed out, alcohol's relationship with

---

[1] Troy Duster, cited in S. Barrows and R. Room, 'Introduction', 1, in S. Barrows and R. Room
(eds.), *Drinking: Behavior and Belief in Modern Society* (Berkeley, CA /Los Angeles, CA/London,
1991), 1-28.

ideas of proper behaviour is complex partly because alcohol is a thing desirable in itself, as well as being a cultural resource in the making and arguing of power.[2]

Drinking crises?

[Drinking] in those times was good. Nowadays it is bad.[3]

Many people in East Africa today, asked about the consumption of alcohol, will express a sense that there is a kind of drinking crisis. People, they argue, used to drink well: 'Men and women would drink wisely, and in a relaxed way. They used mostly to drink at night, so that when the men got drunk the women would take them to sleep. In the past women kept themselves safe, they would never drink a lot, they were good.'[4]

But people now drink badly, and that this drinking reflects – and is responsible for – wider social problems of disorder and disease.[5] 'In the past alcohol was good, and people would be happy with it, but today's alcohol has made people stupid and sick and they have lost their morals.'[6] 'These days it is too much, people are drinking so much more than in the past . . . Today you find children and women take alcohol which was unheard of in the past.'[7]

There is a not insubstantial literature on alcohol in Africa which draws on this kind of discourse and identifies drinking as the cause of social ills; alcohol, far from being the innocent dye of the social scientist, is the venom of modernity coursing unstoppably through the veins of its helpless victim.[8] Such analyses – often, as Ambler and Crush drily note, 'clothed in scientific language as certain in tone as it is devoid of fact' – suggest that small-scale, pre-industrial societies were characterized by 'integrated' drinking, which was essentially problem-free and associated with a minimal level of harm, in terms of damage to individual health or the well-being of society as a whole.[9] And expressions of concern on what one writer calls the

---

[2] Emmanuel Akyeampong, *Drink, Power and Cultural Change: A Social History of Alcohol in Ghana, c.1800 to Recent Times* (Portsmouth, NH/Oxford, 1996), 15.

[3] Interview (Int) Nya29a, 3.

[4] Int Nyoro10a, 8.

[5] Int Nya3b, 5; Nya40a, 1

[6] Int Nyoro33a, 5.

[7] Int Nyoro11a, 4.

[8] B. Hutchinson, 'Alcohol as a Contributing Factor in Social Disorganization: the South African Bantu in the Nineteenth Century', in M. Marshall (ed.), *Beliefs, Behaviors and Alcoholic Beverages. A Cross-cultural Survey* (Michigan, 1979), 340; V. Beckman, *Alcohol. Another Trap for Africa* (Orebro, 1988). More seriously than either of these rather crude works, one detailed study of drink in a Zambian society seems to identify alcohol as an agency of social decline: E. Colson and T. Scudder, *For Prayer and Profit. The Ritual, Economic and Social Importance of Beer in Gwembe District, Zambia, 1950-82* (Stanford, CA, 1988).

[9] C. Ambler and J. Crush, 'Alcohol in Southern African Labor History', in J. Crush and C. Ambler (eds.), *Liquor and Labor in Southern Africa* (Athens, OH/Natal, 1992), 9; Marshall, *Beliefs, Behaviors and Alcoholic Beverages*, 451-7.

'alcoholization' of Africa often imply not only that drinking has changed –
which is very evidently the case – but more importantly that the amount of
alcohol consumed, or the incidence of 'alcoholism' has increased very
greatly.[10]

But expressions of anxiety over drinking are not new. If 'integrated'
drinking is marked by consensus and a lack of concern over drink, there is
little evidence that it ever existed in East Africa. One might argue that
drinking was *always* better in the past: one scholar inspired by the 'integrated'
model drew a contrast between unproblematic banana-wine and dangerous
distilled spirits in 1960s Buganda, presumably unaware of earlier intense
debates in Buganda over the dangers of banana-wine drinking.[11] Nor is
anxiety over drinking a particularly East African, or twentieth-century,
phenomenon. 'It is easy to see the consequences of widespread drunkenness',
wrote Engels, of what he perceived as an increasing consumption of drink,
'the deterioration in personal circumstances, the catastrophic decline in
health and morals, the breaking up of homes'.[12] Later nineteenth-century
French commentators feared that their countrymen were physically
shrinking because they drank so much;[13] in the 1970s (at a time of historically
relatively low levels of alcohol consumption) much concern was expressed
over drinking in the United Kingdom.[14] Perceived increases in the volume
of alcohol consumed are often perceived to be linked to – and productive of
– disorders of society.[15] This goes beyond Horton's celebrated argument
that drinking reveals the degree of insecurity within a society;[16] the literature
suggests that 'integrated' drinking binds societies together, and that the
end of such drinking pulls them apart.

In part, those who talk of a drinking crisis are concerned simply with
volume: they suggest that the amount of alcohol which people drink in
East Africa has increased very greatly over the last century, and adduce

[10] J. Curto, 'Alcohol in Africa: a Preliminary Compilation of the Post-1875 Literature', *Current
Bibliography on African Affairs*, 21 (1989), 3-31; Robert G. Carlson, 'Haya Worldview and
Ethos: An Ethnography of Alcohol Production and Consumption in Bukoba, Tanzania'
(PhD, Illinois at Urbana-Champaign, 1989), 366-7; N. Miller and R. Yeager, *Kenya: the
Quest for Prosperity* (Boulder, CO/San Francisco, CA/Oxford, 1990), 91.

[11] M. Robbins, 'Problem Drinking and the Integration of Alcohol in Rural Buganda', in
Marshall, *Beliefs, Behaviors and Alcoholic Beverages*, 362-74; compare with Nsimbi, 'Village
Life and Customs', 29-30; and with *Uganda Notes*, June 1913. The *Uganda Notes* piece, of
course, argued that in the past banana-wine drinking had been unproblematic.

[12] F. Engels, *The Condition of the Working Class in England* (trans. W. Henderson and W. Chalmer),
(Oxford, 1958), 143.

[13] J.-C. Sournia, *A History of Alcoholism* (trans. N. Hindley and G. Stanton) (Oxford, 1990), 98-
9, 107.

[14] J. Spring and D. Buss, 'Three Centuries of Alcohol in the British Diet', *Nature*, 270 (Dec.
1977), 567-71.

[15] Brennan has shown how the Parisian bourgeoisie expressed their anxiety over the social
pretensions of their inferiors through criticisms of their drinking: T. Brennan, 'Social
Drinking in Old Regime Paris', in Barrows and Room, *Drink: Behavior and Belief*, 61-86.

[16] D. Horton, 'The Functions of Alcohol in Primitive Societies: A Cross-Cultural Study', *Quarterly
Journal of Studies on Alcohol*, 4 (1943), 199-320.

fearsome statistics in support of this assertion.[17] But such statistics have little meaning, for they refer to the consumption of bottled beers, wines and spirits. The bald statistic that 'beer drinking' in Kenya increased by 247 percent in 25 years tells us nothing about overall alcohol consumption since – as this book will suggest – by far the bulk of alcohol consumed in East Africa has always been and still is taken in the form of traditional, or 'informal sector', beverages.[18]

Such arguments on increased drinking are anyway bedevilled by a basic lack of information: in Africa, even more than in Europe, this is an area 'beset with partisans and starved of statistics'.[19] We have absolutely no idea of how much alcohol was consumed in East Africa in the nineteenth century, though we have the impressionistic accounts of a number of travellers. Some suggest sobriety; others describe widespread drinking, and drunkenness: 'Pombe-brewing, the chief occupation of the women, is as regular here as the revolution of day and night, and the drinking of it just as constant', observed Speke, and he alleged that the people of Karagwe were in a 'constant state of inebriety'.[20] Burton wrote of the people of Ujiji that 'they are never sober when they can be drunk', and referred to life on the Indian Ocean coast as 'a continual scene of drumming, dancing and drinking'.[21]

There is just as little real information for most of the twentieth century; and the little we know about East African alcohol consumption in recent years suggests that in per head terms, it is unremarkable by international standards. Internationally, comparative consumption is usually measured in terms of absolute alcohol – that is, the actual amount of ethanol contained in the alcoholic beverages which people consume. Twenty litres of an average beer at 5 percent ethanol by volume would be 1 litre of absolute alcohol; 3 litres of brandy at 33 percent ethanol by volume would also be 1 litre of absolute alcohol. In 1978, Kenyan consumption was estimated at 7.7 litres of absolute alcohol per head of the over-15 population, or less than 4 litres per head of the total population.[22] That compares with an international

---

[17] Some remarkable statistics circulate: one suggests that 'alcohol consumption' in Kenya increased by 105 percent in three years, 1979-82: 'Alcoholism in Kenya', *Daily Nation*, 26 Aug. 1983. See also S. W. Acuda, ' International Review Series: Alcohol and Alcohol Problem Research. East Africa', *British Journal of Addiction*, 80 (1985), 121-6.

[18] The 247 percent figure was, according to the Kenyan press, supplied by the World Health Organization: 'Drinking Soars in Third World', *Daily Nation* (1 May 1985). At present, probably about 80 percent of the alcohol consumed in East Africa is made in the 'informal sector': see Part 3, below.

[19] B. Harrison, *Drink and the Victorians: The Temperance Question in England, 1815-72* (London, 1971), 22, citing the unnamed authors of a British sociological report of 1935.

[20] J. H. Speke, *What Led to the Discovery of the Source of the Nile* (London, 1967 (1st edn 1864)), 354; *idem, Journal of the Discovery of the Source of the Nile* (London, 1969 (1st edn 1863)), 215.

[21] R. F. Burton, *The Lake Regions of Central Africa* (2 vols)(New York, 1961 (1st edn London, 1860)), II, 69 and I, 35.

[22] J. Partanen, *Sociability and Intoxication: Alcohol and Drinking in Kenya, Africa and the Modern World* (Helsinki, 1991), 47.

average of around 5 litres of absolute alcohol per head of total population.[23] My own, very rough, estimates for consumption in 1997-8 suggest figures of about 8 litres per head of the adult population in Tanzania, and only around 5 litres in Uganda. In 1980, French consumption was 20.6 litres per head of the over-15 population; UK consumption in 1996 was around 6.1 litres per head of the over-16 population.[24]

This is not to deny the genuine problems, directly related to alcohol, which exist in East Africa at an individual level; or to understate the dangers which are associated with heavy drinking. But we really have no evidence that the volume of liquor consumed per head is rising rapidly, or at all. There is, on the other hand, ample reason to argue that people have been, and are, faced with profound and urgent challenges to their well-being which come from other directions; that such challenges became more acute in the late twentieth century; and that arguments over the very nature of drinking have been and are involved in central debates over power and authority which occur in the context of these challenges. Ambler and Room have both argued that models of 'integrated drinking' have served as a means for anthropologists and historians to reify and idealize other societies.[25] This book explores how, for people across East Africa, talking about 'proper' drinking, and contrasting past drinking with present drinking, have been ways of arguing about proper behaviour within their own societies. That this has been such an important way of arguing about the present reveals the importance of ideas of drunkenness, proper drinking behaviour and temperance in the making of authority.

Being drunk: culture, physiology & disinhibition

They only made alcohol to make themselves happy.[26]

All the languages which I have come across in East Africa have terms to describe the condition of people who have consumed an intoxicating beverage; 'being drunk' is a distinct and distinctive state, and it is expected that behaviour will manifest this distinction. Alcohol, one man told me,

---

[23] World Bank Group Note on Alcohol Beverages, March 200, paragraph 2.4: citing draft World Health Organization report.

[24] Sournia, *A History of Alcoholism*, 57; UK figure extracted from the official Household Survey, which gives mean adult consumption as 10.7 units of alcohol per week. In the 1930s, Platt recorded that the 156 inhabitants of a village in Nyasaland drank 4,000 gallons of beer a year: which would give a consumption per head of 4 litres of absolute alcohol, assuming a modest alcoholic strength of 3.5 percent v/v: B. Platt, 'Biological Ennoblement: Improvement of the Nutritive Value of Foods and Dietary Regimens by Biological Agencies', *Food Technology*, 18 (1964), 68-76.

[25] C. Ambler, 'Alcohol and Disorder in Precolonial Africa', Boston University African Studies Centre Working Paper No. 126 (1987), 2-3; R. Room, 'Alcohol and Ethnography: a Case of Problem Deflation?', *Current Anthropology*, 25 (1984), 169-80.

[26] Int Nyala, 3.

'makes you a man';[27] another said that alcohol 'can make you do things you wouldn't [otherwise] have done'.[28] That alcohol makes people more adventurous – socially, and sexually – is widely accepted.[29] It is also generally believed that alcohol can make people 'happy': when I enquired why people drink, a Ugandan man said, with some amusement, 'Doesn't it make people happy?'[30] A man in Tanzania drew chuckles from bystanders with a similar comment.[31] The desirability of drinking is often understood precisely in the light of this motivation to individual enjoyment. These assumptions are fundamental to people's understanding of why people drink – and of why their drinking matters.

A discussion of the consequences of these two assumptions – that drink changes behaviour, and that people drink at least in part to be 'happy' – requires that these East African debates over 'being drunk' be set in the context of a wider, and prolonged, debate over the nature of drinking in human societies. Humans all over the world have been using intoxicating beverages for a very long time and have contrived to make these beverages from a remarkable range of ingredients in an extraordinary variety of ways, and the near-ubiquity of alcohol as a drug of choice has caused widespread debates.[32]

In Europe, the nineteenth-century discovery that all intoxicating beverages (at least all the ones that could be drunk with any degree of safety) contain the compound called ethanol[33] became central to a particular understanding of drunkenness which has informed much of the international debate on drunkenness.[34] In this, drunkenness is the product of a predictable interaction between a chemical and the human body, which manifests itself as a collapse of inhibition resulting from a sort of disabling of the brain.[35] Alcohol, the new knowledge suggested, acted first upon the cerebral cortex. 'Self-control is one of the highest functions of the brain', it was argued; alcohol destroyed self-control, deadened 'all higher thought',[36] and 'dethrone[d], be it ever so slightly, the crown of evolutionary progress'.[37] It has been suggested that the development of this particular idea of alcohol as the enemy of self-control was linked to the emergence of a new idea of

[27] Int Nyoro33b, 7.

[28] Int Nyoro36b, 6.

[29] Int Nyoro25c, 4; Nyoro42a, 1.

[30] Int Nyoro4c, 5.

[31] Int Nyala, 3.

[32] P. Ghalioungui, 'Fermented Beverages in Antiquity', in C. Gastineau, W. Darby and T. Turner (eds.), *Fermented Food Beverages in Nutrition* (New York/San Francisco, CA/London, 1979), 3-19.

[33] Since the body metabolizes this quite rapidly, which it cannot manage with other alcohols: R. Ylikahri and K. Eriksson, 'Physiological and Medical Problems Associated with Excessive Alcohol Intake', in G. Birch and M. Lindley, *Alcoholic Beverages* (Barking/ New York, 1985), 183-200.

[34] E. Todhunter, 'A Historical Perspective on Fermentation Biochemistry and Nutrition', in Gastineau *et al.*, *Fermented Food Beverages*, 83-97; Ambler and Crush, 'Alcohol in Southern African Labor History', 4.

[35] H. Emerson, *Alcohol. Its Effects on Man* (New York/London, 1934), v-vi.

[36] V. Horsley and M. Sturge, *Alcohol and the Human Body* (London, 1907), 111, 115.

[37] C. Weeks, *Alcohol and Human Life* (London, 1929), 18.

the nature of order in modern industrial society;[38] and it is clear that this was a discourse which was easily inserted into European debates on non-European populations, who were assumed to be lower in the order of social evolution, less civilized, and therefore in particular danger from the temporary derangement of the cerebral cortex which alcohol wrought.[39]

The physiological approach to intoxication has remained widespread, and dominant in the work of natural scientists,[40] yet the notion that intoxication is explicable simply in pharmacological terms – that ethanol produces disinhibition – has become increasingly problematic. Partly this is simply because, despite the energies of research scientists, there are still many uncertainties about the metabolization of alcohol and the way that it affects the nervous system.[41] Physiologically, it is well attested that ethanol consumption has a biphasic effect on the nervous system: that is, it does two different things, depending on how much is consumed.[42] Small amounts lower the excitation threshold, making people more sensitive to stimuli; larger doses have the opposite effect of raising the excitation threshold. It is by no means clear how this biphasic response fits with the idea of disinhibition: is this the result of reducing or raising the excitation threshold? Are the intoxicated disinhibited because they are more excitable; or because they are worse at processing information, less responsive to stimuli received from the world outside, and therefore more likely to miss or misread the signals of approval and disapproval from others which normally guide and constrain our behaviour? Such questions dog all this research into the pharmacological properties of ethanol: no predictable relationship has been established between human behaviour and the state of the nervous system. As one report cheerfully states, 'very little is known about the C[entral] N[ervous] S[ystem] effects of alcohol on people who drink alcohol in socially normative ways'.[43]

This question has become particularly urgent since the work of anthropologists has consistently demonstrated cultural patterns of difference in the behaviour of the intoxicated. In a seminal book, Macandrew and Edgerton directly challenged the whole notion of disinhibition as an inevitable, pharmacological consequence of drinking, and argued that

---

[38] H. Levine, 'Presenter's Comments', 164-7, in R. Room and G. Collins, *Alcohol and Disinhibition: Nature and Meaning of the Link* (Rockville, MD, 1981).

[39] Ambler and Crush, 'Liquor in Southern African Labor History', 6.

[40] The theory that alcohol influences particular parts of the brain first is no longer widely advocated, though it was persistent: see for example L. Greenberg, 'Alcohol in the Body', *Scientific American* (Dec. 1953), 86-90.

[41] S. Wood and J. Mansfield, 'Ethanol and Disinhibition: Physiological and Behavioral Links', in Room and Collins, *Alcohol and Disinhibition*, 4-23; readers with a taste for truly complicated and inconclusive scientific literature might like to try the papers in M. Gross (ed.), *Alcoholic Intoxication and Withdrawal*, Vols IIIa and IIIb (New York/London, 1977).

[42] H. Wallgren and H. Barry, *Actions of Alcohol* (2 vols)(Amsterdam/London/New York, 1970), I, 254-5; Wood and Mansfield, 'Ethanol and Disinhibition'.

[43] E. Parker and E. Noble, 'Drinking Practices and Cognitive Functioning', in Gross, *Alcoholic Intoxication and Withdrawal*, IIIb, 377-88; also P. Dreyfus, 'Effects of Alcohol on the Nervous System', in Gastineau *et al.*, *Fermented Food Beverages*, 341-57.

drunken comportment is actually culturally defined. Intoxication does not lead to the suspension of inhibition, for even in drink we are bound by rules, acting in ways that are defined by societal expectations.[44] A number of studies have amplified this basic point: drunken behaviour varies over time, and from one society to another.[45] In response, scientists have conducted studies which purport to show a degree of cross-cultural similarity and genetic difference in behaviour and mood changes, as well as in the measurable physiological changes associated with alcohol consumption: seeking thus to show that genetics, not culture, determine how intoxication is manifested.[46]

The study of drunkenness has thus become almost a parody of the relationship between academic disciplines: while natural scientists pour energy into devising evermore complicated experiments and theories on metabolic pathways and neural membranes, social scientists perceive such efforts as irrelevant and devote themselves instead to cross-cultural issues which demonstrate at perhaps unnecessary length the unexceptionable truth that drunken comportment does vary. The work of many social scientists goes beyond this observation of difference: a great deal of the writing on cross-cultural drinking has been informed by a functional approach, which argues that drink performs a particular role in each society.[47] This is, in essence, the argument of Macandrew and Edgerton concerning the disinhibition effect in European society: drunkenness is 'time out', a temporary escape from the rules of society which vents frustration and functions, ultimately, to contain potential disorder.[48] As Ambler and Crush have argued, the cultural approach to drunkenness has often led on to the assumption that because drunkenness is a cultural construct, drink must perform a certain function in society – and therefore that people drink in pursuit of that function.[49] Such functional drinking is presented as an entirely consensual and unproblematic aspect of a society which is a cohesive and interdependent unit: it is non-pathological, and is 'woven into the fabric of social existence', as Marshall puts it, in a typical metaphor.[50] Drinking

---

[44] C. Macandrew and R. Edgerton, *Drunken Comportment: A Social Explanation* (London/Accra/Lagos, 1970), 87-8.

[45] Marshall (ed.), *Beliefs, Behaviors and Alcoholic Beverages*.

[46] J. Hull and C. Bond, 'Social and Behavioral Consequences of Alcohol Consumption and Expectancy: A Meta-analysis', *Psycological Bulletin*, 99 (1986), 347-60; J. Ewing, B. Rouse and E. Pellizzari, 'Alcohol Sensitivity and Ethnic Background', *American Journal of Psychiatry* (Feb. 1974), 206-10.

[47] See for example M. Douglas (ed.), *Constructive Drinking: Perspectives on Drink from Anthropology* (Cambridge, 1987).

[48] Macandrew and Edgerton, *Drunken Comportment*, 166-9.

[49] Ambler and Crush, 'Alcohol in Southern African Labor History', 7-8. The functional implication is rather easily drawn from, for example, W. Madsen and C. Madsen, 'The Cultural Structure of Mexican Drinking Behavior', in Marshall (ed), *Beliefs, Behaviors and Alcoholic Beverages*, 38-54.

[50] Marshall, 'Introduction', 3, in Marshall (ed.), *Beliefs, Behaviors and Alcoholic Beverages*; Macandrew and Edgerton, *Drunken Comportment*, 53, offer a similarly uncomplicated vision of pre-colonial drinking in a number of societies.

behaviour, it is argued, is 'learned':[51] a term neatly redolent of knowledge gravely imparted and respectfully received.

Taken to an extreme, this functional argument implies that drinking in pursuit of 'purely personal enjoyment' is inherently pathological and 'disruptive'.[52] It is hard to reconcile this rather grimly purposive idea of functional drinking with the pursuit of pleasure and the belief in a changed condition of the individual which underlie East African ideas of drinking; surely, people's personal experience of a sometimes euphoric moment of intoxication must play a central role in understanding the use of alcohol.[53] Nor, in East Africa at least, is the idea of unquestioned (integrated) drinking which lurks behind such functional approaches one which sits easily with an evident record of prolonged debate over drinking.

In this book, it is argued that, in East Africa at least, drink has always been regarded with ambivalence. Drunkenness is a cultural construct, but this has never made drinking 'functional, or 'integrated'. People drink, and have drunk, for pleasure, and most people have considered drinking to be a desirable activity. The particular importance of drinking lies in debate over how the effects of drinking on human behaviour should be manifested, and managed. There are two aspects to this. There is a euphoric moment of intoxication which provides occasion for people to idealize their role in society and relationship with others; but they also have a wary sense of the dangers, as well as the pleasures, that altered states may bring. Karp, discussing the drinking of the Teso in Uganda in the 1960s, presented the beer-party as a moment of tension, as well as pleasure. People drank for pleasure, and they conceived of this pleasure as lying in sociability; thus they created an ideal of amity and corporation amongst those who drank. Yet at the same time they were aware of the possibilities of danger inherent in the drinking, for they were aware that in reality human relationships fell short of their ideal of amity.[54] Heald has made the same argument of drinking among the Gisu, also in Uganda; the beer drink was a focus of communality, but also of jealousy and violence.[55] In both these cases, the ideal of behaviour commonly created was one of sociability amongst those who were permitted to drink; but sociability was not always the drinking ideal. As will be argued below, drinking patterns developed in which the moment of drinking idealized an exclusive, sometimes even solitary, pattern of behaviour.[56]

[51] Macandrew and Edgerton, *Drunken Comportment*, 87.

[52] B. Hutchinson, 'Alcohol as a Contributing Factor', 340; K. Fukui, 'Alcoholic Drinks of the Iraqw. Brewing Methods and Social Functions', *Kyoto University African Studies*, 5 (1970), 125-48.

[53] E. Jellineck, 'The Symbolism of Drinking. A Culture-Historical Approach', *Journal of Studies on Alcohol*, 38 (1977), 849-65. Hull and Bond argue that the effect of alcohol in improving mood seems homogeneous across studies: 'Social and Behavioral Consequences', 351.

[54] I. Karp, 'Beer Drinking and Social Experience in an African Society: An Essay in Formal Sociology', in I. Karp and C. Bird, *Explorations in African Systems of Thought* (Bloomington, 1980), 83-115.

[55] S. Heald, *Controlling Anger. The Sociology of Gisu Violence* (Manchester/New York, 1989), 7.

[56] Partanen has argued for the importance of the drinking experience in constructing an ideal of experience, but suggested that in all cultures this lies always towards 'sociability'; J. Partanen, 'Towards a Theory of Intoxication', in Room and Collins (eds.), *Alcohol and Disinhibition*, 34-6. He develops the idea of 'sociability' further in Partanen, *Sociability and Intoxication*.

Drinking, then, is a moment of pleasure, in which people create ideals of behaviour, and at the same time a moment of danger in which those ideals are most threatened. This is why – in East Africa and elsewhere – there have been prolonged debates over who may drink, and how much and under what circumstances; and it is why such debates must be set in the context of wider debates over the nature of authority.[57]

DRINKING TOO MUCH

A physiological understanding of intoxication creates its own notion of temperance; responsible drinking is a matter of body weight and grams of ethanol consumed. Cultural notions of drunkenness set different parameters for argument over drinking, which are rooted in issues of authority: whose ideals of society should be celebrated in the moment of drinking? And which groups were most dangerous, most likely to throw up alternative patterns of behaviour? Akyeampong has argued the importance of the 'indigenous ethic of temperance' as a field for debate over drink and power, and much of this book will be concerned with what were, in effect, debates on temperance.[58]

In East Africa, for much of the period under discussion, this was not principally a matter of the amount consumed; it was a question of the age and gender of the drinker, and the presence or absence of particular categories of person – as in colonial Zimbabwe, it was 'joint drinking' which challenged ideas of propriety.[59] For women to drink with men, or for young men to drink with old, was often argued to be undesirable. There was also an idea of temperance amongst those who perceived themselves as drinkers, but this was a matter largely of avoiding obvious helplessness in front of younger men, or in-laws. On the other hand neither the time of drinking, nor the place, were concerns of popular discourse before the 1960s; one of the most prolonged struggles over drink in the colonial period, and after, was the intermittent campaign by the state to create an idea of temperance which deprecated morning drinking.[60] And while physiology defines excess through reducing all drinks to the standardized measure of ethanol content, people in East Africa argued ideas of temperance which defined particular kinds of drink as being entirely inappropriate for certain groups. In the 1920s and 1930s many African men regarded bottled beer as profoundly dangerous (and many Europeans similarly categorized such drink as dangerous to Africans); from the 1950s, a new model of temperance developed which characterized traditional fermented liquors as unsuited for workers and the waged; throughout the twentieth century, many have regarded distilled liquor as particularly problematic. Notions of temperance

---

[57] P. Morgan, 'Alcohol, Disinhibition and Domination: A Conceptual Analysis', in Room and Collins, *Alcohol and Disinhibition*, 405-20.

[58] Akyeampong, *Drink, Power and Cultural Change*, 15.

[59] M. West, 'Liquor and Libido: "Joint Drinking" and the Politics of Sexual Control in Colonial Zimbabwe, 1920s-1950s', *Journal of Social History*, 31 (1997), 645-67.

[60] For British official attempts to impose a new separation between drink and leisure in the nineteenth century, see Harrison, *Drink and the Victorians*, 40.

made arguments about how drink endangered society, just as idealizations of drunken behaviour made arguments about what society should be. Drinking practice was not integrated, or functional; it was the product of arguments over temperance and drunkenness. And the very nature of drink ensured that drinking practice – and discourse – was central to the making of authority.

DRINK, POWER & AUTHORITY

In arguing the central role which alcohol has played in the making of power, this book relies on a particular formulation of the relationship between power and authority; following the tradition gently mocked by Arens and Karp, it must 'begin anew with a preliminary clarification of the intended usage.'[61] In the classic formulation derived from Weber, power is the ability of one party in a relationship to achieve their objectives, regardless of resistance; and authority is socially accepted power. Power is thus conceived of as a relationship, or rather the potentiality of a relationship – as it is by Giddens when he defines it as 'the capability of actors to secure outcomes where the realization of these outcomes depends upon the agency of others', predicated upon what he calls allocative and authoritative resources, or the ability to command things and people.[62] This book builds on an argument advanced by Akyeampong which, in effect, reverses the direction of the argument, and seeks to understand how control over people and things is the product of people's understandings of power; that is, it casts power not as a relationship, but as a cultural construct, which is in itself the subject of contest. Power is the perceived direct ability to transform, or coerce, or otherwise compel change – 'the cultural notions that compel the many to accept the direction of a few – or suffer the presumed consequences';[63] while authority is the ability to command (rather than directly compel) others, and to control resources.[64] Power can take many forms: direct physical force, control over rain or sickness, the ability to seduce or reproduce. Power lies behind authority: it is the sanction, or incentive, on which authority rests. Forms of power, and therefore potential sources of authority, are multiple, in any society: unequally distributed, but by no means easy to monopolize.

Effective power cannot always be in evidence: soldiers cannot be everywhere, all the time; the rain does not fall every day. Authority which rests on the immediate exercise of power is transient and local, for power is easily exhausted and compromised. Such local, transient kinds of authority abound in any society; yet they are overshadowed by authority which relies on the unquestioned assumption of power. Following Bourdieu's argument of the central importance of practice in creating 'structuring structures', this book argues that these assumptions are reproduced through patterns

---

[61] W. Arens and I. Karp, 'Introduction', in W. Arens and I. Karp (eds.), *Creativity of Power: Cosmology and Action in African Societies* (Washington and London, 1989), xi.

[62] A. Giddens, *Central Problems in Social Theory* (London, 1979), 91-101.

[63] Arens and Karp, 'Introduction', xv.

[64] Akyeampong, *Drink, Power and Social Change*, 12-14.

11

of behaviour and speech which constantly evoke power, for they are suffused with its assumptions.[65] It is through practice and discourse that power assumes its 'capillary' nature, pervading behaviour.[66] This may be true of behaviour in a wide variety of situations, in which assumptions of power are revealed by deference, by avoidance, by abstaining from doing certain things or always doing other things. Kneeling in the presence of certain people is a rather evident way of reproducing notions of power; employing elaborate circumlocutions to avoid using the name of an in-law or spilling a few drops of beer or palm wine before drinking are less obvious. These may not be consciously understood as arguments; they are patterns of behaviour whose significance may well not even be considered by those who follow them. That is their strength; therein lies the unquestioned nature of the assumptions of power which they reproduce, and the dominance of the authority derived from those assumptions of power.

Yet no assumptions of power are ever completely unquestioned. In what people do, and in what they say they do, there is room for negotiation. And, as will be argued in this book, there is often a considerable discrepancy between what they do and what they say they *should* do. Feierman has argued that discourse is itself a sort of practice, evidencing and recreating a 'practical consciousness',[67] and there also exists some room for contest and negotiation within the domain of practice: by its very nature, practice is not perfectly reproduced, time and time again, but involves a series of forgettings and misrememberings which allow practice to be remade in novel ways, sometimes without overt debate.[68] The crucial issues in understanding power, authority and the changing nature of both are then those which relate to the possibilities of change and contest in everyday discourse and practice.

LADEN PRACTICE, LADEN DISCOURSE

The process of making authority feeds back into itself. Assumptions of power lend authority to certain people whose behaviour and action therefore become of especial significance: their discourse and practice are particularly laden. This is central to what Giddens calls the 'recursive' character of society: it is the means of reproducing the system which contain the seeds of change.[69] Those who possess authority may translate the nature of the power on which their authority ultimately rests, through remaking assumptions of power. This is not an instant process, nor is it by any means necessarily concerted, and it may involve a period of intense debate and fracture within the dominant group. Yet it is a process which regularly occurs; so that even where forms of power are debated, authority may rest continuously with a particular group.

[65] P. Bourdieu, *Outline of a Theory of Practice* (Cambridge, 1977), 72.
[66] S. Feierman, *Peasant Intellectuals. Anthropology and History in Tanzania* (Madison, WI, 1990) 19, quoting Foucault.
[67] Feierman, *Peasant Intellectuals*, 31.
[68] C. Kratz, *Affecting Performance. Meaning, Movement and Experience in Okiek Women's Initiation* (Washington, DC, 1994), 308-19.
[69] Giddens, *Central Problems in Social Theory*, 18, 70.

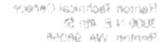

12

In his theorization of shifts in discursive fields among the Shambaa, Feierman has addressed this issue of unequal participation in the remaking of assumptions of power, by arguing that conjunctures of circumstance may make the discourse of certain individuals particularly influential: these are the figures whom he characterizes as 'intellectuals', a group distinct from but somehow connected with those who wield authority in society.[70] The idea that some people's discourse – and practice – may carry especial weight is central to any understanding of the reproduction of power, and this theorization may be expanded to suggest a series of conjunctures which bestow upon certain individuals an especial influence in the remaking of assumptions of power.

First, as suggested above, the existing nature of authority inevitably gives some people a particular influence. Second, not all sources of power are equally efficacious; the actual capacities of sources of power may change over time; and new kinds of power may appear. In the twentieth century the influence which certain individuals brought to the remaking of power was radically affected by the development of bureaucratic colonial states possessing a coercive power which, while weak when measured against the pretensions of these states, was unprecedented in most East African societies. Third, discourse and practice in certain social situations is inherently more influential: though, of course, these circumstances may change over time. In their discussion of the definition of ritual, the Comaroffs fall back on the notion that ritual is that which evokes the transcendent: by which presumably they mean a set of values and understandings which transcend particular, immediate circumstances.[71] As Glassman has argued, the importance which people attach to these moments of special significance ensure that discursive struggles over them are 'a major forum for the contestation of power'.[72] Everyday behaviour and speech may reproduce power; but certain social moments may be of especial importance in that reproduction.

DRINKING AS DAILY RITUAL

The notion that certain situations are of especial importance in reproducing assumptions of power returns us to alcohol. In East Africa, people drink in pursuit of pleasure; and in drinking moments, they idealize social relationships, yet are especially aware of the potentially disruptive effects of deviation from those ideals. In East Africa, as elsewhere, the 'hidden transcripts' of resistance may become suddenly extant in drink;[73] and drink may promote patterns of speech and behaviour which challenge the

---

[70] Feierman, *Peasant Intellectuals*, 17-27.

[71] J. and J. Comaroff (eds.), *Modernity and Its Malcontents: Ritual and Power in Post-colonial Africa* (Chicago, IL/London, 1993), Introduction.

[72] J. Glassman, *Feasts and Riot: Revelry, Rebellion and Popular Consciousness on the Swahili Coast, 1856-1885* (London/Athens, OH/Nairobi, 1995), 23; Akyeampong, *Drink, Power and Cultural Change*, 21.

[73] J. Scott, *Domination and the Arts of Resistance: Hidden Transcripts* (New Haven, CT/ London, 1990), 121.

13

assumptions of power.[74] This is not *why* people drink – it is not simply that 'time out' is a Gluckmanesque ritual of rebellion which serves to maintain order by allowing temporary inversion.[75] People drink for pleasure; but in their drinking they are acutely aware of the particular significance of their behaviour, and that of others, while drunk. If ritual is that which evokes the transcendent, then it might be argued that drinking is always in some sense ritual; and, of course, drinking has very often been drawn into the practice of circumcisions, funerals and offerings precisely because it *does* evoke the transcendent, and confers a particular status on a social moment.

And so drinking moments have always been viewed with ambivalence; as moments of pleasure and of the expression of social ideals, but also as moments of social danger. '[Alcohol] was something very precious, which kept the life of people good', one man told me;[76] but the corollary of this was the view, expressed by another informant that alcohol 'spoils the culture of the people, and morality itself. A drunkard doesn't care about what he say, whether it is shameful or not.'[77] Drinking can make and unmake authority, for it leads the dominant as well as the subordinate out of the normal paths of behaviour, and may make fools of them; undoes the assumptions of power that are recreated in their everyday speech and behaviour. In drink, the ambiguity of power is manifest. The notion of drinking crisis turns this ambiguity into an historical trajectory from 'integrated' drinking to immoral drinking, yet drinking has always contained both possibilities: 'Alcohol is good', one man told me, 'and on the other hand it's bad.'[78]

The research

This book is about the whole of East Africa, but the interviews and observation which provided much of the research material were conducted in only three limited areas: Kajiado District in Kenya; the Rungwe and Kyela districts of Tanzania; and Hoima District in Uganda. The choice of the field areas was largely arbitrary, though there was a degree of systematic selection: one from each country, to cover the considerable variety of the colonial and post-colonial political structures; one very agricultural area, another very pastoral; one sizeable pre-colonial political entity, another determinedly stateless. But other choices would have yielded different contrasts, and this work is inevitably limited by this simple issue of fieldwork location, though in its pretensions to regional coverage it does make extensive use of archival

---

[74] P. Clark, *The English Alehouse: A Social History, 1200-1830* (London/New York, 1983), 340; S. Barrows, 'Parliaments of the People: The Political Culture of Cafés in the Early Third Republic', in Barrows and Room, *Drink: Behavior and Belief*, 87-97.

[75] As is argued, with the drunk cast as a kind of 'jester', in P. Dennis, 'The Role of the Drunk in an Oaxacan Village', in Marshall, *Beliefs, Behaviors and Alcoholic Beverages*, 54-64.

[76] Int Nyoro10a, 7.

[77] Int Nyoro2c, 3.

[78] Int Nyoro9c, 3.

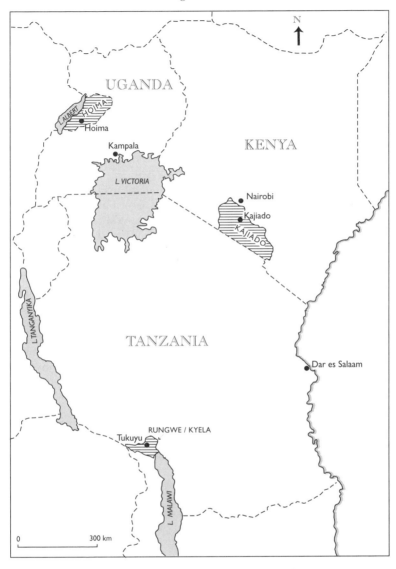

Map 1 *East Africa, showing field areas of case studies*

and secondary material. Yet there are remarkable similarities, amongst the three field sites and with other societies in the region: patterns of difference also emerge, yet the similarities are more striking. So too, in fact, are the similarities in government policies, particularly in the period when the whole region was under British rule; debates over alcohol policy revealed broadly similar concerns – even obsessions – amongst officials in each of the UK's East African territories. In many ways, these similarities carried over to the early years of independence, and there remained a striking similarity in public rhetoric across the region. Overall, this is far more a story of similarity than it is of differences.

TALKING HISTORY

This linkage between power and drink suffuses all that has been said or written about drinking in East Africa; to such an extent, indeed, that the interpretation of accounts of the past becomes a central problematic of any attempt to write a drinking history of the region. The written record of the African past is dominated by the words of Europeans, mostly men, whose observations and comments tell us much about their own concerns and anxieties; and in particular, about their ambivalent attitude to change and tradition, which will be a central theme of one part of this book. Nineteenth-century adventurers and explorers expressed their frustrations over the chronic problem of transporting baggage and their fears of the dreadful possibility of sudden violent onslaught, by moaning about the drunkenness of their porters and characterizing all who challenged them as 'drunkards';[79] white missionaries, in the nineteenth century at least, were prone to see alcohol as a spiritual danger: 'Drinking parties are usually intimately connected with devil worship.'[80]

The attitudes of colonial officials to alcohol were often less censorious, and revealed how many administrators, uncomfortable with the notion of colonialism as a transforming mission, idealized particular models of authority and patriarchy in African societies which they feared were threatened by change. Lugard argued against any attempt to ban – or even to license, in most areas – traditional fermented beverages;[81] but called for prohibition of novel spirituous liquors, the introduction of which might mean that (as one Foreign Office mandarin had put it in the 1880s) 'the process of civilization and demoralization may be simultaneous'.[82] 'Demoralization' was the bogey for many colonial administrators, and alcohol

[79] H.M. Stanley, *Through the Dark Continent: Or, the Sources of the Nile Around the Great Lakes of Equatorial Africa and Down the Livingstone River to the Atlantic Ocean* (2 vols)(New York, 1988(1st edn 1879)), I, 136; F. Jackson, *Early Days in East Africa* (London, 1930), 218; Speke, *What Led to the Discovery*, 267; V. L. Cameron, *Across Africa* (London, 1885)(1st edn 1876), 186, 230, 234-5.

[80] A. Lloyd, *Uganda to Khartoum. Life and Adventure on the Upper Nile* (London/ Glasgow, 1907), 75.

[81] F. Lugard, *The Dual Mandate in British Tropical Africa* (Edinburgh, 1923), 602-4.

[82] Quoted in S. Miers, 'The Brussels Conference of 1889-90', in W. Gifford and P. Lewis (eds.), *Britain and Germany in Africa. Imperial Rivalry and Colonial Rule* (London/ New Haven, CT, 1967), 83-118.

was a focus for fears on this subject. Yet – partly because alcohol was drawn into their idealizations, and their demonization of certain kinds of change – their accounts often reveal frustratingly little about the actual practice of drinking in African societies. Still less do they record African discourses about drink, except in very particular circumstances, where Africans with access to officials used alcohol as a discursive tool in their presentation of their own role as a bulwark of tradition against the threat of modernity: as when Chief Sapi, in Tanganyika, urged the banning of bamboo wine as it was having 'a most deleterious effect on tribal life'.[83]

For African discourses, then, we must rely either on oral evidence collected in the present, or on very scanty documents indeed. The documents are skewed, as well as rare: newspapers had little African input before the 1950s, and even once writers and editors were Africans, they were usually men, based in urban areas with a particular kind of formal education. The archives have hardly any material after the early 1960s, and throughout they record the words of a distinct group of African men which have been preserved. As this book will argue, those whose words were most likely to be preserved in the record have been those who have had the most hostile attitude to drink in general, and to 'traditional' liquor in particular: in 1934, a British official had already noted that 'a class of native exists which despises the native beer'.[84] Complex transformations served to make 'traditional' alcohol the focus of considerable hostility from those who were most likely to find their views recorded; in a very real way, attitudes to traditional liquor set the elite off from others: such as the Bwana Aryakomishna of independent Tanzania, who shied away from the prospect of drinking banana wine with his village relatives and gave them bottled beer instead.[85]

For these reasons, much of the data for this book was collected through qualitative oral interviews – and to a much lesser extent through quantitative questionnaire work. Through an extensive series of oral interviews, I tried to step outside the confines of the elite discourse of the colonial and post-colonial period, and to both hear the voices and – in so far as this is possible – to see the practice of others who were involved in the reproduction of power, and in the exercise of and challenges to authority. Yet retrospective discourse on drinking is also implicated in the reproduction of assumptions of power, in ways which pose obvious and immediate problems for those who seek to follow the history of drinking. The drinking of beer at work-parties is one example of this. In the 1990s, accounts of past drinking in some societies – in Rungwe, for example – identify the feasts which followed work-parties as a central feature of past drinking. Neighbours who had helped cultivate land for planting, or assisted in the harvest, would be rewarded with beer and food; and would in turn host their own work-parties

[83] Hutt, Ag. District Officer (DO) Iringa, to PC Iringa, 16 Apr. 1934, TNA 77/26/12.
[84] E.C. Baker, 'Memorandum on the Social Conditions of Dar es Salaam', 35 (1931) (in African Studies Centre Library, Cambridge).
[85] G. Ruhumbika, *Village in Uhuru* (London, 1968), 151.

when they needed to mobilize labour.[86] It is a picture of drinking redolent of reciprocity and non-commercial relationships, evoking the famous English maxim cited by Harrison 'with beer one thanks; with money one pays';[87] and people – women and men – rue the decline of this kind of drinking and the modern rise of commercial drinking and casual farm labour paid with cash, which they cannot afford.[88]

Yet this neat summary of change conceals a more complex history of dispute, in Rungwe at least. The giving of beer was apparently an early twentieth-century innovation, in work-parties for men: previously, cooked food, rather than beer, would be the centre-piece of the feast.[89] This innovation was presumably associated with the attempt by male household heads – some of them affected by the migration for work by their sons – to increase the cultivation of millet, the crop which they controlled.[90] Preparing land for planting was a men's task, while women sowed and weeded.[91] Men lightened their burden by calling on male neighbours for clearing work, and rewarded them with beer – the product of their wives' labour; meanwhile, women continued with other labour-sharing arrangements for weeding and domestic tasks, which did not necessarily involve beer.[92] The cultivation work-party increased the demand for women's labour, giving them extra beer to make and extra fields to tend: 'He [husband] was the one who would invite people to dig . . . then I would make beer for them to drink.'[93] The decline of the work-party was indeed associated with the rise of the selling of beer, as women tried to insist on selling their product, and escape the new burdens which 'thanking' with beer placed on them in the colonial economy.

Yet now women – feeling themselves multiply disadvantaged by the commercial economy – join men in talking with regret of this change: even a woman who had herself long relied on selling liquor for her income shared in this discursive creation of an ideal past of work-party drinking.[94] People always use the past to argue over the present, often in very conscious and informed ways: alcohol's particular role in the reproduction of power makes talking about past drinking a particularly important way of talking about the present. Accounts of past drinking are (and have been) arguments about present power and authority, closely involved in the reproduction of power

---

[86] Ints Nya4a, 1; Nya5b, 1; Nya26a, 1.
[87] Harrison, *Drink and the Victorians*, 56.
[88] Ints Nya26c, 1; Nya31a, 3-4; Nya32b, 2.
[89] M. Wilson, *Good Company. A Study of Nyakyusa Age-villages* (Boston, MA, 1963 (1st edn Oxford, 1951)), 51.
[90] Several informants identified the beer work-party as something called by men, to deal with men's tasks: Ints Nya4a, 3; Nya11a, 5; another remembered clearly that beer was only offered in cultivation work-parties – that is, those in which men were involved: Nya31b, 2. By the 1940s, some wealthier men were also using work-parties to clear land for planting other crops, like beans or potatoes, for cash sale: Nya41a, 2. Men's control over millet will be discussed further below: see IntsNya5b, 2; Nya9b, 1; Nya19b, 2.
[91] Ints Nya31a, 2; Nya33a, 2.
[92] Int Nya26c, 1-2.
[93] Int Nya41a, 2.
[94] Ints Nya19a, 2; Nya4a, 3.

in modern society. When a man says, 'I saw our fathers, when they were drinking; they would drink silently. Even if you were passing, you would not know that there were people there; not like nowadays, when people are noisy', he is not offering a casual observation; he is making a very direct argument about changing ideals of behaviour.[95] Alcohol is the focus of intense debate, now, as it was in the past, and what that says about drinking in the past. People argue their often contradictory attitudes to the present; just as in their arguments in the past, they struggled for control of the future.

DRINKING HISTORY

The book is divided into four main parts. The first discusses the nature of power and authority in pre-colonial East Africa; it argues that in the mid-nineteenth century authority generally rested with elder men, and that a widely held principle of elder men's power over well-being underpinned this authority against the challenging powers of sex and violence. Alcohol was prominent in the patterns of behaviour which reproduced the assumption of men's power over well-being. The authority of individual elder men was challenged, and there were subversive counter-currents in practice but, except in the interlacustrine, the principle of elder men's power was largely unchallenged. In the later nineteenth century, however, changing circumstances gave new power to men who recruited younger men as warriors, challenging with violence the ritual power of elders. Elder men's authority was increasingly challenged as new forms of drinking practice emerged which did *not* reproduce the assumption of elder men's power over well-being.

Colonial rule offered new resources and opportunities to elder men; the control of drink was one of the shared concerns around which their alliance with the colonial state turned. But, as the second part of this book argues, the alliance was a tenuous one: colonial attitudes to the control of alcohol changed, and African debates over accumulation and tradition were increasingly fractured. By the end of the colonial period the trade in locally-made alcohol had become a major field of entrepreneurship for African men – and, in a more marginal way, for many women – while European officials had shifted their concerns on drinking to the specific issue of illicit distillates. These became the focus for European and elite African anxieties about uncontrolled change in the social world which existed beyond the confines of state patronage and control, and the threats which this posed to the kinds of material development which those associated with the state sought to promote. Development has, indeed, been the dominant theme of post-colonial history, and itself became a form of power, evoked in a distinctive pattern of drinking and temperance which is considered in the third part of the book. The state derived authority from its claims to provide development, just as elder men derived authority from a claim to control well-being. And, in the latter years of the twentieth century, the decline of the state and an accelerating pattern of social inequality and marginalization

[95] Int Nya21a, 3.

produced a widespread pattern of economic and moral diversification, as people seek to draw on multiple sources of income and multiple ideas of authority to survive and maintain their well-being in an increasingly difficult world. It is this diversification which is the subject of the last section of the book, which examines the current sense of drinking crisis and the increasingly intense, fractured and internally contradictory debates over what proper drinking is, and how far modern practice has departed from it.

Throughout this history, alcohol has retained an ambiguous quality: making and unmaking power, the perquisite of those who wield authority, and their undoing. In 1954, a Tanzanian newspaper published a poem by a teacher entitled 'Drunkards and their Ways', composed of alternating stanzas on the contradictory nature of alcohol:

> The drunkard is weak, and has no respect
> The drunkard has no sense, he knows not what he says,
> The drunkard is rude, he passes by without grace
> This is how I see them, drunkards and their stories.
>
> The drunkard is wise, he drinks and is satisfied,
> The drunkard is generous, and people love him
> The drunkard has no anger, and loves to dance
> This is how I see them, drunkards and their stories.[96]

Wise and weak; generous and rude: alcohol lies at the heart of the contradictions of power.

[96] 'Walevi na Visa Vyao', Ramadhani Mwarukwa, Middle School, Utete, in *Mambo Leo*, May 1954.

One

What are you drinking?
Alcohol & innovation
1850–1999

In the presence of certain strains of yeast and some bacteria, sugar will break down to produce ethanol and carbon dioxide. This is the process called alcoholic fermentation. In the nineteenth century Guy-Lussac rendered as a formula this ancient mystery: $C_6H_{12}O_6 \rightarrow 2C_2H_5OH + 2CO_2$.[1] Such scientific reduction makes an important point: the same basic process lies behind the production of all alcoholic beverages. But this basic homogeneity is more apparent to the chemist than to the casual observer. Sugar, yeast and bacteria may come from many different sources, and the alcoholic strength of the final product, as well as the appearance and the taste of the beverage, will vary, depending on how much sugar is available, how much of it is converted and what else is in the raw materials from which the sugar is derived. Alcoholic drinks can be made from an extraordinary range of ingredients, and take an immense range of forms: people all around the world have shown remarkable ingenuity in the production of intoxicating beverages. It is customary to talk of 'traditional liquor'; yet it is important to emphasise that, in East Africa as elsewhere, people have been very willing to innovate in what they drink and how they make it. The basic simplicity of the fermentation process, and the readiness with which the materials for it may be obtained, has encouraged innovation and eclecticism. As a background to the study of power and authority which follows, this chapter offers an introduction to the changing techniques of alcohol production in East Africa over the last 150 years.

In doing so, it seeks to stress a simple point: there have been two contrasting themes in debates on the physical nature of locally-made alcoholic beverages in East Africa. One has presented former drinks, as well as former drinking patterns, as superior to contemporary ones. Particular alcoholic beverages have been condemned as undesirable innovations – stronger, less nutritious – just as the circumstances of their consumption are denounced. An opposing tendency has cast all 'traditional'

---

[1] Todhunter, 'A Historical Perspective on Fermentation Biochemistry and Nutrition'.

drinks as dangerously unhygienic. Each of these approaches makes an argument about change through reference to the changing physical nature of alcoholic beverages; and each underestimates the degree of experimentation which has long characterized the manufacture of liquor in East Africa.

Sweet things

Sugar for fermentation can be obtained from a variety of sources. Honey, of course, is very rich in sugar; and so is the ripe fruit of certain plants, such as some species of banana. The sap of certain plants is very sugary: notably, of course, sugar-cane, but also some varieties of bamboo. The growing flower spathes of a number of species of palm tree may be tapped to provide a very sugary liquid. Generally speaking, those drinks produced from sap or juice are, in English, called wines; that prepared from honey is called mead or hydromel. As important as any of these, however, is the production of sugar from the starch content of grains. If a grain of sorghum, or maize or barley is induced to sprout, by soaking it in water, it will produce diastatic enzymes which turn the starch content of the grain into sugar. This is how plants grow, for the newly-produced sugar is available as an energy source for the growing shoot; but the same process can be used to produce sugar for fermentation.[2] Anyone can make sugar for fermentation by soaking grain and letting it sprout; this process of 'modifying' the grain is the basis of what European brewers call malting, and the beverages which result are called beers.[3]

TURNING SOUR

Natural sources of sugar are plentiful, and alcoholic fermentation may occur quite spontaneously because the organisms which encourage this process – yeasts and some lactic acid bacteria – are also very common, occurring in considerable abundance in many environments.[4] Sweet things turn sour easily, as sugar is turned to alcohol and associated processes produce lactic and other acids. It is widely supposed that fermentation was discovered quite independently by people in different parts of the world, precisely

[2] H.S. Corran, *A History of Brewing* (Newton Abbot, 1975), 12-13.
[3] Platt suggested that bacteria, rather than diastatics from the grain, were responsible for producing sugar: 'Biological ennoblement', 71. It was presumably such bacteria which were responsible for releasing sugar for fermentation in cassava, which was used to some degree for beer in the southeast of Tanzania: F. Fulleborn, *Das Deutsche Njassa- und Ruwuma-Gebiet* (Berlin, 1906), 412.
[4] Yeast is often considered to be the basis of alcoholic fermentation, but in certain conditions lactic acid bacteria, which are responsible for souring processes which in non-industrial production generally occur alongside alcoholic fermentation, may also produce ethanol: J. Taylor and S. Joustra, 'Sorghum Beer Technology' (2 vols) (University of Pretoria/CSIR, 1996), II, 1-2; also M.J.R. Nout, 'Aspects of the Manufacture and Consumption of Kenyan Traditional Fermented Beverages' (PhD, Wageningen, 1981), 48.

because it is such a simple and commonplace process. The very abundance of bacteria and yeasts may cause problems: while sweet things readily turn sour, they do not always do so in a way which leads to a palatable or intoxicating product. Not all fermentations are alcoholic, and even where they are, the resulting beverages may vary widely in strength and taste, depending not simply on the ingredients of the beverage, but on temperature, cleanliness of the vessel and other factors. Yeasts vary in their tolerance of ethanol, and some allow the process of fermentation to go on for longer than do others. The regular production of an alcoholic drink with any kind of consistency of taste or appearance requires some attempt to encourage the activity of particular yeasts and bacteria through the use of what is called an inoculum, a source of desirable organisms which will reproduce rapidly in the right environment and encourage the right sort of fermentation. Alcohol is easily made; but making it come out right each time is a little more difficult.

Stopping the processes of fermentation, and other associated changes, is sometimes more difficult than starting them; the success of industrial bottled-beer brewing lies in its ability to turn the bubbling mess of the ferment into a temporarily quiescent liquid which can be kept in a sealed container. Fermentation produces carbon dioxide, as well as ethanol, and simply putting a fermenting liquid into a closed container will cause the container to explode. And the multiple processes of bacterial multiplication and yeast growth also produce other gases and acids.[5] Fermented drinks are quickly made, and they spoil quickly; they become excessively acidic, then they cease to bubble, and become unpalatable.[6] Makers of fermented alcoholic beverages in East Africa have never really overcome this problem: their products cannot be kept in closed containers, and must be consumed quickly – mostly within a day or two – lest they spoil and are wasted.

Innovation & variety:
nineteenth-century drinks

In nineteenth-century East Africa, people exploited a great variety of sugar sources for the production of alcoholic beverages. There were regional patterns to this variation, with certain kinds of drink being particularly common in certain areas. But there were also considerable degrees of overlap, for many societies were familiar with two or more different techniques for making alcoholic beverages, and there was a clear willingness to experiment and change: the Meru apparently largely abandoned honey wine during the nineteenth century in favour of a banana-based liquor.[7] Such

---

[5] K. Steinkraus, 'Nutritionally Significant Indigenous Foods Involving an Alcoholic Fermentation', in Gastineau *et al.*, *Fermented Food Beverages in Nutrition*, 47.

[6] Nout, 'Aspects of the Manufacture and Consumption', 9, 45, 86.

[7] P. Puritt, 'The Meru of Tanzania: a Study of Their Social and Political Organization' (PhD, Illinois, 1971), 35.

innovation could precipitate arguments over who should be responsible for the actual physical production of alcohol, arguments which particularly ran along gender lines. Generally speaking, people made their usual alcoholic beverage from the most plentiful source of sugar available; and – again, generally speaking – the less work the process of production involved, the more likely it was to be taken over by men.

The scale of production was also similar across the region. There might be a degree of co-operative labour; Speke described an apparently shared cooking of a mash for beer in a Tanzanian village, and sugar-cane for alcoholic beverages might be pounded by groups of women.[8] But even where stages in the process were shared, the overall production was the work of a single woman or man, sometimes assisted by their offspring. Production was small-scale, and the production of alcohol was not a specialized activity.[9] There was a limited production of alcohol for exchange, but there is no evidence that any individual concentrated on this: the production of alcohol was in most societies restricted by gender, but – that crucial restriction aside – it was open to all.

GRAIN BEER

The millet grain is put in a container like a basin. They mix it with water to make the millet wet. After one day the millet starts germinating, after four days the germinating millet is dried. After drying, it is ground into flour. The flour is again mixed in enough water just to wet the flour. When you taste it the smell is of beer. From there you put it in a big pan and fry it. You dry it with fire. When you taste again, the taste is of beer. Then you dry it in the sun. After drying it you transfer it to a pot and mix it with water. You get more flour and add it on. After that it is already beer. To drink it, it is mixed with hot water and taken through a straw with a filter.[10]

In much of the region, grain beers were the staple intoxicating beverage: made mostly from finger millet, though sorghum and bulrush millet were used, as was maize in the areas where this had become established as a crop.[11] Mostly, these beers were made in a two-stage process, which involved the soaking, sprouting and grinding of one batch of grain which would then be kept (in a container which through constant re-use became a store of desirable yeasts and bacteria) to begin fermentation. A second, larger batch of grain would be sprouted and ground; and the first batch would then be added to it; fermentation of the whole would then take place quite rapidly. There were considerable variations in this process, however, as a result of prolonged experimentation

[8] Speke, *What Led to the Discovery*, 355; C. Cagnolo, *The Akikuyu: Their Customs, Tradition and Folklore* (Nyeri, 1933), 110-11.

[9] Even in Bunyoro, where exchange of alcoholic beverages was commonplace, observers stressed that production was a domestic affair: G. Schweinfurth, *Emin Pasha in Central Africa* (trans. R. Felkin) (London, 1888), 77.

[10] Int Nyoro6b, 3.

[11] Nout, 'Aspects of the Manufacture and Consumption', 15, notes the continued East African preference for finger millet for malting.

1.1 *(above). Preparing millet beer
(i) Beer ready to drink*
1.2 *(right). Preparing millet beer
(ii) Germinated grain*
1.3 *(below) Preparing millet beer
(iii) Mixing ground flour*

and adaptation to differing temperatures and levels of humidity. The germinated grain, or malt, might be heated ('kilned'), which reduces enzyme activity but gives a darker colour and may encourage the souring processes of lactic acid fermentation; the second batch of grain may not be malted, but rather just soaked to encourage souring, and the mash of water and malted grain, the mash, was sometimes directly cooked, and sometimes not.[12] One account of Iraqw brewing suggests that no malted grain was used; presumably, the grain was saccharified by bacteria.[13] Across the region, making grain beer was almost always a task of women, and it involved the processing – grinding, as well as soaking – of a large amount of grain, as well as the additional physical labour of mixing the flour with hot water.[14]

This was more demanding than it might sound, for grinding took place by hand with a rubbing stone, and the mixing itself was hard, for the mixture was thick and resistant. The final product was also thick, for there was usually no straining to remove the grain.[15] It would be drunk through straws, with hot water being added, as drinking went on, to make this possible. Speke noted, with characteristic disdain, that '[t]his fermented beverage resembles pig-wash, but is said to be so palatable and satisfying – for the dregs and all are drunk together – that many entirely subsist upon it.'[16] Burton, more cheerfully, noted that 'strangers, who at first dislike it exceedingly, are soon reconciled by the pleasurable sensations to which it gives rise'.[17]

Brewing was also a task with particular uncertainties, for the modification of the grain could go wrong; if it were not soaked for long enough, or for too long, or if it were damaged in harvesting or threshing, the grain would not produce a sufficient quantity of the enzymes required to turn starch to sugar, and the brew would not work. Similarly, any abrupt variation in the acidity of the brew, or the temperature, could ruin the process.[18] These uncertainties compounded the basic unpredictabilities associated with yeast and bacteria strains; even if the brew did not simply fail (and mostly, it did not) then its strength could vary quite considerably. It is sometimes assumed that African grain beers were generally weaker than European bottled beers, but this is by no means necessarily the case, and tests on 'traditionally' produced grain beers show a considerable range of strength, though most brews would lie at the lower end of this range.

[12]   Platt: 'Biological ennoblement', 70-1; H. Ddirar, 'The Art and Science of Merissa Fermentation', *Sudan Notes and Records*, 57 (1976), 115-29; Taylor and Joustra, 'Sorghum Beer Technology', I, 20. While Speke described a vigorous heating of the mash in central Tanganyika, and practice in Bunyoro was similar, an account of traditional millet-beer making in the western highlands of Kenya suggests that the mash was not heated: Int Nyoro6b, 5; J. Peristiany, *Social Institutions of the Kipsigis* (London, 1939), 140-1. Current manufacture of what is considered to be 'traditional' millet beer among the Nyakyusa similarly involves no heating, and description of beer-making by a neighbouring group in the 1920s makes no mention of heating: D. Mackenzie, *The Spirit-Ridden Konde* (London, 1925), 129-30.

[13]   Fukui, 'Alcoholic Drinks of the Iraqw', 127-9, 132.

[14]   See for example Burton, *Lake Regions*, II, 286; Fukui, however, again offers an exception, suggesting that Iraqw men could brew grain beer: 'Alcoholic Drinks of the Iraqw', 129.

[15]   J. Grant, *A Walk Across Africa, or Domestic Scenes from My Nile Journal* (London, 1864), 85.

[16]   Speke, *What Led to the Discovery*, 355.

[17]   Burton, *Lake Regions*, II, 285.

[18]   Taylor and Joustra, 'Sorghum Beer Technology', I, 22-30.

Table 1.1 *Alcoholic content of various beverages, recorded as % ethanol by volume*

	Millet beer	*Maize beer*	*Banana wine*	*Sugar-cane*	*Palm wine*	*Bamboo wine*	*Mbege*	*Sugar ferment*	*Distillate*
Min.	2.3	2.7	2.0	4.6	4.5	5.1	3.3	4.3	21.0
Max.	8.5	8.1	11.0	5.2	7.8	5.5		8.3	44.0

Note: It should be noted that variations in temperature and microbial activity, availability of sugar and other factors will affect the alcohol content of any particular ferment; and also that the alcoholic strength of any ferment will increase in the first 48-72 hours after production. These figures therefore show only the maximal and minimal values recorded in various tests. They are derived from Govt Chemist to DC Njombe, 23 Apr. 1946, TNA 157 A2/8; tests performed by Tanzania Breweries Ltd on samples provided in 1997; D. Mosha, J. Wangabo and G. Mhinzi, 'African Traditional Brews: How Safe Are They?', *Food Chemistry*, 57 (1996); Mwesigye and Okurut, 'A Survey of the Production and Consumption'.

BANANA WINE

In the interlacustrine sweet varieties of banana formed the principal source of sugar for alcohol. There was no need for elaborate processing with bananas: their ripening was artificially stimulated through heating, but after that the process was relatively straightforward, for the juice of ripe bananas is 20-23 percent fermentable sugar.[19] The skins of the bananas would be removed, and the bananas would then be squashed, usually together with some fibrous agent such as spear grass to which the pulp of peel and fruit would adhere, leaving juice to run free.

> . . . the fruit is thrown into the 'lyato'[wooden trough], in which is also placed a quantity of fine dried grass of a particular kind. The bananas are now worked up by hand and pressed and squeezed through the grass till they become a thick creamy liquid. Water is then added, and the result is an intensely sweet and vapid liquor called 'mubisi'. This may be drunk by strict Mahometans and teetotal Europeans, but at best it is a bilious and unwholesome beverage. A malt is added to the 'mubisi' in the shape of a small fine grain, a kind of millet called 'mwemba'[sorghum]; the liquor is then strained off and left for twenty-four hours, when it is ready for use. If kept too long, it soon becomes sour; but when fresh it is a very refreshing and hardly intoxicating drink, unless taken in very large quantities, which unfortunately is usually the case.[20]

The squashing was by no means easy work, however; reducing a heap of bananas to a pulpy mass is hard work. The juice would then be collected

---

[19] P. Mwesigye and T. Okurut, 'A Survey of the Production and Consumption of Traditional Alcoholic Beverages in Uganda', *Process Biochemistry*, 30 (1995), 497-501.

[20] R. P. Ashe, *Two Kings of Uganda, or Life by the Shores of Victorian Nyanza* (London, 1970 (1st edn 1889)), 307-9; see also Burton, *Lake Regions*, II, 287; and S. Baker, *The Albert N'yanza. Great Basin of the Nile and Explorations of the Nile Sources* (2 vols) (London, 1962 (1st edn 1867)), II, 422.

1.4 *Treading banana wine, c. 1900.* (From the Hattersley Collection, Royal Commonwealth Society by permission of the Syndics of Cambridge University Library.)

into fermenting pots or troughs, and kept warm by covering;[21] within a few days, the yeasts and bacteria which survived in the fermenting vessel from one production to the next would have multiplied anew, encouraging fermentation which could give a beverage of a higher ethanol content than grain beers, and considerably less sour.

The production of this kind of alcohol did not lie simply, or even mainly, in the realm of women's work; a crucial element in this was the squashing of the bananas. Where they were squashed by hand this could be the work of women.[22] But they could also be squashed, or rather trodden, with the feet. This allowed them to be squashed without first being peeled (though in some cases bananas were peeled before treading[23]), and it allowed, too, the more rapid production of a large volume of juice: 'when they started making much that is when they started making beer with their feet'.[24] And this was very largely men's work. '[K]wete and *masohi* [maize and millet beer] are cooked and that is a work for the woman, and the *tonto* is for men because they use the legs to tread them and women are not allowed to do this.'[25]

---

[21] Grant, *A Walk Across Africa*, 158.
[22] Ints Nyoro37b, 5; Nyoro38a, 5.
[23] L. Mair, *An African People in the Twentieth Century* (London, 1934), 114.
[24] Int Nyoro33a, 8; Nyoro42a, 3.
[25] Int Nyoro1b, 4. This woman was talking of Bunyoro, but a similar transition was evident in Buganda, where Stanley, *Through the Dark Continent*, I, 301-2, mentions women as being the makers of banana wine by hand; but treading has been men's work: Mair, *An African People*, 114.

1.5 *Treading banana wine, 1998*

Only in Karagwe is there any evidence of women treading bananas in the nineteenth century.[26] Treading was quicker than squeezing by hand, but still hard work, as one observer noted: 'Perspiring considerably, the men, to prevent the perspiration from falling into the beer, wrap the forehead tightly around with dry fibre.'[27] The role of men in treading has been explained as a result of cultural preoccupations with the possibility of contamination by menstrual blood, but it also fitted into the overall pattern in which men dominated the less physically demanding tasks of production.[28] The fermentation of this kind of beverage hardly ever went awry, and so the labour of making it would almost always be rewarded.[29] It is possible that there was a twofold process of male encroachment on the manufacture of alcohol in parts of the interlacustrine. Banana wine displaced millet beer, over an extended period; then treading replaced squeezing to process bananas.[30]

---

[26] Grant, *A Walk Across Africa*, 158.

[27] C. Hattersley, *The Baganda at Home* (London, 1908), 103.

[28] For the idea of 'contamination', see Ints Nyoro10b, 7; Nyoro15b, 5; Nyoro38b, 5.

[29] Informants in Bunyoro suggested that the process was always successful, but problems with fermentation have been reported elsewhere: S. Whyte, *Questioning Misfortune. The Pragmatics of Uncertainty in Eastern Uganda* (Cambridge, 1997), 100.

[30] It is difficult to set precise dates to the increasing dominance of banana wine: Roscoe suggested that even in the early twentieth century, millet beer was more common in Bunyoro than was banana wine, and Grant suggested the prominance of millet beer at the Nyoro court in the early 1860s, but the accounts of Baker and Speke hardly support this: J. Roscoe, *The Northern Bantu. An Account of Some Central African Tribes of the Uganda Protectorate* (London, 1966 (1st edn 1915)), 72; Baker, *Albert N'yanza*, II, 319, 328; Grant, *A Walk Across Africa*, 295.

Around Kilimanjaro, bananas were also used in the production of alcoholic beverages, but this was a technically quite different process to that of the interlacustrine. These were peeled, cooked, starch bananas, and they were mixed with sprouted millet, the freed sugar from which formed the principal basis for fermentation: there is no study which reveals whether the diastatic enzymes released by the grain would also have had the effect of breaking down the starch in the bananas. This beverage, then, revolved around the sprouting and grinding of grain, and it was women's work;[31] it seems that it was generally lower in alcohol content than was the banana wine of the interlacustrine.

SUGAR-CANE & HONEY

The juice of sugar cane was easily fermented. But the extraction of this juice was by no means an easy task, since it involved either smashing the sugar cane in a mortar – sometimes a multi-holed log, for many women to share[32] – or grating it. Both processes were time-consuming and tiring, and they seem to have largely been the work of women, though in some societies, as among the Kamba, this task was performed by men.[33] Elsewhere in central Kenya, the production of beverages was divided, with women doing the physical labour of juice extraction while the men superintended the rather less tiring process of fermentation.[34] Fermentation simply involved keeping the juice in containers, in reasonably warm places; often an inoculum was used in the shape of the dried fruit of the sausage tree, or a fibrous root, which had previously been steeped in a fermented beverage and then dried.[35] The use of this kind of inoculum was distinctive to the societies of what are now central Kenya and northern Tanzania.

Honey was the other principal source of sugar used in nineteenth-century alcohol production, and was particularly common in central Kenya, especially where cultivated sources of sugar were not available, in dry areas and in forests. Making alcoholic beverages from honey was straightforward: the honey would be dissolved in water, an inoculum contained in a dried root added, just as was done with sugar-cane juice, and the mixture would be 'placed near a fire to ferment'.[36] But obtaining honey

---

[31] H. Johnston, *The Kilima-Njaro Expedition* (London, 1886), 175.

[32] L. Hohnel, *Discovery of Lakes Rudolf and Stefanie. A Narrative of Count Samuel Teleki's Exploring and Hunting Expedition in Eastern Equatorial Africa in 1887 and 1888* (2 vols) (London, 1968 (1st edn 1891)), I, 352.

[33] G. Lindblom, *The Akamba in British East Africa. An Ethnological Monograph* (Uppsala, 1920), 518-19.

[34] L.S.B. Leakey, *The Southern Kikuyu before 1903* (3 vols)(London, 1977), I, 284-5; Cagnolo, *The Akikuyu*, 110-11.

[35] Cagnolo, *The Akikuyu*, 111; Lindblom, *The Akamba*, 519; J.L. Krapf, *Travels, Researches and Missionary Labours During an Eighteen Years' Residence in Eastern Africa* (London, 1860), 312; H. Laswai, A. Wendelin, N. Kitabatake and T. Mosha, 'The Under-exploited Indigenous Alcoholic Beverages of Tanzania: Production, Consumption and Quality of the Undocumented "denge"', *African Study Monographs*, 18 (1997), 29-44.

[36] D. Storrs Fox, 'Further Notes on the Masai of Kenya Colony', *Journal of the Anthropological Institute*, 60 (1930), 447-65; W. Chanler, *Through Jungle and Desert. Travels in Eastern Africa* (London, 1891), 220.

1.6 *Extracting sugar-cane juice, c. 1900.* (From C. Hobley, *Ethnology of the Akamba.*)

was by no means easy; often this meant lengthy journeys and involvement in trading networks, particularly for those who lived in arid areas where bees were only active in certain seasons. Obtaining honey in this way was often the task of women;[37] and so the production of alcoholic beverages was often the work of women, although when men chanced to obtain honey they, too, might make alcohol from it.

TAPPING PALMS

All along the East African coast, and in inland areas where palms grew, palm wine was by the later nineteenth century the dominant beverage.[38] This was a remarkably easy beverage to produce; there was skill in climbing the tree and in cutting and binding the flower spathe in such a way as to ensure a steady flow of sap, but once the sap was collected the process was almost entirely self-driven. The exuding sap would probably be inoculated by fermentative agents on the flower spathe itself; it would anyway usually be mixed with a little sap that had already fermented.[39] Since the ambient

[37] Johnston, *The Kilima-Njaro Expedition*, 404.
[38] Krapf, *Travels, Researches and Missionary Labours*, 137, 140; C. New, *Life, Wanderings and Labours in Eastern Africa* (London, 1971 (1st edn 1873)), 85, 115.
[39] Nout, 'Aspects of the Manufacture and Consumption', 14.

1.7 *Tapping bamboo. The juice collects in the sections of stem which have been bent down*

temperature in areas where palms thrive is high, the fermentation proceeded rapidly, and was almost always successful; again, the availability of sugar ensured that this beverage could reach a strength of 7 or 8 percent alcohol by volume, after which it would rapidly become too sour to be palatable. The tapping and preparing of palm wine was a task for men.[40] Along much of the coast it was the coconut palm which was the principal source of palm wine, and this drove a vast expansion in palm planting in some areas from the later nineteenth century, particularly in the immediate hinterland of the Kenya coast.[41] Elsewhere, where coconut palms grew poorly and people tapped instead the rather less productive oil palm or doum palm,

---

[40] As it was elsewhere in Africa: see N. Ngokwey, 'Varieties of Palm Wine among the Lele of Kasai', in Douglas, *Constructive Drinking*, 113-21.

[41] T. Herlehy, 'Ties That Bind: Palm Wine and Blood Brotherhood at the Kenya Coast During the Nineteenth Century', *International Journal of African Historical Studies* 17 (1984), 285-308.

1.8 *Tapping a coconut palm. Note the bottle strapped on to collect the juice*

palm wine did not become the dominant beverage. Wine from other palms tends to be consumed when it is stronger, as the sap emerges more slowly, the containers take longer to fill, and the beverage therefore has longer to ferment.[42]

Watery beers & sugar:
twentieth-century fermented drinks

I don't know how *kangara* is made, but I think it is also made from pineapples [and] they cook it with tea leaves. You drink, it tastes sweet, but then you cannot even move. One day I drank it, and I enjoyed it, I was very hungry, but when it got me I said, "Eeh!" It wanted to come out again![43]

The spread of maize, cassava, rice and of certain varieties of bamboo; new mechanical processes for sugar-cane crushing and grain processing; the availability of granulated sugar and pineapples and tinned dried yeast have all inspired innovation in twentieth-century alcohol production. In a general way, the trend has continued to be one towards the use of the most easily

---

[42] Oil palms were tapped at Lake Tanganyika in the nineteenth century: Burton, *Lake Regions*, II, 59; the tapping of doum palms was reported from parts of the Kenya coast where there are no coconuts, in the twentieth century: Solicitor-General to PC Coast, 12 Jan. 1943, KNA BY/11/60. The explanation of the apparently greater strength of such wine was offered in Philip, Native Hospital Nairobi, to Paterson, Director Medical Services, 10 Dec. 1942, KNA BY/11/60.

[43] Int Nyoro16a, 4.

available sugar source (though commercial change has altered the definition of 'easily available' to a very great extent). But the associated nineteenth-century trend, of male dominance where labour requirements were reduced, has not been so straightforwardly maintained. As will be argued in the second part of this book – and as has been amply demonstrated by previous scholarship – alcohol has become an economic resource of extraordinary importance during the twentieth century, and direct control over the production processes has therefore taken on a new significance.[44]

Some nineteenth-century drinkers preferred their grain beer to be strained, so that it might be drunk from a cup rather than sipped from a pot.[45] During the twentieth century, this practice of serving 'watery' beer, as some called it, became increasingly common, spurred both by changing fashion and by the demands of a new cash market in alcoholic beverages: some people who paid wanted to know exactly how much they were getting for their money, and sellers thought watery beer more profitable: 'I realized the watery one had more money . . . we used to put in more water, so that it would be a lot.'[46] There is an easy argument to make about individualism here. The contrast between shared drinking from a communal pot with long straws and the single toper hunched meanly over his own little gourd is an evident one, and implies that commercialism pushed individual drinking and strained communality. And undoubtedly, where shared pots were the norm, separate pots did convey a simple message of dissociation.[47] But the significance of the shift was not a simple one. Not all the alcohol bought for cash was drunk from individual containers; beer could be sold in pots, to groups who shared it through straws. The individual pot of 'watery' beer could be passed around and shared; some who drank in non-commercial contexts preferred separate containers; Nyakyusa men drank their beer from individual containers, using short straws to do so, and Mijikenda palm-wine drinkers, a resolutely communal gerontocracy in many ways, had long drunk from individual containers, though they might pass these around.[48] But more importantly, there was always an ambiguity about the warm image of communality derived from sitting around the shared pot with straws, as revealed in the twentieth century by the fear of some that they would be poisoned by some substance placed in the

---

[44] For the importance of alcohol sale, see M. Mbilinyi, '"This is an Unforgettable Business": Colonial State Intervention in Urban Tanzania', in J. Parpart and K. Staudt (eds.), *Women and the State in Africa* (Boulder, CO, 1989), 111-29; N. Nelson, '"Women Must Help Each Other": The Operation of Personal Networks Among Buzaa Brewers in Mathare Valley, Kenya', in P. Caplan and J. Bujra (eds.), *Women United, Women Divided* (Bloomington, IN, 1982), 77-98; Carlson, 'Haya Worldview and Ethos', 347-59; T. Beidelman, *The Kaguru: a Matrilineal People of East Africa* (New York/ Chicago, IL/San Francisco, CA, 1971), 25-6.

[45] Burton, *Lake Regions*, II, 286; straining was recorded later in the nineteenth century, too: P. Kollman, *The Victoria Nyanza* (trans. H. Nesbitt)(London, 1899), 147.

[46] Int Nya23a, 4.

[47] As is implied in James' description of beer among the Uduk of Sudan, where merchants drank separately from their own containers: W. James, 'Beer, Morality and Social Relations Among the Uduk', 21, *Sudan Society*, 5 (1972), 17-27, 21.

[48] Int Nya27a, 2.

34

1.9 *Preparing maize beer (i) Brewing drums*

mouthpiece of their straw.[49] The fear of poisoning at a drinking party was a common one, even in the nineteenth century.[50] The move to (watery) beer does not simply show a collapse of supportive social relationships built around the beer pot.

It was particularly maize beers which were strained for drinking; and maize became the main ingredient for grain beers during the twentieth century.[51] Rice, another colonizing crop of the twentieth century, was also used for beer.[52] The use of maize was predicated on the development of mechanical processing: hand-hulling and grinding maize for beer was even more demanding than processing millet.[53] And mechanical techniques also imposed new cash costs on production: hulling and grinding cost money, rather than labour. Maize made it possible to make more beer, a little more easily, but it also introduced a cash cost for doing so. Grain beers have continued to be almost exclusively the preserve of women; but men have sometimes turned to this work, as in western Kenya where men made maize beer from the 1930s.[54]

---

[49] Heald, *Controlling Anger*, 181.

[50] Speke, *Journal of the Discovery*, 423.

[51] Partanen, *Sociability and Intoxication*, 79-80, gives a description and schematic representation of modern grain beer making; see also Nout, 'Aspects of the Manufacture and Consumption', 9.

[52] A. Culwick and G. Culwick, *Ubena of the Rivers* (London, 1935), 18, 228.

[53] Ints Nya3a, Nya4a.

[54] W. Sangree, *Age, Prayer and Politics in Tiriki, Kenya* (London/New York/Nairobi, 1966), 136. Some informants suggested to me that men make grain beer, nowadays, but I have never seen this: Ints Nyoro6b, 5, Nya38a, 3.

1.10 *Preparing maize beer (ii) Straining beer*

Twentieth-century maize beers have mostly involved new, and often prolonged, processes of heating or roasting, which serve to gelatinize the starch and so ultimately release more sugar for fermentation.[55] Other things being equal, this will make fermentation a little quicker, and the final product stronger in terms of its alcoholic content; it also means that there is more continuous labour in the process of making the beer. The addition of sugar or honey to the brew was another way of making beer stronger.[56] Though this was a technique which some had known in the nineteenth century, it was in the twentieth century often described as an innovation: one man emphasised the alien nature of such drink by asserting the 'Swahili', urban identity of the women who made it: 'It started in the cities, the Swahili women used to make that beer . . . They made and drank it; and at that time in the villages they did not know it.'[57] Not all welcomed innovations: as one woman said of straining beer, '[o]ur mothers did not do that, they used to say we were playing with it with our hands.'[58] But some women preferred to make

[55] Taylor and Joustra, 'Sorghum Beer Technology', II, 2-3.
[56] B. Platt, 'Some Traditional Alcoholic Beverages and Their Importance in Indigenous African Communities', *Proceedings of the Nutritionists' Society*, 14 (1955), 115-24 .
[57] Int Nya22a, 3; Burton, *Lake Regions*, II, 286 mentions the technique.
[58] Int Nya42a, 3.

these new drinks, seeing them as more profitable, more in demand (especially from young men) and, importantly, as freeing the brewer from the continued work of providing hot water while the beer was consumed. But overall, maize beer probably requires more labour, and a more consistent input of labour, than millet beer – long hours of heating and stirring, rather than simply leaving the brew to ferment.[59] The availability of metal containers – at first, old petrol tins, then cement and oil drums – have, however, made the new processes easier, for these are easier to heat. They are also larger. It has been argued that oil drums in themselves encourage increased alcohol consumption, because their size makes it possible to produce batches of drink much larger than could be made in earthenware pots.[60] This is an interesting argument, but it is by no means proven, and it is of course true that – since populations have increased greatly – the use of larger vessels may do no more than keep pace, allowing for the maintenance of a constant level of consumption per head.

New techniques have also made the extraction of sugar-cane juice very much easier; but again, at a cost. In some areas, as in central Kenya, the rise of mechanical extraction with hand-mills was apparently associated with an increasing involvement by men who could afford such mills.[61] The spread of the cultivation of species of bamboo, whose sap can be fermented, has been very much a male domain. This technique of alcohol production, which was established among the Kinga of southwestern Tanzania in the pre-colonial period,[62] is even easier than the use of palm sap, since the tapper need not even climb the bamboo. Bamboo wine, like palm wine, has tended to dominate other kinds of alcoholic beverage in areas where the plant thrives: other kinds of beverage survive, but the bulk of consumption comes to be from the easiest sugar source.[63] In the upland areas of Rungwe, where bamboo grows slowly, little is drunk; but in the lowland areas bamboo wine has become almost as common as grain beer in recent years.

In banana-wine areas, there have also been changes, though these are less striking. Principally, treading has almost entirely replaced hand-squeezing.[64] Some people suggested to me that the use of wooden fermenting troughs – rather than earthenware pots – is also an innovation, indicative of a growth in the scale of manufacture.[65] Troughs have, in fact, long been in use, but it may be the case that they have become more

---

[59] Ints Nya2a, 6; Nya7a, 2.

[60] Colson and Scudder, *For Prayer and Profit*, 45.

[61] Watkins, CNC to Attorney-General, 11 Jan. 1923, KNA AG 1/386; C. Ambler, 'Drunks, Brewers and Chiefs: Alcohol Regulation in Colonial Kenya, 1900-39', 177, in Barrows and Room, *Drinking: Behavior and Belief,* 165-83.

[62] Fulleborn, *Das Deutsche Njassa- und Ruwuma-Gebiet*, 116, 448.

[63] Reported as a recent and growing phenomenon in Iringa in the 1930s, it is now the principal intoxicant there: Hutt, Ag. DO to PC Iringa, 16 Apr. 1934, TNA 77/26/12; Beckman, *Alcohol: Another Trap for Africa*, 63-6.

[64] Int Nyoro17b, 3.

[65] Ints Nyoro 17b, 3; Nyoro41b, 2; but see J. Roscoe, *The Bakitara, or Banyoro* (Cambridge, 1923), 206.

1.11 *Making a sugar and yeast drink*

common.[66] Otherwise, there has been very little change in techniques, equipment or ingredients; excepting the very recent and yet limited practice of using dried bakers' yeast to speed fermentation, producing a drink which celebrates the brand name of the yeast: DCL. New varieties of sweet banana have been introduced, which yield more sugar and have been turned to the production of a base for distillation. This produces certain historical ironies. In the early twentieth century British administrators complained that the people of Bunyoro concentrated on production of the *mbidde*, a banana used for beer; in the 1940s British administrators tried to ban the *barwokole* banana because they believed that this was a 'beer' banana which had displaced other traditional varieties of banana; in the 1990s, official anxieties focus on distillates rather than fermented drinks, and local officials complain that people grow too much of the *serere* variety used for distillates, and should plant instead the trusty old *barwokole*.[67] Despite the growth in treading,

---

[66] Both Baker and Grant noted the use of troughs for banana-wine: Baker, *Albert N'yanza*, II, 422; Grant, *A Walk Across Africa*, 158.

[67] Report, 10 July 1907, UNA A43/151; DC Bunyoro to Mukama, 12 May 1947, HDA, NAF/9.

1.12 *Distilling (i) Pot still*

women have continued to play a major role in the making of banana wine, either by using male labour (family members of hired workers) to tread or by treading the bananas themselves, in defiance of opinion against this.[68]

The tendency towards easier ways of making fermented drinks is even more evident in the use of granulated sugar. In 1947, the DC of Kajiado noted that 'sugar [is] mainly required for brewing as it made better beer than honey'.[69] There may be some debate about whether granulated sugar makes *better* liquor, but this is absolutely the easiest way to make an intoxicating beverage; and now it is perhaps the most common way of doing so in some places. Those who wish to make alcohol can just buy a bag of sugar, dissolve it in warm water, add a handful of dried bakers' yeast (and a little baking powder, to nourish the yeast, for quick results) and then leave it. Within 48 hours, the result will be an alcoholic beverage; and while the simplicity of manufacture is often reflected in the limited palatability of the end-product, addition of tea leaves or other flavourings may remedy this defect. It is hard to understate the degree of direct effort required to make this beverage; and it has become a staple in those places where the cost or sheer unobtainability of other ingredients makes the production of other types of alcohol impossible. While

---

[68] Ints Nyoro10b, Nyoro21a; Nyoro16b, 4 and Nyoro16c.
[69] Kajiado District Annual Report for 1948, 18, KNA DC KAJ 2/1/2.

1.13 *Distilling (ii) Oil-drum still*

men do sometimes make this granulated-sugar-based alcohol, it is more often women who do so, as they defend this source of cash income against male encroachment.

DISTILLATION

It would begin like this; you would go and buy your alcohol, *tonto* [banana wine] and your tin or you would go and squeeze your alcohol. And if you don't squeeze it yourself, you would just buy it and put it in the other tin. Then you would get the tin with the *tonto* and put it on a fire, after putting it there you get a tube and fix it in a tin; after that now let me tell you, even what we would use for covering. We would get banana fibre from a banana plantation and use it to cover the other hole, you would put it on the top. And after covering you would get a saucepan and fill it with water, and you bring the tube into the water.[70]

Another new technique for the production of alcoholic beverages became even more important in the twentieth century. Distillation involves taking a fermented drink, and heating it. Because ethanol boils at 79°C, the ethanol content of the beverage will turn to vapour before the water does. By catching the vapour and condensing it, a liquid is obtained which contains a much higher proportion of ethanol than did the original ferment. This is how the drinks which the English call 'spirits' are made. In the twentieth century, people all over East Africa learnt how to make simple stills from readily available materials.

[70] Int Nyoro27a, 4.

Distillation was largely unknown in nineteenth-century East Africa; it was practised a little on the coast, and Arab traders and European travellers both introduced this technique to societies along the caravan routes;[71] the 'Sudanese' troops, on whom the early attempts at imposing imperial domination relied, continued to produce spirits in northern Uganda throughout the 1880s.[72] Yet it was not emulated; perhaps because the desire of those within African societies who possessed political authority to reserve spirits to themselves, led them to discourage the practice. In nineteenth-century East Africa, distilled spirits remained very rare indeed, available only to those privileged few who occupied places of especial importance in the networks of international trade which brought the occasional bottle of imported brandy far inland.[73]

But in the twentieth century, the production of spirits in East Africa grew enormously; by the 1950s, spirits were being distilled from a great variety of fermented bases, from banana wine to simple sugar-based liquors.[74] Distillates, unlike simple ferments, do not spoil rapidly; and since they are not in a state of continuous fermentation they can be kept in sealed containers. The technology began using simple pot stills, adapting earthenware pots to serve as heating vessels and condensers; then petrol tins were employed as heating vessels, with copper tubing used to make coil condensers; now there is a fairly standard pattern of still in operation which uses an oil drum and a length of copper tubing. Technical innovation has increased the scale of production, and in the 1990s locally-made distillates constituted a considerable proportion – in Uganda, the bulk – of absolute alcohol consumption.

Distilled spirits have been the subject of protracted disputes at all levels. Since these disputes form part of the subject of this book, I will mention here only the simple issue of cultural categorization: since spirits were new, they posed direct problems of gender, who should make and control them, and of behaviour, how could their effects be understood? No uniform answer emerged to the question of manufacture: in some places men distilled, in other places women did so.[75] In terms of behaviour, spirits of all kind have tended to be seen as related to fermented beverages, as is of course apparent to anyone who makes them, but also as being in an important way different. The popular Ugandan use of the English term 'alcohol' specifically to describe spirits is revealing.[76] For most people, beer

---

[71] Samuel Baker made spirits from sweet potatoes for the ruler of Bunyoro, Kamurasi, and is often assumed to have been East Africa's first distiller, but Arab merchants had been distilling in East Africa before he arrived (Burton, *Lake Regions*, II, 286) and they continued to do so (Schweinfurth, *Emin Pasha*, 77). Speke had distilled for Mutesa before Baker's famous demonstration for Kamurasi: *Journal of the Discovery*, 306-8; Baker, *Albert N'yanza*, 467-9.

[72] F. D. Lugard, *The Rise of Our East African Empire* (2 vols)(London, 1968 (1st edn 1893)), II, 210.

[73] J. F. Elton, *Travels and Researches Among the Lakes and Mountains of Eastern and Central Africa* (London, 1968 (1st edn 1879)), 409.

[74] E. Babumba, *Report of the Spirituous Liquor Committee* (Entebbe, 1963), 2-3.

[75] Babumba, *Report of the Spirituous Liquor Committee*, 3-4.

[76] See for example Int Nyoro21a, 6.

or banana wine are not alcohol, and in the 1950s one man applied for a licence to sell 'non-alcoholic beers'.[77] Spirits are often considered to be in a distinct, and fearsome, class of their own; just as they were for the nineteenth-century British public.[78] But not an entirely separate category: another Ugandan man assured me that spirits are *omwenge* – the term used in Runyoro in the general meaning of 'alcohol' – and across East Africa, linguistic usage affirms that 'drunkenness' was basically the same, whether induced by distilled spirits or ferments.[79]

Beer & nutrition

A number of studies have shown that unstrained grain beer is, nutritionally, rather good.[80] It has a very high vitamin-B content, and for some grains the process of modification helps make available an element of nutritive value which would otherwise be lost.[81] This has led some to argue that a diet of beer and meat – as was the ideal for men in many East African societies – would be entirely healthy, and to argue further that the modern practice of straining beer has deleterious effects on nutrition: as indeed does the displacement of grain beer by palm wine or granulated-sugar-based drinks, or bottled beer.[82] This offers a kind of nutritional variation on the general theme of increasingly problematic drinking. Another variant on this theme is that the production of alcoholic beverages is a wasteful use of foodstuffs such as maize and bananas and in particular that the development of a cash market in alcohol during the twentieth century led people to make drink at the expense of food.[83] Banning the production of alcohol has been a stock response to famine, in both the colonial and post-colonial state: a telling reflex which reveals the ingrained official belief in the irresponsibility of ordinary people.[84]

Yet even when unstrained grain beer was the norm, there were always attempts to limit the consumption of grain beer to particular groups in society; the straining or disappearance of beer can have had no effect on the nutrition of all those who were not drinking it anyway. And the production of alcoholic beverages for sale in time of hardship, far from wasting food, has in fact been a very successful survival strategy: as will be argued in this book, alcoholic beverages in the twentieth century were among the most

[77] Juma Kidyedye to DC Bunyoro, 7 May 1953, HDA FIN.7.
[78] Harrison, *Drink and the Victorians*, 120-3.
[79] Int Nyoro8a, 4.
[80] Platt, 'Biological Ennoblement', 71-2; *idem*, 'Some Traditional Alcoholic Beverages'.
[81] Steinkraus, 'Nutritionally Significant Indigenous Foods'; Corran, *History of Brewing*, 16.
[82] Partanen, *Sociability and Intoxication*, 180-1; M. Nout, 'Aspects of the Manufacture and Consumption', 21, 31-9.
[83] M. Wilson, *For Men and Elders. Changes in the Relations of Generations and of Men and Women among the Nyakyusa and Ngonde* (London, 1977), 185-6.
[84] DC Bugishu to PC Eastern, 22 Sep. 1924, UNA Z 325/20; Minute, 3 June 1943, TNA SMP 23241, Vol. II; Beidelman, *The Kaguru*, 25.

important items of exchange in increasingly money-oriented local economies.[85] They have been central in accumulation strategies, and in the survival strategies of some – especially women – who have had little control over other items of monetary value. Where entitlements are called into question by crisis – whether chronic or acute – exchange in alcohol of all kinds has been an important way to secure adequate nutrition. The greater nutritive value of unstrained 'traditional' beer is an issue of minor significance compared with the role which alcohol has played in redistributing money within local economies.[86]

HEALTHY DRINKS?

If the native beer were made in clean vessels of clean materials, a little would be perfectly wholesome, but everything that goes to its manufacture is filthy.[87]

As Fabian has recently observed, at least some European explorers of the nineteenth century consumed locally made alcoholic beverages with relish, and without apparent ill-effect,[88] but their twentieth-century successors regarded locally-made beverages with much more suspicion:[89] 'I failed to appreciate the drab, dirty-looking liquid', noted one, somewhat lugubriously.[90] In the 1990s, most expatriates treated grain beer or palm wine as though they were poison: partly because of the unfamiliar appearance of these beverages, but also, explicitly, a reaction informed by the notion that these drinks are a danger to health. This became a central feature of discourse during the twentieth century, and it is not solely Europeans who argue this: officials of the post-colonial state ban the consumption of locally-made alcohol in epidemics, as well as in famines.[91] The evidence that such drinks pose a major danger to health is limited, and there has been no systematic study which would show whether or not locally-made beverages routinely contain pathogens.[92] Palm wine and bamboo wine, being unadulterated with water, are very unlikely to pose a health risk. The

[85] A. Harwood, 'Beer Drinking and Famine in a Safwa Village: A Case of Adaptation in Time of Crisis', paper given at East African Institute of Social Research conference, 1964.

[86] M. Green, 'Trading on Inequality: Gender and the Drinks Trade in Southern Tanzania', *Africa*, 69 (1999), 404-23.

[87] E. Bache, *The Youngest Lion. Early Farming Days in Kenya* (London, 1934), 108.

[88] J. Fabian, *Out of Our Minds. Reason and Madness in the Exploration of Central Africa* (Berkeley, CA/Los Angeles, CA/London, 2000), 70. Burton aside, others too drank local ferments: Baker and Speke both consumed large quantities of banana wine: *Albert N'yanza*, 319; *Journal of the Discovery*, 304.

[89] See for example Ag. PC, Rift Valley Province to all DCs, 15 Jan. 1965, KNA DC KAJ 4/8/2.

[90] K. Weule, *Native Life in East Africa* (trans. A. Werner) (London, 1909), 93.

[91] M. Walsh, 'Village, State and Traditional Authority in Usangu', in R. Abrahams (ed.), *Villages, Villagers and the State in Modern Tanzania* (Cambridge, 1985), 135-67.

[92] There is not a great deal of literature on this. M. Collis, 'Cancer of the Oesophagus and Alcoholic Drinks in East Africa', *Lancet* (19 Feb. 1972), 441, notes a geographical correlation between the use of maize for beer and the incidence of oesophagal cancer, but suggests no cause for this. A recent study has suggested some – but not very threatening – contamination with higher alcohols and with metals: D. Mosha *et al.*, 'African Traditional Brews', 205-9; an earlier study also showed that metal contamination could be dangerously high: P. Nikander *et al.*, 'Ingredients and Contaminants of Traditional Alcoholic Beverages in Tanzania', *Transactions of the Royal Society of Tropical Hygiene and Medicine*, 85 (1991), 133-5.

production of some grain beers does sometimes involve unboiled water, but in all beverages except banana wine the acidity of the beverage and its alcohol content militate against the presence of pathogens: certainly, fermented alcoholic beverages will usually be safer than unboiled water in Africa, just as they were in pre-industrial Europe.[93] As Platt noted, people in Buhaya who shunned water in preference for banana wine were remarkably successful in avoiding dysentery.[94] As will be discussed, the debate over the health risks associated with alcoholic beverages has particularly focused on distillates. Yet here too the overall evidence is far from compelling: well-known public tragedies of poisoning seem to be associated with the adulteration of beverages with industrial ethanol or methanol, rather than with the products of local distillation.[95] In health, as in nutrition, attitudes to alcohol have not been informed simply by the physical nature or properties of locally-made alcohol: they form part of wider debates about propriety and well-being in society as a whole.

Words for drinking

This is a book about the relatively recent past, but its subject inevitably raises questions about the more distant past, and the antiquity of alcohol production in East Africa. It has been argued that the spread of grain cultivation through sub-Saharan Africa may have been propelled by the possibilities for alcohol production which this offered, rather than by the food uses of grain, but this is entirely speculative, and it would be surprising if the population of the region were ignorant of alcohol before the spread of grain cultivation:[96] there would have been plentiful sources of fruit sugar and honey available for fermentation. Nor is there much evidence to argue for the diffusion routes of particular techniques of alcohol production, such as malting, or the use of bananas or a dried inoculum.

Historical linguistic evidence is rather disappointing in this regard: Guthrie offers 'starred forms' of terms for 'beer' and 'intoxicate', and suggests that the latter may be a very ancient term.[97] Reflexes of that form do appear in some East African languages; but terms for alcoholic beverages show not even that limited consistency; indeed, they manifest rather a startling array of terms for kinds of drink, for techniques of production and for fermentation.[98] The

---

[93] Corran, *History of Brewing*, 35; Harrison, *Drink and the Victorians*, 37.

[94] Platt, 'Biological Ennoblement', 72.

[95] 'Five Survivors of Killer Brew Now Blind', *Daily Nation*, 30 Sep. 1999. See also Appendix III of Babumba, *Report of the Spirituous Liquor Committee*, and Nout, 'Aspects of the Manufacture and Consumption', 42, which report levels of higher alcohols, in particular, which are above European safety standards, but record no lethal levels of contamination.

[96] This argument is mentioned in Carlson, 'Haya Worldview and Ethos', 47-8.

[97] Guthrie's c. s. 1107 is -kod-, 'intoxicate'; the modern Nyoro term 'kolwa' is presumably a reflex of the passive of this of this. However, the Nyakyusa term is quite different, -gal-. M. Guthrie, *Comparative Bantu* (4 vols) (Farnborough, 1971), Vol. II.

[98] Guthrie's starred form for beer (c.s. 1892) has no reflex in any language I have come across in East Africa.

historical record, moreover, suggests that the terminology of drink derives from specific moments of cultural categorization which are hard to recapture through the linguistic record alone: in the 1940s, officials in Tanganyika tried to define a kind of drink called *kangara*, which most were agreed was a particularly dangerous kind of alcohol. It became apparent that this drink was made in different ways in different places.[99] The common implication of the term was that the beverage involved was perceived as a novelty, and as unusually strong – rather as the term 'ale' in English usage defines not a particular method or taste, but rather a perceived contrast with some other more innovatory and less 'traditional' drink: the beer of the fifteenth century was the ale of the eighteenth.[100] In the 1990s, a granulated sugar drink flavoured with tea-leaves was called *scud* in some places, *wanzuki* in others and *rorungana* (a term in use since the 1950s, at least) in others: fashion and local circumstance have produced quite different names for the same phenomenon. The term *busaa*, now widely used in Kenya for grain beer, apparently derives from an Egyptian term, and – although grain beer has long been made in Kenya – presumably became current in the twentieth century, when the growing sale of grain beers centred on military encampments which preserved elements of the culture of the 'Sudanese' troops of the early colonial period. On the other hand, while the Sudanese soldiers' term *araki*, for distilled liquor, has given rise to the modern Ugandan term *waragi*, this term did not become widespread in Tanzania or Kenya, even though distilled spirits were often associated with Sudanese soldiers there too. In the colonial period, distilled spirits were called *moshi*, 'smoke', in Tanzania; now they are called *gongo*, 'bludgeon'. The words for drinking reveal not some clear pattern of the movement of ideas and techniques, but a whirl of innovation and borrowing that has shown no respect for linguistic or ethnic boundaries.

IS BREWING SEX?

Suggestive images and terminology cluster around the practice of alcohol production, particularly, around the production of alcoholic beverages from grain.[101] This is a woman's task, it is generally incompatible with pregnancy and menstruation, and in some societies it is apparently compared with the sexual act, with the bubbling ferment as a metaphor for maleness.[102] The use of a fermented inoculum for the malt sustains this image of the reproductive act; linguistic usage in 1940s Dar es Salaam made explicit an idea of the diastased grain as 'the father of beer' and the unmodified grain as 'the mother of beer'.[103] The same imagery may be deduced in the use of

---

[99] Ag. PC Southern to Chief Sec., 19 Jan. 1946, Ag. PC Central to Chief Sec., 12 Feb. 1946, TNA SMP 20945.

[100] P. Mathias, *The Brewing Industry in England, 1700-1830* (Cambridge, 1959), xvii-xviii, 3.

[101] Carlson, 'Haya Worldview', 110-11 suggests that fermentation may be understood as sex.

[102] Green, 'Trading on Inequality', 409; M. Wilson, *Rituals of Kinship Among the Nyakyusa* (London/New York/Toronto, 1957), 139 notes restrictions on pregnant women brewing; Heald, *Controlling Anger*, 67-9 suggests the maleness of the ferment.

[103] 'African Brewing in Dar es Salaam', TNA 157 A2/8.

the sausage fruit in preparing alcoholic beverages made from honey or sugar-cane: each Kamba household head kept his own sausage-fruit inoculum.[104] Even in the production of banana wine, the principle of the addition of a 'fertilizing' element was maintained, for it was throughout the region common practice to add sorghum to the banana juice when it was placed in the fermenting vessel.[105] The sorghum in question had not been germinated, and so could not itself have served any role as a diastatic (which would anyway be unnecessary, as banana juice is full of sugar) nor as an inoculum (since it was fried just before adding, which would have killed off any bacteria or wild yeast present on the grain). Yet people referred to this – and still refer to it – as though it were a fermenting agent.[106] This is even more striking since (in Bunyoro at least) people now also make a kind of banana wine which is intended not for consumption as a ferment but as the basis for distillation. No sorghum is added to this; so people are consciously aware that the sorghum is not necessary to fermentation, but they nonetheless argue that it is. The notion that the preparation of fermented alcohol is sex is a persistent one.

Yet it is not absolutely dominant. The production of palm wine or bamboo wine does not (in so far as I am aware) involve any sexual imagery; nor is there sexual imagery around distillation. And while the sorghum put into the banana juice is regarded as a 'seed' in this context, people talk of the *mbidde* banana used for making wine itself as 'male', in contrast to the 'female' cooking banana, the *nyamunyo*.[107] The imagery of sex may be persistent, but it is not consistent; and it is not clear that this has any further significance in determining behaviour or practice around the making of alcohol. Unlike smelting – around the production of which Herbert has made such a persuasive argument for a 'genderizing' role – the making of alcohol is by no means an esoteric art.[108] It is the consumption, rather than the production, of alcohol that produces and reproduces notions of power; the making of alcohol has been the focus of immediate disputes over the control of labour, and of a potentially valuable resource, but the extent of innovation in technique and gender roles has been very considerable. Practice and discourse have tended to reproduce the idea that brewing, and some other kinds of alcohol preparation, are sex: but the cultural connotations of alcohol production have not determined behaviour. The history of the making of alcohol in East Africa is not one of culturally bound rigidity, nor of technological determinism: it is a history of change and innovation. The story of technical change laid out in this chapter offers a background, and no more than that.

[104] Lindblom, *The Akamba*, 519.

[105] Ashe, *Two Kings*, 308.

[106] Journal, 10 Apr. 1998. Platt cites a description of Ethiopian honey-wine making which records the same use of toasted grain as an inoculum: 'Some Traditional Alcoholic Beverages', 116.

[107] Roscoe, *The Bakitara*, 205; Int Nyoro41b, 4.

[108] E. Herbert, *Iron, Gender and Power: Rituals of Transformation in African Societies* (Bloomington, IN, 1993).

Part One

Drink, sex & violence
The nature of power
in nineteenth-century East Africa

Many young bloods were the worse for liquor, and wanted to fight.
Lugard, *The Rise of Our East African Empire*, I, 325; describing his arrival
in Kikuyuland in 1890

. . . no man who had not had a child of his own initiated was entitled to
drink beer . . . It was quite contrary to law and custom for any unmarried
man or young married man to drink beer and get drunk.
Leakey, *The Southern Kikuyu*, I, 293-4

For the benefit of the missionary and amateur ethnographer, Kikuyu elders
insisted – retrospectively – on the privileged nature of alcohol consumption
in the nineteenth century: only old men could drink. And they spelt out at
length the varied social and ceremonial circumstances in which elder men
might enjoy beer, describing as they did so a world in which well-being
rested on the goodwill of elder men, and the use of alcohol constantly
reminded everyone of this.[1] But Lugard, the insecure representative of the
fragile early colonial presence, saw a different world, in which drink fuelled
the belligerence of young men; and he was not the only nineteenth-century
European observer to suggest that drunkenness was common, and was by
no means confined solely to elder men.[2]

This apparent contradiction – between a discourse which stressed the
controlled, ritual nature of alcohol consumption and practice in which
alcohol spilled constantly beyond the bounds of control – was not confined
to central Kenya. Contrasting accounts of drinking conjure up two, quite
different, images of the African past: one of ordered acquiescence to an
unquestioned gerontocracy, the other of constant, imminent violence and

[1] Cagnolo, *The Akikuyu*, 57, 61, 88.
[2] Speke, *Journal of the Discovery*, 101-2.

disorder – or at least, 'unorder', as Ambler has called it.[3] The next three chapters will locate these conflicting images of drinking and ideas of temperance in gender and generational disputes over power. It is this context which helps us to understand both the ubiquity of alcohol, and the particular linkage of alcohol to the power of men, which Charles New observed in the hinterland of Mombasa in the 1860s, in a description which could have been applied to the ideal – if not always the practice – of drinking in many East African societies in the nineteenth century.

> Nothing is done among the Wanika without drink. Marriages, births, deaths, civil and religious rites and all 'maneno' (palavers) are celebrated by drinking carousals . . . Drunkenness is not common among young men, and among women it is hardly ever witnessed. It may be regarded as the special privilege of the older men.[4]

[3] Ambler, 'Alcohol and Disorder in Precolonial Africa', 3.
[4] New, *Life, Wanderings and Labours in Eastern Africa*, 96.

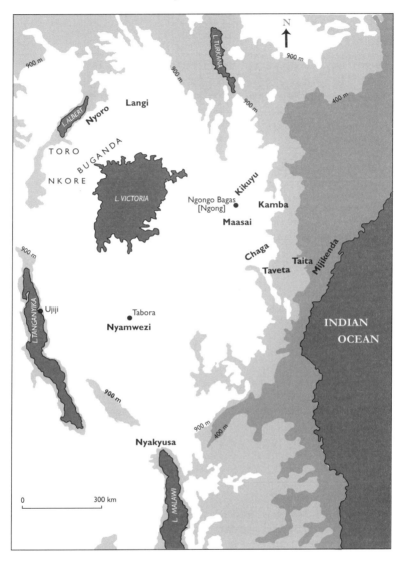

Map 2 *Nineteenth-century East Africa*

Two

Wild women & violent youths

When a young man sees a young woman who is unhappy in her polygynous marriage, if he takes a liking to the woman, he tries to tempt her to elope with him. They meet in secret … [The woman says], 'My fathers have already used the cattle given as my bride-wealth. How will they repay my husband? … If my fathers follow us, do not give me up to them!'

[The youth says] 'Only a fool would give up his wife. We will go tomorrow!'[1]

Patriarchy, kinship & marriage

In nineteenth-century East Africa, wealth was people. Cultivation and harvesting required considerable inputs of labour at key moments in the agricultural cycle; herding and guarding livestock required almost as much labour, and more constantly. People were the basis of food and physical security, and those who aspired to wealth sought to acquire dependants. Wealth begat wealth, for those who could provide acquired more followers; and so transactions in authority over people were central to nineteenth-century society. In many societies, such transactions were marked through the movement of cattle: 'kinship is cattle', as one Nyakyusa man declared.[2]

The senior male has been the central figure in scholarship on these societies, which has seen patterns of accumulation as revolving around the attempts of male household heads to maintain and expand their control over followings of younger men and women. It was senior men who made and marked these transactions in people. In emphasizing the 'colonizing' nature of any of these societies, and stressing the negotiability of identity and the experimentation and enterprise of African economic life in the pre-colonial period, most historians have shared Kopytoff's perception that

---

[1] T. Meyer, *Wa-Konde. Maisha, Mila na Desturi za Wanyakyusa* (Mbeya, 1993), 253-5.
[2] C. Ambler, *Kenyan Communities in the Age of Imperialism. The Central Region in the Late Nineteenth Century* (New Haven, CT/London, 1988), 25; Wilson, *For Men and Elders*, 30.

the 'frontier' society, which constantly expanded and reproduced itself by throwing off new pioneers who established male-headed households, had the ambitious, incorporative senior male at its core and sustained and reproduced a patrifocal model of authority. These societies were colonizing and enterprising, but they were relentlessly patriarchal.[3]

On one level, this analysis raises a straightforward definitional issue: which men were 'elders'? In the twentieth century, some colonial administrators were struck by the imprecision of this category: 'The word "elders" may be somewhat misleading, suggestive of a body of exclusively old men. The majority, it is true, were elderly, but as a body they represented more a grade than an age group.'[4] In some East African societies, such as the Maasai, collective ritual events marked transitions in the status of men, making it relatively clear who was an elder and who was not. But even here, there might be disputes, over the timing of the rituals of transition and over the status of individuals who for one reason or another might be inserted into the hierarchy of age in ways which evaded the normal ritual requirements. Elsewhere, the issue of 'elderhood' was even more vexed, and was involved in a kind of circular definition with the possession of authority: those men were elders who had married, had children and sought to assert their particular authority over children, and those who asserted authority were elders. Quarrels between old men and young men over the right to command and dispose of labour and persons must surely have been a constant feature of nineteenth-century society, played out partly through arguments over who was an elder.

Such contestation over definition was by no means the only problematic of senior male power. The model of unchallenged patriarchy has been questioned by a scholarship which points to women's ability to control and manage resources in some pre-colonial societies.[5] And seniority itself could complicate claims to authority: for notions of seniority were cross-cutting. Marriage and kinship created no unambiguous claims to authority: to any individual, the social world was full of potential 'seniors', defined variously by differing interpretations of kinship, generation, affiliation and marriage. These competing structures of seniority did not simply balance; they created space for rivalry and for contest along the lines of the 'fraught triangle' of elder men, younger men and women.[6] The personal mobility

---

[3] J. Iliffe, *A Modern History of Tanganyika* (Cambridge, 1979), 17; Ambler, *Kenyan Communities*, 14-30. I. Kopytoff, 'The Internal African Frontier', in I. Kopytoff (ed.), *The African Frontier. The Reproduction of Traditional African Societies* (Bloomington, IN, 1987), 17, 18, 36; also J. Lonsdale, 'The Conquest State of Kenya, 1895-1905', in B. Berman and J. Lonsdale, *Unhappy Valley. Conflict in Kenya and Africa* (2 vols) (London/Nairobi/Athens, OH, 1992), 13-44.

[4] C. Dundas, *African Crossroads* (London, 1955), 38.

[5] R. Oboler, *Women, Power and Economic Change. The Nandi of Kenya* (Stanford, CA, 1985), 8-14; A. Talle, *Women at a Loss: Changes in Maasai Pastoralism and Their Effects on Gender Relations* (Stockholm, 1988), 1-9.

[6] Ambler, *Kenyan Communities*, 22-5, argues 'balance'; the 'fraught triangle' is from P. Spencer, *Maasai of Matapato. A Study of the Rituals of Rebellion* (Manchester, 1988), 7.

and enterprise inherent in the notion of the frontier ensured that the claims to authority of any individual elder men were very much challenged, both by the insubordination of young men and women and by the rivalries of elder men. Seniority created rivalries and alternatives, and the maintenance of authority over persons-as-wealth posed chronic problems.

It has been argued that the authority of senior men was maintained through their control of women; that, fundamentally, their control over marriage gave elders the ability to command the labour of young men.[7] Such analysis builds on the classic argument of Meillassoux.[8] Yet it is problematic, for it tells us nothing about how women were actually controlled, and verges on defining authority in terms of itself: old men had power over society because they had control over young men, because they had control over women . . .[9] This chapter suggests that the institutions of cattle transfer, marriage and kinship did not *in themselves* reproduce senior male authority in the face of youthful violence and female sexuality, and so raises a central question: how was seniority continually reproduced as the 'prevailing source of power' in pre-colonial East Africa?[10]

YOUTHFUL VIOLENCE

When, in 1883, an elder Maasai man offered to guide Joseph Thomson and his caravan, disaster nearly ensued: he led them inadvertently into a group of young warriors who were feasting on meat. The consequent stand-off revealed very clearly the elder's fear of the prospect of physical violence.[11] Across East Africa, young men were associated with truculence, and their behaviour constantly evoked the possibility of violence;[12] everywhere, societies were riven by a 'latent hostility between fathers and sons'.[13] Relationships between old men and young were constantly strained by the possibilities of such insubordination. They were even more threatened by the violence and raiding of young men: either the infuriated assault on the person of an elder, or the appropriation of livestock, usually for immediate consumption. Meat was a treat; young men might steal a goat or calf from a father or uncle for feasting; or more often, they might go and steal livestock from neighbouring settlements. Young men's hunger could lead them to take violent hold of the counters with which elder men played their complex

[7] Iliffe, *Modern History of Tanganyika*, 17.

[8] C. Meillassoux, *Maidens, Meal and Money. Capitalism and the Domestic Economy* (Cambridge, 1981), 33-50.

[9] J. Guyer, 'Household and Community in African Studies', *African Studies Review*, 24 (1981), 96.

[10] Lonsdale, 'Conquest State', 26.

[11] J. Thomson, *Through Masailand. A Journey of Exploration Among the Snowclad Volcanic Mountains and Strange Tribes of Eastern Equatorial Africa* (London, 1968(1st edn 1885)), 198.

[12] A.C. Hollis, *The Masai. Their Language and Folklore* (Westport, CT, 1970, (1st edn Oxford, 1905)), xvii; Wilson, *Good Company*, 80.

[13] J. Beattie, *Bunyoro. An African Kingdom* (New York/Chicago; IL/San Francisco, CA/Toronto/London, 1960), 52.

games of transaction in authority.[14]

Violence against, or theft from, uncle or father was an immediate and obvious challenge. Stealing or raiding from neighbours could also be a manifestation of youthful insubordination, and it raised more complex problems. Potentially, it brought useful resources within the domain of the household, and men argued over the distribution and control of any livestock that were not consumed immediately, and over captured persons.[15] Yet raids also brought complications: claims for compensation, if the raided were physically close and were bound by any ties of kinship, marriage or obligation; counter-raids if no such ties existed. Elder men tended to take a less sanguine view of raiding than did young men, for raids compromised relationships of authority and raised the spectre of endless petty conflicts and raids which would turn authority solely into a matter of physical violence. This altered perspective on violence struck European observers very forcibly: 'The married Masai is a changed man. From a lustful, bloodthirsty fiend he becomes a staid, courteous and reasonable man.'[16]

Amongst the Maasai, age-sets institutionalized youthful truculence, and created a physical space for it in warrior-camps. Age-sets may have formalized the 'rituals of rebellion' and so acted ultimately to uphold the dominance of elders;[17] but the very maintenance of the system of age-sets was the product of a constant conflict between young and old men, and warrior behaviour defied and complicated the position of elder men. Institutionalizing the dominance of elder men, age-sets also institutionalized young men's challenges to that dominance. Among the Nyakyusa a widely respected principle of male generational separation existed, and boys moved into their own houses when still quite young, and might move even further away from their fathers when they were teenagers, establishing distinct settlements with other young men from neighbouring households; a degree of generational separation of men was also considered desirable among the Nyoro.[18] Such youthful bids for autonomy were often associated with violence, and this pattern of youthful violence could be drawn into the construction of wider patterns of political authority, as will be argued below.

SEDUCTIVE POWER

The Maasai ritual of *eunoto* revolved around practice in the structure called the *os-singira*. This

> . . . is used as a 'club-house' by the men of the age-group concerned with the ceremony, but there are certain restrictions, and it is these

[14] H. McClure, 'Memorandum on the Masai' and 'District Records for the Guidance of the Officer Administering the Masai Southern Reserve', 7-8, in the library of the British Institute in Eastern Africa, Nairobi; Int Nya25a, 1 refers to pre-colonial disputes over cattle theft.

[15] Thomson, *Through Masailand*, 256; Spencer, *Maasai of Matapato*, 20-1. R. Tignor, 'The Maasai Warriors: Pattern Maintenance and Violence in Colonial Kenya', *JAH*, 13 (1972), 271-90.

[16] Johnston, *The Kilima-Njaro Expedition*, 416.

[17] Spencer, *Maasai of Matapato*, 5.

[18] Meyer, *Wa-Konde*, 151; Int Nyoro10c, 3; Nyoro36c, 6.

restrictions which give the key to the meaning of the whole ceremony. It is considered both ignoble and dishonourable for any man in the warrior groups to have sex with any but the uninitiated girls, but of course cases do occur . . . only those who have strictly observed the above regulation and have never had sexual relations with an initiated girl or marred woman may enter . . . Inside the hut – as mentioned – is a large hole which is used as a cesspool, into which the men who enter the hut must urinate. This cesspool is also bewitched as an extra precaution, and anyone who has falsely entered and evaded the witchcraft of the entrance will certainly die upon urinating in the hole.[19]

Elder men's authority over women revolved around their attempts to control sex, and reproduction. Yet sex and reproduction were forms of power for women, from which they derived an authority of their own. 'Woman's only magic is between her legs', commented a Shambaa man.[20] This was not entirely true, for – as will be argued below – women could and did claim for themselves a power over well-being. Yet the control of the power between women's legs preoccupied men: they argued that this was women's only power, but they feared it. Men struggled to establish their own authority, and to stop their peers succumbing to the seductive and reproductive power of women in ways which would undermine the authority of elder men as a group: men's collective power was threatened by the sexual power of women and the sexual weakness of men.

Marriage was a transaction in authority over reproduction;[21] but it was also a transaction in authority over sex. Across East Africa, there were quite different ideas about what constituted a transgression of the sexual claims created by marriage; yet there was a common concern with the challenge to authority which was created by such transgressions. Ideas of adultery differed; but the idea that adultery was problematic did not. Among the Nyakyusa, marriage was perceived to create a very narrow set of sexual rights, involving the husband alone (though these rights would be inherited by his brothers); among the Nyoro, male kin might claim sexual rights in a bride. Among the Maasai, sexual rights were claimed primarily by the husband but were shared by him with friends of the same age-set. The bounds of sexual activity for men and women might then be relatively wide; but the concern with adultery suggests that these bounds were still frequently crossed.[22] Societies where bride-wealth was paid tended to an imbalance in claims to authority over women: certain men, especially elder men, were more able to pay bride-wealth, and they acquired more wives than younger, poorer men.[23] And so many of these elder men were cuckolds, as their wives

[19] L.S.B. Leakey, 'Some Notes on the Masai of Kenya Colony', *Journal of the Anthropological Institute*, 60 (1930), 195.

[20] A. bin Hemedi 'l Ajjemy, *Habari za Wakilindi* (Nairobi, 1962), 75.

[21] Wilson, *For Men and Elders*, 60; Beattie, *Bunyoro*, 55.

[22] Ints Nya36a, 2; Nyoro11a, 1; Roscoe, *The Bakitara*, 69; Leakey, 'Some Notes on the Masai', 202; Storrs Fox, 'Further Notes on the Masai', 455.

[23] Meyer, *Wa-Konde*, 171.

sought younger, more desirable lovers.

In Rungwe and Kyela rivalry over sexual access to wives, particularly between old men and young, was a regular cause of violence and of claims for compensation. 'A husband is constantly unsure of his wives, and he becomes like a policeman to them as he tries to restrict and frighten them.'[24] Among the Maasai, elder men's anxiety over this issue and the existence of 'extreme inter-generational sexual tension' was revealed in the events at the *os-singira*.[25] Nyoro society too experienced frequent disputes over adultery: authority over reproduction might be contested, through arguments over precedent and the precise provenance of cattle given as bride-wealth, but authority over sexual activity was a much more immediate and constant issue. It was also a much more intractable problem, since children were much more tangible focuses of conflict than sex itself; as the elaborate rituals of the Maasai suggested, elder men were always troubled by the possibility of cuckolding, if unable to demonstrate that it had taken place. And it was not only young men who seduced the wives of others. Among the Nyakyusa and Nyoro, and other societies where the definition of adultery was not so clearly defined by generation, men's authority over women was constantly challenged by their peers; the seductive power of women regularly breached the imagined solidarity of elder men, creating disputes amongst those who claimed to control society.[26]

Men who seduced the wives of their elders and peers faced violent retribution, or at least demands for compensation.[27] Women who cuckolded their husbands faced physical abuse; or they might be divorced.[28] In some East African societies, divorce and widowhood created a number of once-married women of ambiguous status, sexually available but subject to residual claims by former husbands which made them potentially dangerous marriage partners, since a new husband might become embroiled in disputes over the return of cattle originally given for bride-wealth and the control of children born to the woman before the claims of the former husband and his kin had been settled: such women might be married 'cheaply', or might simply become concubines.[29] But divorce for simple adultery was by no means common; for adultery did not in itself jeopardize authority over children, and men were reluctant to deal with the complex sorting-out of multiple entailments which would inevitably follow on from divorce, as the cattle given as bride-wealth were reclaimed, and then argued over.[30] Nor

[24] Meyer, *Wa-Konde*, 173; cf. Wilson, *Good Company*, 161-2; her argument would suggest that this was a twentieth-century phenomenon.

[25] Storrs Fox, 'Further Notes on the Masai', 452-3, 455; McClure, 'District Records for the Guidance', 20; Spencer, *Maasai of Matapato*, 161, 177-82.

[26] Int Nyoro16c, 9-11.

[27] Meyer, *Wa-Konde*, 173.

[28] Leakey, 'Some Notes on the Masai', 202.

[29] Meyer, *Wa-Konde*, 171; M. Merker, 'The Masai', translation for private circulation of *Die Masai. Ethnographische Monographie eines ostafrikanische Semitenvolkes* (Berlin, 1910), 19.

[30] Meyer describes the determined and eventually successful campaign of a man to stop his wife leaving him: *Wa-Konde*, 169-70.

was widowhood very common, for younger women at least, since they would almost always be claimed by the kin of their husbands. More commonly, marriages ended and temporarily single women were created through women's action in running away from husbands.

RUNNING AWAY

Women might defy claims over their sexual and reproductive power by discreetly taking lovers. They might also run away. Women who felt that they were maltreated or neglected by their husbands ran away, not to live alone, but to 'find ways of living':[31] re-establishing relations with men on different terms, going to live, physically, in the household of an uncle, their father, a new lover, or their son.[32] It is impossible to know how common it was for women to run away in the mid-nineteenth century; and how many marriages ended in this way: sometimes with a settlement of the claims of the former husband and sometimes in straightforward defiance of those claims. The Maasai woman who ran to her father in protest at her husband's neglect, and who returned to her husband when he promised better treatment, represented one kind of flight; the woman who fled from her husband to live with her mother, without intention of returning, is another.[33] As the desperate individuals thrown up by violent conflict in the later nineteenth century discovered, young women could always find a household to which to attach themselves.[34] Any attempt to assess the incidence of this in the nineteenth-century is complicated by twentieth-century accounts, largely given by men, which have encouraged the notion of the nineteenth century as a period of extreme marital stability. Yet it is clear that there were runaway and rebellious women; the ease with which caravan porters of the mid-nineteenth century found local lovers suggests this.[35]

MOVEMENTS OF CATTLE, TRANSACTIONS IN AUTHORITY

Elder men did not wrestle only with the rebelliousness of youths and women; such rebelliousness was predicated partly on the lust and acquisitiveness of other elder men, and it constantly threatened conflicts with other men. Cattle transfers might serve to provide a focus for such conflicts, rather than a medium for the self-interested co-operation of a gerontocracy. Among the Maasai, Nyakyusa and Nyoro, marriage was ideally marked by a transfer of cattle from the physical possession of the bridegroom or his kin to the bride's father and/or his kin.[36] Such movements were complex events which

---

[31] Int Maa21c, 1.

[32] Ints Maa15b, 1; Maa12c, 1; Meyer, *Wa-Konde*, 123, 253-5.

[33] Int Maa39b, 1; M. Wright, *Strategies of Slaves and Women. Life-Stories from East/Central Africa* (New York/London, 1993), 52.

[34] Wright, *Strategies of Slaves and Women*, 84-5.

[35] H.M. Stanley, *How I Found Livingstone. Travels, Adventures and Discoveries in Central Africa* (London, 1874), 203.

[36] Wilson, *Rituals of Kinship*, 1; R.B. Fisher, *Twilight Tales of the Black Baganda* (London, 1911), 45; Merker, 'The Masai', 30; Roscoe, *The Northern Bantu*, 39.

reaffirmed and created relationships of authority. The cattle given might be taken from the physical holdings of father, uncle, brother or some other figure; once handed over, they might be kept in the immediate possession of the father or passed on to his uncles or brothers, or (amongst the Maasai, and very occasionally amongst the Nyakyusa) to one or more wives.[37] The distribution of such cattle would be keenly observed by all involved; for they were valuable sources of food, and they could reproduce. Cattle transactions lay at the basis of recruitment to and authority within the male-headed household.

But these movements of cattle were not straightforward transfers of ownership of cattle from one man to another; the cattle were desirable in themselves, but they represented also a transaction in authority over people, and long-remembered ties linked the cattle back to those from whose possession they had come. Idealized accounts of past practice stress that bride-wealth transactions were not simply exercises in cattle accumulation: 'They should consider the dignity of a person, saying "I will not take many cattle, because he has not many."'[38] Should the marriage fail, or the bride prove barren; or should disputes over the fidelity of the bride arise, claims would be made for the return of some or all of the cattle, and these claims could be further controverted by changes in the relationship between the original donors.[39] Some fathers in Bunyoro so much feared these complications that they declined to accept bride-wealth for their daughters.[40] Individuals had often to seek help in paying bride-wealth for themselves and their sons: Maasai men might attach themselves to wealthy patrons with whom they had no kin relationship, Nyakyusa men might pledge an unborn daughter in marriage to secure a loan for cattle, or otherwise 'borrow' in ways which established relationships which could be recalled at some undefined moment in the future.[41] Among the Nyakyusa, it was sometimes argued that this continued interest in cattle extended even to the offspring of those cattle.[42] But of course, the original cattle or their offspring might have been passed on yet further, in the creation or marking of yet further relationships of authority over people.[43] Cattle moved, but not simply as possessions, owned outright by those to whom they were given.[44]

[37] Wilson, *For Men and Elders*, 86-8; Merker, 'The Masai', 19; Meyer, *Wa-Konde*, 172, reported that cattle were sometimes divided amongst 'houses'; all informants to whom I talked said that this never happened: Ints Nya14c, 4; Nya26b, 2; Nya28b, 1.

[38] Int Maa27c, 1.

[39] 'Marriage and Divorce', Note in Southern Masai Political Record Book, KNA DC KAJ 1/1/1; McClure, 'District Records for the Guidance', 21; Int Nyoro10b, 4; Meyer, *Wa-Konde*, 174.

[40] Int Nyoro1c, 2.

[41] R. Waller, 'Economic and Social Relations in the Central Rift Valley: The Maa-speakers and Their Neighbours in the Nineteenth Century', in B. Ogot (ed.), *Kenya in the Nineteenth Century* (Nairobi, 1985), 83-151; Meyer, *Wa-Konde*, 157.

[42] Meyer, *Wa-Konde*, 123.

[43] Wilson, *Rituals of Kinship*, 1.

[44] Talle, *Women at a Loss*, 72-5; a similar argument is made in Oboler, *Women, Power and Economic Change*, 10.

And cattle did not move solely through marriage. Cattle might be lent to poorer relatives or clients, dispersing the cattle and lowering their vulnerability to raiding or disease while at the same time marking new relationships.[45] They might be demanded as fines for misbehaviour or extracted as compensation for injury.[46] Any individual beast might be entailed in multiple transactions in authority over people: given as bride-wealth, lent on by the bride's father, claimed in compensation. Many men actually had very few cattle, and struggled to raise beasts for bride-wealth for themselves or for their sons; arguments over cattle could stretch on for years, and from generation to generation.[47] The system of cattle exchange threatened always to embroil elder men in conflict with their fellows, sparked off by impetuous youth and dissatisfied women.

HOUSEHOLDS & HOUSES

Men aspired to an ideal of polygamy.[48] But, though men might claim to be the absolute rulers of their wives and children, polygamy did not simply create a larger household as an economic unit.[49] Multiple wives did not necessarily occupy the same physical space, and there was constant struggle over the degree of authority which a husband should have over each wife and her children, and the extent to which wives might co-operate. Competing with the household was the alternative notion of the 'house' – that is, the distinct matrifocal unit consisting of a wife and her children. The physical nature of the household reflected conflict and shifting patterns of practice on this. Among the Nyakyusa, wives in the nineteenth century lived in individual, round houses, each wife having her own house and space and granary; but during the twentieth century they were increasingly forced, by their husbands, to occupy adjacent rooms at one end of a great 'long house', at the other end of which the husband had a room.[50] Nyoro households, where wives similarly sought to each maintain their own gardens and granary, underwent a similar physical transformation.[51] One household, or many houses: the variant physical structures revealed a dispute over the fundamentals of household authority and resource control. Among the Maasai, wives – if they all occupied the same settlement, which was not always the case – arranged themselves on either side of the entrance gateway, according to a process of recruitment and alliance-building under which

---

[45] Ints Nya37b, 3; Nyoro13b, 1.

[46] Meyer, *Wa-Konde*, 173, 311-12.

[47] Roscoe, *The Bakitara*, 275-6; cattle numbers in the past are hard to estimate, but some informants' accounts suggest that, among the Nyoro, it was not uncommon for men to have no cattle: Ints Nyoro11a, 1-2; Nyoro12a, 1; Meyer, *Wa-Konde*, 123.

[48] Wilson, *For Men and Elders*, 120; Beattie, *Bunyoro*, 55-56.

[49] Beattie, *Bunyoro*, 51-2; Guyer, 'Household and Community', 99.

[50] Wilson, *For Men and Elders*, 118; Int Nya22a, 2; Int Nya23a, 2; see also Meyer, *Wa-Konde*, 115, 328, 330. Meyer notes that the 'long house' was an innovation of the early twentieth century, initially intended to avoid tax on plural wives: Meyer, *Wa-Konde*, 165.

[51] Ints Nyoro6b, 1; Nyoro7b, 1; Nyoro 9b, 2; Roscoe, *The Northern Bantu*, 69; Roscoe, *The Bakitara*, 264-5; Beattie, *Bunyoro*, 51.

established wives were expected to give a share of 'their' cattle to recruit a new wife to their 'side' of the gate, gambling as they did so on the possibility that the new wife would produce no sons and would therefore not threaten the claims of their own sons to cattle for bride-wealth purposes.[52] Nyakyusa and Nyoro women had no such formalized system of alliance-building, and tension between co-wives over the claims and status of their sons were constant, even though co-wives might also find themselves forging close ties of co-operation in sharing work.[53]

The identification of women with the interests of their sons was based on concern for their own future as much as motherly sentiment. Women were often younger than the men who married them, and might well expect to outlive their husbands. Yet widowed women easily lost their place in the system of authority, claim and obligation on which survival depended. Among Nyoro, Nyakyusa and Maasai, as among most people of pre-colonial East Africa, sex and reproduction were the basis of women's ability to construct relationships with men and often widowed women were old, without seductive or reproductive powers. They relied for their survival on the support of their sons: a woman whose sons were married should find herself cared for in widowhood, but a childless older woman, or one without married sons, faced a bleak future when her husband died. So women were always concerned to assert a degree of autonomy for their 'house', to claim that cattle should be used to help their sons to marry, and to invoke a complex range of arguments of precedent and obligation to suggest that some cattle should only be used to mark transactions in favour of their sons: because those cattle had been given for their daughters in marriage, or because they had been lent or borrowed in some other transaction involving the woman's kin.[54] Across the region, the claims of the 'house' might conflict with those of the male-headed household.

Amongst the Nyakyusa, this matrifocality reached its extreme in the form of household establishment known as 'cock marriage': a marriage in which there was no movement of cattle. Instead, the groom would work for a period for the bride's father, in acknowledgement of his acceptance of a new relationship of authority. The children of the marriage would be considered to be under the authority not of the husband and his kin but of their mother's male kin: hence 'cock' marriage, the analogy being with the cockerel which has no interest in or claim on its offspring.[55] The consequences of such marriage for the household were clear: a man's children acknowledged the authority, and sought the assistance, of men who were not their father's kin. Such marriages were apparently not uncommon amongst the Nyakyusa in the nineteenth century, and they were the norm in many East African

---

[52] McClure, 'District Records for the Guidance', 14; Storrs Fox, 'Further Notes on the Masai', 458-9; Int Maa24b, 1; Spencer, *Maasai of Matapato*, 33-35.
[53] Ints Nya30a, 1; Nya37b, 1.
[54] Storrs Fox, 'Further Notes on the Masai', 459; Meyer, *Wa-Konde*, 173; Wilson, *For Men and Elders*, 89.
[55] Wilson, *For Men and Elders*, 60.

societies, particularly those in the south of the region. Even in societies where cattle bride-wealth was paid and children were expected to be under the authority of their fathers' kin, poor men might enter into arrangements very similar to the 'cock marriage' of the Nyakyusa.

CURSES & HEALTH

The authority of the senior male was, then, an embattled one. The role of men as a collective gerontocracy was constantly subverted by the aspirations of individual 'big men': weak in the face of the sexual power of women and the physical violence of youth, elders were constantly threatened by each other's greed and lust. Marriage, kinship, and age-sets did not in themselves reproduce seniority: they were arenas in which it was contested. Yet in these contests senior men did, collectively, retain their authority, even though individuals might lose out; and this observation returns us to the issue of how such authority was maintained.

Wilson's account of Nyakyusa society offered a simple explanation of this: the physical violence of young men, she observed, was contained by the mystical authority of elder men.[56] An early British administrator of the Maasai made a similar suggestion: 'the morani [warrior] believes the moru [married man] to be a master of the black art, and prefers for this reason not to offend him'.[57] A number of ethnographers have offered similar arguments for other East African societies,[58] adding detail for Aguilar's general argument that 'the old manipulate knowledge and reinvent tradition so as to create a gerontocracy'.[59] Bravman has suggested of Taita society that it was the control of elders over well-being which made their wider authority 'self-evidently proper'.[60] Baldly stated, this sounds uncomfortably like a colonial stereotype of youngsters held in thrall by the constant threat of cursing; and Heald has argued of Gisu society that while there was a clear contrast between the physical violence of young men and the mystical power of older men to curse, the suspicion of witchcraft by elders created hostility, not respect or authority.[61] Yet in many societies it was the ability to bless, as well as to curse, which senior men wielded, and they used it against their peers as well as their juniors. The next chapter will argue that ideas about power over individual and societal well-being were generally the basis of the authority of senior men in the face of the potent forces of sex and violence; and that the ways in which people used alcohol, and talked of its use, were central to the reproduction of these ideas.

[56] Wilson, *For Men and Elders*, 87.
[57] McClure, 'Memorandum on the Masai', 5.
[58] J. Middleton, *Lugbara Religion. Ritual and Authority among an African People* (London, 1960), 23; Sangree, *Age, Prayer and Politics*, 30.
[59] M. Aguilar, 'Gerontocratic, Aesthetic and Political Models of Age', in M. Aguilar (ed.), *The Politics of Age and Gerontocracy in Africa* (Trenton, NJ/Asmara, 1998), 7.
[60] B. Bravman, *Making Ethnic Ways. Communities and Their Transformations in Taita, Kenya, 1800-1950* (Portsmouth, NH/Nairobi/Oxford, 1998), 41.
[61] Heald, *Controlling Violence*, 72, 120.

Three

Drinking power
The construction of authority
in pre-colonial societies

If there's no beer, it's not a ritual.[1]

In 1873, Joseph Thomson stumbled unintentionally into the middle of a striking performance in a village in what is now Tanzania:

> In the square of the village, propped against a tree, sat a poor woman, apparently half-dead with illness of some sort, and looking very much as if she was in the stocks. Round about were some huge pots of native beer . . . In front of the woman the men danced in succession, with movements and gestures the most extraordinary . . . I learnt that they were employed in casting out devils from the woman in front of them, and to do this they required to use the most powerful charms they could think of, namely beer, dancing and music.[2]

Thomson's analysis of this as a casting out of devils may be suspect, yet the visual details of the scene are enough: here was some curative performance, dominated by men, with a woman as the subject, in which beer played a prominent role.

Many other sources affirm the near ubiquity of alcohol in rituals in nineteenth-century East African societies; and attest to the widespread social use of drink. 'The use of mwenge is so universal in Unyoro, and particularly in Uganda, that I believe many people never drink water.'[3] It is easy to be overwhelmed by the sheer abundance of references to the use of alcohol, and to conclude, simply if imprecisely, that alcohol carried great significance. But examination of these accounts reveals a pattern – not an absolute pattern, for there are many exceptions and counter-exceptions, yet still there is a pattern. This chapter seeks to show how the use of alcohol in rituals was

---

[1] Int Nya20a, 4: describing past practice.
[2] J. Thomson, *To the Central African Lakes and Back: the Narrative of the Royal Geographical Society's East Central African Expedition, 1878-80* (2 vols) (London, 1968 (1st edn 1881)), I, 102-3.
[3] Schweinfurth, *Emin Pasha*, 76.

informed by, and constantly recreated, a particular understanding of the nature of well-being: that people had an innate power over the health of others; that this was most developed in elder men; and that elder men, uniquely, possessed the ability and self-control to use this power well.

Everyday drinking was perhaps more important than such situationally defined drinking. Marriages, funerals and crises of health were occasional events; but everyday drinking reproduced the same assumptions of power as ritual; this was how alcohol created authority in daily practice. Yet the power evoked by drink was an ambiguous one: undermined from within, by the weaknesses and rivalries of the dominant, and faced by chronic challenges from alternative ideas of well-being. The next chapter discusses alternative notions of power and well-being, which existed across the region but which played a particularly important part in the making of authority in the interlacustrine area.

Age-sets & blessings:
alcohol in Maasai performance

You would be given alcohol when you had [borne] children, because you too would bless your children with alcohol.[4]

When a man quarrelled with his child, it was brewed, so that they come and speak and the relationship is restored; there was alcohol for shaving children; and alcohol was used for blessing warriors when they became young elders. There was also alcohol for sacrifice to god, but it was not drunk. There was alcohol to be offered to god so that it would rain; alcohol was made and poured on a holy ewe, it was blessed and they prayed, and then when it was uncovered it would shake itself and go back to graze, they did not slaughter it; when it shook itself at that moment it would bring rain; and they would eat meat and drink alcohol.[5]

For Maasai men life was punctuated by a series of performances, which marked movement from one status to another. At the age of about nine years, boys would go through circumcision; some years later they would go through the *enkipata*, a performance which made them into *murran*, or young men, living in separate encampments of their own; a further ceremony of *eunoto* would constitute them as a distinct and named age-set, and make them into senior *murran* who might marry; later still they would pass through further performances which led them to elderhood. The performances around circumcision involved one, or only a few boys; those of further transition tended to be much larger in scale.[6]

---

[4] Int Maa12a, 2.
[5] Int Maa20a, 2.
[6] J. Dawson, 1933, 'Account of the Engapata Ceremony' and ' Milk-drinking Ceremony', typescript in British Institute Library, Nairobi, 3; Leakey, 'Some Notes on the Masai'; Storrs Fox, 'Further Notes on the Masai'. Spencer, *Maasai of Matapato*, gives a clear account of rituals of transition as they appeared in the 1970s.

The circumcision operation was followed by a feast; while the circumcised boy rested indoors with age-mates, drinking blood and milk, his father would entertain with meat and honey-wine other men-kin, affines and neighbours who were of an age to have circumcised children.[7] This feast was an integral part of the process, not an added extra: if the father of the boy lacked the means to provide for guests in this way, circumcisions would be postponed until the drinking was feasible; Spencer suggests that in the twentieth century at least this part of the event was explicitly associated with the power of the father to bless and curse his children.[8] When boys sought elevation to the status of *murran*, they would ply with honey-wine the elder men of the age-set but one above them in the hope of enlisting their support.[9] Should they be successful, the actual performance which changed their status would similarly involve a constant supply of honey-wine to the elders, whose good humour was essential.[10] The boys might drink a little honey-wine mixed with blood, but no more than that; and when the new age-set was given its name, this would be announced through a horn which had been filled with blood and honey-wine.[11] The *eunoto* made even more extensive use of honey-wine. In this case, not only had all the elder men present to be kept well-supplied with drink, but the sacrificial ox had also to be made drunk, to ensure its good will, and honey-wine was used in the blessing of the young men at the end of the event: 'some elders walked round them drinking honey-wine and spraying it out of their mouths over the group as a blessing'.[12] In this event, some of the most senior *murran* might take a little honey-wine with the elders, but most would not. After *eunoto* came the milk-drinking ceremony which ended strict *murran* prohibitions on eating and drinking, and which could only be performed after the young man had sought permission from his father, with a gift of honey-wine.[13]

In the case of a young man – one who had recently ceased to be a *murran*, or still was one – many of the decisions around marriage were actually taken by his elders. But any man who sought to marry, whether a young man wishing to marry a first wife or an older man acquiring a new wife, would take a gift of honey to the father of the intended bride, seeking his agreement: 'when he ferments the honey he will be happy, and he will give you his daughter'.[14] Should the father agree to the match, the bride-wealth offered would also include honey-wine.[15] As with the status-transition events, the honey-wine was not perceived as an optional extra, but as a necessary part

---

[7] Storrs Fox, 'Further Notes on the Masai', 448.

[8] Spencer, *Maasai of Matapato*, 59, 74.

[9] Dawson, 'Account of the Engapata.'

[10] Dawson, 'Account of the Engapata', 9.

[11] Dawson, 'Account of the Engapata', 5, 6, 9.

[12] Storrs Fox, 'Further Notes on the Masai', 452; Leakey, 'Some Notes on the Masai'; Spencer, *Maasai of Matapato*, offers the explanation of the ox's intoxication and describes a 'shower' of blood and honey-wine: 140, 159; see also Int Maa30b, 1.

[13] Dawson, 'Milk-drinking Ceremony', 1.

[14] Ints Maa32a, 1; Maa37a, 2; Merker, 'The Masai', 30.

[15] Leakey, 'Some Notes', 203; Int Maa11a.

of the process, without which the marriage might not flourish. The blessing and goodwill of elders was essential to the success of ritual and alcohol helped secure this; and so it appeared too in the ceremonies to formalize inheritance, and in the final ceremony at the burial place.[16]

In Maasai society, there were few performances intended as responses to specific crises: in contrast to many other East African societies, the deceased, whether relatives or not, were not perceived to have any influence over the well-being of living Maasai, and human or animal illness would usually be treated with herbal cures rather than through appeals for the intervention of spirits.[17] Yet there were occasional appeals to super-human agency for assistance: women routinely offered prayers for well-being to an imprecisely defined creator spirit, and when some major crisis occurred, such as drought or animal disease, elder men and married women would sacrifice an animal – usually a sheep – and utter blessings intended to secure remission of the problem.[18] Again, elder men would drink at this event, and the blessings would involve the sprinkling of honey-wine:[19] 'They would slaughter a sheep there and pray to god, pouring alcohol on the sheep. Then if it shakes and that alcohol pours down, rain starts falling.'[20] And occasional crises over the fertility of women could lead to an *ol-amal*, a complex event involving on one level a high degree of female autonomy – as women formed into a band to demand livestock for offerings from men, and physically and sexually assaulted men – but ending in a performance in which elder men blessed women with alcohol to secure their fertility.[21]

A further Maasai practice in response to sickness should also be mentioned. Individual illness might sometimes be attributed to the curse of a senior man. Cure of such an illness could only be secured by seeking forgiveness from the curser, which would be effected through a gift of honey-wine to, and a public blessing from, the senior man believed responsible for the curse: 'You will be blessed and you will recover'.[22] Similarly, Hollis recorded that a young man who seduced the wife of someone of an elder generation might seek forgiveness and blessing through a gift of alcohol.[23] Some argued that women too could curse – particularly women who had borne children. But such a curse was very rare, and very feared, for there was no cure to this: 'remember', one man told me, 'women have no blessing'.[24] Women's power over others – so men argued – was solely destructive, though women could and did pray for general well-being. This practice made very clear the assumption which ran through the uses of

[16] Leakey, 'Some Notes', 205.
[17] Storrs Fox, 'Further Notes on the Masai', 456.
[18] Hollis, *The Masai*, xviii-xix; Ints Maa12c, 1; Maa21c, 1.
[19] Ints Maa28a, 2; Maa27c, 1.
[20] Int Maa35a, 2.
[21] Int Maa32b, 1; Maa17b, 1; Maa21c, 1: Maa40b, 1; Maa33a, 1. Leakey describes an *ol-amal* for young men: 'Some Notes on the Masai', 188.
[22] Int Maa17b, 1.
[23] Hollis, *The Masai*, 312; Leakey, 'Some Notes on the Masai', 202.
[24] Int Maa27c, 2.

honey-wine in other events: all linked the drinking of intoxicants by elder men to their claim to an especial power to ensure, as well as threaten, the well-being of individuals and of society. Only old men could bless, and 'alcohol is for old men'.[25]

Beer & well-being: Nyakyusa ideas of social health

Beer [is] a drink which is valued, on ordinary days and special days.[26]

The classic ethnographies of the Nyakyusa, based on fieldwork in the 1930s, suggests that, in the nineteenth century, society in Rungwe was characterized by clear physical separation of generations of men: young men would withdraw collectively from their fathers' villages, under the leadership of a new generation of political leaders, and establish separate settlements of their own.[27] However, no such age-villages were ever recorded in their ideal form – residence patterns were much more complicated than would have resulted from this – and it seems likely that the image of age-villages was a retrospective formalization and idealization of a pre-colonial reality in which chronic conflicts between young men and old men could mean that the practice of initiation, or 'coming out' for a small group of boys, might sometimes be the cue for these boys to move away, in defiance of their fathers, in search of new patrons.[28]

Ritual performances among the Nyakyusa were less tied to general moments of transition than they were amongst the Maasai; individual ceremonies of transition, and rituals in response to domestic crises, were more common. Alcohol was common – almost ubiquitous – in these: 'Beer must be present in every religious proceeding', noted a missionary who worked in the Nyakyusa area from the 1890s to 1916.[29] At the birth of a first child the mother would return to her parental home, and then come back to her husband again with the new baby. In this return, she would come accompanied with gifts, millet beer for her husband and his male kin being prominent amongst these. Later children were not greeted so elaborately, unless they were twins, in which case both father and mother would retreat for a period from human contact. The period of their seclusion was defined by the time taken to prepare millet beer; on their emergence the beer would be drunk by the husband and by his father-in-law, with the bride and her mother also participating.[30]

---

[25] Ints Maa7a, 3; Maa8a, 2.

[26] Meyer, *Wa-Konde*, 82.

[27] This literature began with G. Wilson, 'An Introduction to Nyakyusa Society', *Bantu Studies*, 10 (1938); and continued with M. Wilson, *Good Company*; Wilson, *Rituals of Kinship*; *idem*, *Communal Rituals of the Nyakyusa* (London/New York/Toronto, 1959); *idem*, *For Men and Elders*.

[28] M. McKenny, 'The Social Structure of the Nyakyusa: A Re-evaluation', *Africa*, 43 (1973), 91-107.

[29] Meyer, *Wa-Konde*, 82.

[30] Wilson, *Rituals of Kinship*, 148, 152-3.

The initiation, or emergence to adulthood, of men and women similarly involved a pattern of withdrawal, and then return, marked by predominantly male drinking. A woman marrying for the first time would go through a period of seclusion and instruction while beer was brewed. When the ferment was ready, the woman would go to her new father-in-law with beer for him and his kin to consume.[31] 'That beer would be taken and carried to the man who had given you the cow [of bride-wealth]. And he would call his friends and say "This drink comes from my brother, the one to whom I gave a cow, now let us talk, my brothers". . . . It unites them and they talk very well.'[32]

Ritual exchange of beer constantly evoked the importance of amity and goodwill amongst elder men; and linked this to their authority over others. The movement of beer at marriage balanced a flow of beverages in the other direction during the negotiation of the marriage, when the prospective husband would take beer to the father of his intended bride, and young men would also take beer when they went to ask an uncle for help with cattle to marry.[33] The drinking aspect in these performances was essential to well-being: madness threatened brides whose weddings were not attended by suitable drinking events.[34]

Amongst the Nyakyusa, offerings in direct response to sickness or ill-fortune were conducted by men. 'Beer [was] taken in the mouth and spat out' as the man named his ancestors and mentioned his particular troubles as he did so.[35] A missionary observed this practice at the turn of the century: 'Near to a neighbouring house I saw a man standing by a banana plant. In his left hand he held a gourd . . . He took the drink in his mouth and spat it towards the banana plant as he talked . . . Finally he tipped out the dregs on the plant . . . I greeted him and learned that he had a sick child.'[36]

Beer and food might also be left out for the consumption of the deceased even when there was no immediate crisis of health;[37] and generalized problems of disease or poor weather were the cue for large-scale offerings in which cattle, sheep or chickens were slaughtered, the blood poured out, and the meat either set aside for ancestors to consume, or eaten by the male officiants at the events.[38] In such events, millet beer again played an important role, being sometimes poured out or left for ancestors to consume (if it were left, children might later drink it as surrogates for the deceased), or being consumed by the elder men who controlled these performances.[39] 'Beer is drink for men and gods', remarked a missionary who had worked among the Nyakyusa and the neighbouring Ngonde.[40] While political

[31] Int Nya2a, 2.
[32] Int Nya20a, 3.
[33] Wilson, *For Men and Elders*, 91.
[34] Wilson, *Rituals of Kinship*, 99-101.
[35] Meyer, *Wa-Konde*, 70, 74; Int Nya17b, 3.
[36] Meyer, *Wa-Konde*, 75.
[37] Wilson, *Rituals of Kinship*, 180.
[38] Meyer, *Wa-Konde*, 72-4.
[39] Meyer, *Wa-Konde*, 76; Ints Nya20a, 4, Nya21b; Wilson, *Rituals of Kinship*, 182.
[40] Mackenzie, *Spirit-ridden Konde*, 128.

leaders played some role in these events, a role which may perhaps have been exaggerated in retrospect, it was always elder men who dominated these performances, whether they were performed for one sick child or for a whole area suffering from inadequate rain.[41]

In the 1930s, a Nyakyusa man called Kasitile organized a particular event when he himself was sick and when he perceived that there was a problem with the health of society: he held a drinking party of influential men with the aim of encouraging them to 'express' or 'speak out' any resentment or ill-will which they harboured.[42] Missionaries recorded similar Nyakyusa practice in the nineteenth century, when men were encouraged to publicly vituperate, in the hope that the expression of their ill-will would bring general health: there was some disappointment that the missionaries themselves were unwilling to perform a similar 'speaking out'.[43] This practice was paralleled in the particular performance involving an individual young man and an elder, when the youth's illness was attributed to the elder's anger: by presenting the elder man with drink the son sought to ensure the expression of anger and consequent goodwill.[44] 'Long ago there were curses, if you wronged your father, you might become lame. Now, if he wanted to forgive you he would have to call people . . . people would drink there, then those people would say, "Now stand up", and immediately one would stand up . . . The lameness is gone!'[45] In the 1930s, Wilson recorded repeated instances of the centrality of beer in securing remission of illness caused by the wrath of elder men: only thus could their admission of anger, and their forgiveness and blessing, be assured.[46]

Despite the evident contrast between a system which made much of the mention of deceased ancestors and one in which the dead played no apparent part, there was a remarkable similarity between Nyakyusa and Maasai practice in the use of intoxicating beverages in performances related to well-being. Consistently, alcohol flowed towards elder men; others might taste it, but elder men were supposed to drink deeply of it, for this encouraged in them the goodwill and amity which cured the sickness, made the marriage fertile, ensured that the child was healthy – which, in short, ensured well-being.

---

[41] Ints Nya3a, 4, Nya12b, 1; Wilson, *Rituals of Kinship*, 182; Wilson, *Communal Rituals*, 25, 74.

[42] Wilson, *Communal Rituals*, 133-41. To 'speak out' is *ukusosya*: a term linguistically connected to the whole set of practices around the 'emergence' after initiation and the 'emergence' of parents from seclusion after a twin-birth. Wilson, *Rituals of Kinship*, 119, 152-3; *idem, Communal Rituals*, 52.

[43] Meyer, *Wa-Konde*, 87.

[44] Wilson, *Good Company*, 240.

[45] Ints Nya10a, 5-6; also Nya20c, 1.

[46] Wilson, *Good Company*, 70-1, 76, 107, 238, 240.

Elders & alcohol

Long ago the alcohol belonged to elders, not juniors. It was made purposefully for elders.[47]

The particular association of drink with elder men was widespread in other nineteenth-century East African societies.[48] New, noting the ritual role of alcohol, noted too that it was the elder men of 'Wanika' society who drank, not the young men or women.[49] Among the Kamba an early twentieth-century observer noted that 'according to the old custom, beer drinking is a privilege for the old men . . . not only women but also young men and boys are forbidden to drink it'.[50] Kamba men would take beer to the father of the woman they wished to marry, and the circumcision of a boy would be followed by general drinking by elder men.[51] In the early twentieth century, young Langi men waiting for initiation would be daubed with beer by elder men, apparently in blessing, and during the ceremony the young men had to serve elders with beer; the elaborate ceremony which followed the birth of twins similarly involved men drinking beer along with the mother of the twins.[52] Kikuyu elders used honey-wine to bless initiants; and Kikuyu suitors presented honey-wine to prospective fathers-in-law, lest their brides be cursed and infertile.[53]

The use of alcohol in offerings to deceased men – particularly in those offerings made in response to immediate crisis – has led some to analyse drinking by living elders as a way of allowing communication, which put the living elders in touch with those who had died: Akyeampong has argued that alcohol 'bridged the gap between physical and spiritual worlds'.[54] But the way in which drinking by the living was interwoven with the offering of drink to the dead suggests an alternative interpretation, within a wider context in which alcoholic beverages flowed towards elder men and were largely the privilege of elder men. Drinking by the dead and by the living was essentially similar: the dead drank because that was the practice of the living:[55] 'Beer is the drink of the country', one Nyakyusa man said, when asked why it was used in rituals.[56] Elders, dead and living, were given drink because their goodwill was sought; and the giving of drink constantly

[47] Int Maa20b, 1.

[48] J. Roscoe, *The Bagesu and Other Tribes of the Uganda Protectorate* (Cambridge, 1924), 59; J. Driberg, *The Lango. A Nilotic Tribe of Uganda* (London, 1923), 231; Chanler, *Through Jungle and Desert*, 220.

[49] New, *Life, Wanderings and Labours*, 96.

[50] Lindblom, *The Akamba*, 519.

[51] C. Hobley, *Ethnology of the Akamba and Other East African Tribes* (Cambridge, 1910), 63, 68, 72.

[52] Driberg, *The Lango*, 142-3, 248.

[53] Cagnolo, *The Akikuyu*, 90, 91.

[54] Akyeampong, *Drink, Power and Cultural Change*, 21; Carlson, 'Haya Worldview and Ethos', 222, 253.

[55] A local opinion recorded by Carslon, 'Haya Worldview and Ethos', 252, though his interpretation is different.

[56] Wilson, *Rituals of Kinship*, 62.

reproduced the idea that their goodwill was necessary.

That the giving of drink was principally concerned with ensuring the goodwill of elders, not with establishing communication with the deceased, was clear enough in Maasai practice, since deceased elders played no perceived role in this. Maasai concerns – at least, as explained in retrospect – were very much focused on living elders: 'If elders don't drink, they become unkind.'[57] That was why Maasai insisted that there should be inebriate goodwill at the *eunoto* and that even the sacrifical ox had to be happy when it died. Maasai elder men needed alcohol to bless: as a medium to convey their blessings, sometimes, but even more to ensure that they were in the mood to bless. The giving of drink to elder men argued their ability to bless, and the danger of their ill-will. For while the ill-will of elder men was inherently dangerous, it could be countered by encouraging the public, intoxicated, expression of grievances. Alcohol 'makes [elders] happy and they become very frank, they will say all that is in their hearts during blessing'.[58] This was the essence too of the Taita practice of *kutasa*, in which men spat sugar-cane beer while uttering blessings, casting out the dangerous anger that lay within them.[59]

Nyakyusa practice revealed the same concerns with the innate power of elder men over well-being, as Kasitile's performance suggests. Wilson, in the 1930s, reported the Nyakyusa conceptualization of this power as 'the breath of men'.[60] Goodwill was not only important to subordinates. Meyer recorded that a Nyakyusa man who swore a false oath would fall ill unless he gave beer to those who had witnessed the oath and sought their forgiveness; and that a man's children might fall ill if he were in dispute with another man, or his wife refused to share food with neighbours.[61] The goodwill and forgiveness of elders were as important to their peers as they were to their subordinates. So drink featured at the division of the inheritance, where some potential heir who failed to assert claims to a share might miss out on that share, and thereafter bear a grudge.[62] Drink helped them speak out, and grievances, actual or potential, might be addressed once they were aired. In many societies, the peaceful settlement of cases between men required drink, and such was the importance of alcohol in this that when public discussion amongst elder men failed to secure resolution of a dispute, people in central Kenya would say: 'The case has drunk water.'[63]

BLOOD, MILK & WATER

The use of alcohol in rituals of well-being, coupled with the privileged access of elder men to alcohol, evoked the notion of men's innate power, the importance of their goodwill and the expression of their opinion. No other

[57] Int Maa13b.
[58] Int Maa26a.
[59] G. Harris, *Casting Out Anger. Religion among the Taita of Kenya* (Cambridge, 1978), 25-8.
[60] Wilson, *Good Company*, 100-1, 107, 121.
[61] Meyer, *Wa-Konde*, 77-9.
[62] Ints Nya27b, 2; Nya32b, 2.
[63] Wilson, *Good Company*, 137; Lindblom, *The Akamba*, 152.

sacred fluid made this clear linkage, though there were a number of other fluids which might play a role in ritual, all across the region. Blood, milk, water and saliva could be, and were, all used. But each of these occupied a more definitely distinct role; and none had the cross-cultural ubiquity of alcohol. And blood was not – as has been argued elsewhere – seen as somehow equivalent to alcohol.[64] Maasai used milk to bless, usually by sprinkling it, and milk had clear connotations of fertility;[65] Maasai men also blessed simply by spitting saliva.[66] Nyakyusa spilled blood on the ground, or left it in containers, when animals were slaughtered in events intended to ensure the goodwill of the deceased.[67] The intention was, explicitly, that this provided a means for the deceased to share in the feast, an attempt to satiate them. Water might be blown by Nyakyusa when they mentioned the names of the deceased and spoke out their grievances; water was a medium which might carry the dangerous anger away from the body, and disperse it.[68]

Strikingly, alcohol could be used in any of these ways; its employment was a constant ritual possibility. No other fluid possessed this versatility, this adaptability to circumstance. The Nyakyusa did not blow milk when they mentioned ancestors; no one poured water in the hope of appeasing the deceased or indicated their forgiveness by spitting blood over repentant youngsters. Some, in retrospect, explain the ritual role of alcohol through the associations of its ingredients: arguing that honey-wine was used by the Maasai because it implicitly invoked the fecundity of the bee; or that grain beer was used because it was associated with the success of the harvest.[69] Such arguments may have featured in discourse within particular societies; yet none explain why alcohol, made in such different ways from so many different ingredients, should have been so important in so many societies. The explanation for this surely lies much more clearly in the idea that men's goodwill – and frankness – was necessary to the well-being of society. Certainly in the nineteenth century, alcohol existed alongside other sacred fluids; it had not entirely displaced them, and might be poured, blown and sprinkled alongside them. But its use did create the assumption of power as men's possession, in the way that no other fluid did.

[64] S. Klausner, 'Sacred and Profane Meanings of Blood and Alcohol', *Journal of Social Psychology*, 64 (1964), 27-43.
[65] Int Maa20b, 1-2; J. Galaty, 'Pollution and Pastoral Antipraxis: the Issue of Maasai Inequality', *American Ethnologist*, 6 (4) (1979), 803-16. Kamba men used milk and alcohol together in blessing: Lindblom, *The Akamba*, 184.
[66] Thomson, *Through Masailand*, 166.
[67] Meyer, *Wa-Konde*, 74.
[68] Meyer, *Wa-Konde*, 37, 81.
[69] Ints Maa11b; Maa24a, 1.

Social drinking

Only men drink.[70]

By no means all, or even most, drinking, took place in the context of ritual events. Unreliable as European travellers' accounts of East African drinking are, they suggest widespread (if seasonally varying) intoxication. 'Perhaps in no European country are so many drunken men seen abroad as in East Africa', said Burton.[71] Drinking was very common, and drinking parties formed one of the main foci of social activity. But these were – at least ideally – events for elder men. Young Maasai men were not supposed to drink; nor were women.[72] In East Africa, as among the Tswana, beer drinking 'physicalized senior men's dominance of social consumption'.[73] Among the Nyakyusa, the millet used for beer-making was a man's crop, unlike food crops, and was kept in a special store by the husband.[74] When a husband wished to drink, he would give his wife millet: 'You make [beer] with this. I will invite my friends.'[75] These companionable drinking events were the scene of transactions in authority over juniors:

> Because in those days it was like they were finding things out from one another. If someone has given birth to a child, he is asked what kind of child it is, and how it was growing; so that the child would be married or would marry. That was the reason for gathering in their groups.[76]

Notions of temperance focused on preventing or controlling the drinking of young men and women. Where young men were allowed to drink beer, it was supposed to be taken in a manner which affirmed, strikingly, the dominance of elders.

> [The elder] took the straw himself, and drank. When he, with the straw, had the alcohol in his mouth, he would give you the [other end of the] straw to sip. You would sip the alcohol from his mouth, you drank like that. You took like that from his mouth, not through the straw because that was forbidden! You would not drink through the straw, it was forbidden. Because you were a young person and you could not drink with the elders.[77]

Women were similarly supposed to drink in ways which reproduced their subordination. 'A woman did not have permission to drink without being told by her husband to drink. She waited until she was told to drink. Then

[70] Int Maa32a, 1.
[71] Burton, *Lake Regions*, II, 295-6.
[72] Thomson, *Through Masailand*, 251; Hollis, *The Masai*, xvi; Int Maa32b.
[73] P. Landau, *Realm of the Word. Language, Gender, and Christianity in a Southern African Kingdom* (Portsmouth, NH/London, 1995), 83.
[74] Int Nya28b, 1.
[75] Int Nya22a, 3.
[76] Int Nya29a, 2.
[77] Int Nya32a, 3.

she gave thanks, and moved away'.[78] Such statements are idealizations, but they do reflect a discourse about what should have happened, and there are nineteenth-century accounts which evidence this same notion of temperance. Burton suggested that Nyamwezi women could only drink separately from the men, having 'private pombe', as he put it,[79] and a missionary described Nyamwezi drinking as very much an affair of elder men:

> I remember arriving at an Unyamwezi village one morning, just as the elders were about to hold a beer drinking. They came out and solemnly seated themselves in a circle under a spreading tree; a huge cauldron of 'pombe' or beer, was brought out and ladled into gourds and cups made of basket work from which not a drop of the liquor escaped. These were silently passed from hand to hand until the cauldron was emptied.[80]

This notion of temperance argued the dangerous nature of women's power and young men's power: the powers of sex and violence. Drunken women would engage in sexual adventures, drunken young men might run amok.[81] Elders, on the other hand, possessed an innate power over well-being which was, if anything, more benevolent when they were drunk, and their dangerous 'secrets' and angers were expressed.[82] Restrictions on drinking, and the pattern of drinking parties, affirmed the triangle of power between sex, violence and power over well-being, and asserted the primacy of power over well-being in this triangle.

DRINK & SELF-CONTROL:
THE UNDOING OF POWER

The one who has drunk his fill, spills beer on himself.[83]

The 'indigenous ethic of temperance' of most of nineteenth-century East Africa constantly reproduced a set of assumptions about the contrasting powers of elder men, women and young men. Young men possessed the power of violence; women the power of sex: but men had the power to cure and harm, and so they could and should drink. Yet at the same time social drinking practices underlined the potential weakness of men: elders should not drink with women and young men, lest they make fools of themselves. For elder men, frankness was desirable, but helpless inebriation was not.[84] Elder men were expected to drink, but they were not expected to become incapable in front of women and young men. Maasai men drank inside, for preference, and one would put his stick on the roof of the house to warn

---

[78] Int Nya27a, 2.
[79] Burton, *Lake Regions*, II, 28, 295-6.
[80] Ashe, *Two Kings*, 308-9.
[81] Ints Nyoro35c, 8; Maa36b, 2.
[82] Int Nya16c, 11.
[83] 'Kila ashibaye pombe hujimwagia'; proverb quoted in letter from Batamaha, *Mambo Leo*, Apr. 1946.
[84] Int Nyoro10c, 4.

women and young men not to approach.[85] The hopelessly drunkard elder was regarded as disgraceful – the drunkard was the archetype of the *olwishiwishi*, the Maasai term for a feckless elder, and he encapsulated the dangers which faced men if they lost respect:[86] 'Alcohol has no respect. It can make you fall in front of your in-laws and sisters and show your nakedness.'[87] For alcohol revealed men's weakness, as well as arguing their strength: when drunk, Kamba elders 'generally so careful of their dignity, forget it'.[88] Quarrelsomely drunken elder men were helpless in the face of physical insubordination by younger men; and they were doubly helpless in the face of the sexual power of women, unable to perform yet prone to initiate sexual adventures which could only provoke conflict with their fellow men. When Maasai men were blessed – with honey-wine – to indicate that they had reached the status where they might start to drink, they were warned: 'Drink, but do not cause a disturbance, do not destroy prosperity with alcohol'.[89] And social drinking events also manifested the contradiction in elder men's relationships with one another. They potentially embodied an ideal of conviviality and openness amongst elder men, yet in practice they were also the occasion for conflict: the expression of grievances might lead not to reconciliation but to immediate violence.[90]

Alternative ideas of power: Prophets & sacred places

The use of alcohol constantly reproduced the idea that power over well-being was innate in elder men. But behind the drinking predominance of elder men, there was a startling array of practices across the region, only partially revealed by the limited evidence, which suggests a considerable tendency to eclecticism and the constant emergence of new practices in response to new crises; yet suggests too a repeated cycle through which new principles of power were contested, reinterpreted and finally incorporated by elder men.

Some claimed an influence over well-being through their relationship with some reputed place of power. In essence the power that they claimed was an intercessory one; a power to speak for or seek the assistance of some kind of spirit which was not ancestral, nor human. Meyer described the activities of

[85] Int Maa29a, 1.
[86] Int Maa12a, 2. Similar ideas on 'respect' and drink are expressed in Ints Nya2c, 1; Nya5c, 1.
[87] Int Maa20b, 1.
[88] Lindblom, *The Akamba*, 521.
[89] Int Maa14a, 1.
[90] At least, on evidence from the early twentieth century: Weule, *Native Life*, 186; Mackenzie, *Spirit-ridden Konde*, 129.

one man who demanded cattle and wives for his spirit in return for securing general well-being.[91] In Nyakyusa and elsewhere there was often a prophetic or mantic element to this: those who claimed such power delivered messages which enjoined people to avoid certain activities in order to avoid sickness or drought, or they offered predictions as to the success of raids and other, less tangible, visions into the future.[92] There was considerable fuzziness in the definition of such power and in people's understanding of its relationship to other kinds of power; yet such individuals could build a local authority which challenged the authority of elder men through the claims which they made on labour or resources. Prophets who demanded gifts of cattle, or young women, for the satisfaction of the spirits on whose behalf they spoke, posed a direct challenge to the authority of elder men.

The most clearly tense relationship was perhaps that between Maasai *il-oibonok*, or 'prophets', and Maasai elder men. Maasai men feared the power of the *il-oibonok*, sought their services in times of crisis and valued their opinions on the timing of raids, but they also despised them, sought to evade their demands, and perhaps resented the claim of the *il-oibonok* to have a power over the fertility of women.[93] *Il-oibonok* asserted also a different role for alcohol, which they consumed not in pursuit of a state of cheerful sociability, nor yet to allow them to express their angers. Drink influenced *il-oibonok* in a much more direct way, putting them into contact with their possessory spirits.[94] Their drinking, however, was a private affair, rather than an exercise in openness and sharing: it evoked a lonely, secret power, quite unlike the much more widespread assumption of the innate power of elder men.

Some people claimed a particular power over well-being based on some unusual ability or knowledge which they possessed, through inheritance or through purchase.[95] Sometimes the envious or resentful might do more than mutter their ill-will or privately wish ill upon those who had offended them; they might seek the help of the other people to cause harm, or employ substances which were believed to give the power to bring harm.[96] Women might invoke the help of their own ancestors through ritual performance,[97] but even more importantly they might turn to these ideas of inherited or learned power. Sorcery and witchcraft existed, and posed an implicit challenge to elder men. But they existed in an ambiguous way: people sought to distinguish varieties of power over well-being, creating distinct categories for the power of ancestors or living elders, the inherited particular power of some individuals and the learned power of others.[98] Scholarly analysis has

---

[91] Meyer, *Wa-Konde*, 63-4.

[92] R. Waller, 'Kidongoi's Kin. Prophecy and Power in Maasailand', in D. Anderson and D. Johnson (eds.), *Revealing Prophets. Prophecy in East African History* (London/Nairobi/Kampala/Athens, OH, 1995), 28-64; M. Wright, 'Nyakyusa Cults and Politics in the Later Nineteenth Century', in T. Ranger and I. Kimambo (eds.), *The Historical Study of Religion in Africa* (London, 1972), 153-70.

[93] Merker, 'The Masai', 14-16; Galaty, 'Pollution and Pastoral Antipraxis', 805-6; S. L. and H. Hinde, *The Last of the Masai* (London, 1901), 72.

[94] Hollis, *The Masai*, 324.

[95] Meyer, *Wa-Konde*, 86-92; Waller, 'Kidongoi's Kin', 31-2.

[96] Meyer, *Wa-Konde*, 88-9.

[97] Meyer, *Wa-Konde*, 72-3.

[98] Meyer describes a whole range of distinct kinds of practitioner: *Wa-Konde*, 86-100; and see Nya20c, 1.

picked up these fractured arguments about the nature of power.[99]   But in daily practice the use of drink guided such debates back towards the notion of an innate power which was strongest in (if not unique to) men: as in Nyakyusa society, where this power was conceived, strikingly if ambiguously, as taking the form of 'snakes', living in the belly.[100] 'Everyone has a snake', one man told me.[101] Power over others might be innate, but if so it was unequally distributed; elder men alone could use it wisely.

ALTERNATIVE DRINKING

Women, also, frequently appear intoxicated.[102]

Across much of East Africa, the notion of elder men's exclusive claim to drink was widespread, the basis of an ideal in which '[w]hilst the women look after the house and field, the men squat idly in little knots, drinking, laughing and talking together'.[103] But this principle was not always strictly observed in practice, and drink might actually flow very freely at certain moments. Women and young men drank – sometimes away from elder men,[104] but sometimes publicly, with elder men. 'The expression of the countenance, even in the women, is wild and angry, and the round eyes are often reddened and blurred by drink', said Burton of the people of Ugogo.[105] Thomson's caravan was welcomed in one place by an all-night party with 'unlimited pombe (native beer) and a dance' in which men and women participated.[106] The young Kikuyu men who alarmed Lugard might really have been drunk, though they existed in a society which asserted the undesirability of such drinking. Speke observed in northwestern Tanzania a wholesale drinking binge and party, in which 'all the men, women and children, singing and clapping their hands in time, danced for hours together'.[107] Such events emphasised the subversive as well as the authoritarian possibilities of drinking: young men and women danced and drank with elder men, creating multiple possibilities for sexual rivalry. On occasion, women might also appropriate alcohol in rituals of well-being, as well.[108] And where the assumptions of elder men's power were most challenged, patterns of drinking moved quite beyond the control of elder men: as among the Nyoro, and other societies in the interlacustrine.

[99] Wilson argued a distinction between the power of neighbours – as the 'breath of men' – and that of senior kin; and distinguished both from the power resident in certain substances: *Rituals of Kinship*, 3. Yet the idea of 'pythons' as the basis of power recurs: *Good Company*, 91-4, 96-8, 101, 106; *Rituals of Kinship*, 32.

[100] Meyer, *Wa-Konde*, 86-7.

[101] Int Nya16c, 7.

[102] Burton, *Lake Regions*, II, 296.

[103] Krapf, *Travels, Researches and Missionary Labours*, 356-7.

[104] Both Burton and Cameron noted the existence of separate drinking-houses for women in Unyamwezi: Burton, *Lake Regions,* II, 28; Cameron, *Across Africa*, 140.

[105] Burton, *Lake Regions*, I, 305.

[106] Thomson, *To the Central African Lakes*, I, 106-7.

[107] Speke, *Journal of the Discovery*, 101-2.

[108] J. Last. 'A Visit to the Masai People Living Beyond the Borders of the Nguru Country', *Proceedings of the Royal Geographical Society*, ns, v (1887), 522.

Four

Chiefs & caravans
Alternative sources of power

In the palace there was always alcohol.[1]

Samuel Baker was an unhappy visitor to the capital of Kabarega, king of Bunyoro. One of the things to which he objected most was the nocturnal merrymaking of Kabarega's following of young men: the *barasura*, as the Nyoro called them, whom Baker described as 'lounging by day and drinking and howling with drums and horns as an accompaniment throughout the night'.

> I could never learn the exact number that formed Kabba Rega's celebrated regiment of blackguards, but I should imagine there were above 1,000 men, who constantly surrounded him and gained their living by pillaging others.
> Any slave who ran away from his master might find an asylum if he volunteered to enlist in the bonosoora. Every man who had committed some crime or could not pay his debts could find a refuge by committing himself to the personal care of the young king, or enrolling himself within the ranks of the royal guards.[2]

The characterization of both king and followers as young men is significant. Bunyoro was a state ruled by a young man, with a young army, who were a regional by-word for violence and raiding; and the army drank very publicly and noisily.[3] Kabarega also drank: Baker several times suggested that Kabarega was drunk when they met.[4] While societies across much of East Africa were dominated by elder men, whose authority rested on assumptions of power reproduced in drinking practices, authority in Bunyoro lay in the hands of younger men with armies of drunken blackguards. This pattern was reproduced in other parts of the

---

[1] Int Nyoro15a, 1.
[2] S. Baker, *Ismailia. A Narrative of the Expedition to Central Africa for the Suppression of the Slave Trade* (London/New York, 1895 (1st edn 1874)), 343-4.
[3] H.M. Stanley, *In Darkest Africa, or the Quest, Rescue and Retreat of Emin, Governor of Equatoria* (2 vols) (New York, 1890), II, 310.
[4] Baker, *Ismailia*, 351, 354.

interlacustrine too, but it was most evident in Bunyoro, where two phenomena were combined. One was the existence of unusually overt competition between different notions of well-being, which allowed the elaboration of new political forms which exploited generational tensions amongst men. The other was a new competition over control of people and resources – including alcohol – consequent on the growing caravan trade. The first of these phenomena was largely confined to the interlacustrine; the second was widespread across East Africa, and particularly affected societies along the main caravan routes across what is now central Tanzania. Both profoundly affected relationships between old men, young men and women, in ways which were manifest in contests over the use of alcohol.

The gatekeepers

Mandara, Chaga ruler of Moshi on the slopes of Mount Kilimanjaro, made a martial impression on those who met him.

> He was not difficult to distinguish from his bodyguard. With a natural feeling for effect he had grouped his soldiers in a semi-circle round him, and placed himself somewhat in front, with a crescent of fierce-looking warriors behind, each man holding his shining spear-blade erect.[5]

While his young warriors imitated Maasai weaponry and dress, Mandara himself had a decidedly more catholic set of tastes and desires, which were most apparent in his dealings with the various European travellers who stayed with him, and whose accounts have made Mandara one of the best-known East African potentates of the nineteenth century.[6] Mandara was absolutely aware of the possibilities which such travellers offered, in terms of an immediate supply of relatively sophisticated weaponry and manufactured goods, and in terms of links to a wider world from which these items were flowing into East Africa at a rapidly increasing rate. The new items brought by the caravan trade were, by their novelty and sometimes by their nature, quite different from the things which had long been the subject of exchange transactions in the region – salt, iron, earthenware, grind-stones. As Glassman has argued, this was not a simple difference between 'necessities' and 'luxuries'; it was rather a matter of the changing social meanings ascribed to things.[7] Johnston soon learned that the men around Mandara's court who wore cloth and bore guns perceived themselves, and were treated, as quite different from the ordinary spear-carriers.[8] Guns were violence embodied – their power was clear enough. Cloth declared its

---

[5] Johnston, *Kilima-Njaro Expedition*, 103.
[6] Johnston, *Kilima-Njaro Expedition*, 89; New, *Life, Wanderings and Labours*, 387-97; Thomson, *Through Masailand*, 76; Jackson, *Early Days*, 118-19.
[7] Glassman, *Feasts and Riot*, 36-7.
[8] Johnston, *Kilima-Njaro Expedition*, 87-8.

wearer to be a privileged participant in a system of commerce that led to the coast and beyond. So too, in a lesser way, could beads or wire be transformative, their possession marking status among women and men across the region. The items of the caravan trade *were* power – at least for a time, until the 'trajectory of meanings' put them all (except for guns) back into the realm of everyday items possessed by many but esteemed by none.[9] Yet for the time that they embodied power they created new kinds of authority – and new tensions over authority; offering new models of accumulation and new paths to autonomy.

So Mandara, and others like him, obtained guns, cloth, mirrors and a host of other items, and used these to support a campaign of violence and of patronage politics which catapulted him to prominence in the space of a few years and which – according to some observers – led to a period of prolonged insecurity and general violence around Kilimanjaro, as Mandara and others sought to meet the demands of the visitors who supplied them with weapons and cloth: slaves for coastal traders, porters, food and protection for the much smaller but generally wealthier assortment of evangelists, explorers, botanists and egotists from Europe.[10]

In all this, Mandara turned to new effect the long-standing tensions between old men and young men, for the availability of new forms of wealth and new resources of violence gave a new direction to what Wrigley has called the 'band phenomenon', of young men coming together into raiding parties.[11] Mandara used violence to enable him to act as a 'gatekeeper', controlling contact between traders and local society and exacting as a toll the resources which allowed him to continue the exercise of violence.[12] Mandara was a prominent, though by no means unique, example of a quite widespread phenomenon: a youthful ruler, whose power was explicitly associated with violence, and who relied on youthful followers. Mirambo, who pursued a similar trajectory to power in central Tanzania, told Stanley of his contempt for older men, and his reliance on young men, who were 'obedient and brave'.[13] Mandara, Mirambo and others based their power on access to things, which gave them authority over their followers; and on youthful violence, which gave them authority against others.

Their ability to do so was predicated on the chronic tension between young men and old men over authority. Elder men wished to control the labour of their sons; they sought to prevent the fission of the household, and sought too to add to the household by marrying new wives. Young men sought to evade this control, and to accumulate on their own account. The possibility that they might do this by seeking a new patron was a constant one; the existence of aspirant political rulers, who rewarded their followers

[9] Glassman, *Feasts and Riot*, 50-1.
[10] Johnston, *Kilima-Njaro* Expedition, 96-8.
[11] C. Wrigley, *Kingship and State. The Buganda Dynasty* (Cambridge, 1996), 222.
[12] Johnston, *Kilima-Njaro Expedition*, 96-7, 108, 165; for the concept of gatekeepers, see Lonsdale, 'Conquest State', 22.
[13] Stanley, *Through the Dark Continent*, I, 386.

with the spoils of war and the proceeds of engagement in trade, made this possibility more attractive. Some, like the blacksmith and his companions whom Cameron met on their way to join Mirambo in 1873, travelled far to seek such patronage.[14] Other men began to build up their own little followings of violent raiders in imitation of Mirambo, Mandara and others: the petty 'sultan' with whom Grant lodged in Unyamwezi had 20 young men as his little army.[15] The young follower of a successful gatekeeper might acquire a captured woman as a wife, would eat well and come in for a share of captured cattle and traded manufactures.[16]

> In such states as Mos[h]i, where there is a relatively large standing army, the chief will generally distribute the female slaves captured in war among his soldiers, and dower them himself with cattle. Thus his soldiers become indebted to him for their domestic happiness, and are consequently very much attached to the person of their monarch who is, to them, the sole dispenser of benefits.[17]

Mandara also displayed another characteristic of this group of new men: he was as eclectic in his search for paths to well-being as in his taste for gadgets. Johnston had barely arrived in Moshi when he was beset by demands, made through Mandara, for treatment for ailing wives and children of the chief. By contrast, Johnston had commented that an ordinary man in Taveta, on his way to Moshi, had snubbed his offer of medical advice; Mandara had no such reservations.[18] Violence was one characteristic of these new men; chronic uncertainty about their ability to secure the well-being of their followers was another.

Such was unsurprising, for violence was an unsteady foundation for authority. Youthful followers, and the gatekeepers themselves, grew older and faced the everyday crises of health and ill-luck against which neither coloured cloth nor violence offered remedy. They sought also to exercise their own authority as elders over wives and children in the face of the demands of others and the insubordination of their juniors, against whom the constant use of physical violence was scarcely practicable. The violence on which they relied challenged generational authority and the principle of elder men's power: but offered nothing in place of this. Mandara and his followers wrestled with an intractable problem: immediate authority could be built through the power of patronage and the power of violence, but the power of youthful violence slipped away with time, and they must either compromise with the power of elder men, or provide an alternative path to well-being.

[14] Cameron, *Across Africa*, 58.
[15] Stanley, *Through the Dark Continent*, I, 397; Grant, *A Walk Across Africa*, 85, 103.
[16] New, *Life, Wanderings and Labours*, 387, 458.
[17] Johnston, *Kilima-Njaro Expedition*, 437.
[18] Johnston, *Kilima-Njaro Expedition*, 111-12, 215.

Power of violence, power of ritual

The King would give you a cow, a goat, or even a woman if you worked diligently.[19]

In many respects, the two nineteenth-century rulers of Bunyoro about whom we know most, Kamurasi and his successor Kabarega, were similar to Mandara. Like Mandara, Kamurasi and Kabarega were both entranced by firearms, which – as tools of coercion and desirable patronage items – embodied the two kinds of power on which the gatekeepers based their authority.[20]   Both traded ivory and slaves for guns and ammunition, and served as gatekeepers for traders operating south along the Nile; both Kamurasi and Kabarega surrounded themselves with followings of violent young men, attracted to this powerful patron, who lived in the distinctive settlement around the palace.[21] 'The *Barusura* would loot during war, just like those [soldiers] of today. They would bring the loot to the King and he would give them their share . . . he would give them goats, cows and wives.'[22] Kamurasi and Kabarega were 'receivers and distributors of women', as Beattie has put it: they obtained women as war captives, or as runaways from their husbands, or as daughters given by men who hoped thus to secure protection, and they gave these women to those who served them.[23] 'He used to give away all the women in the palace'; said one woman, and a Nyoro man recounted the popular memory that '[o]nce you went to the king he would give you a wife'.[24] The *abaranga*, the women of the court, were there 'to entice one'.[25] As rulers, the immediate ability of Kamurasi and Kabarega to enforce their will relied on the coercive power of these young men.[26]

Descriptions of the Bunyoro court consistently stress the physical violence which surrounded it, while noting that this was less extreme than in Buganda.[27] It was a violence implicit in the constant presence of armed young men, and explicit in the looting through which these young men supported themselves.[28] It was explicit too in the way that the ruler's decisions were conveyed and enforced: when the king wished the court to

[19] Int Nyoro6c, 2.

[20] Speke, *Journal of the Discovery*, 396-7, reveals the importance which Kamurasi attached to firearms; as do Baker's complaints of Kamurasi's begging for particular weapons: *Albert N'yanza*, II, 416. These European witnesses were themselves, of course, peculiarly passionate about guns: *Albert N'yanza*, II, 341.

[21] Baker, *Albert N'yanza*, II, 437-40; Schweinfurth, *Emin Pasha*, 63; Baker, *Ismailia*, 284; Int Nyoro36b, 1-2.

[22] Int Nyoro8a, 2.

[23] J. Beattie, *The Nyoro State* (Oxford, 1971), 142; Speke, *Journal of the Discovery*, 433, recorded one instance of a man being provided with wives; Schweinfurth, *Emin Pasha*, 87, refers to the women of the court: Ints Nyoro15b, 1; Nyoro22a, 1-2.

[24] Int Nyoro10a, 2; Nyoro16a, 3.

[25] Int Nyoro4c, 4; Nyoro10b, 4.

[26] Speke, *Journal of the Discovery*, 413.

[27] Grant, *A Walk Across Africa*, 288.

[28] Grant, *A Walk Across Africa*, 307.

be cleared, his followers set about the crowd with bludgeons; when he sentenced a man to death the sentence was carried out at once: they [*barusura*] were brutal.[29] Even more clearly than in Mandara's domain, the power of the Nyoro ruler directly challenged the authority of elder men and the principle of elder men's power over well-being; 'everybody was a servant of the King'.[30] Mandara dispossessed the subjects of his rival potentates, and challenged elder men indirectly by competing with them for the allegiance of young men and women; in Bunyoro, the ruler's young men simply dispossessed the old and paid no heed to the consequences.[31] The Nyoro state inverted the authority of elder men and defied the structures of marriage and household. People in Bunyoro still perceive that state authority and domestic authority are fundamentally distinct, and in many ways opposed.[32]

Kamurasi and Kabarega, however, ruled over a political entity which was much larger and more structured, and had a much longer history, than Mandara's little domain of Moshi: the ruler of Bunyoro presided over chiefs and lesser chiefs, to whom responsibilities and authority were delegated.[33] Mandara and Mirambo both built on a local authority which they had possessed as inheritors of a claim to special power over well-being; and built their position through exploiting the new possibilities offered by the caravan trade and the new tools of violence and patronage which it made available. Kamurasi and Kabarega drew on a much longer tradition of authority and on an established principle of eclecticism in the search for well-being.

While East Africa was in the pre-colonial period largely characterized by small-scale societies, without centralized power, there had long been rulers in the interlacustrine – in Bunyoro, Buganda, and to a degree in Nkore and Toro – who were able to exercise a degree of control over people and resources that was unparalleled in the region. These societies were in other ways quite diverse: Buganda was an agrarian society dominated by a system of clans; Nkore, Toro and the lesser states of the southwest were marked by a clear social divide between agriculturalists and pastoralists in which the pastoralists were dominant and political power rested largely in their hands; in Bunyoro the division into agriculturalist and pastoralist was rather less clear.[34] It is generally argued that political power in the west grew out of the adroit manipulation of cattle as patronage resources;[35] and in Buganda out

---

[29] Int Nyoro9c, 3; Nyoro16b, 5; Baker, *Albert N'yanza*, II, 420, 436.

[30] Int Nyoro8a, 1.

[31] Ints Nyoro38a, 3; Nyoro39b, 5; Baker, *Albert N'yanza*, II, 349-50; *idem, Ismailia*, 353.

[32] One informant described these two domains of authority as *omubulemi* and *omunzaarwa*: roughly translated as 'the space of the state' and the 'space of kinship': Int Nyoro 27a, 7. For the distinctive notion of *obulemi*, see Beattie, *Nyoro State*, 7.

[33] Baker, *Ismailia*, 322.

[34] E. Steinhart, *Conflict and Collaboration: The Kingdoms of Western Uganda, 1890-1907* (Princeton, NJ, 1977), 3-7, 18-24.

[35] E. Steinhart, 'The Kingdoms of the March: Speculations on Social and Political Change', in J. Webster (ed.), *Chronology, Migration and Drought in Interlacustrine Africa* (London, 1979), 189-214; J. Sutton, 'The Antecedents of the Interlacustrine Kingdoms', *JAH*, 34 (1993), 33-64.

of brokering resources derived from a very productive banana-based economy and from the possibilities of trade around Lake Victoria.[36] In each case, these resources made it possible for rulers to assemble a following of young men who offered the possibility of organized violence against recalcitrant subjects or against neighbouring societies who chose not to recognize the authority of the ruler. Such violence yielded further patronage resources, in the form of captives, foodstuffs and livestock, and so the cycle of violent accumulation continued. Long before the caravan trade of the nineteenth century, rulers in the interlacustrine were using patronage resources to direct the violence of young men towards the construction of authority.

These material possibilities aside, the rulers of the interlacustrine states possessed another kind of resource; in this part of the region, alternative ideas of control over well-being were very apparent. In the nineteenth century, Kamurasi and Kabarega sought medicine from their European guests as well as manufactured goods and firearms, just as Mandara did;[37] they believed in the possibility that power over well-being could be contained in a bottle. But long before the arrival of tartar-emetic in explorers' medicine chests, rulers of Bunyoro had been experimenting with alternative ideas of well-being, and it was their ability to do this that had made their authority more than transitory. Their authority was bound up with their success in incorporating and subordinating multiple ideas of well-being, notably that associated with the non-human, possessory spirits which influenced the well-being of individuals and of groups: the *embandwa*.

Among the Nyoro, deceased men were assumed to have some power over well-being, and practice which involved living elder men and offerings to deceased elders were one resort in time of problems, in which drink could be spilled or consumed.[38] Such practice evoked the idea, widespread across the rest of the region, that the goodwill of elder men was necessary to the well-being of all, and that the anger of elder men – their 'bad heart', as Nyoro put it – was a fearsome, dangerous thing.[39] Drinking at funerals and marriages similarly evoked this idea, with drink being given to elders – and especially in-laws – to make them happy and to ensure that their 'hearts were clean'.[40] 'Alcohol is very important in this land. When marrying, there has to be alcohol. Someone is dead – alcohol is brought. Alcohol is very important.'[41]

But among the Nyoro there existed alternative forms of practice, to which

[36] Wrigley, *Kingship and State*, 232-6.

[37] Speke, *Journal of the Discovery*, 410-11; Baker, *Albert N'yanza*, II, 427. Given the amateurish prescription and the nature of the pharmacopeia at the time, it is perhaps surprising that the ministrations of the explorers produced no effects more serious than temporary discomfort: *Albert N'yanza*, II, 428.

[38] Int Nyoro11b, 6; Nyoro 10b, 11.

[39] Int Nyoro2c, 5; Int Nyoro8c, 4; Int Nyoro15c, 2.

[40] Int Nyoro10a, 8; Nyoro2a, 4; Nyoro4a, 2; Nyoro6b, 5; the terms for 'make happy' and ' make clean' are close in form: -*shemeza* and *semeza*.

[41] Int Nyoro6b, 6.

many had recourse in time of sickness and might also become involved in the rituals of status transition. There were specific, locational kinds of power over well-being, claimed by particular lineages and associated with particular shrines. And there were *embandwa*, possessory spirits who were believed to be able to cause a whole range of problems far more serious than those attributed to the anger of living or deceased elders.[42] The nature and extent of *embandwa* practice suggest that the development of such practice downgraded the perceived power over well-being of elder males.[43]

Relationships with the *embandwa* revolved around initiated cult groups in which both women and young children could play central roles. There were itinerant individuals, many of them women, who claimed to have special relationships with possessory spirits, and who provided ritual recourse in time of sickness or ill-fortune. In return for their services, they were rewarded, and they acquired their own little followings.[44] This role of the *embandwa* in establishing a degree of religious autonomy for women has been stressed by some authors;[45] but *embandwa* could also become associated with the particular power – and the sorts of freedom – offered at the court of the ruler.

Some *embandwa* practitioners apparently operated under the patronage of the Nyoro ruler, and became a part of the shifting population around the court, lending their services to the ruler and offering him a new form of power through control over well-being.[46] There was a distinctive notion of the power possessed by rulers in Bunyoro: the idea of *mahano*.[47] But this was a terrible and destructive power, and the ingenuity of the Nyoro kingship lay in its appropriation of healing powers alongside this. The accounts of Speke and Baker tell us little about ritual, but the prominence in royal ritual practice of horns filled with magical substances suggests the belief that certain substances contained power, and could bestow this power,[48] and it is likely that the fantastic costumes which were adopted by the young soldiers of Kamurasi and Kabarega were associated with *embandwa* practice. Popular memory identifies the rulers as involved in *embandwa*, or even as a kind of *embandwa* themselves, and the kings of Bunyoro became involved in a distinctive kind of ritual performance at each new moon, associated with the *embandwa*, which was supposed to ensure the well-being of the kingdom

---

[42] Grant, *A Walk Across Africa*, 292-3.

[43] D. Schoenbrun, *A Green Place, A Good Place. Agrarian Change, Gender and Social Identity in the Great Lakes Region to the 15th Century* (Portsmouth, NH/Oxford, 1998), 233-5.

[44] Speke, *Journal of the Discovery*, 218.

[45] I. Berger, 'Fertility as Power: Spirit Mediums, Priestesses and the Pre-Colonial State in Inter-Lacustrine East Africa', in Anderson and Johnson, *Revealing Prophets*, 65-82.

[46] Fisher, *Twilight Tales*, 53-68. R. Tantala, 'The Early History of Kitara in Western Uganda: Process Models of Religious and Political Change' (PhD, Madison, WI, 1989) argues that there is a long history of possessory spirit activity in the region, and that a particular strand of this became associated with rulers' power over well-being.

[47] Beattie, *Nyoro State*, 118.

[48] Speke referred repeatedly to Kamurasi using 'horns' of magic: *Journal of the Discovery*, 401, 407, 419.

as a whole.[49] In all of these ways, *embandwa* practice became involved in establishing a royal claim to power over well-being, in clear competition with the notion that the goodwill of elder men was central to well-being: Kabarega was believed – by some, at least – to control the rain, as well as his blackguards.[50]

In *embandwa* in Bunyoro, it would seem that alcohol may not have been used at all,[51] though in rather similar possessory practices around the court of Buganda, women mediums plied the king with drink.[52] In either case, the pattern of *embandwa* was associated with drinking which reproduced no assumption of elder men's power, and *embandwa* challenged the authority of elder men as directly as did the recruitment of dissatisfied young women and men. The challenge between these different notions of power over well-being could be very manifest: the kings of Bunyoro allegedly retained ritual specialists to protect him from the spirits of those he had robbed and killed.[53] This was the fundamental difference between the states of the interlacustrine and the new political creations that sprang up under the immediate influence of nineteenth-century trade. Both were characterized by youthful violence, but in the interlacustrine an alternative model of well-being existed to underpin the authority of rulers, and to offer a model for the longer-term translation of power: so that the authority of ruler, and of the men whom he ruled, might rely on something more than constant resort to coercion.

DRUNKEN YOUTHS, DRUNKEN CHIEFS

...people who stayed with the king ... were always drinking alcohol from the villages[54]

Drink flowed freely among the youthful retainers of the Nyoro rulers, and of men like Mandara.[55] The *barusura*, in popular memory, 'would always be drunk'.[56] Sometimes they drank to prepare themselves for battle. At Kabarega's tomb the vessel, the *entigiro*, which was allegedly used to serve banana wine to his soldiers before battle was still displayed in the 1990s, and in the 1880s Johnston had witnessed Mandara's warriors topping up

---

[49] Int Nyoro38c, 5-6; Nyoro43a, 3; Baker, *Albert Ny'anza*, II, 347-9; Schweinfurth, *Emin Pasha*, 66; G. Casati, *Ten Years in Equatoria and the Return with Emin Pasha* (trans J. Clay) (London, 1891), 265.

[50] Lloyd, *Uganda to Khartoum*, 52.

[51] There is no mention of alcohol in Lloyd's account of *embandwa*, *Uganda to Khartoum*, 70-2; or in Fisher's, *Twilight Tales*, 53-68. See also J. Beattie, 'Spirit Mediumship in Bunyoro', in J.M. Beattie and J. Middleton, *Spirit Mediumship and Society in Africa* (London, 1969), 159-70.

[52] Speke, *Journal of the Discovery*, 211.

[53] Int Nyoro10c, 2.

[54] Int Nyoro10a, 10.

[55] Baker clearly valued his sleep; years before writing his complaints about Kabarega's drunken followers, he had made exactly the same criticism of Kamurasi's men: *Albert N'yanza*, II, 443. New complained about the inebriate nocturnal carousing of the soldiery of one of Mandara's rivals: *Life, Wanderings and Labours*, 443.

[56] Int Nyoro38a, 3.

on beer in mid-battle.[57] And sometimes they drank in celebration of military success: Mutesa of Uganda rewarded his successful warriors with drink on their return from the field.[58] Krapf watched Kivoi, one of the first of East Africa's 'gatekeepers', ply his followers with honey-wine before persuading them to accompany him on a dangerous expedition.[59] Such gestures emphasized the extent to which the recruitment of these followings exploited the tensions between elder and younger men. In other societies, young men were denied drink – and even among the Nyoro, one strand of discourse asserted the desirability of drinking by the elderly, rather than the young.[60] But in the interlacustrine, rulers extracted drink from household heads. Grant said that in Karagwe one pot in three of banana wine was taken by the palace, and drink was given to young followers.[61] It is perhaps unsurprising that in the early years of the twentieth century, the 'king's police' in Bunyoro remained notorious for drinking and riotous misbehaviour.[62]

This created a distinct pattern of drinking, evident in Bunyoro and elsewhere, which focused on the centres of political power and involved young men, and which revolved not around the open expression of grievance in the hope of reaching consensus and avoiding conflict, but rather on the release of the violence of younger men. Drinking in this case evoked not the danger of elder men's power over well-being, but the immediate reality of young men's power of violence. The very pattern of distribution of drink showed how political authority both parodied and inverted generational and gender authority. In Bunyoro, household heads brought banana wine to local chiefs, and they, or local chiefs, also took banana wine to the palace of the ruler: the *ebihotoole*, as it was called.[63] In so doing each giver implicitly cast themselves as a junior, seeking the goodwill and blessing of the ruler through gifts of drink. Yet the ruler might then distribute this drink to his following of younger men.[64] Drink flowed towards power; to the ruler, and through him to the young warriors.

There was an ambiguity, though; men like Mandara or Kabarega, though they exploited the tensions between young and old, and sometimes directly defied the authority of individual elders, might hesitate to snub all elders; for while violence and trade goods were the basis of their authority, their immediate followings remained a small part of the populace. Their ability to accumulate followers was predicated on the existence of the male-headed household, which they tended to undermine. Even where, like Kabarega, rulers claimed a distinct power over well-being, their long-term interest lay in a degree of accommodation with the elders on whom they were, in many

---

[57] Int Nyoro8c, 6; Johnston, *Kilima-Njaro Expedition*, 175.

[58] Speke, *Journal of the Discovery*, 324.

[59] Krapf, *Travels, Researches and Missionary Labours*, 312.

[60] Int Nyoro3a, 2.

[61] Grant, *A Walk Across Africa*, 143.

[62] Int Nyoro15a, 1; Lloyd, *Uganda to Khartoum*, 58.

[63] Ints Nyoro2b, 5; Nyoro4a, 2; Nyoro5a, 4; Nyoro16a, 4.

[64] Ints Nyoro6c, 1; Nyoro36a, 5.

ways, predatory . Rather than distributing to young men the alcohol brought as tribute, the ruler might therefore drink with those who brought it, in a social drinking practice which both marked favour and evoked the notion of co-operation and openness among equals inherent in the principle of elder men's power.[65] While the drinking of young men was wild and uproarious, rulers seem more usually to have drunk very heavily, but sedately: Thomson refers to Mandara's 'continual quaffing of beer', and many observers commented on the drunkenness of 'gatekeepers' across East Africa – with a sly glee derived from European ideas that such behaviour represented reprehensible lack of self-control.[66] The chiefs of nineteenth-century East Africa – in the interlacustrine, but even more so elsewhere – were poised between different principles of power, balancing the demands of their youthful followers and the realities of maintaining longer-term authority.[67] The drunkenness of the young followers of chiefs embodied a challenge to the authority of elder men; the drunkenness of chiefs themselves might rather manifest a willingness to reach temporary accommodations with that power. One woman described how the *ebihotoole*, destined for the ruler, might be diverted on the way in a manner that intertwined male power and the power of the ruler, while implicitly challenged the unique claims of elder men:

> In those days, when you were going to marry and your prospective father-in-law has asked for five gourds [of banana wine], if the person you have chosen to lead you is bright enough and he has at one time lived in the palace, if he met people taking *ebihotoole* for the King, he might grab some and send the people to the King to tell him, 'Your servant, so and so, has taken two gourds from your *ebihotoole*, because he is taking his son to marry'. In that case there was no crime, because what you were doing was not bad, you would be instead adding to the kingdom.[68]

SPIRITS & POWER

Mandara himself treated one of his visitors to an extended eulogy on Chaga beer, which stressed the physical strength which drink bestowed. 'He extolled toddy as not only exhilarating, but really nutritious and strengthening, pointing to his own thews and sinews in proof of the statement.'[69] Others exploited their position as gatekeepers to use new kinds of alcohol in ways which came to serve as an evocation of the notion of particular or mantic power over well-being which had long existed alongside the principle of elder men's power. Distilled spirits, unknown in East Africa before the

---

[65] Stanley, *In Darkest Africa*, II, 371.

[66] Thomson, *Through Masailand*, 76; Stanley, *Through the Dark Continent*, I, 120; Grant, *A Walk Across Africa*, 24.

[67] This dilemma was observed by Casati, who was in most ways an unsympathetic – and occasionally mendacious – chronicler of Bunyoro: *Ten Years*, 264-5, 273.

[68] Int Nyoro2a, 4.

[69] New, *Life, Wanderings and Missionary Labours*, 397.

expansion of commerce in the nineteenth century, were central to this, as more than one explorer sought to seal their alliances with local potentates by offering them spirits.[70] Famously, both Kamurasi of Bunyoro and Mutesa, the ruler of Buganda, were delighted when European visitors turned their hands to the production of spirits and presented these to their hosts: in each case, the ruler was anxious to obtain a regular and exclusive supply of this new kind of alcohol.[71] More widely available drinks were the source of contest between old men and young which political rulers could exploit; this new kind of alcohol was a form of power, exclusively available to those who already wielded authority, and much sought by them.[72] Like the bottled medicine in the explorers' chests, spirits were a kind of power that could be consumed, as Stanley was anxious to show his hosts: '"Here", I said, uncorking a vial of medicinal brandy, "is the Kisungu pombe' (white man's beer); take a spoonful and try it . . . a little of it makes men feel strong, and good; but too much of it makes men bad, and they die." "Let me have some," said one of the chiefs.'[73] Sadly, neither Baker nor Speke recorded quite how spirits were perceived, in terms of their relationship to other kinds of alcoholic beverage, but clearly those with authority constantly sought access to spirits from European travellers or visitors; not to share this with their followers but to consume it themselves.[74] In this alternative formulation of drinking, drink was power, and its consumption should be a secret activity.

Aspiring rulers: Balafyale

Amongst the Nyakyusa, no individual ruler of the stature of Mandara emerged, but the very ethnonym, Nyakyusa, suggests that not dissimilar processes were at work in this society. In the later nineteenth century, the people at the north end of Lake Nyasa were known by a variety of names.[75] Mwakyusa was one of a number of aspirant local leaders in the later nineteenth century.[76] He achieved sufficient prominence to bring him to the attention of missionaries, who recorded his name and the derivation of it, Nyakyusa, which was used to describe those who acknowledged a degree of obedience to this man and his descendants.[77] In the 1920s and 1930s, British policy and practice were to turn this into the general term for the populace of the area.[78]

Mwakyusa was a *mlafyale*, a local political leader. The *balafyale* were very numerous, and most of them commanded very small domains, of a few

---

[70] Grant, *A Walk Across Africa*, 69; Fabian, *Out of Our Minds*, 70.
[71] Speke, *Journal of the Discovery*, 307-8; Baker, *Albert Ny'anza*, II, 467-9.
[72] Krapf, *Travels, Researches and Missionary Labours*, 182-3.
[73] Stanley, *How I Found Livingstone*, 258.
[74] New, *Life, Wanderings and Labours*, 165; Hohnel, *Discovery of Lakes Rudolf and Stefanie*, I, 173.
[75] D. Kerr-Cross, 'Geographical Notes on the Country Between Lakes Nyassa, Rukwa and Tanganyika', *Scottish Geographical Magazine*, VI (1890), 281-93; Lugard, *Rise of Our East African Empire*, I, 56-57, 131.
[76] Ints Nya8c, 4; Nya4c, 7; Kerr-Cross, 'Geographical Notes', 282; Mwakyusa's name appears on a map of the late 1880s: Lugard, *Rise of Our East African Empire*, I, 94.
[77] Ints Nya1c, 2; Nya16a, 1.
[78] Wilson, *Good Company*, 2.

hundred people only. The standard ethnography of the area argues that the *balafyale* were an immigrant ethnic group, of different origin from the rest of the populace, who wielded a political power which was bound up with a system of male residence in age-villages, and rested largely on their assumed control over well-being and their involvement with a rather vaguely defined ritual hierarchy centred on one or more shrines.[79] But it is by no means clear that age-villages really existed, and it is quite evident that while chiefs played a role in collective ritual practice, this was in some ways subordinate to that of elder men.[80] Sources are by no means consistent on the point of the distinct origin of the *balafyale*; modern oral accounts and evidence collected in the period from 1890 to 1930 tend rather to suggest that the ancestors of all the population were immigrants, and to divide the *balafyale* into several unrelated lineages.[81] The title *mlafyale* implies descent in the female line, and the form of Mwakyusa's name reveals that he was named for his mother, Kyusa, a practice popularly explained by Nyakyusa as a consequence of the polygamy of the wealthy: the sons of men who have many wives choose to assert their identity and their claims to inheritance through their mother, not their father.[82] It would seem that the *balafyale* were actually not a single group but rather that they emerged from (and often merged back into) the rest of the populace, briefly exploiting the generational tensions of society to raid and build a degree of authority, but never constructing any lasting domain.[83] This was the basis of the identification between the emergence of a new chief and the emergence of a new generation of men; a brief alliance between chief and young men, as the chief gathered round himself a following of young men to whom he would distribute the spoils of raiding.[84] Thus the apparently rapid shifts from periods of peace to periods of raiding and insecurity, such as that which attended the attempt by Mwakyusa's son to establish his own independence.[85]

The area populated by the Nyakyusa was off the caravan routes, walled in by high mountains. Aspirant leaders here could not derive patronage resources through playing gatekeeper, and so the scale of political experimentation here was small. But Mwakyusa's position near to the northern shore of Lake Nyasa gave him a limited degree of contact with coastal traders and, from the 1880s, with Europeans. He was therefore able

---

[79] Wilson, *Communal Rituals*, 1-3.

[80] Meyer, *Wa-Konde*, 133, but see also 205-9. On age-villages, see chapter 2.

[81] For the assumption that the *balafyale* were ethnically the same as the rest of the populace, see Meyer, *Wa-Konde*, 28; Ints Nya16a, Nya32a, Nya36b; see also 'Historical-Tribal Legends', in the Rungwe District Book, TNA MF 28. For conflicts between unrelated groups of *balafyale*, see Int Nya21c, 3.

[82] Ints Nya1c, 2; Nya4b, 1; Nya3c, 2-3; Wilson, *Communal Rituals*, 17.

[83] One man recalled how his grandfather had been effectively robbed by an aspiring chief, and forced to flee: Int Nya1c, 1.

[84] Meyer, *Wa-Konde*, 132, 134-5; Int Nya36b, 3.

[85] L. Fotheringham, *Adventures in Nyasaland* (London, 1891), 285, 287-91; a few months earlier Kerr-Cross had described the same area as a model of peace: 'Geographical Notes', 281-4.

to command a little more in the way of patronage, and to build a slightly larger reputation and following than his fellows.[86] Like other accumulators, Mwakyusa faced the problem of how to manage this reliance on violence and dispossession with the establishment of a longer-term authority. The *balafyale* sought to reinterpret their power partly through engagement with elder men, and partly through building a relationship with the particular, mantic form of power over well-being connected with certain ritual sites.

But patronage, even for Mwakyusa, was limited, and the *balafyale* offered no clear ritual alternative to the principle of elder men's power. Nineteenth-century accounts suggest that the authority of most *balafyale* was very limited indeed; they were able to launch youthful followers on to a trajectory of accumulation as household heads, but once that accumulation had begun, the *mlafyale* and his claims were inconvenient, and largely ignored: Mwakyusa himself disappeared rather abruptly from the historical record.[87] Ritual practice was dominated by elder men, and patterns of drinking clearly showed the dominance of the principle of elder men's power; pre-colonial Nyakyusa society was, if anything, characterized by the chronic ineffectuality of a plethora of 'chiefs' competing for the loyalty of a limited number of potential subjects.[88]

MARKETS & DRINK

Mandara built his authority through trade; Kabarega of Bunyoro used the possibilities of commerce to revive the flagging fortunes of the state of Bunyoro, in a remarkable resurgence which was curtailed only by British intervention. The caravan trade offered new resources for the concentration of authority; but it also offered new challenges to authority, and opened new possibilities of accumulation for the subordinate. The nineteenth century saw processes of change which, while drawn-out and gradual, changed the pattern and possibilities of conflict over the control and exchange of a range of things. It has been argued that in most societies the dominant will tend to resist the commoditization of things;[89] contests over the nature of exchange in East Africa suggest that this is all the more so when those things play a role in the practices which make and remake power.

Almost anything could be exchanged: even where there were no formal markets – as among the Nyakyusa – people moved and bartered.[90] Some things were, by virtue of limited geographical supply, inevitably involved in

---

[86] Wright, 'Nyakyusa Cults and Politics', 160; Fotheringham, *Adventures in Nyasaland*, 285.

[87] Wilson, despite her idea of 'divine kings' with ritual power, believed that British policy had exaggerated the former role of the *balafyale*; *Good Company*, 13. British administrators generally shared this opinion: see 'System of Government in Practice', Rungwe District Book, TNA MF 28.

[88] S.R. Charsley, *The Princes of Nyakyusa* (Nairobi, 1969), 69-70.

[89] A. Appadurai, 'Commodities and the Politics of Value', in A. Appadurai (ed.), *The Social Life of Things. Commodities in Cultural Perspective* (Cambridge, 1986), 3-63.

[90] For the pre-colonial lack of markets and the existence of considerable barter trade, see Meyer, *Wa-Konde*, 117, 118, 127-9.

exchange: salt, dried fish, or iron worked from good ores.[91] But there was exchange in other, more everyday items, usually over a shorter distance: pottery, basketwork, hides, ghee, grain or fruit.[92] Yet there were limits to barter, for certain kinds of exchange posed threats to authority. Women sought a degree of autonomy through exchange: a control over the product of their own labour and how its product might be used. They had some success in this, but across much of the region practice and occasional argument defined and reaffirmed the boundaries of two distinct domains of exchange, one involving women and the daily needs of the household; the other involving men and the tools of violence and household reproduction. Women bartered with other women for certain goods which they used and had control over: basic foodstuffs and domestic items.[93] Men bartered small livestock, weapons and hunting equipment.[94] And across most of the region, cattle (and sometimes other livestock) were rarely bartered because they were bound up with a quite different kind of transaction, which dealt in authority over people, and because they were by virtue of this entailed in multiple relationships. The movement of cattle rested firmly in the hands of elder men. Among the Nyakyusa, so too did the use of millet, the main ingredient of beer.[95]

Alcoholic beverages occupied an ambiguous place in contests over exchange. They were desirable in themselves; and being ephemeral they could never be entailed by complex patterns of authority and relationship in the way that cattle might be. In many societies they were very clearly the product of women's labour, so that women had ample opportunity to divert them into exchange, and arguments for doing so. Yet beverages were mostly consumed by men, so that their exchange would violate the boundaries of the distinct gender domains of exchange. And barter disrupted a simple principle: that drinking practice was a central element in the construction of power and drink flowed towards power. The involvement of alcohol in straightforward barter undermined the principle of restricted access to alcohol, and could threaten the practices which made men's authority; and so men sought to prevent the sale of alcohol. They were by no means wholly successful in doing so. This was, unsurprisingly, most apparent in Bunyoro, where the whole pattern of elder men's power was challenged: millet beer was for sale near the palace when Speke and Grant visited in 1862.[96] The caravan trade brought a new kind of demand, and within a few years there were 'women with enormous gourd-jugs full of foaming beer' in the markets.[97] Elsewhere elder men's attempts to prevent the barter of alcohol were increasingly contested as the caravan trade brought new possibilities.

---

[91] Ints Nya19c, 3; Nya37a, 1; Stanley, *In Darkest Africa*, II, 315; for a general account of the importance of trade, see H. Kjekshus, *Ecology Control and Economic Development in East African History: the Case of Tanganyika, 1850-1950* (London/Nairobi/Ibadan/Lusaka, 1977), 111-12.

[92] Speke, *Journal of the Discovery*, 376; Ints Nya39b, 3; Meyer, *Wa-Konde*, 127-9.

[93] Ints Nya14c, 2; Nya16c, 9; Nyoro1b, 2.

[94] Int Nya6b, 1.

[95] Wilson, *For Men and Elders*, 93.

[96] Grant, *A Walk Across Africa*, 295.

[97] Schweinfurth, *Emin Pasha*, 113; Casati, *Ten Years*, 268. Baker, *Albert Ny'anza*, saw banana wine sold by women in the 1860s: II, 326, 328.

Caravans & drink

Caravans relied entirely on human porterage, and by the scale of the time, they were very substantial bodies of men; often 70 or more, sometimes several hundred.[98] Some gatekeepers sought to provide foodstuffs, as well as protection and trade items, giving 'gifts' of supplies in return for cloth, beads or gunpowder.[99] Thus they attempted to monopolize imported goods for themselves, and prevent 'commoditization': Mutesa of Buganda was the most determined exponent of this technique.[100] Stanley expressed his preference for this method of procuring supplies, noting drily that 'it is very economical to be the guest of a powerful African king'.[101] Yet neither Mutesa nor any other ruler was able to fully meet the demand or to control the entrepreneurial inclinations of ordinary women and men. Glassman has argued that in the 'struggles for the caravan trade', an urban coastal elite tended to triumph over upcountry rural male accumulators.[102] Yet there were other participants in these struggles: rural women and young men, for whom the caravan trade offered new opportunities, as well as new forms of oppression and servitude. The caravans offered new access to imported goods, and old and young, men and women, vied to provide services, as the caravans became a new factor in the generational and gender disputes of East African societies. Hohnel recorded how young Kikuyu men helped his caravan, in what was effectively a brief alliance against the authority of elder men, and both he and Thomson benefited from the assistance of elder Maasai men, who helped him avoid the imposts of the *moran*.[103] Young men living near to the caravan routes found that they could acquire trade goods for themselves by enlisting as porters for a little while, for caravans were plagued by desertions (often the new recruits would in turn desert soon after being taken on and receiving advance payment).[104] And where the caravans passed, new markets sprang up: permanent ones in the great new centres of the trade, at Tabora and Ujiji;[105] temporary ones where circumstances demanded, as in the vicinity of Kabarega's itinerant capital or in any place where a caravan stopped for a few days, as at 'Zungumero' in central Tanganyika, where the porters of caravans delayed by rain 'drank beer, smoked bhang, and quarrelled among themselves'.[106] While some travellers, especially those who strayed off the main caravan routes,

---

[98] Cameron, *Across Africa*, 34.
[99] Cameron, *Across Africa*, 35; Johnston, *Kilima-Njaro Expedition*, 78.
[100] Speke, *Journal of the Discovery*, 246.
[101] Stanley, *In Darkest Africa*, II, 343.
[102] Glassman, *Feasts and Riot*, 55-78.
[103] Hohnel, *Discovery of Lakes Rudolf and Stefanie*, I, 135, 296-320; Thomson, *Through Masailand*, 198.
[104] Cameron, *Across Africa*, 54, 115, 130, 132.
[105] Cameron, *Across Africa*, 182; Speke, *What Led to the Discovery*, 207; Stanley, *How I Found Livingstone*, 232.
[106] Burton, *Lake Regions*, I, 156; Casati, *Ten Years*, 268.

complained of the difficulties which they faced in securing supplies – presumably because of disputes over control of foodstuffs within local societies – it is remarkable how well the demand was met, and how quickly contests between old and young and women and men over resources tended to push the development of exchange, as women brought things to sell and then their husbands and fathers tried to take over this new arena of exchange.[107] So the market at Ngongo Bagas, on the boundary between forest and plain in central Kenya, grew in less than a decade from a series of tense, petty exchanges between caravaneers and women into a large, more formalized, affair dominated by men.[108]

This trade ran beyond the control of rulers partly because of the nature of the caravans. While some European travellers tried to buy food themselves for their followers, most trading caravans expected porters to arrange their own sustenance.[109] Porters divided themselves into little groups which shared cooking, and were issued a small amount of beads or cloth at each stop with which to buy food.[110] Porters, or the better-waged caravan guides and guards, might also engage in a little trade on their own account, usually with the aim of acquiring a slave. Having done so, they would have to feed their new acquisition.[111] Beads were threaded into smaller and smaller strings and cloth cut into ever smaller strips to buy a single hen or a cup of milk or a bunch of plantains.[112] In a few places cowries were accepted by some as a token of value but very generally people bartered their foodstuffs for things which they wanted for themselves; as was evidenced from the problems which travellers experienced with choosing exactly which kind of cloth or beads to take with them for purposes of trade.[113]

Sex was also much in demand along the caravan routes. Accounts of caravans frequently mention the temporary relationships which caravan men formed with women, especially during the prolonged stays at the great centres which the caravan trade often involved.[114] These 'black Delilahs'[115] may have been challenging the power of men; but some men were able to turn their authority over women's sexuality into trade items: one of Speke's

---

[107] Hohnel, *Discovery of Lakes Rudolf and Stefanie*, II, *passim*, is much concerned with the problems of supplying a caravan.

[108] Thomson bought supplies from Kikuyu women at Ngongo Bagas, with great difficulty, in 1883: *Through Masailand*, 180; in 1893, Colvile's porters got 'gloriously drunk' by selling their blankets to young men at Ngongo Bagas, which was a regular caravan stop and supply point: H. Colvile, *The Land of the Nile Springs. Being Chiefly an Account of How We Fought Kabarega* (London/New York, 1895), 13.

[109] Speke, *Journal of the Discovery*, 31; Cameron, *Across Africa*, 49, mentions argument over this point: porters clearly preferred to buy for themselves.

[110] Cameron, *Across Africa*, 28.

[111] Speke, *What Led to the Discovery*, 264.

[112] Burton, *Lake Regions*, I, 334; II, 72-3.

[113] Schweinfurth, *Emin Pasha*, 79-81 mentions limited circulation of cowries in Hoima; pipe-stem beads were used as tokens of value in the market at Ujiji: Cameron, *Across Africa*, 183.

[114] Hohnel, *Discovery of Lakes Rudolf and Stefanie*, I, 59, 103; Stanley, *Through the Dark Continent*, I, 68.

[115] Stanley, *How I Found Livingstone*, 203.

men 'rented' a woman from her husband for 20 strings of beads.[116] Elsewhere more temporary liaisons were formed at overnight stops, presumably providing women with cloth and beads:[117] how the fathers and husbands of women reacted to this is not always apparent, though in some cases consequent conflict suggests that men were inclined to demand compensation for adultery, and thus to claim for themselves some of the imported goods which these liaisons yielded.[118]

And women sold drink, as well as sex. Some gatekeepers tried to pre-empt such trade by providing alcohol as well as food;[119] but supplying a whole caravan strained the extractive powers even of Mutesa. While looting alcohol with Mutesa's permission, one of Speke's men was killed by enraged villagers.[120] Women figure most prominently in the accounts of such sale: as at Taveta where porters, buying drink with cloth and beads, tried to push the 'tasting' system to its limits:

> There was plenty of pombe, or banana wine, too, in anything but appetising-looking earthenware vessels. Our Zanzibaris, however, tossed off the contents, taking a pull first from one and then from another jar, with the air of experienced connoisseurs, till the women selling the wine became impatient and gave vent to shrill cries of protest.[121]

At the coast, where the caravans assembled; at Ujiji; in Buganda; at Kabarega's capital, drinks of many kinds were available for sale.[122] Burton noted that palm wine was cheap at Ujiji, but grain beer along the caravan routes was expensive.[123] Stanley noted the constant danger of violence from drunken porters in Ujiji;[124] in the 1880s, 1,000 jars of banana wine were sold each day to the population of court followers, porters and freebooters gathered around the capital of Kabarega.[125] Sometimes alcohol moved quite abruptly into the sphere of barter: far from the established caravan routes, Thomson's porters demanded that he provide them with beer in celebration of their arrival at Lake Nyasa – having prudently arranged before hand that such beer would be available for purchase.[126] Seeking access to imported goods which elder men sought to deny them, women and younger men quickly developed a whole new pattern of exchange in alcohol.

[116] Speke, *Journal of the Discovery*, 122.
[117] Thomson, *Through Masailand*, 160.
[118] Stanley, *Through the Dark Continent*, I, 68; Hohnel, *Discovery of Lakes Rudolf and Stefanie*, I, 59, 103.
[119] Speke, *Journal of the Discovery*, 167; Stanley, *In Darkest Africa*, II, 336, 384.
[120] Speke, *Journal of the Discovery*, 360.
[121] Hohnel, *Discovery of Lakes Rudolf and Stefanie*, I, 98.
[122] Speke, *What Led to the Discovery*, 207; Stanley, *Through the Dark Continent*, I, 41, 142; Schweinfurth, *Emin Pasha*, 79.
[123] Burton, *Lake Regions*, II, 59; 285.
[124] Stanley, *Through the Dark Continent*, II, 7.
[125] Casati, *Ten Years*, 268.
[126] Thomson, *To the Central African Lakes*, I, 256.

THE IDEOLOGY OF DRINK

Yet the increasing involvement of drink in barter did not lead to total change in the use of drink. The caravan trade brought change and new conflict, but even at its peak the trade was seasonal, and affected some areas very little; across the bulk of the region the passage of a caravan was an infrequent phenomenon. The drunken revelry of the caravan centre remained very much the exception. At the end of the nineteenth century, alcohol remained a central feature of ritual across most of the region, and in most societies drinking remained hedged around with restrictions, even though these restrictions were often challenged and occasionally ignored. Even where sale had become relatively common, this did not lead to the abrupt 'vulgarization' of alcohol and its disappearance from ritual. Yet it did cause change. In some societies, the control of alcohol was a matter for open dispute. As the authority of elder men was subject to increasing challenges, from ambitious chiefs and from dissatisfied women and young men anxious for a share of new kinds of wealth, the drinking practices which had been central to the largely unargued reproduction of the principle of elder men's power were increasingly under threat. In Ujiji, Burton observed not only that people are 'never sober when they can be drunk', but also that there was no gendered separation of drinking: 'in no part of the world will the traveller more often see men and women staggering about the village with thick speech and violent gestures'.[127] Nineteenth-century contests over ideas of proper drinking were at their most intense in the interlacustrine; where women drank in royal courts and soldiers' concubines bartered cloth for liquor, the nature of temperance had already been contested.[128] Elsewhere, such open contest came only in the twentieth century, under the new circumstances of colonial rule.

[127] Burton, *Lake Regions*, II, 69-70.
[128] Speke, *Journal of the Discovery*, 255; Lugard, *The Rise of Our East African Empire*, II, 291.

Part Two

Native liquor, money
& the colonial state

1900–60

> It must be realised that the native-brewed liquor is extremely potent and often creates a sort of frenzy which changes an ordinary decent man into a howling menace.[1]

It was a commonplace of European conversation that Africans were without any notion of temperance: that was why they must be ruled by others. 'The native knows no moderation, and when he begins, has no intention of leaving off until every drop is finished.'[2] 'A native did not drink for drink, he drank for drunk', observed one missionary, and another missionary called for total prohibition, saying that 'it was just as necessary for the native to be prohibited from having liquor as it was for him to be prevented from having firearms. We knew that they were children and they had got to be treated as children.'[3] Drinking was believed to be the principal cause of African crimes of violence; the 'alcohol nuisance' interfered with the labour supply; and the drink itself was 'manufactured under the most absurdly disgusting conditions'.[4] Some Europeans liked to add depth to their ethnic categorizations of Africans with allegations about the particular propensity to drink of certain groups; but nonetheless held that drink rendered all Africans both 'stupid' and 'quarrelsome'.[5]

But on another level, many Europeans were aware of the impossibility of prohibition and some were more ready to believe in the possibility of an African temperance. In reply to the calls for prohibition in 1930, one

---

[1] 'Natives and Drink – Growing Evil in Uganda', *Tanganyika Standard*, 17 Aug. 1935.
[2] Bache, *The Youngest Lion*, 108.
[3] Bemister and Leakey, quoted in the report of a Legislative Council debate: 'Closer Control of Native Drinking', *East African Standard*, 19 Apr. 1930.
[4] R. Buell, *The Native Problem in Africa* (2 vols) (New York, 1928), I, 626; H. Johnston, 'Alcohol in Africa', *The Nineteenth Century and After* (Sep. 1911), 476-94; 'Closer Control of Native Drinking', *East African Standard*, 19 Apr. 1930.
[5] Bache, *The Youngest Lion*, 45; N. Strange, *Kenya Today* (London, 1934), 74.

administrator observed that 'drinking in the reserves was connected with the social life and customs of the natives . . . He trusted that the old men would see that that the young men did not drink too much. In the town, drinking in what were called "clubis" did need stern control.'[6] This idyll of rural drinking as an integral aspect of elders' authority had considerable influence on the making of policy. But it faced another idea of temperance, implicit in one administrator's denunciation of elder men with 'their beer and their drums, their sorceries and their superstitions'.[7] British administrators were long torn between the idea of temperance as a desirable attribute of the past, and the contrasting belief that new kinds of temperance must be imposed by a state with a commitment to change.

Imported European liquor, on the other hand, was for much of the colonial period definitely identified as a problem of the modern world, and far from encouraging the consumption of such liquor (as has been alleged of West Africa)[8] colonial states in East Africa sought for 50 years to deny it to Africans. In 1890, the parties signatory to the Brussels Act had agreed to forbid the importation of spirits for African use in central, eastern and southern Africa.[9] Laws passed early on in the period of British rule in Uganda and Kenya created a legal distinction which has endured to this day. The kinds of alcohol familiar to Europeans – grape wines, spirits, hopped beer – were defined as 'intoxicating liquor', and were forbidden to Africans: it was an offence to supply such drinks to Africans, or for Africans to possess or consume them.[10] Kinds of alcoholic beverage made by Africans were defined as 'native intoxicating liquor', or more briefly, 'native liquor': the precise definition of this was to exercise various officials over the years, particularly when cantankerous magistrates chose to dismiss criminal prosecutions on technical grounds, but the concept of two distinct categories of alcoholic beverage went largely unquestioned.[11] In German East Africa, the details of the categorization differed, only spirits being forbidden to Africans, so that those Africans who were rich enough to do so were permitted to drink imported beer or wine or the hopped bottled beer produced by a brewery in Dar es Salaam.[12] British rule curtailed this right, spreading to Tanganyika the rigid demarcation between European drinking and African

---

[6] 'Closer Control of Native Drinking', *East African Standard*, 19 Apr. 1930. For a similar statement of policy, see Annual Report for Tanganyika Territory, 1922, 20, in Despatch 269 of 27 Apr. 1923, PRO CO 691/62.

[7] P. Mitchell, *African Afterthoughts* (London, 1954), 88, 96.

[8] Curto, 'Alcohol in Africa', 6.

[9] Articles 90-5 of the General Act for the Repression of the African Slave Trade, Brussels, 2 July 1890; printed as an appendix in S. Miers, *Britain and the Ending of the Slave Trade* (London, 1975).

[10] For British East Africa, see Regulations of 12 July 1897, in *British Foreign and State Papers, Vol. 89, 1896-97* (London, 1901), 1177-81; for German East Africa, see *British Foreign and State Papers, Vol. 84, 1891-92* (London, 1898), 358.

[11] Commissioner of Police to Colonial Sec., 4 Mar. 1938, KNA AG 1/395.

[12] Ordinance dated 17 Feb. 1894, *British Foreign and State Papers, Vol. 86, 1893-94* (London, 1899), 1050-2.

drinking; between 'intoxicating liquor' and 'native liquor'.[13]

This prohibition meant that, while much of the debate over African drinking in West Africa revolved around the conflict between the demands of temperance and those of the colonial treasury (which relied heavily on import duties on spirits, in particular), the colonial states of East Africa drew a relatively small (though not insignificant) proportion of revenue from liquor duties: as Johnston pointed out, they taxed the populace directly, rather than earning revenue from liquor.[14] Where revenue issues did become an element in debate, as they did with increasing regularity from the 1930s, these were connected not with central government and 'European liquor' but – as in southern Africa – rather with the attempts by local councils to derive revenue from the sale of 'native liquor'.

Created in the context of metropolitan debates about drink, self-control and responsibility, the restrictions on 'European' drink became part of a particular infantilizing discourse about Africans which might be used both to argue the need for colonial stewardship and to express and mediate concerns over the disruptive effects of commerce and change on African societies: the gin bottle epitomized modernity's threat to Africa. And the ban maintained a clear social distance between the drinkers of whisky on the one side and those who took *pombe* on the other: the rulers were masters of modernity, fearlessly imbibing its potent spirit, while their subjects were preserved safe in the familiar hand of tradition. Some Africans circumvented the ban on imported liquor, but for most, imported spirits and bottled beer were quite out of reach. Most Africans were concerned rather with debates over the making and drinking of 'native liquor': that was what they made and drank, and increasingly bought and sold.

---

[13] Sale of Liquor Regulations, *Official Gazette*, 30 Sep. 1919. Again, this ban went beyond international obligations: the terms of the League of Nations mandate required only that the British exercise 'strict control over the sale of spirituous liquors': B. Chidzero, *Tanganyika and International Trusteeship* (Oxford, 1961), 259.

[14] F. Lugard, 'The Liquor Traffic in Africa', *The Nineteenth Century*, 42 (1897), 766-84; Johnston, 'Alcohol in Africa', 489-90; Akyeampong, *Drink, Power and Cultural Change*, 68-70; E. Akyeampong, 'What's in a Drink? Class Struggle, Popular Culture, and the Politics of *Akpeteshie* (Local Gin) in Ghana, 1930-67', *JAH*, 37 (1996), 216-18; L. Pan, *Alcohol in Colonial Africa* (Helsinki/Uppsala, 1975), 16-18.

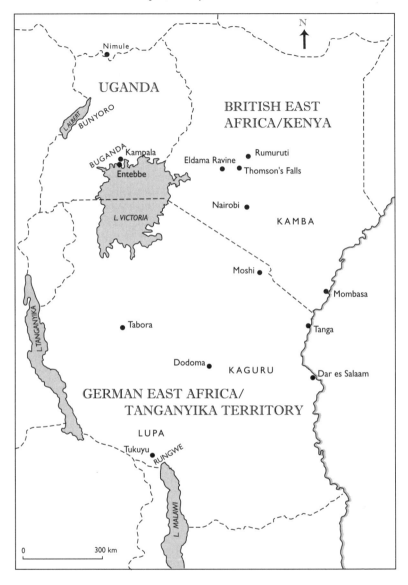

Map 3 *East Africa in the colonial period*

Five

Selling drink
1900–60

> It was hunger, if you would find hunger is disturbing you or perhaps you do not have salt or soap, or you do not have oil, then you decide to make and sell [beer] so that you can buy soap, salt and groundnuts, that was why we used to make it.[1]

In 1952, a judge in Kenya described a case which had come before him:

> A girl convicted of brewing and selling illicit liquor asked if she could speak in her own defence. 'I did it to earn my dowry', she said. 'My parents wish me to marry but I will not be an old man's donkey.' African women . . . are seeking independence through illicit means, since there are no other opportunities open to them.[2]

This vignette encapsulates one aspect of twentieth-century liquor sale: an illicit field of entrepreneurship for women in chronic conflict with the state and patriarchy. In 1963, a Ugandan government commission stated that the income from liquor sale was 'the only money a woman can claim'.[3] And undoubtedly, many of those who began to sell locally-made alcohol in the colonial period were women.[4] Many of them lived in the new urban spaces created by colonialism, often in uneasy sexual relationships with men who had more clearly defined access to the structures of the colonial state. In towns across East Africa, women – often the wives and concubines of soldiers, policemen, chiefs and 'messengers' – were the sellers and makers of intoxicating beverages.

But they were not the only makers and sellers of drink. Men also became involved in this trade, sometimes using their privileged relationship with the state to establish positions as middlemen or managers; sometimes in more humble roles. To some degree, events in East Africa followed the

---

[1] Int Nya41a, 3.

[2] M. Macmillan, *Introducing East Africa* (London, 1955 (1st edn 1952)), 118.

[3] Babumba, *Report of the Spirituous Liquor Committee*, 4.

[4] A pattern which has, of course, been noted in much of Africa: Ambler and Crush, 'Alcohol in Southern African Labor History', 30; H. Bradford, '"We Women Will Show Them": Beer Protests in the Natal Countryside, 1929', in Crush and Ambler (eds.), *Liquor and Labor*, 208-34.

pattern which Ambler and Crush have noted in southern Africa: while women played a central role in the illegal liquor trade, men dominated legal trade.[5] And, while the attention of officials tended to focus on the sale of alcohol in urban areas, a great many rural women and men also became involved in this business. East Africa was still an overwhelmingly rural society throughout the colonial period: even by 1960, only a small proportion of the population lived in towns or cities. In rural areas, as much as in the towns, drink was to play a central part in new contests between women and men and young and old over access to money and the ideas of proper behaviour. This chapter will argue that men played a major role in selling, and often in making, drink; and that the demands of the state and of husbands, fathers and neighbours established a context in which the selling of drink might be neither very profitable, nor very rebellious.

Easy money?

If you brewed and sold it all then you would brew again soon. But if you didn't sell it well, it would take some time for you to brew again.[6]

In 1931, one Kenya Provincial Commissioner (PC) called for higher licence fees for 'native liquor' sellers, as the trade 'provides motor cars for its licensees'; the spectacle of Africans driving cars was evidently as alarming as that of Africans drinking.[7] Characterizing liquor sale as a source of 'easy' money became part of a moral commentary on the fundamental undesirability of alcohol sale by private individuals, and colonial officials bandied around extravagant calculations of the profits realized by sellers: in 1927 it was alleged that women brewers in Dar es Salaam were earning more than 1,000 shillings each month (about 20 times the monthly wage of a skilled worker); in 1945 palm-wine sellers in Tanga were said to be earning a similar amount.[8] But the European men who made these calculations were distant from a reality in which many factors combined to make the manufacture and sale of alcohol an often marginal pursuit; they assumed that every brew was successful, that all the liquor made was sold, and that all that was sold was paid for.

The demands of the state were a major factor in constraining profits. One official, having expounded on the extreme profitability of brewing for women in Nairobi, then rather lamely noted that actually, in the particular case in point, the woman had earned less than nothing, since her entire brew had been impounded and she had been fined.[9] As systems of licensing

[5] Ambler and Crush, 'Alcohol in Southern African Labor History', 30.
[6] Int Nyoro27a, 2.
[7] PC Nzoia to Colonial Sec., 2 June 1931, KNA AG 1/402.
[8] PC Eastern to CS, 21 June 1927, TNA SMP 10491, Vol. I; PC Tanga to CS, 28 Sep. 1945, TNA SMP 33144, Vol. I. See also, for example, Chief Inspector of Labour to PC Lake, 22 Nov. 1938, TNA SMP 12694, Vol. III.
[9] Ag. Senior Commissioner Nairobi to Colonial Sec., 11 Jan. 1927, KNA AG 1/388.

and permits to brew and sell crept across the region, followed by experiments in local state monopolies in the legal making and selling of alcohol, sellers had either to pay fees and submit to unwelcome regulations or subordination, or they had to defy the law and run the risk of fines, or bear the cost of bribes and protection money. The colonial state in East Africa was, like its southern African counterpart, always too weak to suppress illicit drink sale;[10] but it was strong enough to ensure that many of those involved in the trade were constantly vulnerable to exactions from corrupt officials of the state.

The marginality of brewing economics was compounded by the marginal status of drink-selling as an activity. Many men deprecated the ability of women to acquire money for their own use through selling drink (and sex) to men; some disapproved when their male neighbours sold alcohol which they should rightly have shared; elder men criticized the youthful drinking which was made possible by sale. The selling of alcohol was not simply an issue between a repressive colonial state and women; it was a focus for multiple tensions within African society. And while the focus of state concern was on urban sale, African debates were not so confined: legislation was for many years restricted to urban areas, and police activity was limited to towns and European-owned farms and plantations, but arguments between men and women over who could sell alcohol and where were a feature of life across most of the region.

'SWAHILI' WOMEN & URBAN DRINKING

Selling drink . . . started with people in the towns, Muslims.[11]

As the colonial administration developed, first in the established commercial centres of the old caravan routes and then in the new towns of the colonial state such as Nairobi and Dar es Salaam, it began to pay its soldiers and other employees in coin, rather than in the cloth and beads of nineteenth-century commerce. The selling of locally-made fermented beverages for cloth and beads, which had been a feature of the 1880s and 1890s, turned into sale for cash. In 1891, drink was sold for cloth in Buganda; but by 1913 it was being sold for money.[12] Men in the service of the colonial state drove the spread of cash sale in urban areas; particularly soldiers and policemen, who were outside local networks of exchange and reciprocity and could obtain drink in no other way. In western Kenya in 1906, porters, paid for their service on a punitive expedition, went on a wild drinking spree, apparently buying drink from women living in the police lines.[13] There had been such women sellers in the nineteenth century too – at Ujiji or Tabora, or in the entourage of the rulers of Bunyoro. But the spaces in which sale occurred grew in the twentieth century, as did the number of women who found a kind of refuge in them. It was these women who made

[10] Ambler and Crush, 'Alcohol in Southern African Labor History', 21.
[11] Int Nya1b, 2.
[12] Lugard, *Rise of Our East African Empire*, II, 291, 328; *Uganda Notes*, June 1913.
[13] R. Meinertzhagen, *Kenya Diary, 1902-1906* (London/Edinburgh, 1957), 293.

the camps and *bomas* (administrative headquarters) of the colonial states into centres of a new cash trade in alcoholic beverages; for all of them, selling alcohol was a way to get hold of the money which the colonial state tended to put into the hands of men. In 1915, a PC in Kenya reported the cases of two African women who had been convicted of selling liquor without licences. One was the wife of a policeman; the other was a 'Sudanese', that is, she belonged to the shifting group of men and women of various origins which had developed around the settlements of serving or former members of the colonial army.[14] The status of these two women locates them clearly within a widespread pattern of drink selling in the early twentieth century; camp-followers of the motley army of colonial occupation.

As urban populations grew, they continued to be dominated by men; and those who obtained waged employ were almost all men. This population created a thriving alternative economy, in which women could seek refuge from the authority of fathers and husbands;[15] selling sex, food and alcohol. Men also sold liquor in early colonial towns; in Buganda, and along the coast in British and German East Africa, where palm wine – tapped by men – was widely consumed.[16] From the second decade of the twentieth century, as the whole region came under British rule, the role of men in urban sale was to grow, as a result of colonial regulation which wrestled with a fundamental problem: while officials consistently viewed drink as a potential cause of violence, and thought that drinking might undermine their ideals of time-discipline, of sober work-hours and restricted leisure, yet all concurred in the view that '[n]ative beers are necessary and wholesome to adult natives, so long as they are drunk in moderate quantities', and shared the opinion of the PC in Tanganyika who noted that '[i]t is of course well understood that to keep native labour happy and contented there must be plenty of beer'.[17] The regulations which they devised to allow drinking to be conducted with 'orderliness and sobriety'[18] (which will be discussed in chapters 6 and 7) had either of two effects. In Kenya and Uganda, they offered women a choice. Either they could work for male entrepreneurs, or they could produce illicitly, with the attendant risks of fines and extortion. In Tanganyika, in contrast, the laws allowed a small group of women in any town to establish favoured relationships with the state: others had to seek the patronage of these women or produce illicitly.

So, for example, in the small town of Eldama Ravine in Kenya, it was by 1921 the appointed headmen who were profiting most from the sale of liquor. Each held a licence, and gave permission to anything from five to ten women each day to sell on their premises, taking 3 shillings from each who did so, thus vastly augmenting their official salaries.[19] It was male licence holders

[14] PC Nyanza to CS, 14 Sep. 1915, KNA AG 1/401.
[15] L. White, *The Comforts of Home. Prostitution in Colonial Nairobi* (Chicago and London, 1990).
[16] See for example the list of those convicted for illegal sale in Mombasa in 1908, who were largely, though not exclusively, men: KNA PC Coast 1/1/138.
[17] Memo, Ag. PC Nairobi to CNC, 21 Aug. 1919, KNA AG 1/381; *Provincial Commissioners' Reports on Native Administration for 1930* (Dar es Salaam, 1931), 84.
[18] 'Control of Native Beer Trade', *Tanganyika Standard*, 8 Sep. 1934.
[19] Ag. District Commissioner (DC) Eldama to Crown Counsel, 13 June 1921, KNA AG 1/388.

who came to make the real money from urban liquor sale in Kenya; it was they who drove the cars which so offended officials. Some evaded the law – particularly in Uganda, where enforcement around Kampala was very poor, and where brewing women acquired considerable wealth and status as property-owners and money-lenders[20] – but in the more closely administered towns this carried considerable risks. Police raids could lead to arrest and fines, and to the loss of equipment and liquor.[21] In 1926, there were 356 convictions for 'possession of liquor off licensed premises' in Nairobi.[22] Those who wished to avoid prosecution resorted to alliance with the police, selling illegally under their protection.[23]

In towns in Tanganyika, men played less of a role in this period. Palm wine was effectively banned by the British from 1923 – being perceived as dangerously strong for 'up-country' Africans – and grain beers dominated legal sale.[24] In 1923, women in Dar would take out a licence and then charge other women to sell in their premises;[25] by the end of the 1920s this had been transformed into a system of entrepreneurship and waged labour located in a beerhall owned by the municipality. There 12 independent women licensees each employed up to six women brewers on a monthly basis, for a wage of 10-15 shillings;[26] it was the 12 licensees who excited some of the more exaggerated reports of brewers' incomes.[27] Not only women were involved, however: there were allegedly 100 men and women supported by this business;[28] and when a brief attempt to impose an official brewing monopoly drove these brewers into illicit production, the courts evidently assumed that men, rather than women, were the organizers of such brewing.[29] Elsewhere in Tanganyika, some men did manage to build

[20] P. Gutkind, *The Royal Capital of Buganda. A Study of Internal Conflict and External Ambiguity* (The Hague, 1963), 142.
[21] 'Native Brewery', *Uganda Herald*, 31 July 1935.
[22] Ag. Senior Commissioner Nairobi to Colonial Sec., 11 Jan. 1927, KNA AG 1/388.
[23] Buell, *Native Problem*, I, 626.
[24] PC Eastern to CS, 17 Oct. 1922, TNA SMP 3214, Vol. I; PC Eastern to CS, 29 June 1931, TNA SMP 12356, Vol. I. The 'ban' on palm wine actually only covered those areas to which the Native Liquor Ordinance was applied, but administrators contrived to give the populace the impression that it was a total one: PC Eastern to CS, TNA SMP 12356, Vol. I. Palm wine selling was permitted again in Tanga from 1935, and in Dar from 1940: PC Tanga to CS, 25 July 1936, TNA SMP 24575; 'Tembo Kali', *Tanganyika Standard*, 20 Oct. 1934.
[25] Note, AG, 2 Aug. 1923, TNA SMP 3214, Vol. I.
[26] Ag. PC Eastern to CS, 12 Aug. 1930, TNA SMP 10491, Vol. I.
[27] In 1931 another source suggested that these women earned around 150 shillings a month; still a very substantial sum: Baker, 'Dar es Salaam'.
[28] Memorandum submitted by the African Commercial Association, *Tanganyika Standard*, 3 Nov. 1934. In a brief period when the women were excluded from holding licences, one reported prosecution involved a man and a woman working together to brew and sell. Interestingly, the man was in waged employment: 'A Saturday Night Brew', *Tanganyika Standard*, 24 Aug. 1935.
[29] When a man and a woman were brought to trial for illicit brewing, the man received a much heavier fine and prison sentence than the woman: 'A Saturday Night Brew', *Tanganyika Standard*, 24 Aug. 1935.

positions as licensees/rentiers, but over most of Tanganyika – including the,
town of Tukuyu – women were the legal sellers of grain beer in urban areas.[30]
In the early 1950s the dominance of women was still apparent; the little
town of Tukuyu contained 41 women who made their living by making and
selling beer.[31] And in many Tanganyika towns – or just outside the town
boundaries – women made and sold beer without permit or licence, for
some thought the price of the licence too high, or the conditions offered by
those who had licences too demanding.[32]

In official eyes, the premises of urban women who sold alcohol were all
'disreputable places, lacking hygiene and morality'.[33] But African men were
more ambivalent in their attitudes. Mbilinyi has suggested a degree of
popular male support for urban women brewers – manifested, in her eyes,
by concerted action in 1935 when the administration in Dar tried to force
these women out of business by selling industrially-made ' native liquor'.[34]
Yet the evidence for this is a little unclear: accounts of the Dar 'boycott'
actually suggest that drinkers shunned the 'official' beer because it tasted so
terrible, and because they were used to buying liquor on credit, rather than
from any sense of solidarity with women brewers.[35] In the eyes of many
men, women liquor sellers were 'Swahilis', who had defied the claims of
marriage and household authority.[36] Perham's description of 'a dirty,
crowded place with half-drunken women pushing among the men' reflects
the disdain which her educated African host felt for the beer-market women
of Dar;[37] and in 1946, when British officials drove women out of Dodoma
town in Tanganyika, a correspondent wrote, 'we thank the British empire
for ridding us of these worthless enemies'.[38] But in the clearly commercial
environment of towns across east Africa, the most successful urban women
brewers, who ran their own premises, might command respect and status –
even if they did not earn on quite the fantastic scale alleged by officials. As
the more perceptive officials noted, the 'superior and salaried classes of
Africans' preferred to drink in 'the quiet and illicit drink shops' which
provided a welcome and discreet alternative to the public, and often rowdy,

---

[30] There were *pombe* sellers in Tukuyu in 1919 (see the revenue figures in Neu Langenburg
Annual Report, 1919-20, TNA library); informants accounts insist that all were women.

[31] Zuhura bti Ndemele *et al.* to DC, 25 Feb. 1952, TNA 18/T2/6.

[32] Producing just outside towns, where the regulations were different, as will be explained in
chapters 6 and 7, was a common tactic of brewers: DO Bukoba to PC Lake, 5 May 1932,
TNA SMP 12694, Vol. II; but there was also simple widespread evasion of the law: Chief
Inspector of Labour to PC Lake, 22 Nov. 1938, TNA SMP 12694, Vol. III.

[33] PC Tabora to CS, 22 Feb. 1923, TNA SMP 3214/1.

[34] Mbilinyi, '"This is an Unforgettable Business"', 122.

[35] 'Kazi ya Pombe', *Mambo Leo*, Jan. 1935; 'A Saturday Night Brew', *Tanganyika Standard*, 24
Aug. 1935. For retrospective accounts stressing the issue of taste, see Minute, 31 Jan. 1939;
Baker, Social Welfare Officer to CS, nd 1945, TNA SMP 33144, Vol. I.

[36] Nyala, 4; it is not clear whether any of these women were investing in the rural economy in
the way that some Nairobi prostitutes did: White, *Comforts of Home*, 110-16.

[37] 'Tanganyika Tour, 1937', 28, RHO, Mss Perham 49(2).

[38] 'Mabibi wahuni wanaondoka Dodoma', *Mambo Leo*, Mar. 1946.

licensed drinking places.[39] As one literate African put it: 'There is nothing more horrible in this lovely town of Dar es Salaam than the African bars which have been constructed by Government for us'.[40]

MEN, WOMEN & MONEY IN RURAL AREAS

In 1941, 31,291 men paid a total of just over 290,000 shillings tax in the Rungwe District. Of these, 8,095 obtained the money to do so from working at the Lupa goldfields to the north, 6,364 from the sale of livestock (which would have been mostly cattle), 4,987 from the sale of rice grown in the lowlands, 3,497 from the sale of maize and other grain in the higher lands (much of which went to feed the Lupa workers), 2,286 from other waged employment (some local and some as far away as South Africa), 1,599 from government work; and the remaining 4,463 obtained it in a variety of other ways, borrowing from friends, working locally as artisans, or selling coffee or sweet potatoes.[41]

Some of these activities, such as long-distance migrant labour or cattle sale, were clearly only really open to men.[42] Others might involve a struggle with women over the right to dispose of produce: women too might wish to sell maize, or other vegetable crops but, as an official noted 'economic crops are largely the property of married and settled men'.[43] Young men were more likely to earn from wage labour, but elder men sold cattle and had wives to work on their land to produce crops. This range of activities had built up in a few decades: labour migration had been considerable since the 1920s, and men's life histories are full of episodes of migrant labour.[44] Rice production had grown extraordinarily rapidly, as had the sale of food grains.[45] And most of them put cash into the hands of men, though women found ways to earn cash: carrying firewood to sell in Tukuyu town, selling

---

[39] Memo, DO Tanga, 21 Feb. 1937, TNA SMP 24571. The dislike shown by many Africans for the crowded and mixed drinking conditions of beerhalls was not restricted to East Africa: C. Ambler, 'Alcohol, Racial Segregation and Popular Politics in Northern Rhodesia', *JAH*, 31 (1990), 295-313.

[40] Letter, 'African Bars', *Tanganyika Standard*, 24 Aug. 1946.

[41] Rungwe District Annual Report for 1941, RHO Mss Afr s. 741 (3).

[42] There was some waged work available locally for women, on European tea plantations: see the papers of Monica and Godfrey Wilson, held at the University of Cape Town library (hereafter 'Wilson papers') Book E1, 27, 34, 65.

[43] Wilson suggested that maize and beans were sold by women, but also that men might take some or all of the money from sale: Wilson papers, Book E13, 6; 'Labour', Rungwe District Book, TNA MF 28. Some informants recall their mothers' generation selling crops for cash: Int Nya26b, 1-2; Nya23b, 1.

[44] Int Nya22a, 1-2; Nya24a, 1; Nya29a, 2.

[45] In 1923, 2,823 men had worked as migrants (Rungwe District Annual Report for 1923, 7, TNA Library); the lowlands produced 19 tons of rice for the market in 1919, 800 tons in 1934 and 3,500 tons in 1944 ('Native Foodstuffs in District' and 'Rice' in Rungwe District Book, TNA MF 28. The growing of Arabica coffee by Africans was discouraged from 1927, but this policy was reversed from 1934: 30 tons were produced in 1935, 46 tons in 1941/2 ('European Coffee' and 'Coffee' in Rungwe District Book, TNA MF 28; Rungwe District Annual Report for 1935, 9, TNA Library).

thatching grass, selling chickens.[46] Much of this cash went into the hungry maw of the colonial government, although not all did: rice sales alone in 1941 would have brought 156,000 shillings into the district.[47]

Before 1914, money was in very limited circulation in most places; outside urban areas, it moved in a limited orbit defined principally by tax demands. But by the 1930s money was widely used in minor transactions across the region. The activities of hawkers and the establishment of shops meant that money was more than a way of buying freedom from harassment by the minor functionaries of the state. 'You can get anything you want in the shops. Men and women are wearing smart clothes and shoes from Japan', reported a correspondent in Tukuyu in 1935.[48] Significantly, a hawker in Rungwe complained in 1935 that people were paying him in cash, rather than kind – he had found it much more profitable to barter his cloth and salt for maize and beans.[49] Some turned established patterns of barter into cash sale, hoping that by selling pots or beans for cash instead of exchanging them for salt or fish they could give themselves the luxury of choice in the conversion of their labour. This compounded the problem for others: now old as well as new domestic requirements could only be met through cash.[50] Money could be turned into desirable goods; and so money itself became desirable. It became a form of power, possessed of the ability to transform things into other things, and to change the relationship of the individual to other individuals: 'You know, when one has money, whoever he sees he makes pregnant', opined one man, in explanation of his father's many children.[51] One man told me that 'work led me to travel elsewhere, so that I could get cash to marry a woman'.[52]

A woman in Bunyoro sold beans and cassava to repay her bride-wealth and free herself from her husband, when her father refused to do so;[53] a Maasai woman coming back from a life as a prostitute in the town could use money to buy cattle, turning herself from marginal outcast into surrogate household head as she did so.[54] But this was a form of power which was very unequally available. As the availability of goods which could be bought for cash gradually grew, the very spread of these emphasized men's preferential access to money and things. There were places where women played a major role in the new cash economy, notably trading in foodstuffs:[55]

---

[46] Ints Nya26b, 1-2; Nya23b, 1; Wilson, *For Men and Elders*, 182; Wilson papers, Notebook E1, 58.

[47] Working on the figures of 1,200 tons and a selling price of 13 pence a kilo given in the annual report.

[48] 'Sifa za Mji', *Mambo Leo*, Mar. 1935.

[49] Wilson papers, Notebook E13, 6.

[50] Ints Nya23b, 1; Nya24b, 4; Nya26b, 1-2.

[51] Int Nyoro29b, 5.

[52] Int Nya10b, 2.

[53] Ints Nyoro28a, 3; Nyoro28b, 6.

[54] DC Narok to OiC Masai, 17 July 1940, KNA DC NGO 1/9/1.

[55] C. Robertson, *Trouble Showed the Way. Men, Women and Trade in the Nairobi Area, 1890-1990* (Bloomington, IN, 1997).

but more widely, men dominated cash and the economy of exchange which developed around cash. Cloth and other items were given to men as advances by Asian traders, and the men established little shops or worked as hawkers carrying their wares through the district before going back to repay the advance, and take a new one.[56]

In Bunyoro, tax demands on men led many into periods of work in Buganda, for European, Asian or African employers, while others found work more locally with saw-mills or cotton ginneries; here too some worked as hawkers for Asian traders.[57] In the later 1940s and 1950s a significant number of women in Bunyoro found waged work, as teachers or nurses.[58] Before then, the sale of bananas or sweet potatoes was the principal source of cash income for women and there was strong disapproval of married women who worked for wages: 'Immediately she would be married her work would be to stay at home.'[59] The administration sporadically encouraged the planting of coffee for the market and cotton cultivation, but the marketing system for cotton, in particular, was such that most people viewed its cultivation as an obligation imposed by 'the government's law' rather than a field for enterprise.[60] It was chiefs who were most successful in deriving income from land; up to 1933, chiefs were able to extract a 'rent' from their subjects, and there was widespread use also of corvée labour (*oruharo*) to work lands for private profit.[61] In 1933 the 'rent' was commuted in favour of a salary for chiefs, but the descendant of Kabarega who had become the Mukama, the head of the 'native government' subsumed under British rule, contrived to supplement salaries by providing chiefs with personal estates – sometimes of only a few households – from which they might derive rent in cash or kind.[62] Chiefs had the best access to money in Bunyoro. And women had very little; in the later 1940s and 1950s, when returns on cotton improved, men sought determinedly to deny women any of the returns from cash crops; the Mukama issued instructions which effectively banned women from the areas which had been set aside for cotton cultivation, insisting that women should be at home ensuring the supply of food for their husbands and families rather than becoming involved in the money economy.[63] Some men, fearing that access to money would make their wives more sexually adventurous, supported this restriction; others, anxious to bring money into the household, helped their wives to sneak past the chiefs who patrolled the roads to enforce the restriction.[64]

---

[56] Wilson papers, Notebook EXIII, 5; Wilson, *Good Company*, 62; Int Nyoro18a, 1.

[57] Int Nyoro14a, 2; Nyoro18b, 2; Nyoro19a, 2, Nyoro22a, 2-3.

[58] See for example Ints Nyoro15a, 2; Nyoro16a, 1,3; Nyoro23a, 2; Nyoro39a, 2; Nyoro 40a, 3.

[59] Ints Nyoro2b, 2; Nyoro10b, 7; Nyoro 39b, 2.

[60] This opinion was established early on: Masindi Monthly Report, Sep. 1907, UNA A 43/73; Hoima Annual Report, 1909-10, UNA A 46/252; see also Ints Nyoro 5b, 2; Nyoro4c, 1.

[61] Int Nyoro19b, 2; Fisher, *Twilight Tales*, 33; Northern Province Quarterly Reports, Mar. 1926, UNA A 46/798; Perham, 'Uganda Trek', 23, 30, RHO Mss Perham Box 41(3).

[62] Beattie, *Bunyoro*, 38-9.

[63] Mukama to Katikiro, 7 Apr. 1949, HDA AGR A/1.

[64] Int Nyoro35c, 9.

Among the Maasai too, men went away to work for wages: though not to anything like so great an extent as occurred among the Nyakyusa or Nyoro. Young men, in particular, served as cattle-herders for European farmers in the Rift, or went to work as guards in Nairobi. But it was sale of resources – and especially cattle – which brought most cash into Maasai society: 'during the colonial tax we first saw cattle being taken to market to get the money'.[65] Almost from the start, the British encouraged, cajoled, ordered and forced Maasai men to sell cattle.[66] Official cattle markets were established at particular places, and officials devoted much time to compiling records showing how many cattle had been sold at these events.[67] Wages put money into young men's hands; but cattle sales brought money into the hands of elder men; and among Maasai, as among the Nyakyusa, bride-wealth served to transfer wealth to elder men.[68]

So colonial circumstance created a need for cash, and encouraged the use of cash; but directed it towards men, rather than women; and towards some men more than others. And so, like the women along the nineteenth-century caravan routes, rural men and women turned to the selling of drink which they made. 'The man would plant bananas for making liquor. *Barwokole*, from which he would get tax and the rest.'[69] They did so in a piecemeal, little-by-little way – not absolutely depending on this as some of the women of the town did, but trying it, first as a one-off activity to meet a specific need, then perhaps a little more regularly. Wherever they did it, they faced a crucial moment of argument, when drink, which would previously have been shared or given, came instead to be sold.

Rural selling, 1900–40
innovation & contest

Every man had a banana plantation, they would squeeze [to make wine] and make money.[70]

By the end of the nineteenth century, the barter of alcoholic beverages for other goods was not unknown, even in areas away from the main caravan routes and centres of trade.[71] Cash sale in rural areas came more slowly. In the 1920s, Maasai men would take goats to trading centres and exchange them for drink produced by women of uncertain marital status, whom the men chose to regard as Kamba, and therefore beyond the bounds of behaviour prescribed by Maasai identity.[72] By the late 1930s, Maasai women

---

[65] Int Maa22a, 2.
[66] See for example Kajiado District Annual Report, 1933, 13, KNA DC KAJ 2/1/1.
[67] Kajiado District Annual Report, 1932, 9; KNA DC KAJ 2/1/1; Kajiado District Annual Report, 1945, 4-5; KNA DC KAJ 2/1/2.
[68] Int Maa15b, 1.
[69] Int Nyoro25b, 5.
[70] Int Nyoro37a, 2.
[71] Sub-Commissioner Western to Commissioner, 27 Mar. 1903, UNA A 12/3.
[72] Int Maa12a, 2.

evidently no longer had to retreat from their identity and homes to sell alcohol; sale in Maasai settlements had become so common that the Local Native Council was struggling, unsuccessfully, to suppress it.[73] A few years later the residents of a Maasai settlement near to the Kenya Marble quarry in Kajiado District were selling liquor to the workers.[74] In Rungwe in the 1920s or 1930s, Nyakyusa men were pawning tools for beer, a transaction that lay on the cusp of barter and cash sale: the hoe might be redeemed with money, but if it were not it became the possession of the beer-maker.[75] By the mid-1930s the sale of beer for cash was common enough for Wilson to have recorded several instances of this.[76]

Among Nyakyusa and Maasai, selling was an activity of women; though amongst the Maasai, the beverage involved was honey- or sugar-wine, which might be made by men or women. Money sale in these areas, as in the town, was a direct result of the difficulty which women had in gaining access to money: 'I used to make that one so that I can get money to buy food. So when I get from the beer, you would find I have bought food and clothes.'[77] But it raised much more serious issues than did sale in town. The women of the town were, in many cases, already in ambiguous positions, often living outside recognized marriages and beyond the authority of husbands and fathers. Rural women were much more closely confronted with the claims of patriarchy, and the disputes over the sale of drink and the household economy reflected this. Beer was not necessarily a source of economic autonomy: Hehe women made beer for sale in the 1930s, but it was their husbands who sold it and women in central Tanganyika – at least by official account – sought to sell grain to buy 'hoes, salt etc', rather than use it to brew beer for their husbands.[78] In central Tanganyika in the early 1930s, men – not women – were selling beer to railway labourers.[79]

Among the Nyoro, the sale of banana wine was very largely a male preserve from the 1890s up to the 1930s.[80] It was also men, who 'had their families and banana plantations', who made banana wine.[81] The selling of drink involved the continued conflict between chiefs and people, in which alcohol served now as an economic resource. Lesser chiefs made and sold banana wine, or got their subordinates to make and sell it for them, partly to a clientele of younger men;[82] and married Nyoro men, with few other ways of obtaining cash before the later 1930s, sought to sell wine to those who did

[73] Minute 8, Kajiado LNC Minutes, 15-16th Dec. 1938, KNA DC KAJ 5/1/4.
[74] Handing-over Report, 15, Wainwright to Wilkinson, Jan. 1946, KNA DC KAJ 3/1.
[75] Int Nya3b, 2.
[76] Wilson, *Good Company*, 110, 140-1; though Wilson, *For Men and Elders*, 26, 131 suggests that sale was rare in the 1930s.
[77] Int Nya42a, 1; Int Nya37b, 3.
[78] G. Brown and A. Hutt, *Anthropology in Action* (London, 1935), 259-61; PC Central to CS, 9 May 1929, TNA SMP 13427.
[79] 'Lions Conjured up by Brewer', *Tanganyika Standard*, 18 Nov. 1933.
[80] Ints Nyoro40a, 4; Nyoro41b, 1.
[81] Int Nyoro35a, 3.
[82] Int Nyoro21b, 15-16.

have money.[83] The ability to sell liquor played here on a tension over the disposal and control of alcohol. The Mukama expected a steady supply of liquor, which he used to entertain his guests; chiefs were expected to extract this from the populace, and would keep back some for their own use, to share with their favourites.[84] For married men, control over banana wine became another aspect of their chronic and often contradictory struggle with the authority of chiefs: they might resent it when the chief 'took drink without paying for it',[85] but they might also be happy to give drink to the chief when they sought his favour or support. It is not clear how profitable selling was, for men or chiefs; in the 1930s it was suggested that banana wine was 'the most profitable present-day commodity' in neighbouring Buganda, but there is no direct evidence on this.[86] Certainly, making banana wine to sell was a way to obtain cash and a process which in itself articulated the householder's claim to control over junior labour: 'It was the men [who made it] . . . the house holder, with the assistance of his youths, the sons . . . the young girls could of course assist in bringing water. And the wife could assist in preparing the sorghum, to grind it, to fry it, and turn it into flour.'[87]

Those selling drink in the rural areas did so at their own homes; only in rural Buganda and on the Kenya coast do 'clubs' seem to have been common in the first half of the twentieth century.[88] And in their homes they struggled to extract payment in return for drink. Men refused to pay for drink; or they drank with vague promises of future payment, and then never cleared the debts, arguing if challenged that they had been drinking free, as was their right. Unpaid debts and refusals to pay were an almost inevitable consequence of the ambiguity which hung around sale: 'That's why I failed [to make money]. He will come and deceive you, you give him alcohol and he will not pay you. He has cheated you.'[89]

CONTAINING COMMODITIZATION:
THE NATURE OF SALE & THE CONTROL OF MONEY

. . .[men] protested [against the selling of drink] because if alcohol is drunk by all people it is not good, because people will forget about the cows and they will run mad, especially these young people.[90]

The sale of liquor threatened to undermine the rituals of drinking and the social event of the drink-party. Sale made drink available to any who could pay, rather than just to those whose age and sex fitted them for the responsibilities of drink. It also, conversely, excluded those who could not pay, striking directly at the notion that open conviviality amongst elder men

[83] Ints Nyoro8c, 1; Nyoro11b, 2-3.
[84] Int Nyoro23a, 4.
[85] IntNyoro31a, 1.
[86] Mair, *An African People*, 130.
[87] Int Nyoro21a, 5.
[88] Gutkind, *The Royal Capital*, 142-3.
[89] Int Nyoro27c, 4.
[90] Int Maa36b, 2.

was the basis of well-being. Who could know the dark grudges of men who could not afford to drink with their peers? And sale by women mocked the ideal of the household head's control over resources and the subordination of women's trade to certain limited spheres: instead of making beer to be drunk by her husband and his kin and neighbours, a wife made beer to sell. Through selling beer, women could themselves acquire the power of money, could aspire to step outside the authority which the household head claimed: if Swahili women sold beer, would all who sold beer be Swahili women?

Yet men relied on sale; sometimes for their own income, sometimes as a way of meeting the cash needs of their dependants: as has been argued of central Kenya, women's enterprise might simply give men more freedom in choosing how they spent their cash.[91] The commoditization of liquor came in some ways to support the male-headed household. Its effects were contained, for people treated the sale of drink as a contingent activity and argued still the propriety of a limited, non-commercial pattern of drinking. And developing patterns of cash use guided women's spending into the simple reproduction of a 'house' which was increasingly less autonomous.

In Bunyoro, the sale had already been well-established in the nineteenth century, alongside a discourse about the restricted nature of proper access to drink. The twentieth century saw this pattern, with its contradictions, maintained and extended. Chiefs expected that 'you would put one gourd [of drink] aside for the chief',[92] and those men who sought favour from authority would go with banana wine to the chief, or even to the palace of the king, to 'be known' (*okukurata*).[93] Married men also sold banana wine for cash; and they continued to idealize the *ekitekanwa*, the drinking-party of male friends at which liquor oiled open and frank discussion amongst elder men who dealt in authority over young men and women.[94] An elderly man described the drinking-parties of his father's generation:

> They would say, let us go to so-and-so's place, there is alcohol. In drinking, friendship would build up, wives would be given to those who did not have wives . . . they would say, 'So-and-so's daughter or son is well-behaved, he or she is the one to stay with my child.'[95]

The selling of alcohol by women in Bunyoro met with more hostility: 'a woman was not allowed to sell alcohol'.[96] 'How would my mother sell beer? The beer was for the husband.'[97] But by the 1940s sale here too became established as an activity of women, mostly married and with children, who came into selling first by making and selling maize beer, partly for sale to the migrants from the north who some people in Bunyoro employed as

---

[91] Robertson, *Trouble Showed the Way*, 280.
[92] Int Nyoro19a, 4.
[93] Int Nyoro22b, 3.
[94] Int Nyoro29b, 10-11.
[95] Int Nyoro15a, 3.
[96] Int Nyoro29c, 1.
[97] Int Nyoro31b, 2.

labourers to work their gardens: 'All the neighbours used to make it. Now when you went to help to you would also learn.'[98] Women planted their own bananas, in assertion of their rights over the fruit;[99] and (where they did not dare to flout opinion by treading bananas themselves) they found men who would tread in return for a share of the final product.[100] In Rungwe, women who brewed did not use the millet from their granary to do so; they had to buy brewing millet for cash, for the millet of the granary belonged to the husband.[101] When they began to use maize to brew, this too had either to be bought, or had to be unambiguously the product of the woman's labour alone.

Across the region, the selling of drink became the focus for a discourse which insisted on the morality of non-commercial drinking, and treated sale as an aberrant – if temporarily acceptable – activity necessitated by financial circumstance, 'It was just to get the necessities of life.'[102] Women presented their selling as a subordinate activity, intended to meet the daily costs of the household; a prop, rather than a challenge, to the economic control of men: 'You would get money to buy essentials like salt, soap, paraffin only that. Now if you had a family would you buy yourself clothing?'[103] And so, while some men did make it impossible for their wives to sell beer – by simply insisting on their right to drink it with their friends – most accepted this sale, on the understanding that it would provide salt, soap and oil, rather than savings for the woman: 'I cannot forbid her [to sell] because she cannot just depend on me. I cannot meet all her needs. So let her brew alcohol and buy anything she wants because I do not have money to assist her.'[104] Some men, indeed, may have actively encouraged their wives to sell, and then appropriated the money; among the tax-payers of Rungwe in 1941 were 1,731 who declared that their tax money came from 'beer/millet'.[105]

Rural selling took place in homes, not in clubs; those who sold were wives, not the women of the towns: 'We were not going to the clubs, it was the Swahili who we knew had clubs.'[106] Where women sold beer, the domestic setting of sale allowed men to present the purchase as a moment which affirmed male power, as they ordered the seller to carry the beer to some salubrious spot of their choice: 'We would tell her to take it for us, any place we wanted.'[107]

Central to the containment of commoditization, whether men or women were selling, was the notion that drink was not made solely to sell; a part of any batch of liquor might be sold, but another part would be destined for

98 Int Nyoro35b, 4; Nyoro35c, 3.
99 Int Nyoro25b, 2.
100 Ints Nyoro5a, 3; Nyoro5b, 3; Nyoro12b, 2-4.
101 Int Nya18a, 3.
102 Int Nya23b, 3.
103 Int Nyoro15b, 3.
104 Int Nya12b, 5.
105 Rungwe District Annual Report, 1941, RHO Mss Afr s 741 (3).
106 Int Nya25b, 3.
107 Int Nya25b, 3.

non-commercial consumption with friends or neighbours.[108] It has been suggested that some African societies have contained the consequences of commoditization through a rigid compartmentalization between commercial and ritual brewing and drinking: particular brews, and particular drinking moments, have been strictly defined as either commercial or ritual.[109] But more widely, societies contained commoditization through discursive devices which emphasized an ideal of proper non-commercial drinking amid a reality of commerce, and through drinking practices which could – as Appadurai would put it – lead the product of a single brew through a 'social life' in which it was at different times both commodity and non-commodity.[110] 'You must give some of it to the owner of the household! I would give him a certain quantity before I sold the rest.'[111] Men who sold banana wine did this, as did women who sold grain beer: 'I would sell some but then leave like one jerrican for the neighbours. Whoever came, you would give him.'[112] '[My husband] was happy that we were earning an income. And of course he never missed his free share. A certain amount would be reserved for him and his friends.'[113] Such practice constrained the scale of production, by linking the organization of brewing labour to relationships of kin and friendship: though neighbours might occasionally lend a hand (and be rewarded with a little more drink than other neighbours for doing so), men and women mostly produced no more alcohol than could be made by family labour.[114]

Where retail sale occurred outside the household, the distinction between liquor for sale and liquor for neighbourly drinking might be relatively easy to maintain in practice. Where social and commercial drinking occurred together in the home, the possibilities for misunderstandings were manifold. Drinking men exploited the ambiguous status of alcohol, consuming it and then arguing that they were drinking socially, not for cash. Given the immediate imperative to sell drink which spoiled rapidly, sellers were always vulnerable to this technique: much beer had to be sold on credit, and in a sense the spread of sale was no more than the increasing regularity of ambiguous and contested understandings about the possibility of some future cash payment. Men argued about whether they should pay, then when they should pay; then they postponed payment indefinitely and finally refused to pay.[115] Selling crept almost imperceptibly into drinking, sowing the seeds of many arguments as it did so. Women were apparently much more vulnerable than men to losing money in this way, though some men

[108] Int Nya23a, 3.
[109] O. Rekdal, 'Money, Milk and Sorghum Beer: Change and Continuity among the Iraqw of Tanzania', *Africa*, 66 (1996), 367-85.
[110] Appadurai, 'Commodities and the Politics of Value', 16-17.
[111] Int Nya18a, 3.
[112] Int Nyoro 22a, 3.
[113] Int Nya2b, 2.
[114] Int Nyoro35c, 10.
[115] Int Nya23b, 3.

too complained of it: one man in Bunyoro even lost his drinking vessels to defaulting customers: 'The one you'd give a cup to drink from would go with it and I ended up losing.'[116]

But in spite of the unpaid debts and the arguments, sale spread. And while many elder men resisted it, others accepted it, perhaps because they saw in this activity the possibility of a revised pattern of gendered control over household resources: a pattern which did not, in the long run, challenge the authority of household heads but instead made possible a new subordination of women's activities. The innate power of money could not be contained, but men sought to limit the dangers of this, by creating new distinct spheres of spending and investment, which countered the expectation that 'all the responsibility of looking after a woman was the husband's' by tolerating the sale of alcohol.[117] One man remembered how his mother brought him up while his father was away earning – and spending – elsewhere: 'When our father worked in Masindi, we were helped by selling alcohol. My mother would make two tins of liquor and would sell it.'[118]

State enterprise

In 1920, the Secretary of State wrote to the governors of UK's East African territories praising the Durban municipal beerhall, a monopoly enterprise which sold 'native liquor' . As a result of this scheme, he noted, 'a considerable amount of revenue is derived from beer and applied to Sanitary works'.[119] So alluring was this prospect that East African governments sought further information, and while the only immediate result was the acquisition of a municipal beerhall for Nairobi in January 1922 the Durban model was to inspire official reveries, and some policies, for the next four decades.[120]

The essential point about the Durban scheme was that it sought not to regulate and tax the sale of locally-made alcohol, but to take it over entirely as a state enterprise.[121] To quiet the unease of those who thought the sale of alcohol to Africans was fundamentally improper, the profits from the beerhall in Durban were to be applied only 'in the interests of Natives residing in the town.'[122] This model too was adopted in East Africa, where the authorities in Kenya and Tanganyika, and eventually Uganda, all passed legislation allowing monopolies and state-run enterprise on condition that profits were

---

[116] Int Nyoro22a, 3; Nyoro19c, 1.
[117] Int Nyoro23b, 2; see also Int Nyoro32b, 3.
[118] Int Nyoro25a, 1.
[119] Milner, SoS to Governor, 18 Oct. 1920, KNA BY 11/48.
[120] For example 'Report of Enquiry into the Durban System', 1921, UNA A 46/2001; Ag. Dep. Director Medical Services to CS, 18 May 1927, TNA SMP 10491, Vol. I. The model, it should be noted, was not solely a colonial one: during the First World War the town of Carlisle had introduced a public monopoly in alcohol sale, and there continued to be some enthusiasm for such schemes up to the time of the 1931 Royal Commission in the United Kingdom: P. Ford and G. Ford, *Breviate of Parliamentary Papers, 1917-1939* (Oxford, 1951), 509.
[121] P. la Hausse, 'Drink and Cultural Innovation: the Origins of the Beer Hall in South Africa, 1903-16', in Crush and Ambler (eds.), *Liquor and Labor in Southern Africa*, 78-114.
[122] Cited in La Hausse, 'Drink and Cultural Innovation', 98.

to be go to local authorities – rather than the Treasury – and were to be spent on 'such projects on behalf of the natives resident in the area controlled by such local authority as may to the Governor seem best and expedient.'[123] Attempts to expand such monopolies in the 1930s and 1940s will be discussed below; their establishment had a profound effect on the profitability of brewing.

Some local authorities did derive a considerable income from the beerhalls. Nairobi, indeed, made so much money that the municipal authorities struggled to spend it, particularly since a number of their suggestions were held to be in contravention of the requirement that profits be used 'on behalf of natives resident in Nairobi'.[124] Curiously, improvements to the 'facilities' at the cemetery were made, but the use of the money to subsidize actual interments was vetoed.[125] More seriously, there was some debate over the use of the money to finance housing schemes – exactly the sort of infrastructure of social engineering that some had understood the scheme to be intended to cover – with the Chief Native Commissioner (CNC) implicitly raising again the argument over the propriety of any part of the state deriving any income from this source: 'Government insists on a monopoly of brewing native beer and punishes severely anyone who attempts to break through that monopoly. It seems to me obviously wrong that Government should work a monopoly of this nature at any considerable profit.'[126] But the use of brewery profits in this way was approved after pressure from the municipality,[127] and in the later 1930s Margery Perham was to remark – not entirely approvingly – the Nairobi housing schemes had been 'done out of native money – the proceeds of the Government beer markets.'[128] Mombasa's beerhall, established in 1934 (which actually sold palm wine), was almost as lucrative, yielding £7,500 each year by the mid-1940s;[129] and in the 1940s the municipal authorities in Tanga established a similar venture. This was apparently yielding considerable returns within a few years; yet at this point doubts began to be evident, and there were lengthy arguments about whether the Tanga venture was quite as profitable as was suggested.[130] There were doubts in Kenya too. Nanyuki and Thika both ran

---

[123] For Kenya, see Native Liquor Ordinance, 1921, Sec. 29(1) and 30 (9); KNA AG 1/381; for Uganda, see LN 161 of 1945.

[124] By 1924, 3.8 percent of total revenue was already derived from beerhall profits: Ag. Town Clerk to AG, 12 June 1926, KNA AG 1/399; 'Nairobi (Native Beer Shop) Rules, 1926', *Official Gazette*, 7 July 1926.

[125] AG to CNC, 26 Sep 1932, KNA AG 1/399.

[126] Minute, CNC, 17 Sep. 1932, KNA AG 1/399.

[127] There was in effect the threat of an extra tax to cover the cost of the housing scheme if the beerhall profits could not be used: CNC, 3 Dec. 1932, KNA AG 1/399.

[128] 'Kenya Tour', 1937, 132, RHO Mss Perham, Box 49 (1).

[129] Ag. PC Coast to CS, 11 July 1944, KNA PC NGO 1/1/28.

[130] Municipal Sec. Tanga to CS, 30 June 1945, TNA SMP 33144, Vol. I. The municipal authorities earned £3,200 from this venture in 1952: Municipal Sec., Tanga Township Authority to Member for Local Govt, 13 June 1952, TNA SMP 33144, Vol. II. The arguments arose because Tanga occupied an ambiguous status, as it had not been formally declared a municipality, and so the income from the beerhall had to be paid to the Treasury and then clawed back: Minute, 17 Apr. 1953, 28 Mar. 1955, TNA SMP 41407.

briefly successful monopolies.[131] but many up-country towns drew rather less revenue from beerhalls. In 1952 the DC reported that the council-owned beerhall in Kajiado 'works efficiently and produces a good profit', but in the next few years the men who ran this and other beer shops as sub-contractors claimed to be making a loss.[132] Not all believed them, but more than one of these men simply abandoned the beerhalls.[133] While some customers claimed to like the conviviality of the beerhall – 'We thank our Government very much' wrote one[134] – others preferred to drink in more exclusive surroundings; beerhalls faced constant competition from illicit production.[135]

Where beerhalls operated, women were again subordinated. They were employed as brewers of beer, while men worked as managers or sometimes as sub-contractors, paying a set fee to the local authority. The wages of the women who worked in these beerhalls were not low, by the standards of the time – the 12 women brewers in Nairobi reportedly received 50 shillings a month in the 1920s, and even in minor towns they earned 10-12 shillings a month by 1940[136] – but they were lower than those of the male managers and bouncers.[137] The system undermined the profitability of alcohol sale, legal and illegal: the profitability of brewing by urban women was threatened by its illegality; the profitability of state-sponsored alcohol sale was threatened by the very unattractiveness of its setting.

In the 1950s, the spread of a licensed system of 'clubs' to rural areas and in some towns spread the range of these circumstances. These clubs were not state enterprises. They were licensed drinking places, which extended into rural areas a system of revenue collection through private enterprise, and which diverted much of the income from the rural sale of liquor into the hands of men who were part of, or had access to, the local structures of the state. A DC in Tanganyika explained the system simply: an 'overseer' who ran the club was allowed to collect fees from liquor sellers who had permits to sell, and would in return suppress all illicit sale.[138] Beidelman's study of Kaguru beer sales in the 1950s showed that Kaguru women could sell beer, illicitly, at home in the months when the clubs were closed to conserve foodstuffs, but they had to buy – with sex or money – the co-operation of local officials and their 'supporters'. When the clubs reopened, local officials (some of whom had financial interests in the clubs) confined all sale to these clubs, which were owned by men. 'Because of government

[131] DC Nanyuki to Acct General, 2 Aug. 1949, KNA MAA 7/380.
[132] Handing-over Report, Mar. 1952, KNA DC KAJ 3/2; FGPC Minute 17/57, Kajiado ADC, 11 Nov. 1957 and Toshi to DC Kajiado, 27 July 1953 KNA DC KAJ 4/23/8.
[133] Note by Cashier, 5 Jan. 1954; Toshi to DC Kajiado, 3 Sep. 1957, KNA DC KAJ 4/23/8.
[134] 'Lindi: Soko la pombe', *Mambo Leo*, July 1935.
[135] Nangurai to African District Council, 20 July 1960, KNA DC KAJ 4/23/8.
[136] At Narok: OiC Masai to DC Kajiado, 30 Aug. 1940, DC NGO 1/9/1.
[137] In 1927 the manager of the Nairobi beerhall earned 80 shillings a month: 'Memorandum on Native Beershop, Pumwano Location', nd, attached PC Eastern to CS, 18 July 1927, TNA SMP 10491, Vol. I.
[138] DC Chunya to PC SHP, 9 Apr. 1955, TNA 157 A2/8.

regulations and the way these are enforced, a large share of the profit goes to headmen and entrepreneurs with political connections, rather than the brewers themselves.'[139]

Overall, then, the profitability of making alcohol for sale – particularly for women – may actually have been declining in the 1940s and 1950s, as more formalized structures of retailing developed. Some managed to stay outside these formal structures: by the end of the 1950s there was a very large amount of illicit alcohol production and sale going on across the region, in rural and urban areas, and many of those involved in this were women who made and sold alcohol at their homes. They evaded the formal structures of control but exposed themselves to the costs of fines and bribes, and made themselves vulnerable to simple theft from those who knew that illicit alcohol sellers had no recourse to law. They might resist in dramatic fashion, like the two women who killed a chief in Kampala who tried to seize their illegally brewed beer, but this might only bring them more trouble.[140] It is, indeed, largely from the records of prosecutions that we know of the of this trade: in 1959 illicit liquor sale was described as a major element in crime statistics in Kajiado;[141] in 1961 34 of the 411 individuals detained in Kajiado were charged under the Native Liquor Ordinance.[142] The statistics may be misleading, for they reveal only the cases that went beyond informal channels of bribery and favouritism to reach the courts, and these figures see-saw up and down in a manner which probably reveals more about occasional policy crackdowns on a perennial activity than it does about the overall volume of illicit liquor sale.[143] But certainly by around 1960 there was a widespread impression that even as profitability diminished for many of those involved, the sale of 'native liquor' was continuing to grow, and the giving of such liquor was becoming less common.[144] In towns and rural areas, most of the alcohol consumed in the later 1950s was being made for sale, and bought to drink; and it had become a central part of the economic strategy of many women and men all across the region.

---

[139] Beidelman, *The Kaguru*, 25-6.
[140] 'Sentence Sequel to Brewing Dispute', *Uganda Argus*, 14 Jan. 1955. Both women went to prison.
[141] Kajiado District Annual Report, 1959, 9, KNA DC KAJ 2/1/10.
[142] Kajiado District Annual Report, 1961, 9, KNA DC KAJ 2/1/12A.
[143] See for example the cases in the resident magistrate's court at Ngong: in 1949 61 convictions were recorded there, three of these being connected with illicit liquor sale; in 1950, none of the 54 convictions recorded were associated with illicit liquor sale; in 1951, one out of the 56 convictions recorded was connected with illicit liquor sale; in 1952, one out of 44 convictions; in 1953, one out of 153; but in 1954, nine out of 118. Of the 15 individuals convicted over this six-year period, seven were men and eight women: KNA DC NGO 1/6/36. In the same period, native liquor cases in the magistrate's court in Kwale District varied from a peak of 26 out of a total of 502 cases to a low of three out of 614 cases: Kwale District Annual Reports, KNA DC/KWL.
[144] Memorandum from Brewers' Association, 1963, in KNA DC KAJ/4/8/2.

Six

Native liquor, native authority
Drinking policy & practice
1900–40

> The pombe shop is bad enough in a town, but outside in the country it
> is a positive pest. It attracts loafers, promotes drunkenness, gambling,
> prostitution, it tempts the native to waste his substance, gives rise to
> fights and disorders and is generally abominable.[1]

When officials in the colonial states of East Africa talked of African drinking,
they reproduced assumptions about the nature of authority and space;
between town and country, commerce and tradition. These were their
assumptions, which guided and restricted officials themselves, shaping what
they saw as the practical bounds of their authority. But these assumptions
came also to be involved in the construction of authority within African
societies, for European suppositions determined the degree of access which
particular groups of Africans might have to the new coercive and patronage
resources of the colonial state. And hypotheses constructed through talking
about drink passed the other way too, from African to European. Although
Africans and Europeans drank separately their arguments over drinking
overlapped, like two adjacent conversations, each pushed forward by
hearings and mishearings from the other.

   This chapter begins with an account of British policy towards African
drinking in central Kenya, an area which was a focus of official debates. It
goes on to a wider discussion of the relationship between official policies
and African drinking across the region, and argues that between 1900 and
1940 official debates revealed some of the contradictions of colonial states
which were committed to change and to 'tradition'.

Sugar & the Kamba

In the 1890s, the Kamba of what is now central Kenya had already begun to
acquire a reputation for insobriety amongst Europeans: 'the Akamba are

---

[1]   Dundas (SNA), Minute, 6 Jan. 1925, TNA SMP 3214, Vol. I.

great beer drinkers, not to say drunkards', wrote Jackson.[2] By 1912, after
Asian traders established a number of sugar-mills in the area, drunkenness
had come to be a major concern of administrators in central Kenya.[3] Much
of the sugary liquid produced went not into the development of a local
sugar-processing industry, but was instead sold to Africans, for immediate
use in the preparation of alcoholic beverages.[4] There was a brisk demand
for drink from young men who earned cash working for European farmers,
and soon African entrepreneurs were buying sugar-cane mills to crush cane
on their own account: the trade in sugar-cane juice was, Ambler suggests, a
considerable motor of commercial expansion in this area.[5]

Uncomfortably aware of the fragility of their authority, British officials
saw drunkenness resulting from this trade as a potential threat to order and
therefore to the authority of the state.[6] The image of drunkards shrugging
off the weak shackles of the early colonial state was a terrifying one.
'Unrestricted use of these sugar-mills will increase drunkenness one hundred
per cent . . . state of general lawlessness can be the only possible outcome.'[7]

To avert such lawlessness, officials turned to the African agents of the
state. These were the chiefs and headmen recognized by local officials, from
whom support was expected in the collection of tax and the enforcement of
colonial orders, and to whom officials lent the support of such coercive
apparatus as they possessed – the police and messengers stationed at the
district headquarters. Some, in areas neighbouring those occupied by the
Kamba, trumpeted a temporary success in controlling drunkenness with
the support of the chiefs.[8] Yet among the Kamba (as elsewhere across East
Africa) soon the drink issue became not a point of alliance with the
recognized agents of the colonial state but a focus for concern at their lack
of authority. A number of 'regulations' to control Kamba drinking were
introduced under the Native Authority Ordinance,[9] but such rules were
meaningless without enforcement. Headmen seemed quite unwilling to
control public drunkenness and were indeed themselves accused of a chronic
insobriety unsuited to wielders of authority:[10] 'little assistance can be expected
from the headmen and the only effective method of dealing with the
question lies in adopting measures which are not dependent upon their
co-operation'.[11]

---

[2] Jackson, *Early Days*, 180.
[3] Ambler, 'Drunks, Brewers and Chiefs'.
[4] DC Machakos to Ag. PC Nairobi, 2 Oct. 1911; DC Kyambu to AG, 12 Nov. 1913, KNA AG/
     1/384.
[5] Ambler, 'Drunks, Brewers and Chiefs', 168, suggests that there were 55 mills in 1914;
     another source suggests that by 1916, there were about 50 African-owned mills in the area:
     Ag. PC Ukamba to CS, 19 July 1916, KNA AG/1/386.
[6] Ambler, 'Drunks, Brewers and Chiefs', 169.
[7] DC Machakos to PC Nairobi, 18 Oct. 1913, KNA AG/1/384.
[8] Monson, Ag. Secretary to the Administration to AG, 29 Mar. 1911, KNA AG/1/401.
[9] Ambler, 'Drunks, Brewers and Chiefs', 170.
[10] Traill, Ag. PC Ukamba to CS, 6 Jan. 1917, KNA AG/1/386.
[11] Hamilton, for Ag. PC Ukamba to AG, 21 Aug. 1916, KNA AG/1/386.

The demands for labour that came with the First World War intensified the sense of crisis amongst administrators.[12] Despairing of help from headmen some local administrators advocated 'more drastic measures'. If regulation of sale and drinking was impossible, then the answer rested on cutting off the raw materials from which alcohol was made.[13] Though administrators had been warned that they had no power to confiscate sugar-mills, they did this, and a blind eye was turned to their actions.[14] And war offered the opportunity to restrict other sources of supply. Imported sugar was in short supply; and martial law regulations and the increased coercive machinery available to the state were deployed to prevent the supply of processed sugar of any kind to Africans in a large part of central Kenya.[15]

But the end of the war provoked a new crisis; and a new aspect to European debates. Concern was now not just with general drunken disorder, or even with the supply of labour, but rather specifically with the drunkenness of young men,[16] and with the weakness – rather than the disinclination to act – of headmen whose authority was undermined by change: the PC Ukamba saw 'Tribal Headmen' as under threat from a 'large number of discharged Carriers' who would increase the problem of 'intemperance'.[17] The area occupied by Kamba bordered on one of the early foci of European settlement and agricultural endeavour, and during the war European settlers searching for a profitable crop had turned to the production of sugar-cane and the crushing of juice for sale to Africans, and had also diversified into the crushing of African-grown sugar-cane using mechanical mills.[18] By 1918 some were entirely reliant on this trade, by their own admission.[19] Officials blamed the surge in drinking on these settlers,[20] who complained that they could not get enough labour, and demanded physical protection which an overstretched colonial state could barely supply, yet at the same time sought easy profits by selling to Africans the raw materials for alcoholic drinks, heedless of the effect which this might have on headmen's authority and the labour supply. '[I]f Europeans thus encourage the natural tendencies of the Akamba for drink they cannot ever expect a labour supply.'[21] The sugar-planters and mills of Kamba land became, temporarily, a focus for the contradictions of a colonial state which was simultaneously obsessed with

[12] Ainsworth, PC Nyanza (and former CNC) to Traill, Ag. PC Ukamba, 19 June 1916, KNA AG/1/386.
[13] Ag. PC Ukamba to CS, 19 July 1916, KNA AG/1/386.
[14] The Acting PC was specifically warned that confiscation would be illegal, but his letters implied that he had anyway done this: Barth, AG to Traill, Ag. PC Ukamba, 27 July 1916 and Traill, Ag. PC Ukamba to CS, 6 Jan. 1917, KNA AG/1/386.
[15] Draft Martial Law Regulations, attached, Barth, AG to CS, 10 July 1917, KNA AG/1/401.
[16] Drinking by young men is repeatedly mentioned as a problem: Ag. PC Ukamba to AG, 23 May 1918; Report of Special Committee of Legislative Council, AG, 13 Dec. 1918; CNC to AG, 14 Apr. 1919, Memo from PC Ukamba, 21 Aug. 1919; all in KNA AG/1/381.
[17] Ag. PC Ukamba to AG, 12 Feb. 1918, KNA AG/1/401.
[18] DC Ulu to PC, 11 Mar. 1918, KNA AG/1/401.
[19] Settler [signature illegible] to AG, 12 June 1918, KNA AG/1/381.
[20] Ag. PC Nairobi to Versturme-Bunbury, 15 Sep. 1917, KNA AM/1/55.
[21] DC Ulu to PC, 11 Mar. 1918 and Ag. PC Ukamba to AG, 3 Apr. 1918, KNA AG/1/401.

the need to maintain order and committed to change.[22] Drink was symbolic of all the anxieties of officials over the encounter between the 'natural tendencies' of Africans and the temptations of modernity: where young men began to imitate the drinking of elders, 'even ordinary administration [is] difficult to maintain'.[23] With the end of martial law, officials sought a new legal basis for the control on supply, and a quite extraordinarily restrictive measure was discussed, which would have made it almost impossible for Africans anywhere in British East Africa to buy or possess sugar.[24]

Settlers, and some officials in Nairobi, were aghast at this proposal; sugar, after all, was in many ways an emblematic product of civilization, a sweet benefit made available to all through colonialism.[25] Even in wartime, there had been some objection in principle to restrictions on sugar – the attorney-general had opined that 'any prohibition on the means by which sugar may be bought is economically unsound'[26] – and to control it in peacetime raised fundamental questions about the nature of the colonial project. The committee which considered the measure expressed opposition to this in a passage which, significantly, insisted on the desirability of commercial change while accepting that drunkenness amongst young men was the problem:

> Sugar is not only used in the manufacture of intoxicants but is probably more largely used for other purposes and it is felt that to impose restrictions as intended by the Bill will unnecessarily penalize legitimate customers . . . We are further of the opinion that the legitimate use of sugar by the native population should if anything be encouraged. Not only is it a most desirable adjunct as regards diet, but it is one of the means of inducing the natives to spend money.
>
> The Committee is absolutely of the opinion that the question of dealing with the increased state of drunkenness amongst natives, particularly amongst the young men, requires earnest and careful consideration, but we consider that the subject should be dealt with by regulating and restrictive measures.[27]

The measure was dropped; and instead a specific piece of legislation was introduced, 'the Wakamba (Prevention of Drunkenness) Ordinance. This, a remarkable piece of colonial essentializing in its explicitly ethnic approach to drunkenness, gave powers to control sugar supply in particular districts. In explaining this legislation, the attorney-general rather defensively noted that 'It was acknowledged that the native authorities were useless in

---

22 B. Berman, 'Bureaucracy and Incumbent Violence. Colonial Administration and the Origins of the "Mau Mau" Emergency', in Berman and Lonsdale, *Unhappy Valley*, II, 234. Iliffe has identified similar contradictory concerns among British officials in Tanganyika: *Modern History*, 326.
23 Ag. PC Ukamba to Ag CS, 24 Jan. 1919, KNA AM/1/55.
24 Attached, Barth, AG to CS, 19 Apr. 1918, KNA AG/381.
25 Versturme-Bunbury to Ainsworth, CNC, 10 July 1918, KNA AG/1/381.
26 AG to CS, 20 Sep. 1916, KNA AG/1/386.
27 Report of Special Committee of Legislative Council, by Gower, AG, 13 Dec. 1918, KNA AG/1/381.

combating the drink evil'.[28]   Yet the debate did not end there. Officials in Nairobi continued to urge the use of administrative controls, rather than control of materials, to restrict drinking.   Local administrators in Kamba areas, supported by colleagues in other parts of the colony, argued that this was impossible, and pushed still for controls on raw materials.[29] Again and again, central officials urged the use of headmen to control drinking, and local officials said that this was impossible.[30] In 1923 the CNC, who had come to support the position of local officials, argued their case by conjuring up the most potent expression of danger in the colonial vocabulary.

> The vice of drunkenness among young natives is a menace to white women settled among them, to say nothing of black women, and is a danger to life and property . . . Existing laws give us theoretical control, which in practice is impossible without enormous police expenditure . . . The elders who should support us are all addicted to drunkenness. The one narrow point at which we can throttle down is the mill.[31]

By thus linking the fearful image of the 'black peril' to concerns about the threats which modernity – in the shape of the sugar-mill – posed to traditional authority and morality, the CNC won a sort of compromise from the attorney-general's office, the seat of the most determined opposition to controls on materials. The provisions of the local Kamba ordinance were incorporated into a new Sugar Ordinance, which allowed for sugar control in any area by proclamation.[32] This was applied to parts of central Kenya, but never elsewhere, and for some years the administration and the police struggled to enforce its provisions, in the face of widespread evasion. In 1930, an amendment to the Sugar Ordinance imposed higher fines for offences, which could be used to reward informers: a measure which was frankly stated to be necessary because the original ordinance 'has largely failed to achieve its objective'.[33] But during the 1930s, a decline in correspondence on this issue suggests that sugar restriction had ceased to be an important policy. After a brief resurgence in 1945, at a time of sugar shortage, enforcement of the ordinance seems to have lapsed.[34]

   European administrators in central Kenya were particularly anxious about African drunkenness – probably as a result of the inherently tense situation

---

[28]   'Statement of Objects and Reasons', Barth, AG, 14 Apr. 1919, KNA AG/1/386.
[29]   See Buxton, Asst. DC Kiambu to DC Kiambu, 10 Apr. 1922 and CNC to AG, 13 June 1922; the AG's opposition was still being expressed in 1922: AG to CNC, 13 June 1922, KNA AG/1/386.
[30]   Lyall-Grant, AG to CNC, 25 July 1922 and Senior Commissioner, Nyeri to CNC, 21 Aug. 1922, KNA AG/1/386.
[31]   Watkins, CNC to AG, 11 Jan. 1923, KNA AG/1/386.
[32]   Law, for AG to CNC, 13 Jan. 1923, KNA AG/1/386.
[33]   'Objects and Reasons: Sugar Ordinance', *Official Gazette*, 25 Mar. 1930.
[34]   See the contents of KNA AM/1/55. Ambler, 'Drunks, Brewers and Chiefs', 176 suggests that debate on the whole issue died off from the later 1920s, to be superseded – as will be argued below – by debates over the relationship between state control and African entrepreneurship.

created by the presence of a settler community, rather than of the inherent insobriety of the local people. Throughout the colonial period, debates in Kenya over drinking were more intense than elsewhere in the region, and the detail of legislation more painstakingly restrictive. But similar anxieties were reflected in debates and policy across the region. And the pattern of the central Kenyan debates – shifting from an early anxiety over lawlessness, to a concern to maintain the authority of local headmen – was evident everywhere.

LICENSING SALE, 1900–14

In 1906, German East Africa buzzed with rumours that the outbreak of popular violence which Europeans called the Maji-Maji revolt had begun with drinking; there had been great beer parties at which medicine was distributed which was alleged to protect the drinkers from bullets.[35] This assumed link between drink and disorder was symptomatic: across the region, it was the uncomfortable, lurking possibility of explosive African violence which initially propelled laws on drinking, which actually mostly took the form of laws about the sale of drink.[36]

In British East Africa (BEA), regulations were issued in November 1900 which required a licence for the sale of liquor in specified places: initially, in various coastal towns, in Nairobi and along the line of rail. The regulations set a fee of Rs (rupees) 15 for an annual licence.[37] In 1907, an ordinance replaced these regulations. Applicable throughout the protectorate, this set the annual licence fee at Rs30, and required those making palm wine or honey-wine for sale to take out a further licence at an annual cost of Rs25. It also gave discretion to the issuing officer, who was the district commissioner, to refuse a licence.[38] In German East Africa, regulations were issued in 1904 which set a licence fee of from Rs6 to Rs60, depending on local circumstances:[39] this ordinance was applied to specific areas only until 1911, after which it was (apparently) applied to the whole territory.[40] In Uganda, where the existence of the agreements with the rulers of local states – first Buganda, and later Ankole, Toro and Bunyoro – set a rather different environment for legislation, an ordinance was passed in 1902 which required licences for the sale of liquor in the major townships (which were under direct administration). Here the licence fees were very much higher, from Rs100 to Rs150.[41] In 1906 a supplementary ordinance was introduced to require a

---

[35] Weule, *Native Life*, 51.
[36] Memo, Combes, Crown Advocate, 24 Dec. 1907, KNA AG/1/382; Jackson, Ag. DC Toro to CS, 28 July 1911, UNA A46/796.
[37] 'Palm Wine Regulations', 24 Nov. 1900, copy in KNA AG/1/397.
[38] Ordinance No. 15 of 1907, in KNA AG/1/382.
[39] See in TNA G/3/49.
[40] The application of regulations to the whole territory is not clear from surviving German records (see for example G/1/116, which records a further local extension), but in the 1920s British officials believed that the regulations had applied to all of German East Africa: Minute, Treasurer, 15 Nov. 1923, TNA SMP 3214, vol. I.
[41] *Uganda Gazette*, 1 Nov. 1902.

licence to make alcohol in specified areas, and to prohibit importation of alcohol into those areas: this new law being the result of the difficulty officials had encountered in proving that alcohol found had been bought and sold.[42] So, by 1910, colonial states across the region had made laws regulating the sale of alcohol in at least some parts of the territories they controlled.

Revenue was an issue in this legislation too: early extensions in the area covered by the law in BEA were explained partly as revenue measures, and the imposition of a specific licence fee for making honey-wine was explained as a form of 'duty' resultant on the high alcohol content of the product.[43] As revenue raisers for central government, however, licensing schemes were never a great success in East Africa: in most districts, 'native liquor' licences contributed a minute proportion of revenue, and even on the coast (where licences to tap palms, as well as to sell wine, were later introduced) licence income was never that great.[44] The licensing schemes of the early twentieth century were ineffective in other ways too; most spectacularly unsuccessful in Uganda, where only one licence was taken out in the first six years after the passage of the 1902 Ordinance.[45] The licensee – in Nimule, an administrative station in the far north – was a model individual in official eyes. Ex-Sergeant-Major Mourjhan of the 4th battalion, King's African Rifles, sought to protect his investment in the licence by informing on eight other beer sellers who were all prosecuted.[46] It is not clear whether any other licences were taken out between 1908 and 1917, but no record exists of any revenue from such licences; even though by 1913 more than 10 percent of criminal prosecutions in Uganda were charged under the Native Liquor Ordinance.[47]

In BEA, the enforcement of the law in towns and at the coast, where coercive power was routinely available in support of authority, was a little more successful. In Mombasa, for example, officials managed to impose a system of regulation, and they used this to force out of legal business those entrepreneurs – women, and those who had no fixed premises – whom they considered undesirable. On the mainland surrounding Mombasa licences were issued to a favoured group of men and other sellers were prosecuted.[48] Yet this required a sustained effort: some of the small numbers of police available had to be used, and these police had to be directly supervised since, as one official in Uganda noted, policemen 'seldom, of course, give

---

[42] Wyndham Ag. Collector Busiro to Dep. Commissioner, 14 June 1906; and Native Liquor Ordinance, 1906, UNA 42/96.

[43] Memo, Combes, Crown Advocate, 24 Dec. 1907, KNA AG/1/382.

[44] In Digo/Kwale District, on the Kenya Coast, licences and permits accounted on average for 2.8 percent of revenue in the district in the years 1930-42: figures from Annual Reports, in KNA DC KWL.

[45] Minute, Treasurer, 13 Apr. 1908, UNA A/44/113.

[46] Collector Nimule to Sub-Commissioner Nile, 3 Oct. 1905 and Sub-Commissioner to Dep. Commissioner, 4 Oct. 1905, UNA A12/7.

[47] 118 cases of a total of 1,003: Police Annual Report, 1913, UNA A 46/217.

[48] Asst. DC Rabai to PC, 27 June 1913; DC Mombasa to PC, 20 Nov. 1912 and 4 Jan. 1915, KNA PC Coast 1/10/54.

useful information in matters of illicit liquor traffic'.[49] Such concerns established a pattern: throughout the colonial period, officials were convinced of the corrupting possibilities of a drink trade (in which, after all, the wives and lovers of many policemen were involved) and feared to expose their police to these 'great opportunities and temptations'.[50]

In the period up to 1920 such concerns meant that in most rural areas in BEA there was no attempt to enforce the 1907 Ordinance, with its requirements for licences. The enforcement of any law relied on the recognized headmen, who had inherited the gatekeepers' model of authority, and sought to build up little followings of young men, as their immediate resource of coercive power. They used the power of these young men, supported now by their new accommodation with the state, to enforce their will – and the demands of the state – on their subjects.[51] Their authority was by no means assured, as the growing demands of the colonial system turned them from allies into agents. Through them came demands for labour and then for tax; other men resented these demands, as they or their sons were forced into periods of work and they were forced to sell livestock, or labour, to pay taxes. [52] In other parts of East Africa too, the immediate agents of the state were inheritors of a nineteenth-century model of particular authority which relied on coercion to dispossess elder men and celebrated authority in the drunken carousing of the young followers of 'chiefs'.[53] Mukama and chiefs in Bunyoro still surrounded themselves with personal followings, rewarded with drink and sometimes wives; to such followers they could now offer also exemption from taxation.[54] At the beginning of the twentieth century, the officially recognized chiefs of Rungwe were competing in providing feasts and beer for their followers; one tried to appropriate the idea of power conveyed in the use of beer, 'blowing' beer over his warriors in blessing.[55] In the first years of British rule in Tanganyika this plethora of officially recognized headmen was still competing for followers.[56] Drink was part of the construction of authority of these men, part of their challenge to other elders: but across the region, officials complained of the drunkenness of chiefs and headmen and their reluctance to control drinking , and sought to replace the most blatantly inebriate for pursuing the established drinking practices of power.[57] Their concerns were fed by African debates; for complaining of an increase in drinking became a way for elder men, in

---

[49] Wilson, Sub-Commissioner Unyoro to Special Commissioner, 23 Mar. 1901, UNA A/12/1.
[50] PC Coast to CS, 7 Sep. 1943, KNA MAA 7/424.
[51] Lonsdale, 'Conquest State', 26.
[52] Lonsdale, 'Conquest State', 31.
[53] In 1919, it was alleged that government headmen in Rungwe had become accustomed to seizing the cattle of their subjects at will: New Langenburg District Annual Report, 1919-20, 11, TNA Library.
[54] Ints Nyoro9c, 1; Nyoro34a, 1; Nyoro35c, 4; Nyoro38b, 4; Nyoro39b, 1.
[55] Meyer, *Wa-Konde*, 136; Charsley, *Princes of Nyakyusa*, 67.
[56] There were 168 headmen in Rungwe in 1925: Admin. OiC Rungwe to CS, 15 Sep. 1925, TNA SMP 2724.
[57] DC Hoima to CS, 28 July 1909; Henry [?] to PC Northern, 18 Oct. 1915, UNA A 46/492.

particular, to express their sense of the illegitimacy of headmen's power, and the problem of youthful disobedience.

Talking about drinking

In the early decades of the twentieth century, elder men rather consistently evoked a particular ideal of drinking in conversations with Europeans, whether missionaries, officials or ethnographers. They – like their contemporaries in South Africa – used drink as a vivid illustration of their concerns about their authority, and as an argument about the impropriety of certain kinds of behaviour among young men and women;[58] for the new circumstances of the colonial economy had increased tension along the old fault lines of sex and age. The sale of drink potentially combined the perils of youthful defiance and female insubordination. Around 1910, an ethnographer in central Kenya reported concern over drinking by young men, which breached customary prohibitions based on the fear of sexual competition from young men: 'The old people say that the youths must choose between girls and beer.'[59] Missionaries who complained of drunkenness in central Kenya were similarly guided by this notion of rebelliously drunken youth. 'Formerly it was only the elders who drank, but now it extends down even to boys . . . Among the young men who drink there is a tendency to repudiate the authority of the elders.'[60] Such complaints about youthful drinking offered a usefully indirect way for men to criticize the agents of the early colonial state; and they helped to shift the terms of European debate. In the second and third decades of the twentieth century, the concerns of European officials increasingly paralleled those of the elders: drunkenness was a problem of rural youths and urban women.

RETHINKING CONTROL:
OFFICIAL DEBATES, c.1918–26

The government has forbidden drinking by youths and women.[61]

The period from the First World War to 1925 saw the whole of East Africa under British rule for the first time, and saw too the emergence of a rather brittle and short-lived consensus in official debates on locally-made alcohol: a consensus which rested on the premise that the sale of such alcohol should be an essentially urban phenomenon, and should be regulated by licence in urban areas. Elsewhere, it was drunken youths who were the problem, and to stop them from obtaining drink, sale simply should not exist. Where

---

[58] B. Carton, '"The New Generation . . . Jeer at Me, Saying We are All Equal Now": Impotent African Patriarchs, Unruly African Sons in Colonial South Africa', in Aguilar, *The Politics of Age and Gerontocracy*, 31-64.

[59] Lindblom, *The Akamba*, 519.

[60] Johnston, African Inland Mission to PC Ukamba, 4 June 1916, KNA AG/1/386.

[61] 'Makatazo ya Pombe', *Mambo Leo*, May 1924.

it did arise – as among the Kamba – it might be suppressed not by regulation but by making the ingredients for production unobtainable. There was a striking similarity in official debates on this subject in all three East African territories.

In Uganda, a new Liquor Ordinance came into effect at the beginning of 1917. This was, structurally, quite different from its predecessors and from all legislation passed elsewhere in East Africa on this subject: it covered both 'intoxicating liquor' and 'native liquor' – while maintaining the distinction between the two categories – and simply gave the governor power to make rules concerning the drinking, making and selling of these. Such rules were made: they were only applied to towns, where drinking was to be controlled through regulation of sale, and the manufacture or sale of locally-made alcohol in towns without a licence was prohibited. The rules also substantially reduced the licence fees in an attempt to encourage the emergence of a legal trade: to Rs30-50, from Rs100-150.[62] In 1917 a law was passed by the kingdom government of Buganda – after pressure from European officials – which covered those parts of the kingdom where the Liquor Ordinance was not in force. Although avowedly intended to 'prevent drunkenness',[63] it was, in fact, very largely about preventing sale. It banned the *ebirabo*, or 'clubs', at which locally-made alcohol was sold and drunk, which had spread throughout the kingdom; it banned the selling of alcohol on 'any road' or in any market or in the royal capital, the *kibuga*; and it banned the drinking of alcohol 'along the road' or at the place of sale.[64] Legally, people in Buganda could buy locally-made alcohol only if they were going to take it home and drink it there. No licensing system was introduced – the intention was to discourage sale, not to regulate it.

The division between towns as places of regulated sale, and rural areas as being properly beyond sale, was maintained elsewhere in Uganda into the 1920s, and became a brief focus for debate over the relationship between authority and modernity, and over the nature of the accommodation between colonial officials and chiefs and headmen. In 1919, PCs discussed the possibility of introducing in other parts of Uganda laws based on that in Buganda. After a period of consultation it became apparent that, while district administrators viewed drinking by young men as a possible problem, they simply did not believe that chiefs and headmen, who were themselves prominent consumers of alcohol, could control drinking. District officials cautiously avoided any discussion of sale, merely expressing opposition to the possibility of licensing.[65] Overall, there was a clear concern to downplay

---

[62] 'An Ordinance Relating to Liquor', No. 9 of 1916, *Official Gazette*, 1 Jan. 1917.

[63] Gutkind, *Royal Capital of Buganda*, 143-4.

[64] 'A Law to Prevent Drunkenness', Kingdom of Buganda, 4 Apr. 1917, *Official Gazette*, 31 Aug. 1917.

[65] DC Busoga to PC Eastern, 9 Mar. 1920; Ag. DC Mbale to PC Eastern, 4 Mar. 1920, UNA Z/325/20. There is a reference to the need to control juvenile drinking in Ag. PC Teso to PC Eastern, 17 Mar. 1920, UNA Z/325/20. The file Z/325/20 is a 'stray', not on the UNA hand-list, which was found in the archive cellar; it is evidently part of an uncatalogued Eastern Province deposit.

the issue, as though local officials feared that a panic over drunkenness might lead to them being asked to enforce restrictions which demanded too much of chiefs and headmen:[66] 'Legislation which is not, or cannot, be enforced is more harmful than no legislation at all, since it merely weakens a Government's position and authority', wrote one.[67] There was, however, the suggestion that if drunkenness were considered a problem it might be controlled through restricting the supply of raw materials: by preventing the cultivation of certain kinds of bananas or of sorghum.[68] As in Kenya, controls on raw materials were seen as the simplest answer to the problem of youthful drinking, and the best defence of threatened traditional authority.

Debate briefly re-emerged in the 1920s, in consequence of agitation by the police, who continued to view drunkenness among men of all ages as a widespread cause of crime.[69] When the Police Annual Report for 1923 described drunkenness as 'the chief cause of the backwardness of the people' in Bunyoro, the attention of the Colonial Office in London was suddenly drawn to the issue, and the administration was again forced to consider 'restrictive measures'.[70] The debate was a replay of that in 1919-20. District administrators insisted that there was no major drinking problem, that sale under licence was inherently undesirable in rural areas, and that any system of control – beyond those introduced as a temporary measure to conserve food supplies – 'presents grave difficulties'. To underline the point, one DC then asked for a extension of the rules under the Liquor Ordinance to an area where there was a concentration of railway workers, but only on the understanding that the restrictions 'might well be withdrawn upon the completion of construction to avoid unnecessary interference with native life'.[71] Finally, in 1925, the CS issued a circular to all provincial and district administrators: the governor, he announced, had decided that while drunkenness among 'certain tribes' was a cause for concern, it could not be controlled by legislation. The circular linked drunkenness directly to concerns over morality and the dangers of modernity:

> It should be borne in mind that it is more difficult to introduce new ideas and new conceptions of temperance among an African people than to bring about a reversion to salutary tribal customs which have now unfortunately broken down . . . where drinking on the part of women and children was formerly disallowed by tribal custom, the first step should be to endeavour to re-establish this custom.[72]

---

[66] CS to all PCs, 29 July 1920, UNA A/325/20.
[67] Ag. DC Teso to PC Eastern, 17 Mar. 1920, UNA Z 325/20.
[68] CS's note summarizing PCs' suggestions, attached to CS to all PCs, 29 July 1920, UNA Z 325/20.
[69] For example, see Police Annual Report for 1927, 34, UNA A46/228.
[70] The Colonial Office raised the issue in October 1924, and again a year later: Amery, SoS to Governor, 13 Oct. 1925, UNA A/46/225; see excerpt from report, attached Ag. CS to all PCs, UNA Z/325/20.
[71] DC Busoga to PC, 21 May 1925, UNA Z/325/20.
[72] CS to all PCs, 17 July 1925, UNA Z/325/20.

Chiefs, the governor instructed, should set an example through their 'temperate habits', and it must be made clear that 'the suppression of drunkenness was a primary duty of all chiefs'. The circular made no reference to the regulation of sale: outside the towns, drinking was a matter of 'tribal customs', and control of it should come through chiefs' actions to 're-establish' custom. The circular drew a temporary end to debate on this issue and set chiefs – as the guarantors of 'traditional', non-commercial, drinking – in direct conflict with aspirant drink-sellers and drinkers.

In both Kenya and Tanganyika, a similar division between rural and urban was established in the early 1920s. A new Native Liquor Ordinance had been passed in Nairobi in 1915, but it contained clauses relating to the licensing of palm trees which were deemed impossible of implementation in wartime, and so it was never brought into force.[73] This provides a revealing historical footnote: Hobley, the PC at the coast, observed that since previous legislation had been annulled, this meant that there was no longer any law controlling locally-made alcohol. However, as he pointed out, this made no difference as 'the natives do not read the Official Gazette' and an emergency piece of legislation was quickly passed to fill the gap.[74]

The 1915 Ordinance had differed from the 1907 Ordinance in one important way: it was applicable by proclamation to specific areas only. In 1921, an entirely new Ordinance was passed which was similarly applicable only to specified areas. While some officials believed that previous legislation would remain in force elsewhere, this was evidently not the intention of those who drafted the legislation:[75] the Colonial Office had already questioned the wisdom of this new limitation on the working of the Ordinance, but the Kenya administration refused to amend the bill and so, with its passage, the laws which directly governed the sale of locally-made alcohol ceased to apply to most of Kenya.[76] This, of course, made little practical difference, since the 1907 law had never been enforced in most of the territory: the legal change was not even mentioned in the ongoing debates over Kamba drinking. The new Ordinance was applied to urban areas and some areas of white settlement; elsewhere there was no legislation to control sale. Instead, drinking was to be controlled under the provisions of the Native Authority Ordinance, the great catch-all of colonial rural administration, which gave headmen and chiefs power to make orders 'restricting the manufacture or distilling of Native Intoxicating Liquors and the supply of such liquors to young persons' and 'prohibiting or restricting the holding of drinking bouts' – but did not allow for any system of regulated sale.[77]

[73] Barth, AG to CS, 8 Nov. 1915, KNA AG/1/385.

[74] PC Seyyidie to AG, 13 Sep. 1915; and 'An Ordinance to Keep Alive the Provisions of the Native Liquor Ordinance, 1907', in KNA AG/1/385. Nonetheless, some magistrates continued to convict people under the 1915 Ordinance: Sheridan[?] to Solicitor-General, nd and Solicitor-General to Sheridan, 6 Jan. 1920, KNA AG/1/381.

[75] See AG to Ag. Colonial Secretary, 1 July 1921; cf. CNC to Ag. Colonial Secretary, 4 July 1921, KNA AG/1/381.

[76] For the Colonial Office query, see SoS to Governor, 11 May 1921, KNA AP 1/1203.

[77] Ordinance No. 22 of 1912, *Official Gazette*, 16 Oct 1912. CNC to Colonial Secretary, 4 July 1921, KNA AG/1/381.

In Tanganyika, some local administrators had been using the German law on locally-made alcohol since assuming control, though the police complained of its technical inadequacies.[78] But in 1923 a new Native Liquor Ordinance was passed, closely modelled on that in Kenya – and applicable only to specified townships. As in Kenya, there was some dismay from district administrators in particular areas where sale was very common, who found that they suddenly possessed no legal structure for regulating sale, for the law presumed that there was no sale outside the towns.[79] And the Treasury was appalled at the surrender of potential licence revenue.[80] But there were other local administrators who thought that licensed sale 'increased drunkenness and disorder',[81] and agreed with Dundas, the SNA, who minuted that 'The ideal is that the native should brew his [*sic*] own liquor. If licensed premises for sale are set up they become the resort of loafers and drunkards.'[82] Dundas had elsewhere written enthusiastically of the social desirability of 'traditional' drinking – but evidently he abhorred the sale of liquor.[83] And officials in the secretariat were, for several years, obdurate in their resistance to any extension of the system of regulated sale. They were supported by those district administrators who felt that the real justification of urban beer-markets was that at least they made it less likely that those employed in the towns would go into neighbouring rural areas and 'caus[e] trouble to the Native Authorities' by trying to buy drink.[84] Across the region, the way that European officials talked about African drinking played a central role in constructing assumptions about the nature of African societies as threatened by modernity and commerce. Drinking, even a degree of drunkenness, was quite proper in rural society, amongst elders: but drinking by the wrong people, which was made possible by sale, was an engine of societal demoralization.

In urban areas, by contrast, new legislation offered a highly regulated system of sale. Borrowing from South African practice, the Kenyan legislation provided for licensing boards which would issue licences to individuals, with their own premises, who would make for sale, and sell, 'native liquor'.[85] Where no such board was appointed (appointment being in the hands of the governor), the DC alone constituted the board. Premises were to be inspected, hours of sale were set, and while generally licences were to be issued only to Africans, the law allowed for the vesting in a 'local authority' – by which was meant a municipal or township council – the sole right to make and sell 'native liquor'. And under the 1921 Kenyan law, African women in urban areas were specifically excluded from holding

---

[78] Ag. Inspector Tabora to Senior Commissioner Tabora, 17 July 1922, TNA SMP 3214, Vol. I.
[79] Senior Commissioner Tabora to CS, 3 Apr. 1924; Political Tanga to Sec., 12 Mar. 1924, TNA SMP 3214, Vol. I.
[80] Treasurer, Minute, 10 Dec. 1923 and Treasurer to CS, 14 July 1924, TNA SMP 3214, Vol. I.
[81] Admin. OiC Mahenge to CS, 10 Nov 1924, TNA SMP 3214, Vol I.
[82] SNA, Minute, 19 July 1924, TNA SMP 3214, Vol. I
[83] C. Dundas, *Kilimanjaro and Its People* (London, 1924), 144, 259, 262.
[84] DO Shinyanga to PC Tabora, 10 Dec. 1929, TNA SMP 12694, Vol. I.
[85] AG to Ag. Colonial Secretary, 1 July 1921, KNA AG/1/381.

licences in towns, or from obtaining alcohol from those who did hold licences: they could not sell or buy drink in any township.[86] Further changes to the law in 1927 and 1930 made it impossible for women to make alcoholic beverages in towns even if these were not intended for sale, and forbade men to buy drink to give to women in urban areas.[87] 'Traditional' drinking was thus banned from the towns; and so was any drinking at all by women. In practice, women in Kenya were allowed to make grain beer in towns – but only if they were making this for a male licensee to sell.[88] The policy of the 1920s was predicated on a clear distinction: in rural areas, drink's problematic centred on young men; in urban areas, it centred on women.

The rules issued in Uganda under the 1917 Ordinance had already prohibited there the issue of a licence to manufacture and sell to any woman (though it did not make it illegal for women to buy alcohol).[89] In Tanganyika, however, the legislation differed: there were no licensing boards, the DC being solely responsible for licensing. Nor were there gender restrictions as regards the issue of licences, or sale of drink itself, and a distinct model of legal urban sale emerged, with government-owned 'beer-markets' in many towns. In these each of a number of licensees or permit-holders, mostly women, were allowed to sell their liquor. It is not clear why women were allowed to hold licences in Tanganyika; there is simply no discussion of this in the records. It may simply have been that – as some later correspondence suggests – the expectation was in 1923 that quite soon all these beer-markets would turn into official monopolies on the 'Durban' model: one district commissioner looked forward to official breweries in towns, where selling booths would be run by 'government clerks'.[90] In the event, however, the capital necessary to establish such monopolies was hard to find, and the one brief and disastrous experiment with a monopoly in Dar curtailed further such plans.[91] But, like the Kenyan and Ugandan laws, Tanganyika legislation of the 1920s assumed that rural drinking was to be traditional; while urban drinking was a physiological need, which must be met through sale.

The Kenyan and Ugandan legislation fitted into a particular discourse about urban areas, and the need to keep these as separate and distinct,

---

[86] Sec. 3, Native Liquor (Amendment) Ordinance, 1927, KNA AG 1/388; Sec. 20, Native Liquor Ordinance, 1930, KNA AG 1/391.

[87] Sec. 6(2) and 11(b), Native Liquor Ordinance, 1921, KNA AG 1/381.

[88] Even this was in breach of the letter of the law, but it seems to have been understood that the intention was to allow women to make beer for male entrepreneurs. When the police brought a test prosecution against an employed women brewer in 1945, it was immediately thrown out, with the full support of the AG: Circular, 1 Mar. 1945, KNA AP 1/1203.

[89] Rule 22, Native Liquor Rules, *Official Gazette*, 1 Jan. 1917.

[90] Senior Commissioner Tabora to CS, 22 Feb. 1923, TNA SMP 3214, Vol I; Ag. Director Medical Services to CS, 18 May 1927, TNA SMP 10491, Vol. I.

[91] PC Eastern to CS, 21 June 1927; PC Eastern to CS, 6 June 1928, and draft reply to Legislative Council question, attached, TNA SMP 10491, Vol I; Mbilinyi, "'This is an Unforgettable Business'"; Minute, Kayamba, 21 Dec. 1935, TNA SMP 24575. See below for further comment on the Dar monopoly.

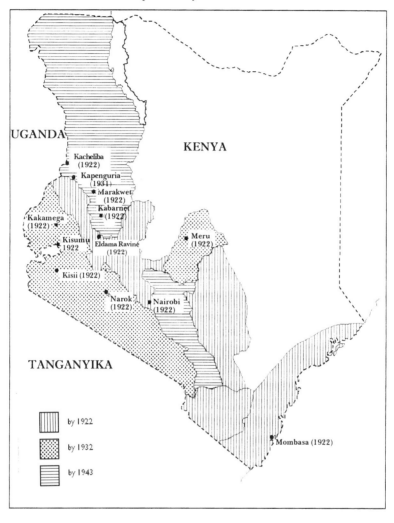

UGANDA

KENYA

Kacheliba
(1922)

Kapenguria
(1931)

Marakwet
(1922)

Kabarnet
(1922)

Kakamega
(1922)

Meru
(1922)

Kisumu
1922

Eldama Ravine
(1922)

Kisii (1922)

Narok
(1922)

Nairobi
(1922)

TANGANYIKA

| by 1922 |
| by 1932 |
| by 1943 |

Mombasa (1922)

Map 4 *Application of the Native Liquor Ordinance, Kenya, 1921–40.* (From information in KNA AG 1/402.)

subject to special rules and suited only for certain activities. A principal element in the discourse was the attempt to exclude women, an exclusion which could form the point of articulation for an accommodation between African men anxious to prevent women from finding an alternative life in the towns which placed them beyond the demands of marriage; officials who feared the disruptive effects of 'detribalization' engendered by urban life; and employers of contract labour, who sought workers who would come to work for set periods, without families to support, and would then return to rural 'homes' maintained by their wives.[92] In many ways, the most liberal European observers were most concerned on this issue: missionaries perceived as advocates of African interests were steadfast in their determination that African women should be kept from involvement in urban drink-selling, as 'such women will begin to drink and ultimately acquire a taste for liquor'.[93] In Tanganyika, however, financial reality prevented the realization of dreams of monopoly sale and women occupied a much more secure role in the urban economy of drink.

MODERNITY, AUTHORITY & RURAL SALE, c. 1926–40

. . . it seems a pity that the profits made from the alcoholic failings of the populace should not be turned to good account.[94]

From the later 1920s, the policy division between urban sale and rural tradition began to break down, as officials sought increasingly to recognize and control the rural sale of alcohol – or to force others to control it for them. Such controls were discussed, usually, in the context of dealing with drunkenness, but it is evident that it was the selling of alcohol which signalled dangerous levels of drunkenness to the official eye. When Tanganyika settlers complained about rural African drinking, district and provincial officials professed themselves unconcerned by the post-harvest binge of neighbourly brewing: 'I do not consider that the brewing of beer is excessive or that there is an extraordinary amount of drunkenness', said one, and a secretariat official noted that the settler complaint was one 'such as Europeans do make without reasonable grounds'.[95] The insobriety of the rural beer-shop was a quite different matter, spawning a much more dangerous type of drunkenness. Beer-shops created a 'highly criminal condition', especially (but not solely) in and around European-owned land where there were concentrations of rural waged workers.[96] Yet despite this anxiety, administrators systematically sought to create such beer-shops from the late 1920s.

---

[92] West, 'Liquor and Libido', 647-9; Ambler and Crush, 'Alcohol in Southern African Labor History', 7.

[93] Reservations, entered by Bemister, in Report of Select Committee on Native Liquor Bill, 1930, KNA AG 1/391.

[94] DO Kajiado to OiC Masai, 17 July 1940, KNA DC NGO 1/9/1.

[95] PC Tabora to CS, 1 May 1929; see also PC Eastern to CS, 28 May 1929, TNA SMP 13427; Minute, 23 May 1928, TNA SMP 12275.

[96] CNC to Ag. Col. Sec., 25 Feb. 1927, KNA AG 1/388; PC Lake to CS, 1 Dec. 1937, TNA SMP 12694, Vol. II; Ag. DO Iringa to PC Iringa, 4 Sep. 1936, TNA 157 A2/8.

The steady spread of controls on rural drinking took two forms. One was a simple expansion of the area in which European officials and police were immediately responsible for regulating sale – that is, the application of the Liquor Rules, or the Native Liquor Ordinance, to new areas. In Kenya, mostly in response to the appeals of district administrators, the Ordinance had by 1940 been applied far beyond the boundaries of towns, or even of white settlement.[97] In Tanganyika, the same trajectory was evident. In 1926 the governor signalled a willingness to apply the the Native Liquor Ordinance more widely when this was necessary to control drunkenness, and over the following years first settler and plantation areas and then an increasing number of other areas were brought under the Ordinance.[98] In settled areas where there were no policemen to enforce the law, administrators encouraged settlers to create their own, extra-legal systems of regulated sale.[99]

The other approach was to force the African agents of the state into regulation of sale. This reversed the policy of the early 1920s which had assumed that the regulated sale of alcohol was really incompatible with 'traditional' authority. From around 1926 – when the Native Authority Ordinance in Tanganyika was amended – chiefs and headmen were given new powers to regulate sale, and from the early 1930s they were increasingly urged to use them.

This expansion of control over the sale of drink was directly involved in the debate amongst officials over authority, tradition and modernity. The distinction between urban sale and rural traditional drinking had been an aspect of the official construction of a distinction between the modern world of towns and the traditional world of rural authority, and the rhetoric of tradition as the basis for the authority of the chosen agents of the state reached an apogee in the mid-1920s, particularly in Tanganyika. In this period, more than any other, district administrators devoted themselves passionately to legitimating the authority of their agents (in the eyes of other officials, at least) through demonstration of their historical antecedents.[100] In Rungwe, the sizeable assortment of headmen who had been recognized by officials since the British occupation were replaced in 1926 by two paramount chiefs and seven lesser chiefs chosen from among the competing *balafyale*. While these were patently not 'traditional', officials went to some lengths to collect genealogies and histories which demonstrated a degree of historically derived

---

[97] For examples of requests for Native Liquor Ordinance extension, see CNC to Colonial Secretary, 5 Nov. 1927; PC Nyanza to Colonial Secretary, 10 June 1937, KNA AG 1/402. The same file contains lists of places to which the Ordinance was applied. See also Proclamations of 15 Jan. and 7 Feb. 1941, KNA MAA 7/378.

[98] CS to PC Northern, 25 Sep. 1926, TNA SMP 3214, Vol. II; Ag. PC Northern to CS, 28 Feb. 1929; TNA SMP 12694, Vol. I.

[99] CS to PC Northern, 27 Aug. 1930, TNA SMP 12694, Vol. I, and ? to Hignell, 16 Sep. 1935, TNA SMP 12694, Vol. II.

[100] Iliffe, *Modern History of Tanganyika*, 318-26.

legitimacy for the rule of the *balafyale*.[101] Yet even as the fevered game of hunt the chief went on, the chronic dissatisfaction amongst officials over the efficacy of the authority of chiefs and headmen began to propel an experimentation with new structures of local rule.

Across the region, a sort of justification through works came to play as significant a role as tradition in official arguments on the legitimacy of authority.[102] By the early 1930s, district officials in Rungwe were dissatisfed with the paramountcies introduced in 1926, which were failing to achieve these aims, and after a prolonged period of debate it came to be accepted amongst officials that the 1926 system had overstated the role of chiefs in Rungwe, and had ignored the role of the commoner advisers or *mafumu*.[103] In 1935, a new system of federation replaced the paramountcy and gave a limited role to *mafumu*, and officials (with no little ingenuity) portrayed this new system as both 'traditional' and able to pursue an effective programme of works.[104] The comic spectacle of the invention of tradition has tended to distract attention from this: native authorities in Tanganyika, like the Local Native Councils (LNCs) introduced in Kenya from the mid-1920s, and like the kingdom governments in Uganda, were not supposed to simply embody reified tradition – they were supposed to transform tradition, if in controlled ways.[105] In 1929 an LNC had been created for the Maasai of Kajiado, and by 1931 this was collecting revenue;[106] in 1933, an Agreement between the Mukama of Bunyoro and the British sought to both formalize and reform the powers of the Mukama's government.[107] These reformed institutions of administration were expected to spend money: on health, on agricultural or livestock betterment, and on education.

Policy towards rural drinking was transformed in the context of this agenda of managed change. Drink was a source of disruption; but it was also a source of money. In Tanganyika, few native authorities took up the opportunity to raise fees from regulating the sale of alcohol when this first became possible in 1926.[108] But in the 1930s they were increasingly encouraged to do so. In the 1920s, the SNA had minuted that 'of all revenue sources, this [native liquor] is the one least to the credit of government';[109] but in 1932 the CS sent out a circular urging native authorities to seek revenue from native liquor. It was cautious in tone, still suggesting that sale might be prohibited in many areas, but it suggested that in some places a

---

[101] Rungwe District Annual Report, 1-5; see also the Rungwe District Book, TNA MF.
[102] See the *Provincial Commissioners' Reports on Native Administration for 1930*, which repeatedly refer to medical, agricultural and educational work: 1-2, 11, 26, 32, 64.
[103] Ag. DO Rungwe to PC Iringa, 10 Aug. 1934, TNA 18/26/3.
[104] PC Iringa to CS, 28 Mar. 1935, TNA 18/26/3.
[105] Barth, Ag. Governor to SoS, 9 Apr. 1929, PRO CO 533 382/13.
[106] Minutes, Kajiado District LNC, KNA DC KAJ 5/1/2; Kajiado District Annual Report, 1931, KNA DC KAJ 2/1/1.
[107] Beattie, *Nyoro State*, 80.
[108] There were some exceptions: DO Shinyanga to PC Tabora, 6 Mar. 1930, TNA SMP 12694, Vol. I.
[109] SNA, Minute, 6 Jan. 1925, TNA SMP 3214, Vol. I.

system of controlled sale might be desirable, and reminded native authorities (or rather, the DCs who dominated them) that they would collect the revenue which accrued.[110] Some authorities, faced by immediate budget crises and pushed by district administrators, soon responded by introducing systems of permits for sale.[111] From the later 1930s, the cautious hinting from the secretariat turned to outright pushing, and draft sets of sale regulations were circulated.[112] The search for revenue was by no means always successful – as in 1935 when the municipal authorities in Dar es Salaam made an ill-fated attempt to establish a monopoly of locally-made alcohol sale[113] – but it was persistent.

In Kenya, the Mombasa municipality had successfully established a beerhall – in fact, a palm-wine hall – in 1934, and LNCs in rural areas began to seek to emulate them: not initially through monopoly sale but through establishing beer-shops at which space was rented out to sellers.[114] Officials were anxious to argue first and foremost that such schemes were primarily intended to control drunkenness – since there was still some sensitivity over the idea of the state profiting from the sale of alcohol to Africans – but their revenue calculations were clear. In the little town of Kajiado, a beerhall owned by the LNC was established in 1940, modelled on one established in Narok town a few years earlier: when the idea was first mooted, the district administrator was careful to argue that as a result of such controlled sale 'drunkenness will decrease'; in 1940 he stated the revenue aims of the scheme more explicitly.[115] In Buganda, the 1917 law was reversed in 1941 by a new law, applicable to the *kibuga* and the area around it, which specifically restricted the sale of drink to *ebirabo* – turning these into an institution for the regulation of sale.[116] The division between towns as an area of sale and the rural areas as beyond sale, built up in the period to 1925, was largely dismantled by 1940.

In Kenya, European private enterprise as well as local government was widely recruited in pursuit of the twin goals of controlling drunkenness and providing revenue for 'improvements'. 'Non-natives' had been barred from holding licences in Kenya in 1907, as it was deemed undesirable that Asians or Europeans should be involved in supplying drink of any kind to Africans.[117] This restriction had been copied in Uganda and Tanganyika, but in Kenya it was steadily loosened. In settler areas, where there were

---

[110] Jardine, CS, 28 Jan. 1932, TNA SMP 13427.
[111] See PC Northern to CS, 13 June 1934 and Ag. PC Northern to CS, 20 July 1934, TNA SMP 12694, Vol. III.
[112] CS to all PCs, 30 Sep. 1944, TNA SMP 20495.
[113] Mbilinyi, '"This is an Unforgettable Business"'.
[114] Mombasa District Annual Report for 1934, 3, 8, KNA DC MSA 1/4; DC Kilifi to PC Coast, 5 Aug. 1938, KNA MAA 2/5/53.
[115] DO i/c Kajiado to OiC Masai, 3 Dec. 1938 and DO Kajiado to OiC Masai, 17 July 1940, KNA DC NGO 1/9/1.
[116] 'Buganda Native Liquor Law', 1941, *Laws of Uganda, 1951* (Entebbe, 1951).
[117] Combe, Crown Advocate to Senior Commissioner, Nairobi, 26 Sep. 1907, KNA AG 1/

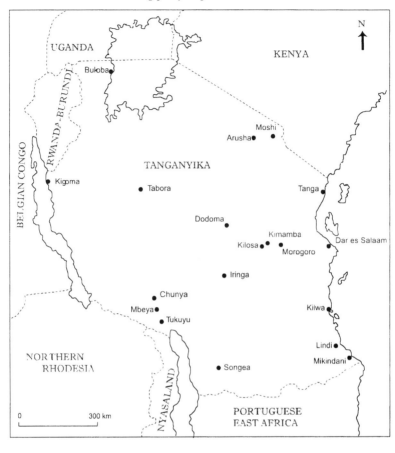

Map 5 *Beer-markets in Tanganyika, 1944*

constant white complaints about brewing by squatters, the 1930s had seen the formalization of a system on large farms and plantations, which gave licences to African men working under the patronage of their white employers (a similar systen was tolerated, extra-legally, in Tanganyika).[118] In 1940 a further amendment introduced Section 9A, which allowed white employers to establish their own beerhalls on the condition that the profits from this were to be used for the 'welfare' of Africans, and a number of large employers did so; in 1943, there were nine such beerhalls in Central Province alone, employing male managers and women as brewers.[119]

The spread of regulated sale was not a straightforward process. There was at first a degree of resistance from some provincial and district administrators, who continued to identify the sale of drink as a symbol of all that was most dangerous about modernity: in Tanganyika, shortly before the CS's 1932 circular, the PC responsible for Rungwe had written that 'I am decidedly opposed to *trading* in native liquor.'[120] When a district administrator in Rungwe implied that rural sale did occur in the district, he was sharply rebuked for allowing it, and hastily revised his assessment of the subject.[121] More importantly, there was a profound lack of enthusiasm from native authorities and LNCs. By the late 1930s, another provincial commissioner was encouraging the imposition of a system of regulated sale in Rungwe and surrounding districts in order to 'check drunkenness' and 'enrich your native treasuries'. After further pushing rules requiring a permit to sell alcohol were introduced in Rungwe, but were evidently ignored by all concerned[122] and in the 1940s, when the issue was raised at a public meeting, chiefs refused to be drawn into support for a system of sale, as 'it would cause a fuss'.[123] By 1945 the native treasuries of Rungwe still derived no revenue from locally-made alcohol.[124] In Bunyoro, rules requiring a permit to sell alcohol in rural areas seem to have been introduced sometime in the 1930s, but informants' accounts suggest that they were not enforced at all.[125] The structures of local government remained unwilling or unable to enforce such laws. In towns, the model of regulated sale of alcohol had provided at least a partial point of articulation for alliance between African men and the officials of the colonial state. But in rural areas, changing official policies on alcohol in the 1930s made no room for any immediate accommodation between officials and elder men.

---

[118] Bache, *The Youngest Lion*, 109; Sec. 17 of the Native Liquor Ordinance, 1930: KNA AG 1/391.

[119] Native Liquor (Amendment) ordinance, 1940, KNA AG 1/396. See the list in KNA MAA 7/379.

[120] Buckley, Ag. PC Iringa to DO Iringa, 18 Nov. 1931, TNA 157 A2/8. Emphasis in original.

[121] Assistant DO Rungwe to PC Iringa, 17 Nov. 1931; PC Iringa to DO Rungwe, 25 Nov. 1931, TNA 157 A2/8.

[122] PC Iringa to DO Iringa, 14 Dec. 1937; DO Rungwe to PC SHP, 21 June 1940, TNA 157 A2/8; for the apparent lack of enforcement, see Ints Nya5b, 2; Nya18a, 3; Nya41a, 3.

[123] Minute 8, Baraza, 25-27 Sep. 1944, TNA 18/26/9.

[124] Minute, 1 June 1945, TNA SMP 33144.

[125] Ints Nyoro5b, 3; Nyoro 11b, 2.

'Men & elders':
drinking practice, 1920–40

A man, to know that he was really a man, and a head of the house, would invite people and they would drink. You had to give them a drink to make them happy. If you wanted to learn something from him you would give him alcohol and he drinks, and he would get drunk then he will tell you everything.[126]

In the 1920s and 1930s, elder men continued to identify a growth in drinking by young men and women, and a growth in the sale of drink, as a threat to their authority.

What brings disrespect is beer; formerly the young did not drink beer, but now they come with their own money and buy and drink. Beer brings pride. A junior quarrels with an elder and seizes a spear. Beer used to belong to the older men. Yes, it belonged to men, there was none for sale, and juniors did not get any.[127]

In Buganda, Mair's informants assured her that the selling of alcohol was an innovation, unknown before the colonial period, and she identified it as a powerful element in driving individualization of enterprise.[128] Yet sale was not so novel in Buganda; and across the region, even as sale became more common, drinking practice continued in many ways to reproduce particular assumptions about power which upheld the authority of men. In 1935, a young educated man called James Mwaikambo married the daughter of a chief in Rungwe. The procession which escorted the bride-wealth to the bride's father was thoroughly modern in form: a squad of cyclists, the school football team and a drill team. But they carried with them 85 pots of millet beer, a gift in deference to the father-in-law's authority.[129] Elders accused young men like Mwaikambo of threatening tradition; but such accusations were in themselves a part of the discursive reproduction of elders' power, and while drink was bought and sold, and consumed in commercial contexts, it was at the same time being given, exchanged and used in ritual in ways which evoked notions of men's particular power. There had always been a contest over control of drink; drinking power had always had to accommodate a degree of alcoholic leakage beyond the circles of those who claimed authority.

In the clubs of Nairobi and Mombasa, with their brick and wire-mesh walls, turnstiles and 'stalwart attendants', the cheerless colonial vision of urban drinking as a physiological function came closest to realization.[130] But other drinking places thrived, offering the possibility of drinking in

---

[126] Int Nyoro10b, 5.

[127] Wilson, *For Men and Elders*, 98: citing the words of a chief.

[128] Mair, *An African People*, 130, 127.

[129] *Mambo Leo*, May 1935.

[130] See the descriptions and sketch in PC Tanga to CS, 11 Dec. 1935 and Memo, DO Tanga, 21 Feb. 1937, TNA SMP 24575.

circumstances which were more salubrious and which allowed customers to choose with whom they drank. Drinkers tried to reproduce their own ideas of proper drinking, even when the law reduced alcohol to no more than a dietary, desirable 'from the point of view of health and of morale'.[131] In their idealizations of drinking, young men themselves reproduced the model of elder men's authority: for the young migrant worker, the dream of acceptance as a man was encapsulated in the idea of giving millet to a wife and saying 'You make beer with this; I will invite my friends.'[132]

In rural areas, most drinking still took place at the homes of married men, either at social gatherings or in ritual practice, and generational separation and deference to men characterized these events. In Bunyoro, men still sought the attention and favour of the Mukama or of lesser chiefs by taking banana-wine to them.[133] Women did drink; but they were supposed to do so discreetly, and separately – although in practice as drinking progressed they might mix with men in circumstances which led to accusations of adultery, actual or intended.[134] Elder men still poured beer in offering to the dead; reconciliation and the renunciation of anger were prized as the basis of well-being. In drinking practice, men accommodated the sale of beer, without accepting its legitimacy: elder men might buy beer, from women sellers in Tukuyu or at markets, yet they sustained the notion that the purchase of beer was disreputable, an activity which no proper man should have to resort to, for surely his wife would make beer for him and his friends? So it was that the elder men of Rungwe were resistant to any idea of permits for sale. Selling beer should not be legitimated by some contract struck with the state; it was rather an activity of dubious status, conducted under often ambiguous circumstances in which, as has been argued above, it was not always clear or agreed whether any sale was actually taking place.

Yet this had begun to change. In the 1930s, accounts of Nyakyusa ritual suggested that in some instances, water was being blown or poured in place of beer.[135] It is impossible to reconstruct the precise circumstances of those events, but the change is suggestive.[136] Across the region, debate and practice were being increasingly shaped by men's engagement with new sources of power. Men found that their claims to authority over women and younger men could be upheld by the courts of the colonial state; and the official search for legitimacy had opened up the possibility of a new kind of engagement between state and married men who derived authority not from tradition but from a particular – and often explicitly Christian – ideal of patriarchal authority within the family. From the 1940s, popular drinking practice and drinking discourse increasingly reflected these alternative possibilities of power.

[131] CS to Produce Controller, 18 June 1944, KNA MAA 7/378..
[132] Int Nya22a, 3.
[133] Int Nyoro19b, 2.
[134] Hill, 'Native Case Law among the Nyakyusa', Southern Highland Province (SHP) Provincial Book, TNA MF 25-26.
[135] Extract from Northcote's Report of 1931, in SHP Provincial Book, TNA MF 25-26.
[136] Akyeampong, *Drink, Power and Cultural Change*, 71, argues that in Ghana the role of water in specifically Christian rituals represented a challenge to elders by youth.

Seven

Clubs & beerhalls
1940–55

In 1940, most of the alcohol consumed by Africans in East Africa was drunk at or near people's homes, and much of it was still being drunk without payment: only in the towns did specialized drinking-places play a prominent role in drinking culture. But by the late 1950s, much – probably most – drinking across the region took place in urban beerhalls or rural clubs. There were exceptions to this trend. Among the Maasai of Kajiado district, while urban drinking was increasingly confined to beerhalls there was no significant spread of rural clubs in this period. Yet overall, this movement in the place of drinking was as significant as the growing predominance of sale, with which it was connected. Neither process was driven simply by legislation, for there was relatively little change in legislation on 'native liquor' in this period, as compared with the period from 1920 to 1940. This fundamental change in drinking patterns was involved in a wider remaking of authority: drinking talk and practice continued to evoke assumptions about power which underlay authority, but the nature of power, if not the location of authority, was becoming more complex.

Courts, clinics & schools

> The white man divided the courts among us. Long ago there were no courts.[1]

In 1944 the DO Rungwe investigated a complaint against a chief for abuse of power. The case is interesting in many ways, for it reveals contention over a series of issues: men's power over women; the rivalry between the recognized agents of the state; and the complex relationship between the power of men and that of these agents. The accused chief, Kasambala, had not been one of those recognized as a chief by the British in the 1920s, but so many people had moved to live in an area which was popularly considered to be under his jurisdiction that the DO had recommended that official recognition be given to his status.[2] Kasambala had subsequently been in

---

[1] Int Nya24b, 2.
[2] DO Tukuyu to PC SHP, 20 Apr. 1939, TNA 77/26/25.

repeated conflict with other recognized chiefs over the geographical boundaries of his authority, as he sought constantly to acquire new followers.[3] It was perhaps one of his aggrieved rivals who encouraged the complaint against him.

The complainant, Anyombile, lived in Kasambala's area but claimed that in the 1930s she had been given a divorce from her first husband by the court of another chief – on what grounds, it is not clear. In April 1944 Kasambala called the woman and her new husband to his court, as her former husband was claiming return of bride-wealth cattle. Anyombile and her new husband brought three cattle, but when she refused to accept a demand for further cattle as 'damages' for adultery, Kasambala ordered her to be beaten by his 'messengers', the young men who enforced his orders. She escaped from the court, and next day went to the DO's office to accuse Kasambala of assault.

The DO's attention having been called to the case, Kasambala was arrested, tried and removed from office.[4] But this exemplary punishment of abuse was not the norm. Kasambala had erred in picking on a woman who was determined to resist, a mistake which compounded his error in alienating his fellow chiefs and offending European opinion.[5] Kasambala evidently felt that there was nothing improper or unusual in the beating as 'The beating took place in the court house and in the presence of a large crowd'.[6] And, as one of the witnesses called in the case casually remarked, 'It is not unusual for women to be publicly beaten in Native Court-houses.'[7] The investigating magistrate chose not to pursue this revelation, but it is suggestive in its ambiguity: women were beaten in courts, and not only physically.

The assault on Anyombile reveals the extent to which courts could function to uphold men's power over women. These were not the courts held at the district headquarters, presided over by the European district administrator: they were the lower-level courts which were empowered to deal with minor criminal cases and with civil offences. Such courts dealt with far more cases than did those at district headquarters, and while they existed under the theoretical supervision of the district administration, record-keeping was limited and supervision was in practice often erratic. Nyakyusa men were famously 'partial to litigation over cattle and women'.[8] When a formalization of the court system in 1925 made events at the courts of chiefs more public and recordable, officials were astounded at the sheer number of cases brought.[9] In the mid-1930s, more than 5,000 cases a year were coming to these courts,[10] and the bulk of them consisted of claims by

---

[3] DC Tukuyu to PC SHP, 5 May 1944, TNA 77/26/25.

[4] DC Tukuyu to PC SHP, 5 May 1944, TNA 77/26/25.

[5] Kasambala had in 1942 been accused of 'insulting' one of the few European planters in the area: DC Tukuyu to PC SHP, 5 Nov. 1942, TNA 18/26/9.

[6] Statement of Prosecution Witness 4, TNA 77/26/25.

[7] Statement of Prosecution Witness 5, TNA 77/26/25.

[8] Thwaites, 'Wanyakyusa agriculture', in Rungwe District Book, TNA MF 28.

[9] Rungwe District Annual Report for 1926, 8, TNA Library.

[10] 'Courts', Rungwe District Book, TNA MF 28.

men against other men, or women, over the control of the sexual and reproductive powers of women: in 1936 it was noted that in Rungwe 'no less than eighty per cent of the cases heard are in connection with adultery'.[11]

The popularity of the courts related directly to chronic problems of power, which meant that 'adultery constitutes one of the greatest difficulties with which native authorities in the Rungwe District have to contend'.[12] The courts represented an attractive new arena for debate partly because they were an alternative, a recourse for those dissatisfied with the outcome of arbitration; but more importantly, they offered a more effective means of enforcing decisions. The settlement of disputes, particularly in cases over women, had always been dogged by the difficulty of enforcing judgements, in the face of physical resistance or – sometimes – simple flight. Among the Nyakyusa an apparent increase in migration to neighbouring areas had exacerbated this difficulty: young men who fled with young women to live under another chief, or in another district, were difficult to pursue,[13] and the simple recourse of seizing cattle from their fathers or brothers might create as many problems as it solved for the injured party by embroiling them in new disputes.[14] The courts established within the formal structure of the colonial state offered some solutions to this problem. The messengers of the chief were available to enforce decision, so that legal action was seen partly as a way of accessing the coercive power possessed by the chief.[15] And courts could also require the support and assistance of other chiefs, in other districts: forcing them to return young men and women who had fled to their protection. This possibility – difficult though it was to enforce in practice – represented an important shift in the context of tensions between young men and old, and between men and women. In 1933 the district administrator told courts that they could imprison women for 'persistent adultery'.[16]

But, up to the 1940s at least, courts did not simply underwrite elder men's power over younger men and women. They were available to women too; one of the witnesses of Anyombile's beating was being taken to court by his wife, and was ordered to pay her 10 shillings for some unspecified offence[17]. And courts – in Rungwe, but also in many other places across the region – tended to be dominated by the chiefs or headmen recognized by the colonial state. In Rungwe, the court was the essential marker of status and point of articulation with the power of the state, and chiefs constantly argued over control and possession of them.[18] Chiefs used control of the

---

[11] SHP Annual Report, 1936: extract on Rungwe, in SHP Provincial Book, TNA MF 25-26.
[12] Extract from the SHP Annual Report for 1935, in SHP Provincial Book, TNA MF 25.
[13] Rungwe District Annual Report, 1924, 5, TNA Library; *Mambo Leo*, May 1935.
[14] 'Labour', Rungwe District Book, TNA MF 28. British officials accepted this practice in the 1920s, but forbade it in the later 1930s: PC Iringa to DO Rungwe, 29 Nov. 1927, TNA 18/ 1 and Tangazo, DO Tukuyu, 14 Mar. 1939, TNA 18/27/1.
[15] 'Execution fees', undated note, 1938, TNA 77/28/2.
[16] DO Rungwe to Headman, Kiwira, 18 Sep. 1933, TNA 18/27/2.
[17] Statement of Prosecution Witness 3, TNA 77/26/25.
[18] DO Rungwe to PC Iringa, 9 Oct. 1930; Ag. PC SHP to DO Rungwe, 13 Jan. 1931, TNA 77/ 28/2.

courts as a source of particular power, against one another, and against elder men: 'our Government has given us courts and everyone [is] enjoying and being paid' wrote one who had a court, while one of the excluded complained that 'those who have been chosen and salaried are happy, thus they despise their unfortunate friends of the same rank'.[19] Other men accused the chiefs of going against 'tribal custom'.[20] Chiefs enriched themselves through courts, and could use them to build up their own following of women: in 1938 the district officer had ruled that if a woman who was suing for divorce went to stay with a chief until the case could be heard, the chief could not be sued for adultery.[21]

In 1949 the power of chiefs in Rungwe was greatly reduced, in an attempt – seen as a model for changes elsewhere – to ensure 'more general representation of the people in local government bodies',[22] which would ensure a 'modernizing of the tribal governing structures'.[23] New councils and new courts were created which took the form of a hierarchy of triumviratic bodies, which gave equal weight to those who represented chiefs, *mafumu* and 'commoners' (*raia*, in the official Swahili of the time).[24] The concept of the *mafumu* was rather vaguely defined, and the early 1950s saw an abrupt mushrooming of *mafumu*, all of allegedly different traditional grades, so that any married man might in fact claim this status. Commoners, who were all apparently elder men, and *mafumu* were increasingly indistinguishable in the new structures of law and government.[25] The chiefs found themselves an endangered minority, with councils encouraged to 'insist upon better service or retirement' from them;[26] by 1951 the district council was discussing removing all judicial functions from chiefs.[27]

By the early 1950s, elder men in Rungwe – not necessarily old men, but married men with grown children – dominated courts and local government. Such rank gave authority, for it conferred a particular relationship with two forms of power: the coercive power of court messengers and police, who could and did enforce the decisions of courts; and the power which came from patronage, for local government was increasingly involved in the expenditure as well as the raising of revenue. The loss of power by chiefs meant also a shrinking of certain kinds of opportunities for young men and women: the protection and patronage of chiefs could no longer provide a ready alternative to the authority of husbands and fathers. The new district council quickly established a decidedly patriarchal agenda: the DC vetoed

[19] Letter attached with Ag. DO Rungwe to PC SHP, 8 Mar. 1937, TNA 18/26/3.
[20] 'Courts', SHP Provincial Book, TNA MF 25-26.
[21] Rungwe District Annual Report, 1926, 8, TNA Library; DC 7/38, recorded in Hill, 'Native Case Law Among the Nyakyusa', in SHP Provincial Book, TNA MF 28.
[22] DC Tukuyu to PC SHP, 15 Jan. 1949, TNA 18/26/9.
[23] PC SHP to Member for Local Government, 26 Sep. 1950, TNA 18/1/27.
[24] DC Tukuyu to PC SHP, 15 Jan. 1949, TNA 18/26/9.
[25] Minute 41 of meeting, 9-11 Nov. 1950 and Minute 52 of meeting, 27-30 Apr. 1952, TNA 157 L5/5/1.
[26] Handing-over Report, Kingdon, July 1949, TNA 77/1/3.
[27] Minute 6, Meeting 23-25 Apr. 1951, TNA L 157 L5/5/1. One man recalled that from 1949 it was clear that the chiefs' 'strength had started diminishing': Int Nya16c, 3.

their idea for imprisoning adulteresses if they or their father could not pay a fine; but accepted new rules which restricted women to seeking divorce from 'native courts' and insisted that a woman must continue to reside with her husband after divorce while the bride-wealth was collected to refund him. A proposal to ban women from attending markets was, however, abandoned as impracticable.[28]

Elsewhere in the region, elder men as a group moved similarly into increasingly close involvement in the late colonial state. From the later 1940s, officials sought constantly to broaden the representative nature of institutions of local government, in particular, as colonial states tried to focus African political ambitions on local objectives.[29] In Bunyoro, the chronology of change was slightly different. Up to 1933, chiefs had been effectively appointees of European officials, and from 1933 to 1955 they were appointed very much at the whim of the king of Bunyoro.[30] Even though there was evident concern over the control of women's sexuality, and the courts were a focus for such activity, men regarded their rulers with some suspicion. It was considered unneighbourly to take a case to the court of the chief, out of the realm of the community and into that of chiefly authority, *obulemi*,[31] and there was little enthusiasm for involvement in councils of any kind.[32] But the period from the late 1940s saw the erosion of this royal and chiefly power, as the colonial government sought to create 'modern, representative and efficient' local government.[33] This began with the appointment of councils (of men) to 'advise' chiefs and then with the creation of a committee to choose new chiefs.[34] In Bunyoro, as in Rungwe, there was soon a struggle for control of these new institutions. In a locally celebrated incident in 1953, a clerk was sentenced to 12 months' imprisonment for showing 'disrespect' to the Mukama in council. The DC set aside the sentence and imposed a small fine instead; when the Mukama appealed against this, he lost the case and was formally advised not to sit as the chair of the council, since this would inevitably expose him to 'disrespect'.[35] Strikingly, the councils in Bunyoro, like their contemporaries in Rungwe, were anxious to ensure male control of women, as well as to wrest power from 'traditional' rulers.[36]

One of the principal activities of local government was the funding of new institutions of health and education; the rationale of the councils lay in the pursuit of 'progress', in the eyes of European officials at least.[37] Spending

[28] Minutes 5, 7 and 66, 9 June 1949; Minute 13, 7 Apr. 1952, TNA 157 L5/5/1.
[29] African Affairs Department Annual Report, 1949, 14, KNA DC KAJ 2/8/1.
[30] Beattie, *Nyoro State*, 150-2.
[31] Beattie, *Bunyoro*, 69.
[32] Beattie, *Nyoro State*, 232.
[33] Uganda Government, *Annual Report for Uganda, 1952*, 11 (London, 1953); see also Uganda Government, *Annual Report for Uganda, 1949* (London, 1950).
[34] Beattie, *Nyoro State*, 162.
[35] High Court Criminal Revision Case 27 of 1953, and attached correspondence, in HDA JUD 6v.
[36] Beattie, *Nyoro State*, 229.
[37] Uganda Government, *Annual Report for Uganda, 1952*, 11.

on hospitals, clinics and schools grew rapidly from the later 1940s,[38] and the scale of the provision offered similarly grew enormously. In Rungwe, clinics and hospitals had already attracted a large clientele of people who were only too happy to experiment with a new and (in their eyes) complementary way of addressing the uncertainties of life and well-being. It is very difficult to know how effectual clinics were in terms of maintaining health, yet evidently people believed that they offered at least some access to well-being, for they made extensive use of them.[39] They also made use of educational facilities offered by Christian churches, the district administration and native authorities.[40] That literacy offered access to power was a simple lesson which none who lived in the colonial state could fail to learn; the commoners welcomed on to the councils in the late 1940s were, by stipulation, only the educated.[41] While the Nyakyusa may be remarkable for the scale and rapidity of this change, the trend of change at least was similar across the region. The local government bodies funding these institutions gave a new kind of authority to a wider circle of elder men: the very act of working in them gave authority to another group of men, who increasingly overlapped with the membership of the representative institutions of late colonial local government. Teachers and medical dressers, like clerks and court messengers, dealt access to new forms of power.

SOBER ELDERS

Every drunk is a beast; let us not put ourselves on the way to be bestial.[42]

Colonial courts, clinics and schools were sober places, for the penalties for obvious drunkenness in these places could be severe: colonial administrators were quick to dismiss chiefs or others who appeared drunk in such places.[43] All cases 'drank water' now. The deliberations of councils were similarly expected to be free from the influence of intoxicating beverages:[44] the European officials who kept a beady eye on the proceedings of these bodies enforced a sobriety which – like the paraphernalia of agenda, minutes, chairs and tables – asserted that the debates of these bodies belonged to a quite

---

[38] The budget of the Native Treasury in Rungwe went from 4,783 shillings in 1935, to 9,936 shillings in 1945, to 59,354 shillings in 1955: 'Native Treasuries', SHP Provincial Book, TNA MF 25-26.

[39] In 1935, 29,712 people attended hospitals or dispensaries in Rungwe as patients, of a total population of 153, 206; Rungwe District Annual Report, 1935, 11, TNA Library; by 1941 this had risen to 121,000 attendances; Rungwe District Annual Report for 1941, 11 RHO Mss Afr s 741 (3).

[40] There are no figures for overall attendance: missionaries were running 'dozens' of bush schools by the 1930s, and by 1944 there were 950 pupils in 'village standard' schools: 'Education', Rungwe District Book, TNA MF 28.

[41] DC Rungwe to Chiefs, 25 Feb. 1949, TNA 18/26/9.

[42] *Mambo Leo*, Oct. 1924.

[43] For examples of dismissals for obvious drunkenness, see DC Bunyoro to PC Northern, 4 Mar. and 18 Oct. 1915, UNA A46/492; Kajiado District Annual Report, 1933, 8, KNA DC KAJ 2/1/1; Wilson, *Good Company*, 144.

[44] Kajiado District Annual Report, 1933, 7, KNA DC KAJ 2/1/1.

different world of authority; and that the resolution of disputes lay in the state's coercive ability to enforce the law, not in the restoration of good relationships amongst elder men. And the involvement of Christian missionaries in much educational and health work encouraged the personnel of courts and councils and clinics to regard drunkenness not as a necessary attribute of authority but as a surrender to base instincts, which rendered the inebriate unfitted for responsibility.[45] Europeans were only too ready to believe that Africans were weak in this way: school clerks could easily overawe teachers by threatening to denounce them for 'bacchanalian propensities'.[46]

Since the nineteenth century, some missionaries in East Africa had been vocal in their condemnation of the drinking of locally-made alcohol, which lent itself rather easily to a rhetoric which stressed the moral degradation of African life in which the day finished with 'a devil dance and a drunken feast, when men, women and children alike participate, and evil passions and sins are let loose.'[47] Members of Protestant denominations were particularly persuaded that drink was a source of 'great evil', linked to 'licentious practices',[48] and they distinguished themselves by calling for total prohibition.[49] While some missionaries used alcohol as a symbol of the dangers of modernity rather than those of barbarism the conclusion of either argument was similar: the drinking of alcohol, and especially locally-made alcohol, was a threat to morality, and the 'progressive' would naturally be against it.[50] 'Those who brought religion did not like drink.'[51] Public preaching and weekly sermons made this discourse widely available, and from the 1930s it was evidently being taken up in innovative ways by African men and women, who used it in pursuit of their own agendas.

The effects of this discourse became increasingly apparent during the 1940s; partly because a generation of men born under colonial rule had married, had children of their own, and were coming more and more to occupy the position of elder men. Literate members of this generation, in particular, had much exposure to official and missionary discourses which condemned drink. In 1930 *Mambo Leo*, the government-subsidized newspaper in Tanganyika, began a series on 'two enemies which are destroying our nation'. The two enemies were syphilis and gonorrhoea, but before the series ended it had turned into 'three enemies which are destroying our nation'; the third enemy was drunkenness.[52] Those who saw the possibility of individual wealth increasingly resented the claims of the

[45] Int. Nyoro10b, 13.
[46] E. Mang'enya, *Discipline and Tears. Reminiscences of an African Civil Servant on Colonial Tanganyika* (Dar es Salaam, 1984), 83.
[47] Lloyd, *Uganda to Khartoum*, 90-1.
[48] J.B. Purvis, *Through Uganda to Mount Elgon* (London, 1909), 338, 352.
[49] 'Closer Control of Native Drinking', *East African Standard*, 19 Apr. 1930.
[50] Overseas Temperance Council (for the protection of indigenous peoples from the liquor traffic), Report, 1949-50, in Overseas Temperance Council to Under SoS, 9 July 1951, PRO CO 822 630; Mackenzie, *Spirit-Ridden Konde*, 130-1.
[51] Int Nyoro35c, 8.
[52] *Mambo Leo*, April-July 1930.

gerontocracy; and European discourses concerning drink offered these men a ready critique of the drinking practices which sustained the levelling collective power of elder men. So some stressed instead a sober basis for order: 'if we drink pombe and kangara we lose all our respect.'[53]

In Kenya, the ambitious self-improvers of the Kavirondo Taxpayers Welfare Association promised to plant trees, dig pit latrines, kill rats, dress cleanly, provide their families with bedding – and 'not to abuse beer'.[54] In Bunyoro, European concerns that 'drink and play come before work and well-being'[55] found an echo in the rhetoric of the educated men who were gaining in influence in local administration: 'A drunkard cannot do things properly; and in the same way, if a country is full of drunkenness that country cannot progress.'[56] In Tanganyika and Kenya, European officials frowned on those who profited from the sale of alcohol but looked much more fondly on entrepreneurs who dealt other beverages; 'a progressive native has erected a tea-shop', one noted.[57] As 'progress' and 'native liquor' became established as anathematic, status in the world of literacy, employment and the state increasingly accrued to advocates of temperance. 'He never drank alcohol, he used to drink tea only because he was a teacher in a school', explained one woman of her father, as though the two activities were self-evidently exclusive.[58] Courts, schools and clinics offered a kind of authority which did not rely on assumptions about the innate power of men over well-being, and it gave many men ample personal reason to seek an escape from the limitations placed on accumulation by the drinking practices intended to avert the dangerous consequences of the anger of fellow men. Parkin has shown how Islam provided Mijikenda men with a means to distance themselves from the demands of a redistributive drinking culture:[59] more widely across the region, both Christianity and a secular discourse about progress and development could play exactly the same role in framing a critique of drinking practice.

In western Kenya, some women appropriated this anti-drink rhetoric in their struggle to escape the task of brewing beer for their husbands without payment: women elsewhere were turning to the sale of drink, but here some women were simply escaping brewing altogether, able to do so because their explicitly Christian, temperance rhetoric ensured the support of the local administration.[60] In Rungwe, alcohol became involved in a prolonged struggle over the control and nature of rituals of social health. Missionaries

---

[53] Letter, H.M.Z. Kapwesi bin Mtemi Mlanda, *Mambo Leo*, Feb. 1930.
[54] Quoted approvingly in 'The Progress of the Native' (Nairobi, 1927), copy in PRO CO 533 377/11.
[55] Ag. Officer to Katikiro, 1 Apr. 1947, see also DC to Mukama, 11 June 1947, HDA NAF 9.
[56] Katikiro to Chiefs, 14 Aug. 1947, HDA NAF 9.
[57] Native Affairs Department Annual Report, 1937-8, PRO CO 533 380/10.
[58] Int Nyoro24b, 2.
[59] D. Parkin, *Palms, Wine and Witnesses. Public Spirit and Private Gain in an African Farming Community* (London, 1972).
[60] Sangree, *Age, Prayer and Politics*, 135-6.

condemned drink, and the rituals which involved it – 'the Christians forbid beer'[61] – and they offered Christian ritual as an exclusive alternative to these practices.[62] The public performance of rituals of offering to ancestors diminished, and practice changed.[63] As drink disappeared from the public performance of case settlement and political deliberation, so also it began to disappear from offerings to ancestors. So it was that Meyer described the 'blowing' of beer; Wilson the blowing of water.[64]

African criticism of drinking was evident partly because those who criticized it were particularly likely to record their views in writing, and in places where they were likely to be preserved for the record: *Mambo Leo* regularly ran cautionary tales, supplied by correspondents, entitled 'the danger of drunkenness', detailing the mishaps which befell drinkers.[65] Drinking – and particularly, the drinking of locally-made alcohol – was associated with poor health and hygiene, and with a surrender of responsibility. 'I saw that some have become weak and thin because of drink, since some no longer eat food, they only drink; I must admit that these people have a real problem.'[66] This was two-edged: in part, it identified drunkenness as a problem of urban culture, as with the poem which ran 'I see the drunks, it is they who fill the towns, It is they who are the thieves, they are always in court'.[67] But it also identified drink as a danger to all, leading to carelessness and conflict: 'So, parents, beware of any drunkenness'.[68] A distinctively new ethic of temperance was being promoted in the way that people talked about drink, which stressed the danger of drunkenness for anyone, even elder men: a drunkard 'is ruled by the devil of drink . . . he is not in his right mind'.[69] Drink, far from reproducing authority, might lead to its abuse or collapse: 'You can find someone pissing in his trousers, other men beat their wives and children to death . . . That's why Protestants gave up drinking.'[70]

This discourse about drinking was drawn into complex remakings of assumptions of power. Others watched how clerks and members of councils drank. But other ways of drinking, and ways of talking about drinking, survived. Drinking behaviour and discourse became increasingly fractured, and the conflict was not simply between sober councillors and drunken elders. Many individuals straddled these alternative notions of power, aware of the demands for sobriety but aware too of the importance of convivial drinking among elder men, unwilling to cast aside the drinking practices and discourse which affirmed their innate power over the well-being of

[61] Int Nya31b, 3.
[62] Int Nya33b, 3-4.
[63] Int Nya39b, 3.
[64] Meyer, *Wa-Konde*, 74; Wilson, *Rituals of Kinship*, 182, also 70 and 101.
[65] 'Hatari ya Ulevi', *Mambo Leo*, Feb. 1932; Mar. 1935; Nov. 1935.
[66] *Mambo Leo*, Jan. 1930.
[67] *Mambo Leo*, June 1947.
[68] 'Hatari ya Pombe', *Mambo Leo*, Apr. 1936.
[69] 'Ulevi', *Mambo Leo*, July 1930.
[70] Int Nyoro23c, 2.

others. And some found that their role in the new institutions of local government gave them – and their friends – a new financial interest in alcohol; liquor might be neither the exclusive preserve of elder power, nor the mark of the 'backward', but rather a source of wealth for the well-connected entrepreneur, as state policy and individual enterprise combined to create a new and particular model of entrepreneurship.

Beerhalls & male entrepreneurship

This Council is perturbed to hear that the Provincial Commissioner does not favour seeing individual Africans in the district become rich.[71]

In Kenya in the 1940s the spreading system of company canteens – and the wider attempts at control of beer-brewing made in the context of war-time grain shortages[72] – encouraged another surge of official enthusiasm for local government monopolies in liquor sale.[73] In 1946, PCs in Kenya agreed that the policy of monopolizing the sale of liquor in the hands of the local authorities should be accepted in principle.[74] They were evidently thinking both of 'native liquor' and of the sale of European beer to Africans, which was soon to be legalized. Once again, it was the financial needs of local government that pushed this policy, and in 1948 the Commissioner for Local Government again canvassed the idea that the sale of alcohol (to Africans) should cease to be a source of private profit and should instead start to contribute to the revenue of local government.[75] The CNC supported the idea that no private licences or permits should be issued: '[p]rofits made out of the sale of intoxicating liquor should be used for the benefit of the population at large'.[76]

Some PCs began to put this policy into practice;[77] but it was soon undone by the effective non-co-operation of the members of those institutions of local government which it was allegedly meant to benefit. From the outset, local authority control had been a bone of contention. In Kajiado, the LNC had only agreed to establish a monopoly beerhall on condition that the man who held the only existing native liquor licence in Kajiado town should be taken on as manager of the new beerhall;[78] another LNC insisted that it

---

[71] Petition from Nyanza LNC, 13 Oct. 1949, KNA MAA 2/5/166: raised in response to the declaration of a local government monopoly in 'native liquor'.

[72] The brewing of grain beer in Kenya had been prohibited in 1943: Proclamation 12, 8 Feb. 1943. The prohibition had been hastily declared in response to a wartime grain shortage, and was soon perceived to be unworkable. It was replaced by a general encouragement to administrators to control brewing through 'administrative action': Minute, nd Aug. 1943, KNA MAA 7/378.

[73] Tomkinson, PC Central to CS, 19 Nov. 1945, KNA MAA 2/5/166.

[74] Minute 33/46, PCs' meeting of Jan. 1946, KNA MAA 2/5/166.

[75] Colchester, Commissioner for Local Govt, 16 Oct. 1948 KNA MAA 2/5/165.

[76] Brayne-Nicholls, for CNC to PC Nyanza, 25 July 1951, KNA MAA 2/5/166.

[77] PC Nyanza to DC North Nyanza, 18 Apr. 1950, KNA MAA 2/5/166.

[78] Minute 13, Kajiado LNC meeting, 15-16 Dec. 1938, KNA DC KAJ 5/1/4; Minutes of meeting, 14-15 Aug. 1940, KNA DC KAJ 5/1/5.

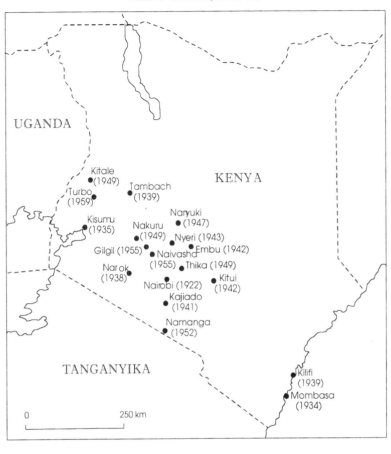

Map 6 *Municipal/LNC native liquor monopolies, Kenya*

would not establish a monopoly, as this should be a field for African private enterprise.[79] Officials admitted that the establishment of monopolies was 'contrary to certain shades of African opinion',[80] and in 1945, one PC anxious to establish a monopoly sourly identified self-interest on the part of LNC members as the principal obstacle: 'A number of members no doubt are hopeful of obtaining licences for their personal profit rather than considering the revenue which can accrue from an exclusive licence and be devoted to the general betterment of the district'.[81]

This clash between European officials intent on public monopolies and a body of newly-institutionalized African opinion enthusiastic for entrepreneurship led to a distinctive system of private enterprise sponsored by local government – particularly as local authority beerhalls became more and more involved in the selling of bottled beer, as well as 'native liquor'.[82] In 1953 the manager of the Kajiado beerhall was fired for misappropriating more than 15,000 shillings.[83] The local authority – now styled the African District Council – sought to change the basis on which the beerhall was run, turning into a concession leased out to an entrepreneur for a fixed rent of 800 shillings per month.[84] The entrepreneur in question was Harry Nangurai who, it transpired, had already contracted some debts to East African Breweries in earlier business dealings, but who nonetheless ran the beerhall for a number of years, in chronic arrears with his rent.[85] He succeeded in persuading the council to reduce his rent very largely over these years; finally he abandoned the beerhall, still a whole year in arrears with his rent.[86] There was considerable competition for the right to run the beerhall after his departure; and after debate and a close vote the council awarded the contract to Julius Keboi, an ex-warrant officer from the King's African Rifles.[87] As a former soldier, Keboi perfectly fitted a model for beerhall stewardship which derived directly from Sergeant-Major Mourjhan in Nimule, 50 years earlier. Yet Keboi fitted a rather different model too; that of the well-connected and ambitious entrepreneur, making the most of contacts. Keboi was evidently an ingenious straddler of ethnicities as well as models of accumulation: shortly after his arrival in Kajiado he was being dunned by men who claimed that they were his 'real' Kikuyu family, from

[79] Minute, Elgeyo LNC, 14 June 1940, KNA MAA 7/378.

[80] Minute 33, PCs' meeting, June 1946, KNA MAA 2/5/166.

[81] PC Central to CS, 19 Nov. 1945, KNA MAA 2/5/166.

[82] The Kajiado beerhall was selling 80 crates of beer a month by 1952: DC Kajiado to Sales Manager, East African Breweries, 7 Oct. 1952, KNA DC KAJ 4/23/8.

[83] Kajiado District Annual Report, 1954, 12, KNA DC KAJ 2/1/6; Commissioner for Local Govt to PC Southern, 22 July 1954, KNA DC KAJ 4/23/8. This was not the first difficulty with the accounts: Kajiado District Annual Report, 1948, 20, KNA DC KAJ 2/1/2.

[84] Contract, 1 Apr. 1954, KNA DC KAJ 4/23/8.

[85] DC Kajiado to Sales Manager, East African Breweries, 17 July 1954; Agreement, 9 Dec. 1955, KNA DC KAJ 4/23/8; Kajiado Monthly Report, Mar. 1954, PC NGO 1/1/8.

[86] FGPC Minute 17/57, 11 Nov. 1957; DC Kajiado to Nangurai, 16 June 1961, KNA DC KAJ 4/23/8.

[87] See list of applications in KNA DC KAJ 4/23/8; and Minute 39/61, Kajiado African District Council, KNA DC NGO 1/9/16.

whom he had borrowed a considerable sum to launch his new business, and who clearly resented his acquisition of the material markers of prosperity, including a Mercedes car.[88] Doubtless fortified by his local alliances, Keboi seems to have seen off these claimants without too much difficulty.[89]

This story of effective resistance to local authority monopoly, and of the emergence of beerhalls which combined the sale of bottled beer and locally-made liquor as an area for private enterprise under local authority patronage, was to become common. In Mombasa, such patronage came to exist extra-legally alongside a technical monopoly: the local authority allowed six men to establish private beer-shops, without licences of any kind, and (with the connivance of the district commissioner) protected them from prosecution while suppressing all other unlicensed sale.[90] In Kenya, this local authority patronage of entrepreneurs existed to some degree in competition with an alternative model of entrepreneurship built up by European DCs. While local councils had control of licensing in places where formal monopolies had been declared, DCs had control over 'native liquor' licences elsewhere, and they used this to try to locate the sale of liquor in what they viewed as reliable hands: those of former government servants, preferably policemen or soldiers.[91] There were limits to this enthusiasm for sale by government servants – as in the case of the corporal in the prison service who was found using detainee labour to brew and sell beer[92] – but the general trend was clear: where licences were issued to individual entrepreneurs, European officials preferred that they should go to placemen of limited ambitions, as a reward for loyalty rather than as a route to accumulation. Given a 'native liquor' licence in Fort Hall after a year of letter-writing and string-pulling, Obadiah Chege (late of the Maize Control Board) knew the appropriate way to express his gratitude: 'I promise to be loyal to God and the King,' he wrote.[93] From 1951, licences might also be given to another group of individuals whose talents for entrepreneurship DCs were willing to recognize: Indian shop-owners, who had been legally barred from this trade since 1907. In 1956 the licensed sellers of 'native liquor' in Kajiado comprised (apart from Nangurai) three ex-sergeants, one ex-teacher, six Asian and one Arab merchants, and a European-owned company.[94]

Meanwhile in Tanganyika, attempts to establish local government monopolies had run quickly to grief, and had not sponsored the same growth of local authority patronage in towns. Yet, by a different route, licensing practice here too came to locate legal liquor trade in the hands of individual

[88] Ex-Chief Kigathi Kinyanjui to DC Kajiado, 28 Aug. 1962, KNA DC KAJ 4/23/10.
[89] DC Kajiado to Anand (Advocate), 19 Oct. 1962, KNA DC KAJ 4/23/10.
[90] Handing-over Report, Mombasa District, 1962, 16, RHO Mss Afr s. 831.
[91] Kajiado Handing-over Report, Mar. 1949, 16; Handing-over Report, July 1950, 16, KNA DC KAJ 3/1; DC Loitokitok to DC Kajiado, 28 Mar. 1956, KNA DC KAJ 4/10/22.
[92] Kajiado District Annual Report, 1956, 9-10, KNA DC KAJ 2/1/8.
[93] Chege to Ag. CS, 12 June 1951, KNA MAA 7/380.
[94] DC Kajiado to all licence holders, 16 Feb. 1956, KNA DC KAJ 4/10/22.

7.1 *Tukuyu beerhall, showing the windows through which beer was sold*

male accumulators. The Tanga monopoly created in 1945 had provoked immediate opposition from sellers in Tanga, and from the African representatives now sitting on the Legislative Council who accused the government of 'discouraging private enterprise on the part of the African'.[95] Some other very local monopolies were created,[96] but in 1954 a committee reported unfavourably on the monopoly system, particularly on the grounds of its unpopularity with Africans, and after a further review in 1957 the whole policy of monopoly was dropped.[97] In Tukuyu, the administrative headquarters for the Nyakyusa, the township authority tried in 1952 to increase their revenue from beer by handing the beerhall established in the town over to a man called John Kasyupa, in place of the various women who had previously been licensed to sell there.[98] Kasyupa's tenancy was ended when he became involved in a court case; after some uncertainty the authority returned to licensing several women at a time;[99] then Kasyupa was given the beerhall again for a period, and finally it reverted to the women who called themselves 'we Swahili of the town'.[100]

[95] Omari bin Salim to CS, 3 Sep. 1945, TNA SMP 33144, Vol. I; Kidaha Makwaia, Legislative Council question, Dec. 1946, recorded in TNA SMP 33144, Vol. I.
[96] Apparently only in Lushoto and (informally) in Mtwara: PC Tanga to CS, 27 Feb. 1948, TNA SMP 37507; PC Southern Province to CS, 22 Oct. 1950, TNA SMP 41407.
[97] Tanganyika Government, *Intoxicating Liquor Report* (Dar es Salaam, 1954), 9; Minute, 7 Jan. 1957, TNA SMP 41407.
[98] Kasyupa to DC, 16 Feb. 1952, and marginal note, TNA 18/T2/6.
[99] Yates and Co. to Executive Officer, Tukuyu Township Authority, 21 Jan. 1953; Note, nd Apr. 1953, TNA 18/T2/6.
[100] DC to Kasyupa, 21 July 1953; Executive Officer to Mbagulile et al, 25 Jan 1954, TNA 18/T2/6.

While this local struggle was in progress, a government committee was considering whether regulated sale should be in the hands of small-scale – and mostly women – producers who shared space in public beer-markets or whether it should rather be in the hands of better-capitalized individual licensees. The committee, composed of two European men and two African men, came down heavily in favour of the latter option, which they saw as central to social improvement. Beer-markets, they argued, failed to provide for the 'better-educated class of African'. Recurring to the identification of uncontrolled female sexuality and physical dirt which had already characterized European – and elite African – attitudes, they described beer-markets as 'unhealthy, overcrowded, smelly and noisy, and many of the women present were said to be prostitutes'.[101] In place of these dens of iniquity, a small number of privately-owned licensed premises of high standard – with 'proper buildings' and wirelesses – should be encouraged, suited to the 'less primitive and better-educated kind of African'. This encouragement of private enterprise and improved drinking, the committee argued, was more important than generating revenue for local government: the private entrepreneur was the key to proper drinking.[102]

In Uganda, policy moved to a similar emphasis on the need for local government to encourage private enterprise. Despite a brief enthusiasm for the idea of state liquor sale, the major experiment in the Nakivubo beer garden in Kampala proved unsuccessful; nor was there here the kind of unease which European officials in Kenya felt about the very idea of Africans profiting from the sale of liquor. This might not have been seen as an ideal field for entrepreneurship (loan schemes intended to provide capital for African business ventures could not be used for 'beer-shops'[103]) but, in Bunyoro at least, district officials began to encourage the dominance of urban liquor sale by well-capitalized 'progressive' men, as the institutions of local government developed in the late 1940s and early 1950s.

In Hoima township, a plan to allow only one beer-club was floated, then relaxed in an attempt to incorporate and formalize the businesses of some of the men who had been running illicit clubs in the town.[104] By the 1950s there were four clubs operating, the most prominent being that of Yusto Kwezi, a successful accumulator who had by the mid-1960s become a councillor and the minister of finance of the Bunyoro Kingdom government.[105] Women were refused licences, even when the Mukama, in his traditional role as patron of women who sought to live outside the male-headed household, asked that certain single urban women be given licences.[106] In Masindi township John Kasigwa, already the proprietor of

---

[101] Tanganyika Government, *Intoxicating Liquor Report*, 2-3.
[102] Tanganyika Government, *Intoxicating Liquor Report*, 4.
[103] DC Bunyoro to George Kabaleega, 5 Apr. 1956, HDA FIN 30.
[104] DC Bunyoro to Asst. Health Inspector, 7 Apr. 1953; DC to Kiiza *et al.*, 9 Jan. 1954, Executive Officer Township Authority to Officer Commanding Police, 17 Apr. 1954; HDA FIN 7.
[105] DC to Mutuba, 25 June 1954 HDA FIN 7; list of councillors, 1964, HDA MUN 4/7.
[106] Nyanjura to DC, 14 Jan. 1954, and marginal note, HDA FIN 7; Mukama to DC, 19 Jan. 1956, HDA NAF 9.

an eating house, the Masindi Modern Hotel, was 'selected' to hold the only 'native liquor' licence issued, and he signalled his appreciation by inviting the DC to open his new brick-and-corrugated-iron club.[107] European officials thereafter sought to suppress any competition to Kasigwa's club,[108] and a chief who allowed alcohol sales, outside the township boundary but near to Kasigwa's club, was criticized in revealing terms: 'By your thoughtless and disobedient action in permitting rival clubs to be established nearby in cheap, badly-built hovels the future of African trade has received a setback'.[109] Kasigwa was the standard-bearer of the future, who required support against refractory chiefs.

These regimes of urban sale embodied a new accommodation between local government and male entrepreneurship, an accommodation initially propelled by colonial dreams of the riches which might accrue to local government through its own ventures into liquor sale, but which came increasingly to be based on the ability of public regulation to sponsor and favour particular individual entrepreneurs through selective application of the law and access to resources. They were favoured through suppression – albeit incomplete – of competition; or through the provision of premises afforded from the public purse. In return they offered a place to drink which was regulated and formalized and set aside; a place to drink, just as the hospital was a place to be ill and the court was a place to judge; a place within the world of chairs and tables and written (if rather misleading) accounts. This was a model of drinking in which temperance was defined as controlled and regulated sale in defined places: 'everything requires wisdom and moderation'.[110] This was distinct from the prohibitionism of the missionaries and from that of the gerontocracy: the beerhalls and clubs of men like Julius Keboi and John Kasigwa were another product of the new authority possessed by educated men with Christian names, another ideal of drinking.

CLUBS & RURAL ENTERPRISE

In Bunyoro, men's dominance in urban alcohol sale was extended into rural areas during the 1950s in a pattern which was also evident, if less pronounced, elsewhere in East Africa. The indirect rule structure of Bunyoro, the Kingdom government, was pushed into a much more rigorous system of regulating drink sale: DCs were fired with a new enthusiasm for this 'excellent source of income' as a way of funding the rapidly growing activities of local government.[111] At the same time, this became a major field for conflict between the Mukama and his chosen chiefs and a succession of

---

[107] Assistant DC Masindi to PC Western, 17 Feb. 1953, HDA MUN 4/2; DC Bunyoro to J. Kasigwa, 16 Sep. 1953, HDA NAF 9.

[108] Assistant DC Masindi to Kimbugwe, 18 Jan. 1955, HDA FIN 7.

[109] Assistant DC to Musale, Buruli, 23 Apr. 1954, HDA NAF 9.

[110] 'Pombe huleta kujuana', letter, *Mambo Leo*, Aug. 1947.

[111] Assistant DC Masindi to DC Hoima, 4 Oct. 1948 and DC Bunyoro to Katikiro, 20 Nov. 1952, HDA NAF 9; for the Bunyoro government's chronic shortage of revenue see the Annual Report for 1951, HDA ADM 14.

reform-minded Katikiros, or prime ministers, who had the support of many educated men (and of European officials) for a campaign against chiefly power and against the perceived growing autonomy of women. In 1952, a by-law was passed which restricted the retailing of locally-made liquor to licensed rural clubs, or *ebirabo*, and required anyone who was making alcohol (except for a marriage, a funeral, or to present to the Mukama) to take out a 2-shilling permit.[112] Club licences could only be issued to men (the DC opined that licensees should be 'men of good character'[113]); and the Katikiro sought to claim a sole right to issue licences and to restrict these to suitably well-capitalized individuals,[114] following the DC's policy that '[w]e want to have fewer clubs than at present but of a higher standard'.[115] The Mukama tried to ensure that his favourites got licences; some chiefs undermined the whole system – claiming that popular resentment made it unenforceable – by issuing large numbers of permits, and allowing permit-holders to sell alcohol.[116] After 1955 the changed system of chiefly appointments and increasingly close supervision from the Katikiro overcame chiefly opposition, and forced drinking into the 'clubs' and the revenue from drinking into the Treasury.[117] In the late 1950s the Kingdom government was routinely deriving more than 10 percent of its income from licences and permits for locally-produced liquor.[118] The male-owned *ekirabo* was the central place of drinking in rural Bunyoro.[119]

The male-owned *kilabu* emerged as the drinking place of rural Tanganyikan society in the same period. In Rungwe this was a rapid transformation. It was apparently women who, around 1950, began to establish the first rural specialized drinking places among the Nyakyusa, *vilabu* in the villages. Such clubs represented a new departure in another significant way, for they involved a shared economic enterprise rather than informal co-operation between neighbours.[120] The women built simple structures, on land borrowed from husbands (or from the village headmen who had a limited right to assign land which was not under cultivation).[121] In establishing these clubs women hoped to minimize disruption at home, and to create an unambiguously commercial atmosphere.[122]

---

[112] By-law, 4 Apr. 1952, HDA NAF 9.

[113] DC to Katikiro, 20 Nov. 1952; the exclusion of women was made explicit elsewhere, see for example Omuketo (Treasurer) to all Masaza (county chiefs), 3 Jan. 1955, HDA NAF 9.

[114] Katikiro to all Masaza, 23 Feb.1953, and Mukwenda to Katikiro, 5 Mar. 1953, HDA NAF 9.

[115] DC to Mukama, 23 Dec. 1952, HDA NAF 9.

[116] Mukama to Katikiro, 1 Feb. 1955; District Team minutes, 16 Nov. 1954, HDA ADM 5/1.

[117] From 1954, the Katikiro set chiefs targets for collecting revenue from locally-made alcohol: Katikiro to all Masaza , 24 Feb. 1954, HDA FIN 7.

[118] In 1953-4, these licences and permits provided £2,290 of a total revenue of £59,498. In 1955-6 they provided £7,624 of £63,479; in 1956-7 £8,115 of £73,656, in 1959-60 £11,349 of £102,000: HDA FIN 28 and FIN 28/2.

[119] There were exceptions: one woman of the royal family acquired a share in a club by providing the land on which it was built: Int Nyoro 38c, 2.

[120] Int Nya42a, 2.

[121] Int Nya14b, 3-4.

[122] Int Nya3a, 2.

The introduction of clubs reflected another pressure. In 1949 the very first meeting of the new Council in Rungwe had – after dealing with adultery – determined to establish an effective system of permits and licences for clubs and brewing.[123] The new structures of local government were willing to seek revenue from regulating liquor sale, in a way that their predecessors had not; and they were encouraged in this by European officials.[124] When the revenue from these was not as great as had been expected, the council set some of the rapidly multiplying *mafumu* to the task of collecting permit revenue; and when problems persisted the council agreed that *mafumu* should be allowed to keep a portion of the revenue collected.[125]

The increasing role of these *mafumu*, married men raised to new authority through their relationship with the state, was associated not only with increased state demands, but with an increased dominance by men. One woman recalled the disapproving attitude of officials: 'they used to say the women are selling from a dirty place, that is when we found they were giving us papers to stick on the side of the room'.[126] The magical, cleansing, permit was not always forthcoming for women, and within a few years almost all clubs were owned and run by men, who charged women a fee to come and sell.[127] Men's access to land and relationships with the state gave them dominance in these rural clubs: as in rural Bunyoro, the new structures of the late colonial state gave men in rural Rungwe control over the drink trade.

SUBVERSIVE DRINKING

Urban beerhalls and rural clubs presented a new model of regulated drinking, open to all adults who could afford to pay. And increasingly, the public discourse of those who possessed authority stressed a new model of drinking, which laid emphasis on moderation and the notion that drinking was appropriate only in certain, closely defined situations. Yet much drinking took place in ways and places which defied this new ideology of drinking. Even those who were supposed to be the standard-bearers of modern temperance drank 'native liquor' in clubs – however much they might profess to disdain it.[128] As a critique of modernity, in defiance to the demands of the colonial state, and in pursuit of a degree of economic autonomy, people drank, and sold drink, far beyond the bounds of the clubs or the hours set by the newly zealous agents of local authority. 'At every ceremony which gathered people together, they would drink.'[129] In the towns and in some rural areas women and men made and sold alcohol in their houses, in spite of the law.

There would seem to have been considerable variation in the degree of this, and in how much contest there was over the relocation of drinking to

---

[123] Minute 8, Dec. 1949, TNA 157 L5/5/1.
[124] Circulars. 4 July and 9 Aug. 1950, TNA 18/1/27.
[125] Minute 32 (vi) 22-24 Oct. 1951 and Minute 69 (a) 5-9 Oct. 1953, TNA 157 L5/5/1.
[126] Int Nya42a, 2.
[127] Ints Nya4a, 3; Nya5b, 2; Nya19a, 3; Nya40a, 2.
[128] Mang'enya, *Discipline and Tears*, 106-17, 300.
[129] Int Nya12a, 3.

clearly commercial spaces. Overall, the speed with which Nyakyusa women shifted the location of selling from house to rural club was remarkable, and women's accounts insist that this was in large measure because they themselves saw potential value in this move.[130] But it was also because the new councils were zealous in their pursuit of those who failed to move. In Bunyoro, there was more resistance to the enforcement of the rural *ebirabo* licences, partly expressed in the unsubtle traditional idiom of burning down chiefs' houses.[131] There were, after all, many who were left out of the new dispensation; not educated, not Christian or Muslim, without access to the new institutions of government. For those who resented the new status of the educated, who struggled to assert their authority over wives and children through the courts, drinking yet remained a way of arguing their authority; and of challenging the right of others to exercise authority. And so they drank at rituals – and reminded others of the risk of resentment against those who did not drink: 'people will not allow you to do this . . . you can even die.'[132] And they drank at home, and drank publicly to excess at inappropriate times; ironically, challenging the new ideology of temperance partly through collusion with the women drink sellers who had long challenged the authority of elder males.

In some areas, local government itself resisted change. The officially recognized representatives of the Maasai in Kajiado resisted any spread of clubs or licences to sell beyond the confines of towns and market-places;[133] they vigorously asserted that the sale of alcohol should not be part of life in such places, and that drinking was an activity for homes, for weddings, circumcisions and the deliberations of elder men. But there was little consistency to this, for those who defended the authority of traditional drinking might also have an interest in selling liquor. One Maasai section council resolved to end the sale of liquor; but then approved a licence for a senior man to establish a club.[134]

Sometimes an element of wider, nationalist, politics could be involved in these debates over licensing. Refusing to pay licences, and drinking at the establishments of those who so refused, could be a statement of resistance to the colonial state; and in some places it was seen as such: during the 1950s a police patrol raiding a Nairobi drinking den found the patrons singing 'Jomo Kenyatta songs', and sparked a riot by arresting them.[135] But the most prominent members of nationalist movements were committed to the model of regulated, taxed drinking. They were also, of course, committed to another kind of alcoholic beverage, which from the mid-1950s dominated the drinking practices of the region's elite: bottled beer and bottled spirits were to be the tipple of those who ran the post-colonial states of East Africa.

[130] Ints Nya3a, 2; Nya42a, 2.
[131] Mumyoka Bugahya (sub-chief) to Mukwenda (chief), 7 Oct. 1946, HDA NAF 9.
[132] Int Nya16c, 6.
[133] Minute 6/56, Chiefs' meting, KNA DC KAJ 4/10/22.
[134] Minutes 27/57 and 38/59, Loitokitok section, meetings of 23-24 July 1957 and 21-23 July 1959, KNA DC NGO 1/9/16.
[135] 'Disturbances in Pumwani', *Uganda Argus*, 13 Jan. 1959.

Eight

Whisky in the club
'Intoxicating liquor'
1900–47

. . . whisky infests the colony.[1]

The spirit of empire

Wonderful days those, a case of whisky 22 shillings – Scotch at that – one could afford to entertain a few friends occassionally [sic] . . .[2]

Whisky and soda, as Weule observed, was the 'national drink of all Germans in East Africa'.[3] Statistics from the 1920s and 1930s show a similar preference among British empire-builders. And very largely, this whisky was Scotch. Other kinds of drink occupied particular places in European drinking practice: wine marked personal rituals and the rituals of the state, just as consistently as did the wearing of special costumes or the hoisting of flags. On the king's birthday even the isolated European population of Hoima drank claret and hock;[4] and there was champagne for weddings and at grand events, such as those at Government House in Entebbe where it 'flow[ed] like a river' in the 1930s.[5] Bottled beer, in contrast, was a manly drink for explorers and administrators in the bush: Hohnel and Chanler (or rather their porters) carried 96 bottles of Pilsner on their expedition – 'What nectar it seemed!'[6] – and in 1913 Arthur Champion, besieged in camp by rebellious Giryama, began the day with a bottle of beer.[7]

---

[1] W. McGregor Ross, *Kenya from Within. A Short Political History* (London, 1968 (1st edn 1927)), 179.

[2] 'My Arrival at Nairobi Station, Feby 1911', anon, nd, Box 6, RHO Mss Afr s. 1456.

[3] Weule, *Native Life*, 43-4. I can find no evidence for Rodwell's suggestion that whisky was brought cheap to East African by German shipping lines anxious to make up tonnage in order to qualify for subsidies: E. Rodwell, *Sixty Years of Kenya Breweries* (Nairobi, nd), 2.

[4] Lloyd, *Uganda to Khartoum*, 45.

[5] Elkington, 'Recollections of a Settler in Kenya', 35, RHO Mss Afr s. 1558; Perham, 'Tanganyika and Uganda', 19, RHO Mss Perham 49 (3).

[6] Chanler, *Through Jungle and Desert*, 45.

[7] Dundas, *African Crossroads*, 76.

But everyday drinking was whisky drinking. During the First World War, deprived of Scotch, the settler and official populace of German East Africa turned to distilling their own spirits locally (a special ordinance having been passed to regulate this):[8] jokingly, they called the product 'Kriegswitzki'.[9] The Second World War caused a different kind of switch in drinking habits.

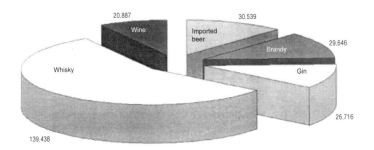

Figure 8.1 *Total consumption of imported alcohol, Kenya/Uganda, 1930, in litres of absolute alcohol*

British administrations were unwilling to countenance any breach of the treaty obligations which prohibited local distillation for consumption, although limited shipping space and the drinking habits of a greatly expanded military populace meant that overall imports of whisky and other beverages from Europe dropped and the amount of whisky getting through to settlers and district officials dropped even more.[10] The bars and hotels of Bukoba District received 227 cases of spirits in 1941, but only 40 in 1942.[11] In Tanganyika a Greek entrepreneur had offered to establish a local distillery, saying that his product 'will suit the Greeks and the Indian particularly. The small quantity of British whisky and gin available can then be more freely distributed among the British people';[12] this magnanimous offer had been rejected.[13] South African produce partly filled the gap; imports of brandy soared during the war, encouraged by the introduction of preferential import duties (an important point, since a special war duty had doubled the price of other imported alcohol).[14] Up to 1940, however, whisky had held sway as the drink of the non-African population: it was the spirit of a colonial modernity, too potent for Africans, but entirely proper – indeed, desirable – for the men of empire.

[8] Regulations of 28 July 1915, TNA G 1/154.
[9] Dundas, *African Crossroads*, 98.
[10] Crown Counsel to Tisdall, DC Nairobi, 4 Nov. 1942; and AG to CS, 4 May 1944, KNA AG/ 1/369.
[11] PC Lake to CS, 16 Mar. 1943, TNA SMP 23241, Vol. II.
[12] Lambrides to CS, 8 May 1941, TNA SMP 29622.
[13] As had other similar proposals: Ag. CS to PC Central, 21 June 1940, TNA SMP 31839.
[14] East African Hoteliers' Association to CS, 25 Apr. 1942, TNA SMP 23241, Vol. II.

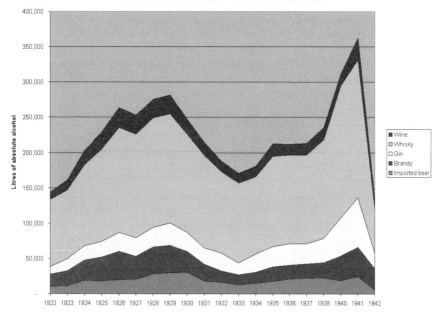

Figure 8.2 *Imports of alcohol to Kenya/Uganda, 1922–42*

DRUNKEN SETTLERS?

I once asked a chap how the cost of living in Uganda compared with
BEA as it was then, his reply was, 'Oh, much the same, about three
shillings a bottle.'[15]

The Europeans of East Africa – and of Kenya in particular – acquired a
remarkable reputation for insobriety as well as immorality.[16] McGregor Ross's
lengthy denunciation of settlers suggested that their violent excesses were a
result of drink, and both mocked and bewailed their willingness to squander
their wealth and prestige on liquor: this is the Kenya of Rumuruti, the 'Town
of the Thirsty Ten', with three licensed premises for ten residents.[17] Accounts
of pre-1914 Kenya heighten this image: Lord Delamere, doyen of the white
settlers, once wrecked his own hotel in the course of a drunken binge; a new
police officer's first assignment involved arresting two drunks who were
shooting up a hotel bar.[18] In the 1930s, a visitor to Dar es Salaam, noting
the protracted nature of 'sundowner' drinks parties, enquired drily as to
whether Tanganyika was the land of the midnight sun.[19] Impressionistic

---

[15] 'My Arrival at Nairobi Station, Feby 1911', anon, nd, 4, Box 6, RHO Mss Afr s 1456.

[16] 'Kenya Highlands', *East African Standard*, 2 Dec. 1922.

[17] McGregor Ross, *Kenya from Within*, 179-80, 377.

[18] E. Huxley, *White Man's Country. Lord Delamere and the Making of Kenya* (2 vols) (London,
1935), I, 149; W.R. Foran, *A Cuckoo in Kenya. The Reminiscences of a Pioneer Police Officer in
British East Africa* (London, 1936), 109-11.

[19] 'Dar es Salaam Sundowners', *Tanganyika Standard*, 20 July 1935.

accounts aside, the statistics are hardly compelling, though they do suggest a peak of drinking before the First World War. Statistics are aggregated for the non-African population, so that it is not possible to determine how much was drunk by Asians and how much by Europeans: perhaps Europeans drank most of the imported liquor (although there is plentiful evidence of Asian whisky-drinking[20]). Yet even so, such consumption would hardly have been extraordinary by European standards.

Table 8.1 *Consumption per head of intoxicating liquor, expressed in terms of absolute alcohol, for the European and Asian population, 1908–36. Figures derived from* Blue Books.

	Kenya/Uganda	Tanganyika
1908	6.1	N/A
1930	2.75	4.0
1936	2.1	2.39

But in British culture, temperance occupied a moral high ground, and accusations of drunkenness served as a useful rhetorical tool for critics of the multiple injustices and excesses of colonial society. The binge-drinking of settlers on occasional visits to town offered ready encouragement for such characterizations: Delamere, allegedly, rarely drank while on his farm but race week in Nairobi offered the occasion for wild indulgence.[21] Anxiety over drunken behaviour was anyway rooted in the colonial situation, where Europeans perceived a constant need to maintain their prestige and were always ready to deplore those of their fellows whose drunken improprieties exposed them to potential ridicule. European drinking was very much a subject of debate in East Africa; this too was a way of talking about authority and the nature of power. European discourses stressed the authority which Europeans derived from rationality, and argued their own superiority over an African populace unable to control its base instincts: 'Africans cannot, unfortunately, drink in moderation'.[22] An ability to hold drink manifested European superiority, but drinking always carried it in the danger of a drunken surrender of rationality and a consequent loss of prestige.

DRINKING PLACES

This is the Englishman's paradise. The Club, with its golf, dancing, the happy-go-lucky chatter over a sundowner at the bar, the happy foregathering of old friends at luncheon on market day.[23]

[20] 'Serious stabbing affray sequel to convivial bout', *Dar es Salaam Times*, 24 Mar. 1923; 'Hikima ya Mlevi na Rafiki Yake', *Mambo Leo*, Oct. 1924; Commissioner of Police to Editor, *Official Gazette*, 19 June 1924, KNA AG 1/365.
[21] Huxley, *White Man's Country*, I, 148, 254-6.
[22] Minute, CNC, 2 Oct. 1951, KNA MAA 2/5/166.
[23] N. Farson, *Last Chance in Africa* (London, 1953 (1st edn 1949)), 83.

It was a basic principle of colonial administration, German and British, that the consumption of 'intoxicating liquor' was an entirely legitimate and proper activity for the non-African population. As the Crown Advocate of British East Africa put it, 'liquor within the meaning of the Ordinance is both more palatable and more wholesome than the other liquids obtained in the Protectorate'[24]. The trade in bottled spirits, wines and beers had to be regulated and controlled, and given the profitability of this trade this should be done in a way which yielded revenue; but this was only possible through a system which served what one official (rather unfortunately) called the 'public convenience.'[25] Drinking laws should not be made difficult to observe, or they would be broken. This anxiety to make legal drinking possible was balanced against the perception – rooted in British domestic experience – that too many licences led to excessive drinking.[26] In serving the 'public convenience', licensing legislation pursued remarkable detail: by 1909, Kenyan law boasted a range of licence categories from wholesale merchants to railway station canteen; from steamship licence (for the lake steamers) to theatre.[27] In 1925, the licensed railway restaurant car was added to the suite of drink-selling venues.[28] This variety was necessary to accommodate the different hours – and different levels of profitability – involved in different drinking contexts: licensed railway dining-rooms, for example, were essential public ventures, required to open sometimes at unusual hours, and the administration was open to a degree of bargaining in the setting of licence fees, at least when dealing with the Uganda Railway.[29] Such regulatory sophistication was far removed from practice with regard to 'native liquor', the sale of which was necessary to meet a physiological need for some individuals, but which demanded no refinement. European (and Asian) drinking by contrast was a social activity; regulation and revenue-raising should not make it unreasonably difficult to drink.

The idea of convenience was built into the licensing system in British territories, which was based on liquor licensing courts which decided on licence applications, and which represented unofficial as well as official interests. 'Inconvenience' was, however, to be defined by Europeans. Asians formed the majority of prospective customers, and held many of the grocers and wine merchants' licences under which general stores sold alcohol for 'off' consumption, but almost all liquor licensing courts were exclusively European, in Kenya, at least: when Karve, a prominent Mombasa doctor, was nominated

---

[24] Minute, 12 Dec. 1909, KNA AG 1/351.
[25] Combes, AG to Commissioner of Police, 6 June 1912, KNA AG 1/363. For more felicitous phrasing of the same principle, see Combes, AG to CS, 17 Oct. 1913 and Chair, Nyanza Liquor Licensing Court to Col. Sec., 24 Sep. 1928, KNA AG 1/366.
[26] A point made, for example, by the 1932 Royal Commission: Ford, *Breviate of Parliamentary Papers*, 508.
[27] Intoxicating Liquor Ordinance, 1909, KNA AG 1/351.
[28] Intoxicating Liquor (Amendment) Ordinance, 1924, KNA AG 1/354.
[29] Manager, Uganda Railway to HM Commissioner Nairobi, 27 Jan. 1904; and Minute, nd, 1904, KNA AG 1/363.

to one court, a law officer had to support this by pointing out that there had never been any legal restriction on Asian membership of courts.[30]

A great deal of drinking was, however, not conducted in licensed premises. Some drank at home: given the policies of racial exclusivism operated by many bars and hotels this would have been the only option for many Asians. More often Europeans – and some Asians – drank in the clubs, which were central to non-African drinking culture. So central, indeed, that the 'railway head club' had advanced inland with the permanent way, finally coming to rest at Kisumu.[31] The smallest concentration of Europeans would form a club: Thomson's Falls had a club before there was a bank or even a township there.[32] The first club at Thomson's Falls was, in fact, just a room with a bar, but many clubs offered sporting facilities as well as food and alcohol; some also provided accommodation. The Thomson's Falls Club closed, apparently over a debt to a local supplier, to be superseded by a golf club, in which there were a number of 'non-playing' members and the quality of the whisky seems to have aroused as much concern as the state of the fairway.[33] By 1936 there were 52 clubs across Tanganyika; even little Tukuyu had two.[34]

Clubs were of two types: members' clubs and proprietary clubs. The latter category was relatively straightforward, legally: a proprietary club was owned by an individual or company and operated on a for-profit basis but with restricted access – only those accepted as members might attend. Members' clubs were similarly exclusive, in that (in theory at least) they could only be patronized by their members, but they occupied a different legal space, for they were jointly owned by all their members and did not run for profit. Members' clubs were very much more common: in Kenya, for example, there were only two proprietary clubs in 1932.[35] Members' clubs held a particular attraction. Not being run for profit, they tended to sell their drink more cheaply than bars or hotels; they were also more ready to run accounts for chronically impecunious members: a vital issue in Kenya, particularly, where the reluctance of drinkers to redeem their chits led a growing number of hotels to refuse credit.[36] They were cheap for other reasons too. Because all the members of a club owned it jointly, legal opinion held that the sale of liquor in such clubs was not really a sale at all; it was merely a redistribution of assets between the members. Members' clubs were therefore spared the expense of acquiring a licence to sell intoxicating liquor.[37] This allowed them to sell liquor more cheaply; and it also excused

[30] Minute, ? Oct. 1936, KNA MAA 7/385. There were Asians on licensing bodies in Tanganyika in the 1920s: Government Notice 871, *Official Gazette*, 3 Sep. 1929.
[31] Blencowe, 'Kenya: Recollections of a Sailor', Box 6, RHO Mss Afr s. 1456.
[32] 'History of the Thomson's Falls Country Club', I, 53, RHO Mss Afr s.1540 1-3.
[33] 'History of the Thomson's Falls Country Club', I, 5, 17, 15, 54-5, RHO Mss Afr s.1540 1-3.
[34] See list in TNA SMP 24462, Vol. I.
[35] Commissioner of Police to Col. Sec., 12 July 1932, KNA AG 1/359.
[36] 'History of the Thomson's Falls Country Club', (2), 12, RHO Mss Afr s.1540 1-3; 'My Arrival at Nairobi Station, Feby 1911', 2, anon, nd, Box 6, RHO Mss Afr s. 1456.
[37] Solicitor-General to Commissioner of Police, 4 Mar. 1925, KNA AG 1/366; CS to PC Iringa, 26 Nov. 1935, TNA SMP 24698, Vol. I.

them from the ban on employing African barmen, which was imposed on licensed premises, both to prevent 'leakage' of spirits to Africans and to preserve the European 'prestige', which might be undermined if such barmen were to witness the drunken antics of their masters. Since all other licensed premises had to employ European or Asian barmen, who cost a great deal more than African staff, this too meant that members' clubs had a further competitive advantage.

Retailers of intoxicating liquor greatly resented the competition from these cheap drinking places, and their resentment regularly spilled over into accusations that clubs were breaking the rules by selling liquor to people who were not members at all; a practice which might or might not be disguised through 'signing in' guests, or through the issue of 'temporary' memberships.[38] It would seem that these accusations were not pursued with complete diligence by the administration; the club system always benefited from the relationships which it sponsored with local representatives of the state.

But in the 1930s, when economic depression severely affected the hotel business, pressure mounted for some limit to the widespread abuses of the club system; perhaps partly because the Royal Commission on licensing in Britain had recently raised metropolitan concern over the issue of club licences there.[39] The Commissioner of Police, apparently concerned over the drunken misbehaviour of club-goers, supported these calls, in the hope that this would give the police powers of entry which they did not possess for unlicensed members' clubs.[40] In Kenya, after a lengthy process of inquiry which included the creation of a Select Committee of the Legislative Council – in evidence to which a number of witnesses insisted that the clubs were essentially a 'family' affair, and served as 'homes' for their members[41] – an amendment to the Liquor Ordinance was passed in 1934, requiring that members' clubs should henceforth take out a licence. After considerable debate, it was also decided that – rather than force clubs to employ more expensive European or Asian barmen – all licensed premises should be allowed to employ Africans as barmen. Concerns over the effect which this might have on prestige were answered with a simple argument: Africans were already employed in various ways in clubs and hotels, and had ample opportunity to witness European inebriation at its least prestigious.

This was an economic decision: the 1934 amendment in no way represented any lessening of racial restrictions on drinking, nor was it a sign of diminished concerns over this issue among the European population. Giving evidence to the Select Committee, the East African Hoteliers' Association had asked for legal enforcement of a system of separate bars for Asians.[42] This call for further exclusion did not make its way into law, but the

---

[38] Crown Advocate to PC Kisumu, 11 Jan. 1909, KNA AG 1/363.
[39] East African Hoteliers' Association to Colonial Sec., 19 Dec. 1931 and 4 Feb. 1932, KNA AG 1/359; Ford, *Breviate of Parliamentary Papers*, 509.
[40] Commissioner of Police to Colonial Sec., 12 July 1932, KNA AG 1/359.
[41] Harrison *et al.* to Chairman, Select Committee, 11 Apr. 1934, KNA AG 1/370.
[42] 'Memorandum on Liquor Licensing', East African Hoteliers' Association, KNA AG 1/370.

amendment as finally passed did increase the penalties for supplying 'intoxicating liquor' to Africans, introducing a minimum sentence of two years for a third offence of this kind. Officials in Nairobi and London concurred on the importance of this restriction.[43] Meanwhile in Tanganyika and Uganda members' clubs could still operate unlicensed – and African barmen were still forbidden in licensed premises.[44]

In Kenya, the new licensing requirement for members' clubs imposed in 1934 was hardly a financially onerous one. An annual licence for a members' club cost only £3, while a 'general retail' licence, required to operate a bar selling beers, wines and spirits, cost £60 in Nairobi, or £45 in any other town. Unsurprisingly, members' clubs continued to offer a cheap and popular alternative to bars and hotels across the region, and the bulk of drinking continued to take place in these clubs. Resentment over this issue boiled over again in northern Tanganyika in the early 1940s, when the liquor licensing court for Moshi increased liquor licence fees in its area as a special wartime measure. Hoteliers were outraged: their business had anyway been greatly diminished by the desperate shortage of imported spirits, and as they pointed out, the members of the liquor licensing court all drank at the Moshi club, which under Tanganyika law required no licence. The chronic suspicion of official favouritism towards clubs having been publicly raised, the administration was forced to act. Fortuitously, it was discovered that the liquor licensing court had anyway been irregularly constituted, and so its decisions were declared void and the increased licence fees were withdrawn.[45]

But the issue did not go away. Indeed, it became in some ways more acute, for the post-1945 surge in the European population in East Africa led to further expansions of the club system. 'Dar es Salaam is waking up', read one cheering leader on the burgeoning social life of postwar East Africa;[46] and newspapers of the late 1940s are full of reports of 'sundowner' events at up-country clubs where the technocrats washed inland by the second colonial invasion danced with the daughters of settlers and administrators.[47] By the mid-1950s Nairobi alone had 36 members' clubs and five proprietary clubs.[48] The brief gaiety of the late colonial moment confirmed the place of the club as the focus of elite drinking.

INCLUSION & EXCLUSION

In 1934, the defenders of Kenya's members' clubs had insisted on their family nature. Perhaps so: but these were decidedly exclusive and patriarchal families: in 1907, the spectacle of European women, excluded from the

---

43 Flood, Minute, 13 Mar. 1935, PRO CO 533 455/5; Harragin, AG to Colonial Sec., 2 May 1935, KNA AG 1/360.
44 Memorandum, 12 Aug. 1937, TNA SMP 24698, Vol. I.
45 Davids *et al.* to CS, 27 Apr. 1942; Minute, 18 May 1942; CS to PC Northern, nd June 1942, TNA SMP 23241, Vol. I.
46 *Tanganyika Standard*, 29 Mar. 1947.
47 'Shinyanga now on social map', *Tanganyika Standard*, 19 Apr. 1947; see the letters of Mrs R. B. Joly for a rather dizzy insider's account: RHO Mss Afr. s. 737.
48 OiC Nairobi to Secretary for Legal Affairs, 24 Feb. 1956, KNA MAA 2/5/212.

Mombasa Club, waiting outside for the emergence of their menfolk in the evening attracted unfavourable comment in the local press.[49] Men were the principal patrons, propping up the men-only bars where their drunken indiscretions were concealed from their women (if not from the bar staff). These were places of business as well as gossip, where deals were done and agreements reached, off the record and out of view, where mutual interests were recognized and shared prejudices reconfirmed.

And European men in East Africa were not a homogeneous group bound together by the conviviality of the club billiard room. Club membership was all to do with employment and social status, and people soon found where they were not welcome, and where they were; particularly in centres like Nairobi, Mombasa or Kampala which were large enough to support a number of clubs. A junior policeman who found himself unwelcome among the administrators at the Nairobi Club took his custom to the Railway Club;[50] few administrators ever gained entry to the Nairobi settlers' lair at the Muthaiga Club.[51] A police officer newly posted to Mombasa soon found his natural social environment – not the Mombasa Club, but the Mombasa Sports Club.[52]   Kampala in the 1930s had both the Kampala Club and the 'progressive and popular' Kampala Sports Club.[53] In the early 1920s, Dar es Salaam already boasted four clubs: the Dar es Salaam Club, where the elite of the administration gave a farewell dinner to a departing Chief Secretary, and the GPO Club, the Gymkhana Club and the Government Service Sports Club, which were presumably for lesser mortals.[54] While police and hoteliers complained of the ease with which outsiders could buy drinks from clubs, exclusivity was a much more important quality of the club system. Racial exclusivity was a standard part of this: most clubs were European only; some Asian communities founded their own exclusive clubs, such as the Oriental Sports Club in Tabora.[55] Colonial policy and European social practice emphasized that drinking lent itself to exclusion and patterns of relationships which were opaque to those outside the drinking circle of the select: the socially exclusive drinking patterns which had emerged in nineteenth-century UK were transported to the colonies.[56] Pre-colonial drinking patterns had argued that drink's relationship to power lay in open drinking amongst men of similar age; the model of club drinking was one of secrecy, in which drinking sociability was determined by wealth and achieved or ascribed status, rather than age. Throughout this period Africans were excluded from clubs, but the ethos of exclusivity which built up around

---

[49]   *East African Standard*, 23 Feb. 1907.
[50]   Foran, *A Cuckoo in Kenya*, 117-18.
[51]   Perham, 'Kenya Tour, 1937', 48, RHO Mss Perham Box 49 (1); J. Gunter, *Inside Africa* (London, 1957 (1st edn 1955)), 318.
[52]   Griffiths, Diary for 1932, 28 Feb. 1932, RHO Mss Afr r 132.
[53]   *Uganda Herald*, 14 Aug. 1935.
[54]   20 Jan., 31 Mar., 2 June, 4 Aug. 1923, *Dar es Salaam Times*.
[55]   'Oriental Sports Club', *Tanganyika Standard*, 14 Jan. 1935.
[56]   Harrison, *Drink and the Victorians*, 45-6.

the clubs was to play a particular role in the development of new drinking patterns amongst Africans from the 1950s.

African drinking

Whisky drinking among chiefs is a matter requiring attention.[57]

British commentators liked to imply that German colonialism was careless of the ban on supplying spirits to Africans;[58] such implication was a useful shorthand assertion that the British were better colonialists, more mindful of the well-being of empire and its subjects. In fact, while the authorities in German East Africa – unlike the British – did not extend the ban on spirits to cover all 'intoxicating liquor', they would seem to have enforced the law relating to the sale of spirits to Africans. The records survive of one prosecution brought under this law, and at one point an edict was issued reminding administrators of the importance of this restriction.[59] German practice did, however, reproduce the idea that distilled spirits were the mark of especial and individual power, through the institution of '*jumbe* cognac', a liquor – the recipe of which is sadly lost to posterity – presented to favoured headmen, or *jumbes*.[60]

The British administration in Tanganyika, having extended the prohibition to cover the supply of any 'intoxicating liquor' to Africans, put some energy into preventing what they called 'leakage,'[61] the illicit supply of drink to Africans, going so far as to try to entrap those suspected of this offence.[62] In Kenya and Uganda, policemen and administrators were always ready to assert 'the very great necessity of preventing Natives from becoming addicted to European liquors'; this was 'in the native interest', and a ready example of the need for European trusteeship over Africans vulnerable to the heady temptations of modernity.[63] Accusations over leakage were usually directed at Asian shop-keepers, a reminder of the alleged threat to African social stability posed by the practices of these most effective agents of commerce, whose competition was generally resented by European entrepreneurs.[64]

It is difficult to tell how much intoxicating liquor did leak to Africans; anecdotal evidence about pilferage by domestic servants reveals much about

---

57 DC Busoga to PC Eastern, 17 Sep. 1924, UNA Z 325/20.

58 Minute, Kitching, 26 May 1930, TNA SMP 13560, Vol. I.

59 See the contents of TNA G 21/268; Ordinance, 17 July 1902, *British and Foreign State Papers, Vol. 95, 1902* (London, 1905), 603.

60 Weule, *Native Life*, 115-16, 213. Weule does record that it smelled of attar of roses (!).

61 Sandford, Memo, 3 Aug. 1937, TNA SMP 24462, Vol. I.

62 'Liquor Trapping Case: Accused Discharged', *Dar es Salaam Times*, 14 Apr. 1923. 'Trapping' for this offence was also accepted in British East Africa: Commissioner of Police to AG, 23 Dec. 1916, KNA AG 1/364.

63 Commissioner of Police to AG, 9 June 1924, KNA AG 1/368.

64 See for example Ag. Commissioner of Police to CS, 5 Nov. 1929, TNA SMP 13560, Vol. I. Some Asian storekeepers did supply beer to Africans: Int Nya8b, 3.

European insecurity but rather less about actual amounts consumed.[65] 'Where would one buy it?', asked one man, incredulously, when I asked him if he had drunk beer at this time.[66] African consumption of spirits intended for industrial or medical use was apparently considered more of an issue by the mid-1930s.[67] This was unsurprising: given the level of import duties, few Africans would have been able to buy imported whisky, even if shop-keepers had been prepared to sell it, but methylated spirits and other kinds of denatured alcohol were sold very much more cheaply.[68] By the late 1930s, discussion on African spirits drinking had moved away from allegations about the unscrupulous character of Asian shop-keepers, and had come instead to dwell – at remarkable length – on the most effective techniques for denaturing alcohol (that is, making it taste terrible), with the rival repellent properties of pyrrhidine and caoutchoucine as the main subject of official debate.[69]

Some Africans could afford to buy whisky, however. In 1927 a Ugandan man was imprisoned for violating the liquor laws, after he had obtained whisky from a shop, alleging it to be for his European employer (this was common and tolerated practice, as 'it would appear to be a hardship if a native servant could not be sent for liquor'[70]) and had then 'delivered it to certain natives of high rank'. He refused to name the customers.[71] Later nineteenth-century experience had established a particular place for spirits in the drinking construction of authority: spirits were the prerogative of those who claimed a distinctive, individual power of their own and who had acquired some preferential access to the imported goods of the caravan trade. The linkage between consumption of 'European' liquor and particular power was maintained into the 1920s and 1930s: the British had no '*jumbe* cognac' but some Europeans gave whisky to chiefs, sometimes in return for helping them to recruit labour: 'for two bottles of whisky you can get all the porters you want'.[72] Others allowed it to their most trusted servants as a mark of favour: 'I don't mind you drinking my whisky,' one settler told his staff, 'but don't drink out of the bottle.'[73] Access to the closely guarded spirit of the colonial state enhanced prestige: even bottled beer was perceived to

---

[65] *Mambo Leo*, Jan. 1934; Strange, *Kenya Today*, 74.

[66] Int Nya25b, 3.

[67] Director of Medical Services, Note, 28 June 1937, TNA SMP 12802, Vol. II.

[68] Memo, 29 Apr. 1936, TNA SMP 12802, Vol. II.

[69] Govt Analyst to Director of Medical Services, 29 Mar. 1932, KNA MOH 1/174; Attached, Govt Analyst to Colonial Sec., 21 Jan. 1935, KNA AG 1/360; CS Tanganyika to CS Uganda, 19 Nov. 1936, TNA SMP 12802, Vol. II. The debate was protracted partly because Uganda had commercial interests in industrial alcohol, which was produced by sugar refineries there, and the Uganda government was reluctant to agree to expensive means of denaturing which might harm this industry.

[70] Commissioner of Police to Crown Advocate, 29 Apr. 1911, KNA AG 1/363.

[71] Police Annual Report for 1927, 32, UNA A 46/228.

[72] Extract from report by Mitchell, nd 1929 and Ag. Commissioner of Police to CS, 29 Oct 1929, TNA SMP 13560, Vol. I; Elkington, 'Recollections of a Settler in Kenya, 1905-70', 20, RHO Mss Afr s 1558.

[73] Elkington, 'Recollections of a Settler in Kenya', 28, RHO Mss Afr s. 1558.

be strong, 'like medicine'.[74] As in the nineteenth century, spirits became part of the complex straddling process through which certain men used local authority to access an external source of power, and turned this access to external power back into local authority.

Officials of the colonial state might look favourably on the supply of 'intoxicating liquor' to Africans who possessed political status: in the late 1920s the governor of Tanganyika gave a broad hint that he would have no objection to the chiefs of Buhaya – showpiece region of indirect rule – consuming beer, agreeing with the PC that 'it would be much better for them if they drink our beer instead of the strong alcoholic stuff they now decant'.[75] By the 1930s other favoured Africans in Tanganyika were allowed to drink beer, and a blind eye was turned to the smuggling of Scotch by the *kabaka*, or king, of Buganda:[76] a sort of drinking evolution was perceived to be under way. In Kenya, a steady tightening of racial definitions in the 1920s and 1930s deprived Somalis and Abyssinians of the right to drink which they had possessed, but maintained it for those Arabs of high status who played a role in the administration of the coast; like Sir Ali bin Salim, Liwali of Mombasa, who needed to obtain liquor 'for the entertainment of his European friends'.[77] Colonial preference, as well as colonial exclusion, confirmed the notion that European liquor was in itself a drink of power: restricted to those who held authority, and by its very nature imbuing them with authority.

BREWING

There is little record of the first brewery in East Africa to produce bottled, European-style, beer. Founded in Dar es Salaam by Wilhelm Schultz, a former plantation assistant, it was already producing beer by 1907; by 1910 its products were being exported to British East Africa.[78] But it ceased production in the First World War – the only extant photograph of the brewery building shows damage from the British shelling of 1916 – and was never revived.

In 1919, the Colonial Provision Society proposed to the government of British East Africa that it might establish a new brewery at Uplands, near Nairobi. The proposal met a discouraging response; any such venture would be expected to pay excise duty at a rate equivalent to the duty on imported beer.[79] The plan lapsed, as had an earlier scheme in 1907.[80] Official caution

---

74 Int Nya6b, 2.
75 Extract, PC Bukoba to SNA, ? 1928; Governor's Minute, 28 Oct. 1928, TNA SMP 12797.
76 Minute, Kayamba, 8 July 1935, TNA SMP 12275; Gutkind, *Royal Capital of Buganda*, 150.
77 Sec. 4, Intoxicating Liquor (Amendment) Ordinance, 1925, KNA AG 1/355; Sec. 2, Intoxicating Liquor (Amendment) Ordinance, 1938, KNA AG 1/361; Ag. Senior Commissioner Coast to CNC, 31 Oct. 1923, KNA PC Coast 1/12/218.
78 Weule, *Native Life*, 43-4; Fulleborn, *Das Deutsche Njassa- und Ruwuma-Gebiet*, 12; Rodwell, *Sixty Years of Kenya Breweries*, 2.
79 AG to CS, 25 Sep. 1919, KNA AG 1/365.
80 A similar fate had presumably overtaken the East African Brewery Company, founded in 1907 with £2,000 capital: *East African Standard*, 4 May 1907.

was unsurprising. McGregor Ross mockingly noted that the import duties paid on alcohol were the only significant contribution which settlers made to the exchequer,[81] and the products of an East African brewery might simply displace drinks made in the UK, an undesirable development from the point of view of imperial economics. But two years later, the Kenya government looked with considerably more fondness on ideas for a local brewery; after some pushing by senior administrators, a Beer Ordinance was passed which established a distinctly favourable environment for East African beer production, setting excise at one-quarter of the level of import duties.[82] In December 1922 the rather makeshift new establishment of Kenya Breweries Limited (KBL) came into production.[83] It is not clear why the attitude of government changed so much in this period. There is no evidence for Colonial Office direction on this issue, and the brewery was not greeted with any official fanfare.[84] The Kenya Breweries legend identifies the two Hurst brothers, failed farmers, as the driving force behind the establishment of KBL; they and one other founder each put up £2,500 capital; by 1924 the company's capital was already being increased to £20,000, and the surviving Hurst brother (one was killed by an elephant in 1923) was only one of a number of directors.[85]

KBL struggled for two years, despite the level of protection which it enjoyed (which attracted some criticism from those who felt that 'the public pays, in the long run'[86]). But by 1925 the company was showing a healthy profit, and was beginning to export beer to neighbouring territories.[87] By 1931 the brewery was sufficiently well-established for the government to be able to reduce by half the degree of protection it received.[88] In 1933, a new brewery was started in Dar es Salaam by the Tanganyika Breweries Limited (TBL), a company in which KBL held a large interest.[89] Newspaper reports stressed the modern, scientific methods of this new industry, and evidently encouraged by the commercial success of the Nairobi brewery, the government of Tanganyika Territory welcomed this new venture with considerably more enthusiasm than had greeted KBL's first faltering steps.[90] The CS opened the new brewery and announced his pleasure that, instead of producing luxuries like tea and coffee, Tanganyika was now 'embarking on an industry which will provide one of the real necessities of life'; and he called on 'the people of Tanganyika' to 'give the Brewery their fullest

---

[81] McGregor Ross, *Kenya from Within*, 151, 259-62.
[82] The Beer Ordinance, 1922. The excise rates are mentioned in Commissioner of Customs to Ag. Colonial Sec., 13 Sep. 1921; administrative support for the idea is evident in Asst Secretary to AG, 16 Dec. 1921 and Colonial Sec. to AG, 2 Jan. 1923, KNA AG 1/371.
[83] Rodwell, *Sixty Years of Kenya Breweries*, 4.
[84] 'Local Beer', *East African Standard*, 16 Dec. 1922.
[85] Rodwell, *Sixty Years of Kenya Breweries*, 4-5; for the death of Hurst, see *Dar es Salaam Times*, 22 Sep. 1923.
[86] 'Our Own Beer', *Dar es Salaam Times*, 20 Oct. 1923.
[87] Rodwell, *Sixty Years of Kenya Breweries*, 6.
[88] Beer (Amendment) Ordinance, KNA AG 1/372.
[89] Just over half of the 12,250 shares were taken up by Kenya Breweries: Rodwell, *Sixty Years of Kenya Breweries*, 9.
[90] '"In Cellar Cool" Up to Date', *Tanganyika Standard*, 16 Sep. 1933.

support'.[91] He was addressing a European audience, and the speech was an interesting example of the kind of jocularity which the topic of drinking among one's social peers may induce amongst Europeans. The vast majority of the people of Tanganyika were, of course, legally disallowed from extending their support to the brewery, but for those permitted to buy bottled beer the relative cheapness of the new product offered an incentive beyond the CS's exhortations: 'Cost of Living Down', trumpeted the advertisements for the new beer.[92]

In 1936 a new holding company called East African Breweries Limited (EABL) was created, owning both KBL and TBL.[93] The government of Tanganyika had followed precisely the model of protective tariffs established in Kenya, and TBL enjoyed the same modest success as KBL; the degree of co-operation between governments and breweries is evidenced in invitations to senior officials to attend the opening of the Dar brewery, and in the alacrity with which governments in both colonies responded to brewery suggestions for reforms to the excise system.[94] In 1938, Kenya bottled beer production was 712,100 litres and Tanganyika production 196,500 litres; excise revenues yielded £7,674 in Kenya and about £2,000 in Tanganyika.[95]

Yet this was still small beer: a small amount of consumption, and a very small part of the total revenue from 'intoxicating liquor'. Locally bottled beer still faced considerable competition from imported beer;[96] and it remained very much less popular than spirits, particularly whisky. Less than 10 percent of 'intoxicating liquor' consumed in Kenya and Uganda in 1938 was in the form of locally bottled beer; and in Kenya, revenue from import duties on liquor in 1938 was £167,602; more than 20 times the excise revenue from beer. It was the Second World War which transformed the fortunes of the brewing industry in East Africa.

Table 8.2 *Apparent intoxicating-liquor consumption in Kenya/Uganda, 1938–44, measured in litres of absolute alcohol. Figures from* **Blue Books.**

	Total	Beer	Whisky	Brandy
1938	263,877	28,484	140,060	21,483
1942	295,664	159,164	63,630	29,855
1944	582,707	215,328	91,364	83,052

A diminished supply of whisky caused many drinkers to switch to South African brandy in the war years. But more switched to beer. The growth in beer production between 1940 and 1945 was phenomenal. KBL benefited from increased protection, as well as the simple disappearance of rival products. At the start of the war, the Kenya government had announced

[91] 'A New Industry for Tanganyika', *Tanganyika Standard*, 2 Dec. 1933.
[92] *Tanganyika Standard*, 1 Sep. 1934.
[93] Rodwell, *Sixty Years of Kenya Breweries*, 9.
[94] Evans, TBL to CS, 7 Nov. 1933, TNA SMP 21891; Commissioner of Customs to Colonial Sec., 20 Apr. 1932, KNA AG 1/373.
[95] Figures from Blue Books.
[96] Rodwell, *Sixty Years of Kenya Breweries*, 9-10.

patriotically inspired increases in import and excise duties to help fund the war effort. Acute eyes in the Colonial Office had noted that the effect of these increases was actually to considerably enhance the protection offered to local brewers, and since there had already been concern expressed that Kenyan beer production was depriving Scotch of an established market, the SoS had asked for some explanation of this.[97] The Kenya government had delayed replying, and the acute shortage of imported drinks consequent on the series of military reverses suffered by the UK from mid-1940 to late 1942 meant that the issue was forgotten, and the two brewing companies owned by East African Breweries Limited both came out of the war very much larger than they had gone into it.

But 1946 was something of a crisis year for KBL and TBL, however. Imported spirits were still in short supply and subject to controls (even at Christmas 1947, news of a special ration allowance of whisky for the festive season caused great excitement[98]), but there was the clear expectation that this situation would soon end, that local bottled beer would soon face

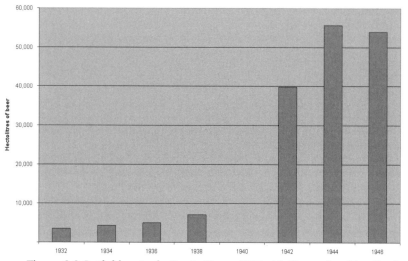

Figure 8.3 *Bottled-beer production in Kenya, 1932–46. Figures from* Blue Books.

competition from a full range of imported products – and that the additional wartime protective duty would be removed. KBL laid off many of the greatly expanded staff it had taken on. But in fact, from 1947 the market for locally bottled beer and production of this beer grew strongly (if not quite as extraordinarily rapidly as it had done in the early 1940s). Partly, this was a result of the 'second colonial invasion' of Europeans after the war. But it was also due to an ultimately much more significant shift in drinking patterns: from 1947, Africans across the region were legally permitted to buy and drink bottled beer.

[97] Ag. Governor to SoS, 14 Nov. 1939, PRO CO 533/515/8. SoS to Officer Administering the Government of Kenya, 2 Dec. 1939, CO 533/515/8.

[98] 'Whisky for Xmas', *Tanganyika Standard*, 29 Nov. 1947.

Part Three

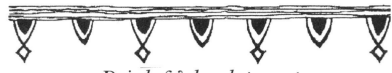

Drink & development
c.1950–90

The black-coated consumer

> To meet the wishes of the wealthier sections of the African population a bill is now before the Kenya Legislative Council to make it permissible for Africans to purchase English beer and wines.[1]

In 1946, a series of letters from Africans appeared in the newspapers in Tanganyika, calling for an end to the ban on bottled beer consumption by Africans. 'Natives are now well civilized . . . We stood shoulder to shoulder in those critical days [the Second World War], should we be kicked off in these Victorious days?'[2] As well as evoking wartime solidarity, the writers made another point: the law restricted urban drinking to unhygienic beer halls, forcing 'decent Africans' to drink, illegally, in private houses and face the risk of arrest or extortion from police patrols.[3] Their complaints fell on sympathetic ears; the East African governors had already decided in principle that the ban on bottled beer and wines might be relaxed in all three of Britain's East African territories.[4] There was a little hesitation from some quarters; a Medical Officer in Tanga solemnly opined that 'consumption of alcohol had a much more detrimental effect on the health of an African than on that of a European'[5] – but by mid-1947, with remarkably little debate, the laws in Kenya, Uganda and Tanganyika had been changed to allow Africans to drink wine and beer.

It was a change which revealed a considerable shift in the grounds of official European debate on temperance – and therefore change and social differentiation – amongst Africans. The end of the prohibition on bottled beer was explicitly intended to cater for the 'wealthier sections of the African population' and encourage the 'best elements of the African population' to

---

[1] 'Unscrupulous People Behind Nairobi Africans Boycott', *East African Standard*, 24 Oct. 1947.
[2] Letter, 'EJC', and Letter, 'Overwhelmed', *Tanganyika Standard* (Weekly), 24 Aug. and 21 Sep. 1946.
[3] Letter, 'Non-abstainer', *Tanganyika Standard* (Weekly), 24 Aug. 1946.
[4] Mitchell, Governor to SoS, 11 Feb. 1947, PRO CO 533/557/1; 'Africans to Have Beer and Wine', *Tanganyika Standard* (Weekly), 24 Aug. 1946.
[5] 'European Wines May Affect African Health', *Tanganyika Standard* (Weekly), 31 Aug. 1946.

distinguish themselves from the rest of the populace:[6] the 'black-coated African consumer' should not have to 'seek refreshment with the Hoi-Polloi in the Pombe market'.[7] This policy of differentiation – which contrasted sharply with policy further south in Africa[8] – was even more apparent in the early 1950s, when the government of Tanganyika selectively granted the right to drink spirits to a small group of African men who were judged by administrators to be of 'reliable character'.[9] Again, drinking privilege would distinguish the 'intelligent, educated, African', in a policy which explicitly sought to replace 'racial discrimination' with 'social or cultural discrimination'.[10]

Such a distinct group of educated men was central to the emerging late colonial vision of reformed, representative institutions of local government which would be led by the educated, and of rapid economic change which would produce stabilized urban populations and make East Africa a much more significant part of an imperial economy which was facing the imminent loss of its Far Eastern possessions. Suddenly colonial governments buzzed with schemes for economic and political change;[11] and while some veteran administrators viewed these changes with some alarm – and evoked the fear of social disruption which had guided policy up to 1940[12] – it was development, not tradition, that was the watchword of colonial rulers after 1945. 'European' alcohol was now a desirable drink for respectable Africans, the communion wine of responsible modernity. A journalist described the role of alcohol in defining the status of a social occasion in 1950s Uganda: 'After the ceremony came a reception by the Kabaka in his small palace . . . Some male guests wore morning dress, and a few carried top hats. No banana wine here! Sweating waiters tore through the packed room with trays of punch.'[13]

Patrimonialism, developmentalism & the new ambiguities of power, 1960–90

After political independence the elite of the new post-colonial states did distinguish themselves from the rest of the populace through what they drank and where they drank it. Like their contemporaries in West Africa,

---

[6] 'Africans to Have Beer and Wine', *Tanganyika Standard* (Weekly), 24 Aug. 1946.

[7] PC Eastern to CS, 10 Feb. 1953, TNA SMP 38758.

[8] In Southern Rhodesia, the state refused to extend drinking privileges to the African elite which sought them: M. West,'"Equal Rights for All Civilized Men": Elite Africans and the Quest for European Liquor in Colonial Zimbabwe, 1924-65', *International Review of Social History*, 37 (1992), 376-97.

[9] Minute, Solicitor-General, 17 Jan. 1953, TNA SMP 20309.

[10] 'Council Discusses European Beer for Africans', *East African Standard*, 1 Aug. 1947; *Intoxicating Liquor Report*, 6.

[11] Farson, *Last Chance in Africa*, 13-25.

[12] Dundas, *African Crossroads*, 39, 135.

[13] Gunter, *Inside Africa*, 432.

they created a distinctive drinking pattern, a model of temperance based on socially exclusive drinking, which came to be a ready focus for popular resentment.[14] 'Except for those very few people who believe in putting a piece of cloth around their necks, called a tie, to look like Europeans, all the people in this country prefer local drinks. The black Europeans are the ones who are encouraging the foreign drinks.'[15]

The 'black Europeans' came into possession of states whose range of activities and material resources had grown enormously between 1945 and 1960. They continued to grow in to the 1970s. Across the region, position within and relationship to the state came to be of central importance: the state was, as Haugerud has argued, the ultimate source of patronage.[16] At one point the state employed 80 percent of wage-earners in post-independence Kenya; state employment in Tanzania grew by an extraordinary 13 percent every year between 1966 and 1976.[17] In 1965, a PC urged the Maasai to 'come forward for being employed in any Government department, as everyone else [does]'.[18] Not all who came forward were chosen, however. One man in Bunyoro explained how his lengthy career in the civil service differentiated him from his fellows. 'Most people who worked for the Government were very comfortably off. And so far as farming went, they were not involved – like me, I wasn't involved. Because we were very comfortable: I ate, I drank, things were sufficient. So I wasn't really concerned with farming.'[19]

In the patrimonial states of post-colonial Africa, having a job somewhere within the machinery of the state meant more than a wage, housing and access to the occasional use of official vehicles and medical treatment – important though all those were.[20] It gave an ability to mediate the access of others to some particular bureaucratic benefice: even if this were only a form, or a signature of approval. Involvement with the state offered access to sources of power: the healing power of medicine, the power to redistribute material patronage, the power of courts, sometimes the power of violence embodied by the erratic coercive force available to local administrations. Of course the state as a category conceals significant institutional fissures: between the structures of local government (to which late colonial policy gave great importance) and the machinery of central government (which in the post-colonial period tended to eat up the autonomy and resource base of local government); and between party political structures and administration. Yet the abstraction is by no means entirely misleading, for there has been an interconnectedness between the different institutions and

[14] Akyeampong, *Drink, Power and Cultural Change*, 145-8.

[15] Mr Abdallah, in *Kenya National Assembly Debates*, 23 Sep. 1971, col. 453-4.

[16] A. Haugerud, *The Culture of Politics in Modern Kenya* (Cambridge, 1995), 146.

[17] Miller and Yeager, *Kenya: the Quest for Prosperity*, 40; N. Chazan, P. Lewis, R. Mortimer, D. Rothchild and S. Stedman, *Politics and Society in Contemporary Africa* (Boulder, 1999 (3rd edn)), 55.

[18] Monthly Report, Kajiado District, Aug. 1965, KNA DC KAJ 4/1/11.

[19] Int Nyoro36a, 3.

[20] Chazan *et al.*, *Politics and Society*, 329-30.

factions of the state, with individuals moving between them and seeking support across them; in each country, access to one aspect of the state could lead on to access to others. Not all who had such access shared it equally, and those at the centre always fared best – better a clerk in the Customs department than a chief in a rural location – yet any handhold on the slippery hide of the Leviathan was better than none.

But the focus on patrimonialism, on the state as a 'lame Leviathan' which exercises authority largely though the arbitrary operation of patron-client relationships,[21] may obscure an essential element in the making – and unmaking – of authority in post-colonial East Africa. For there has been an ideological element to the exercise of authority: the state is more than just a 'facade masking the realities of deeply personalized political relations',[22] for through its formal institutions the state is involved in an international economy which provides patronage resources, yet mediates access to these resources through the notion of development. So the very idea of development came, from the 1960s, to constitute a form of power in itself, a power over well-being and prosperity. Development became synonymous with health and wealth; development was the central term in political rhetoric and popular discourse, argued over and evoked in every dispute, great and small, in parliamentary debates over tax and in domestic arguments over bride-wealth and control of crops. This was an argument inherited from colonial administrators who, particularly in the last years of empire, sought to answer nationalist criticisms of their rule with assertions that the 'real enemies' were 'poverty, ignorance and disease'.[23] The unholy trinity of poverty, ignorance and disease played a prominent role in discursive justifications of state policy and authority after independence.[24] As Haugerud has argued, '[t]o reward citizens' compliance and obedience the state would bring the material benefits of "progress" and "development."'[25] Increasingly, temperance and development became intertwined in official and popular rhetoric.

But development had its own ambiguities and could challenge as well as make authority. The state – or rather the multiple, competing actors whose shifting rivalries composed the state – could be criticized for failing to provide development. And both state and development stood in an uneasy relationship to the chronic conflicts of age and gender. Some scholarship has stressed the patriarchal nature of post-colonial as well as colonial states, in which the operation of law, local authority and the increasing shortage of land have consolidated men's authority: the vision of the male-headed 'family' dwelling in a single home reproduces male authority while destroying

---

[21] Callaghy makes an articulate argument for a Weberian view of the state as a patronage-based instrument of dominance: T. Callaghy, 'The State as Lame Leviathan: the Patrimonial Administrative State in Africa' in Z. Ergas (ed.), *The African State in Transition* (London, 1987), 87-116.

[22] P. Chabal and J.-P. Daloz, *Africa Works. Disorder as Political Instrument* (Oxford, 1999), 16.

[23] J. Golding, *Colonialism: the Golden Years* (Ashford, 1987), 192-3.

[24] 'Socialism Must Govern', *Uganda Argus*, 8 Jan. 1964.

[25] Haugerud, *Culture of Politics*, 81.

such limited autonomy as the multiple wives in their distinct 'houses' once possessed.[26] Yet this was not the perspective of most men. In Bunyoro, European observers noted in the 1950s and 1960s that men had an uneasy sense that women were escaping their authority.[27] Men saw women's access to courts and money as the undesirable results of modernity imposed by the state: 'we are under the women. We are following the law of the Government.'[28] Accumulators themselves, elder men in post-colonial East Africa were threatened by the accumulation of younger men and women, and evoked against it alternative ideas of temperance, based on visions of a past well-being derived from the unencumbered and distinctive sociability of elder men.

FROM TRADITIONAL TO INFORMAL

The contradictions in the state's commitment to development and elder men's evocation of sociability were revealed through the flourishing of the unplanned, irregular entrepreneurship which came to be known as the informal economy. In the 1960s, the 'native liquor' of colonial discourse became (somewhat slowly and unevenly)[29] the 'traditional liquor' of post-colonial rhetoric. This latter term is problematic: not only is it technically misleading, but it casts locally-made ferments as part of the past, vestigial rather than vital. In an important way, the post-colonial history of locally-made liquor has revolved around the tension between their identity as traditional liquor, which has been bound up with debates over development and authority; and their identity as informal-sector alcohol, which has been bound up with the functioning of an economy beyond formal regulation which thrives within the ubiquitous structures of petty patrimonialism.

The label 'informal-sector alcohol' has its own problems. Enthusiasts for the informal economy, a sizeable group from the 1980s, have shied away from discussion of this most active area of entrepreneurship, guided no doubt by the official characterization of informal-sector alcohol as anti-developmental, or a danger to health, or both.[30] And anyway, these drinks

---

[26] Talle, *Women at a Loss*, 1; Oboler, *Women, Power and Economic Change*, 67, 160; J. Parpart and K. Staudt, 'Women and the State in Africa', in Parpart and Staudt (eds.), *Women and the State in Africa*, 1-19.

[27] J. Beattie, 'Nyoro Marriage and Affinity', *Africa* (1957), 11; A.R. Dunbar, 'Mutala Survey of Bujenje (Kisonga), Bunyoro', 71, *Uganda Journal*, 29 (1965), 61-74.

[28] Int Nya27a, 2.

[29] Both great and small might stumble over the changed terminology of drink: Kelaino to DC Kajiado, 25 Oct. 1967; S. Oloitiptip, Asst Minister for Commerce to Chair, Kajiado Liquor Licensing Board, 19 June 1968, KNA DC KAJ 4/25/2.

[30] M.McCall, 'Rural Brewing, Exclusion and Development Policy-making', *Gender and Development*, 4 (1996), 29-38. There is, for example, only one reference to the alcohol trade in the whole of K. King, *Jua Kali Kenya: Change and Development in an Informal Economy, 1970-95*, (London/Nairobi/Athens, OH, 1996) (50 ; and little more in T. Maliyamkono and M. Bagachwa, *The Second Economy in Tanzania* (London/Athens, OH/Nairobi/Dar es Salaam, 1990), 42, 46. A. Tripp, *Changing the Rules. The Politics of Liberalization of the Informal Urban Economy in Tanzania* (Berkeley/Los Angeles/London, 1997), 219 makes only rather vague reference to the importance of 'beverage production.'

did not simply slip out of the world of culture and into that of commerce. The kinds of alcohol which people made for themselves continued to evoke alternative ideas of health, as well as alternative paths to wealth. People in East Africa used hospitals, attended clinics, took their pills; but alongside this system of well-being, other ideas continued to flourish, within which well-being rested not on development but on relationships with elders, with ancestors, with possessory spirits and a series of other sources of power. Debates over drinking, the next three chapters argue, revealed the multiplicity of sources of power in post-colonial society.

Nine

'Beer is best'
Formal-sector alcohol,
1947–90

> When we got independence, and started ruling ourselves, that was when
> we started drinking [bottled beer].[1]

States and breweries deepened their relationship after the end of the
prohibition on beer sales to Africans in 1947.[2] The local brewing industry
continued to receive tariff protection; planning an expansion in capacity,
Tanganyika Breweries dangled the possibility of greatly increased excise
revenue before the government and was rewarded with priority shipping
space for equipment from the UK[3]. Alliance went beyond such occasional
governmental favours; the whole tenor of colonial attitudes to bottled beer
and Africans had changed entirely. Now there was active encouragement
for African bottled beer drinking: the CS of Tanganyika allegedly told an
executive of EABL that it was 'Government's policy to encourage the African
to drink European beer as opposed to other less wholesome drinks'.[4] District
officials sought to 'encourage the sale of the higher-quality product at the
expense of locally-brewed beer [traditional liquor]', believing that bottled
beer was 'a much more wholesome drink than pombe, which is often
unhygienically prepared from dubious ingredients', and that 'the better type
of beer' would supercede home production as inevitably and completely as
it had in Europe.[5] New investment pursued this new market; in 1946
Allsopps, a British brewer, had taken control of a small brewery near Nairobi

---

[1] Int Nya6b, 2.
[2] It is not clear whether breweries lobbied for the end of the prohibition, as they were to do
     in South Africa: A. Mager, 'The First Decade of "European Beer" in Apartheid South
     Africa: the State, the Brewers and the Drinking Public, 1962-1972', 370-71, *JAH*, 40 (1999),
     367-88.
[3] Ag. Comptroller of Customs to Member for Finance, 26 July 1948; EABL had informed
     the government that excise revenue would be tripled as a result of the expansion: EABL to
     Comptroller of Customs, 22 July 1948, TNA SMP 21891.
[4] Sales Manager, EABL to DC Mbeya, 23 July 1952, TNA SMP 21891.
[5] DC Hoima to Verjee, 4 Dec. 1954 and Commodore, East African Railways and Harbours,
     Butiaba to DC Hoima, 8 June 1954, HDA FIN 7; PC Eastern to CS, 10 Feb. 1953, TNA
     SMP 38758.

which had been set up a few years earlier in rivalry to EABL;[6] and another new brewery was established in Kenya (with European capital) under the name City Breweries. EABL itself received new capital from Symonds, another British brewer, for its Kenya and Tanganyika operations, and opened a new brewery in Mombasa in 1952.[7] In 1950, Uganda Breweries was established at Port Bell, near Kampala; a second Ugandan brewery, near Jinja, began production in 1956.[8] These concerns tended to co-operate, rather than compete. EABL bought a controlling interest in Uganda Breweries in 1959, and took over the Allsopps operation in 1962;[9] with the other brewers they formed a Brewers' Association, which EABL inevitably dominated, and which had by 1960 organized what was in effect a pricing cartel across the region.[10]

As the bottled-beer industry grew, the advertising campaigns of EABL (and its smaller rivals) played on the notion of cleanliness and modernity, and looked to a market of young Africans. The first advertisements specifically aimed at Africans appeared in 1954, in the Tanganyika government monthly *Mambo Leo*; simple text messages which asserted the 'cleanliness' of bottled beer, set amidst pages of advertisements for pens, soap, bicycles and the other consumer paraphernalia of modernity.[11] By the 1960s (mid-1960s in Tanzania, a few years later in Kenya) Africans began to dominate pictorial adverts, which initially emphasized beer drinking as an activity of the young and moneyed.[12] In Tanzania, they featured suited men in ties and women in evening dress, sometimes attended by waiters;[13] in Kenya the drinkers were smart young urbanites.[14] There was an air of exhilaration and rebellion in some of this drinking. In the early 1950s, a woman in Tanganyika wrote of the delights of a bar where she and her fellows might drink beer with cash they earned: 'we get great pleasure . . . whoever sells vegetables goes in and relaxes with a beer, and listens to music'.[15] The bar could be a potent meeting place of alcoholic and economic autonomy; in the 1960s, one advert showed a woman on her own, in evening dress, downing a beer.[16]

In the context of such rebellion bottled beer became a focus for new political campaigns, which were for a brief period more vocal – and more violent – than any earlier agitation for the legalization of beer. These were campaigns against beer. In Buganda in 1960, newspapers recorded violent assaults on African beer drinkers and sellers. 'Two men have been arrested

[6] Rodwell, *Sixty Years of Kenya Breweries*, 11.
[7] Rodwell, *Sixty Years of Kenya Breweries*, 11-12.
[8] *Uganda Argus*, 11 June 1956.
[9] Rodwell, *Sixty Years of Kenya Breweries*, 13-14.
[10] *Uganda Argus*, 7 Jan. 1960.
[11] *Mambo Leo*, Aug. 1954.
[12] *Nationalist*, 30 Jan. 1965, 8 Jan. 1966.
[13] *Nationalist*, 22 and 24 Jan. 1966.
[14] *Daily Nation*, 27 Jan. 1967.
[15] Letter, Maria bti Paulo, *Mambo Leo*, Dec. 1953.
[16] *Nationalist*, 24 Jan. 1966.

after two Baganda threw stones at people drinking in the Steel Bar, Nakulabye Kampala, and shouted that they should not drink European-type beer . . . A shopkeeper has told police that he was threatened for buying European-type beer. A man was arrested.'[17] In Kenya, bottled beer was subject to a political boycott in the early 1950s,[18] and in the Emergency bottled beer became a distinguishing characteristic of Loyalists; Mau Mau oaths (at least in rumour) were administered in 'traditional liquor'.[19] In each case bottled beer offered itself as a useful icon for those who sought to stress the moral dangers posed by change; and who resented the ways in which colonialism offered wealth, and new sources of power, to others. After independence the campaign of violence against bottled beer came to an end; but a discursive undercurrent remained which used bottled beer – and other 'European liquor' – as a way of talking about the social dangers of change and unequal wealth.

Selling beer: the economics of the new elite

. . . people have a feeling that once one has a liquor licence [one] has an easy way of making money, which is of course true.[20]

Bottled beer was very much more than a symbol; as Mager has argued of South Africa, it was an economic field of great importance.[21] The sale of formal sector spirits was also important – once sale and consumption by Africans was fully legalized in 1955 – but the cost of these was kept high by the level of duties, and it was bottled beer which was to dominate the consumption of formal-sector alcohol in East Africa from the 1950s onwards. The growth in production and consumption of bottled beer was phenomenal, even in the context of the extraordinary growth in worldwide bottled beer production after 1950.[22] It was most marked in Kenya, where production grew by over 4,000 percent in four decades, from 78,000 hectolitres in 1950 to over 3.25 million hectolitres in 1990; but in Tanzania and Uganda there was also rapid growth in the 1960s and early 1970s – consumption was growing by more than 30 percent a year in Tanzania in 1971-3.[23] This extraordinary growth in the making and selling of bottled beer is a central feature of the drinking history of East Africa since 1950.

[17] 'Two Arrests after Beer Stoning', *Uganda Argus*, 6 Jan. 1960; see also 19 Jan. and 2 Feb. 1960.
[18] 'Record of Meeting on Bill to Amend the Liquor Ordinances, 5 June 1955, KNA MAA 2/5/212; Gunter, *Inside Africa*, 362.
[19] DC Narok to OiC Masai, 26 Oct. 1952, KNA DC NGO 1/9/10. See the retrospective account in *Daily Nation*, 24 Jan. 1964.
[20] Officer Commanding Police Station, Ngong to Officer Commanding Police Division, Kajiado, 5 Nov. 1967, KNA DC KAJ 4/25/2.
[21] Mager, 'The First Decade of "European Beer"'.
[22] On average, bottled-beer production in the developing world was doubling every eight and a half years in the 1960s and early 1970s: J. Keddie and W. Cleghorn, *Brewing in Developing Countries* (Edinburgh, 1979), 14.
[23] *Daily News*, 5 Jan. 1973.

While the brewing industry remained dominated by European (and some Asian) capital until the nationalizations of the the late 1960s and 1970s, the distribution and retailing of beer came very largely into the hands of African men by the end of the 1960s. The possibilities of this had been seen by some enterprising individuals as soon as African consumption was legalized.[24] John Rupia, an established restaurateur of Dar es Salaam, sought to obtain a licence to sell beer in 1947; and was finally favoured with a special permission which allowed him to do so (the change in the law had made African consumption of bottled beer legal, but until the mid-1950s

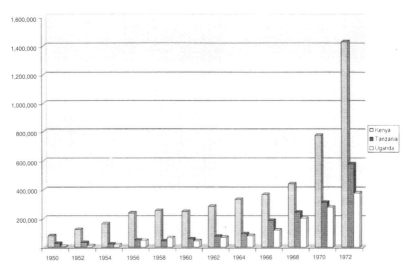

Figure 9.1 *East African bottled-beer production for domestic consumption, 1950–72, in hecolitres*

an African wishing to sell such liquor still required the special permission of the governor).[25] Rupia was a political as well as commercial entrepreneur, and in 1954 he was one of the founding members of the Tanganyika African National Union (TANU), which was to become the ruling party at independence. Across East Africa, Rupia was followed by a select group of other 'reputable African retailers' in the next few years.[26] In Tanganyika, 108 licences had been issued, all to men, by 1954; the giving of a licence was viewed as an 'experiment in good citizenship'. One applicant in Mbeya was rejected as being 'not of sufficient standing in the township'.[27] In Kenya

[24] Waithaka s/o Kimani to DC Nairobi, 14 Nov. 1947, KNA MAA 2/5/166.
[25] John Rupia to PC Eastern, 9 May 1947; Minute, 12 Jan. 1949, TNA SMP 38758.
[26] PC Eastern to CS, 10 Feb. 1953, TNA SMP 38758.
[27] List of licencees in TNA SMP 38758; Minute, Commissioner for Social Development, 27 Oct. 1950, TNA SMP 38758; Political to Province, 26 Mar. 1954, TNA 157 A2/25.

and Uganda, 250 licences had been issued to Africans by mid-1952.[28] In the mid-1950s this policy of close control was abandoned, and with the new legislation of 1955 Africans were able to obtain licences in the same way as Europeans and Asians. It had come to be accepted that space had to be made for African entrepreneurship as well as African drinking: 'Africans should be given their fair share of liquor licences.'[29]

EABL and its lesser rivals were more than willing to share in this social engineering, boasting that licences to sell its beer went to 'responsible Africans who are nearly all doing an excellent trade and have thus made a useful start in profitable private enterprise':[30] selling more beer was a socially desirable activity. Nairobi Council, concerned that its beerhall revenue would collapse as Africans turned to drinking bottled beer in bars, protested vigorously at the 1955 legislation: 'the Bill was the outcome of pressure from a small minority of Africans who wished to make an easy living selling bottled beer, and by the owners of the breweries'.[31] In later years, the breweries were to boast of how path-breaking their attitude had been: 'East African Breweries went ahead and showed that Africanisation was not only the right thing to do but was needed as a firm foundation for the future.'[32] In the 1950s, however, there were limits to the possibilities of this incorporative approach. Officials wished to encourage beer drinking, but still feared that too many licences would encourage an undesirable degree of drunkenness.[33] There were enormous numbers of licence applications from Africans in the 1950s (even with increased licence fees from 1955[34]) but many were rejected.[35] In 1956 there had only been 11 non-club licences in the whole of Kajiado District; the November 1962 Licensing Court meeting had to deal with 79 applications.[36]

The possibilities for the issue of new licences were limited by the existence of an established body of licence-holders – mostly Asian entrepreneurs. In the later 1960s, the effective removal of many of these Asians opened up new space for African licensees. In a process which is best documented in Kenya, an official policy of 'Africanization' of business (sometimes phrased rather as the exclusion of 'non-citizens') coincided with the interests of brewing capital to create a new field for the operation of political patronage. The bodies which issued licences to deal in bottled beer and spirits had acquired their first African members in the late 1940s; by the mid-1960s they were

---

[28] Sales Manager EABL to DC Mbeya, 23 July 1952, TNA SMP 21891.
[29] Circular, Secretary for Defence, 6 Apr. 1956, KNA MAA 2/5/212.
[30] Sales Manager EABL to DC Mbeya, 23 July 1952, TNA SMP 21891.
[31] Record of Meeting, Nairobi Council, 5 Jan. 1955, KNA MAA 2/5/212.
[32] Rodwell, *Sixty Years of Kenya Breweries*, 21.
[33] Province to Political Mbeya, 24 Mar. 1953; PC Mbeya to DC Iringa, 2 Apr. 1953, TNA 157 A2/25.
[34] In Tanganyika, the upper limit for fees more than doubled: Ordinance No. 46 of 1955.
[35] DC Central Nyanza to Secretary to Asian Minister Without Portfolio, 8 Jan. 1957, KNA MAA 2/5/212.
[36] Minutes of Liquor Licensing Court, Nov. 1955, KNA DC KAJ 4/10/22; Monthly Report, Nov. 1962, KNA DC KAJ 4/1/11.

largely composed of African administrators, politicians and local businessmen.[37] These bodies were useful sources of petty cash to some members (whose expenses claims were 'little short of fantastic'[38]); more importantly, they gave a considerable power of patronage, for the issue of a licence could be the key to a lucrative distributorship or bar business. In his capacity as chair of the licensing body, the DC Kajiado gave one man a 'To Whom It May Concern' letter suggesting that the man be given a beer distributorship;[39] another entrepreneur who sought a distributorship through the office of the DC noted that the beer supply was a little irregular and in the hands of an Asian, but that 'our business whose partners are purely Africans with no mixture of races want to rectify this supply'.[40] When some aspirant entrepreneurs suspected the Kajiado district administration of favouring Asian distributors and bar-owners they secured political help from higher quarters who evidently agreed that 'it is high time that they [Asians] are challenged by genuine African businesses' and the administration was ordered to 'exercise a considerable amount of restraint when considering liquor applications from non-Kenya citizens'.[41] The DC then encouraged the breweries to give a distributorship to one individual; then withdrew this suggestion and proposed to advance some alternative names.[42] The next year, an African manager with EABL found a bar business for his wife in Kajiado through the intercession of another DC, who asked the DC Kajiado to let her take over a bar that had been run by an Asian.[43] Space for such patronage increased further in 1969 when a group of 'non-citizen' traders were simply ordered to leave the district.[44] Bars were a good source of income; distributorships were even more desirable, for EABL's desire to Africanize was such that they offered generous credit terms to their distributors, and beer propelled the success of a new generation of African entrepreneurs. In 1978, one source estimated that 30 percent of Kenyan businesses were in some way related to the selling of bottled beer.[45] Local contacts and prestige could be parlayed into a bar licence; wider renown and better contacts could lead to a distributorship, and set individuals off on a path to accumulation and national economic and political

---

[37] For the first appointment of an African to such a body in Tanganyika, see GN 524 of 22 Apr. 1949; for the composition of the Kajiado body in 1963 see President, Liquor Licensing Court to Permanent Secretary for Constitutional Affairs, 25 Mar. 1963, KNA DC KAJ 4/8/3.

[38] Ag. Civil Secretary to Regional Govt Agent (the equivalent of a DC in the short-lived regional constitution), 28 Mar. 1964, KNA DC KAJ 4/8/3; also Provincial Accountant to DC Kajiado, 18 Apr. 1968, KNA DC KAJ 4/25/2.

[39] DC Kajiado to To Whom It May Concern, 18 May 1967, KNA DC KAJ 4/25/2.

[40] Orumoy to EABL via DC Kajiado, 28 Nov. 1966, KNA DC KAJ 4/8/2.

[41] Masai Distributors to DC Kajiado, 10 Apr. 1967; PS, Ministry of Commerce to President, Kajiado Liquor Licensing Court, 22 Apr. 1967 and PC Rift Valley to all DCs, 26 Oct. 1967, KNA DC KAJ 4/25/2.

[42] DC Kajiado to KBL, 13 and 17 Apr. 1968, KNA DC KAJ 4/25/2.

[43] DC Kiambu to DC Kajiado, 28 Feb. 1968, KNA DC KAJ 4/25/2.

[44] Feb. 1969 Monthly Report, KNA DC KAJ 4/1/11.

[45] *Weekly Review*, 15 Dec. 1978: the figure presumably refers to formal retail undertakings.

prominence.[46] The selling and distributing of bottled beer showed very clearly how the regulatory systems created by the colonial state led on to post-colonial patrimonialism.

In these patterns of accumulation, women played a relatively minor role. There was no legal obstacle to women obtaining licences to deal in intoxicating liquor, for the laws passed in 1955 were entirely free of racial or gender restrictions. But few women obtained bar licences, and fewer still secured distributorships.[47] Bottled beer was made in a factory process, and was distributed and sold by male entrepreneurs: women's place in this sector was as barmaids. The barmaid came to occupy a particular and unenviable role in popular culture, pitied, despised and mistrusted: 'There is only one song sung by all barmaids. Woe.'[48] Barmaids were usually young women, unmarried, vulnerable to dismissal and harassment, sexually available to any willing to augment their meagre wages, liable to accusations of theft.[49] And yet men feared them; for the drunkenness of men offered even these women a degree of sexual power, and so occasional extravagant and unenforceable schemes circulated in which administrators required that 'in future all the barmaids and people who served the public in a bar should be first medically examined and have uniforms.'[50]

The pattern of patrimonialism varied in each of the three East African countries. In Kenya, distributing and retailing beer were important fields for the incorporative alliance between entrepreneurship and the state which characterized the post-colonial economy to the late 1980s.[51] In Tanzania, such an alliance was apparent in the 1960s, and there was a brief period of private investment in which Jayant Madhvani, the Asian entrepreneur who had put money into a Ugandan brewery in the 1950s, established a new brewery at Arusha in 1961 (a venture in which EABL took a 40 percent stake in 1964).[52] TBL, meanwhile, invested £800,000 in an entirely new brewhouse in their Dar establishment which began operation in 1966.[53] But the Tanzanian government took a controlling stake in TBL and in Madhvani's brewery in 1967, and took complete control in 1977. EABL, the name which the Kenya-based brewing company had used increasingly since

[46] N. Swainson, *The Development of Corporate Capitalism in Kenya, 1918-1977* (London, 1980), 182, 205.

[47] In the early 1970s, Obbo found that successful bar owners in the Kampa suburb which she studied were all men; and that men also dominated the unlicensed sale of bottled beer: C. Obbo, *African Women. Their Struggle for Economic Independence* (London, 1980), 126-7.

[48] Ngugi wa Thiong'o, *Petals of Blood* (London, 1975), 75; 'Behind the Barmaid's Smiles and Sweet Words', *Daily Nation*, 11 Nov. 1984.

[49] Y. King'ala, *Anasa* (Nairobi, 1984), 85-6; Obbo, *African Women*, 128.

[50] Minutes, Liquor Licensing, 30 Dec. 1969, HDA MUN 4/2/M; for an almost identical form of words, see '35 Applicants for Bar Trade Rejected', *Daily Nation*, 7 Nov. 1983.

[51] Chazan *et al.*, *Politics and Society*, 264-5.

[52] Rodwell, *Sixty Years of Kenya Breweries*, 14.

[53] 'Babu Visits Brewery', *Nationalist*, 21 Jan. 1965; W. Mwingiza, 'A History of Tanzania Breweries', typescript kindly supplied by author. The costs of the new brewhouse had risen to £1 million by the time it opened: 'Brewery Director Coming Today', *Nationalist*, 24 Jan. 1966.

the 1950s, fell out of use. Now each country had its own brewery: Kenya Breweries (KBL) in Kenya, Tanzania Breweries (TBL) in Tanzania (the former Madhvani operation having been subsumed within this in 1971). In Tanzania TBL then took control of the distribution of beer; and finally, to an extent, the party and state took over the retailing of beer through state shops.[54] In Kenya, administrators might sometimes control access to entrepreneurial space; in Tanzania, the state itself occupied this space as its own, and positions in brewery management or regional trading companies were allotted by the state and party. A similar shift in control was evident in Uganda, where the 'move to the left', Amin's 'economic war' and wholesale expulsion of Asians left distribution and retailing in the hands of favoured

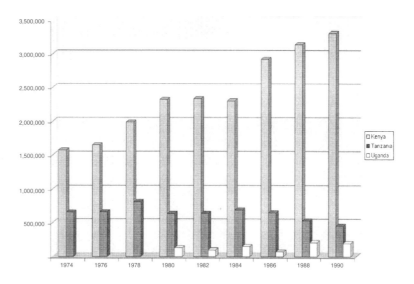

Figure 9.2 *East African bottled-beer production for domestic consumption, 1974–90*

– often rather briefly favoured – individuals who had contacts in the army or the local administration, many of whom failed to maintain themselves in these businesses. Under the increasingly chaotic rule of Amin, arbitrary dispossession by bands of soldiers drove other bar owners out of business. One woman described how her husband had in 1968 'talked to some people in [Hoima] town' and with their support established a bar just outside town.

> He built the bar and put in it the modern processed alcohol. That's how we started, but later my husband became weak, also the regimes

[54] The TBL policy of taking over distributorship was mentioned in 1971: 'Imported Beer Won't Affect Market' *Standard, Tanzania*, 7 Jan. 1971; by 1974, bottled beer was being distributed through Zonal Managers employed by TBL: Zonal Manager to Mwasangu, 14 Nov. 1974, Rungwe Archive L3/2.

changed and everything was spoiled. Everything took a different direction, I think you also witnessed what took place... Things got messed up, people looted whatever they wanted, and from then on our bar and everything else collapsed.[55]

In 1972 the Madhavani's brewery in Jinja was nationalized, in 1976 Uganda Breweries was, too.[56] It was not until the end of the 1980s that a new network of distributors and retailers began to emerge in Uganda.

In Tanzania and Uganda, nationalization meant that brewery management posts became, in effect, state appointments. The consequences of this, and of increasing difficulties in securing supplies and spare parts, were distinctly unfortunate for the bottled-beer industry. Rapid growth in production and consumption during the 1960s and 1970s was followed by an extraordinary decline, as mismanagement and shortages crippled production and distribution. Meanwhile in Kenya production and consumption of bottled beer continued to grow. Visiting Uganda Breweries in 1975, the colonel whom Amin had made minister for industry encouraged them to produce more – but was told that in fact production was in decline 'because of the problems explained to the minister'; the annual report of Uganda Breweries for the same year lamented that they were unable to fulfil demand because of shortages of spare parts and water.[57] The state continued to identify the breweries as of prime importance – launching an 'action plan' to revive them in 1977 – but production did not recover.[58] By the late 1980s, regional dependence on Kenyan beer symbolized the dominance of Kenya's economy.

In Kenya – where by the end of the 1960s KBL was the sole brewer, having finally swallowed up the last of its little rivals, City Breweries, in 1969 – alliance between brewery and state took a different form. EABL, and then KBL, had launched a series of schemes under which workers bought shares in the company.[59] This created a large number of individual shareholders who held a relatively small part of the equity, and allowed the rather disingenuously phrased claim that already by the mid-1960s the majority of the company's shareholders were African.[60] There is no available study of the actual shareholdings of KBL, and rumours of the equity held by prominent politicians cannot be substantiated; but a close involvement with administrators and politicians was evident in other ways. The first African directors were appointed to the board in 1959.[61] Opening a new building in

[55] Int Nyoro24b, 3.
[56] Rodwell, *Sixty Years of Kenya Breweries*, 18.
[57] 'Colonel Sabuni Tours Industries', *Voice of Uganda*, 18 Jan. 1975; Chairman's Note, Uganda Breweries Annual Report, 1975 (copy in Makerere University Library).
[58] D. Nabudere, *Imperialism and Revolution in Uganda* (London and Dar es Salaam, 1980), 307.
[59] 'Brewery Workers Given Chance to Buy Shares', *Nationalist*, 25 Jan. 1965; *Daily Nation*, 23 Jan. 1965.
[60] In 1965, 4,000 out of 7,100 shareholders were African, according to the company: 'Brewery Workers Given Chance to Buy Shares', *Nationalist*, 25 Jan. 1965; by 1973 there were 14,500 Africans out of a total of 21,675 shareholders: *Daily Nation*, 24 Jan. 1973.
[61] The first African directors were Thuo and Muchura: Rodwell, *Sixty Years of Kenya Breweries*, 13.

1966, the minister for industry commended KBL on its role in Africanizing distributorships, but urged further steps in Africanization. The managing director cheerfully trumped him by announcing that an MP and a senior civil servant had just been appointed to directorships.[62] The relationship continued; notably in the person of Kenneth Matiba, whose rapid rise up the political hierarchy in the late 1970s was mirrored by an equally rapid ascent within KBL.[63]

Taxing beer:
revenue & the post-colonial state

We in Government are not blind to the achievements of very successful and progressive companies.[64]

All three East African states have faced chronic problems of revenue collection since independence, partly consequent on the reduction or abandonment of direct taxes on the bulk of the populace; in these circumstances, the bottled-beer industry became a revenue source of great importance. As beer production grew, excise on beer grew too, making up for the loss in earnings from customs duties on spirits which followed the fall in European and Asian populations from the early 1960s. In 1963, even little City Breweries paid £400,000 in various taxes to the Kenya government.[65] From the early 1970s, beer in all three East African countries was paying a sales tax, as well as excise; and when the breweries' contributions in terms of income tax and profits tax were included, they became very significant payers of tax.[66] Uganda Breweries alone claimed to have paid more than £2,500,000 in taxes in 1971, around 4 percent of total government revenues;[67] in 1978, it was claimed that KBL had paid £135,600,933 of tax to the Kenya government over the preceding five years, around 5 percent of the government's total revenues.[68] And excise, at least, was relatively easy to collect; whereas there was widespread evasion of other kinds of tax.

It was particularly important in Uganda and Tanzania, even though the breweries there were so very much less successful than those of Kenya, for Kenya's economy offered a far greater range of revenue sources. This was, indeed, one of the problems of the breweries: in both Uganda and Tanzania, taxes on bottled beer rose to extraordinary levels as the fiscal crises of the

---

[62] *Daily Nation*, 21 Jan. 1966.

[63] Rodwell, *Sixty Years of Kenya Breweries*, 19.

[64] From a speech made by the then vice-president of Kenya, Moi, praising KBL and criticizing other companies: 'Moi Warns Companies', *Daily Nation*, 25 Jan. 1973.

[65] *Daily Nation*, 21 Jan. 1964; total government revenue at the time was around £40 million.

[66] Keddie and Cleghorn, *Brewing in Developing Countries*, 101n.

[67] 'Shops Warned over New Beer Price', *Uganda Argus*, 9 Dec. 1971; total revenue was around £70 million.

[68] *Weekly Review*, 15 Dec. 1978.

state worsened: in the second Obote regime the excise on beer in Uganda was set at 250 percent of the ex-factory price; in the late 1980s beer excise in Tanzania rose from 240 percent to 250 percent.[69] While this tax burden was a heavy one, the state offered in return not simply a degree of protection, but a complete ban on imported beers. In Kenya this was secured through exchange control regulations, under which no money was allocated to anyone who wished to import beer;[70] in Tanzania imports of beer – including beer from Kenya – were simply forbidden.[71] The state gave the brewery a monopoly; the brewery in return provided revenue. In the first year after restrictions on imports were imposed, EABL's profits rose by more than 25 percent.[72] In both Kenya and Tanzania, the state also created a monopoly in the importation of other kinds of alcoholic beverage, giving this to companies partly or wholly owned by the state.[73]

EXCLUSIVE DRINKING

Only big men would go into bars. The low class wouldn't go in.[74]

Despite the success of the breweries, and despite the efforts of government to enforce controlled beer prices, bottled beer remained at best an occasional luxury for many people; 'only the rich people would take it'.[75] Access to drinking places was an even more important marker of social distinction.

In 1964, a party was held to bid farewell to the Polish envoy to Tanzania; attended by various ministers and the second vice-president, it was a gathering of the great and good of the new independent state; and it was held at the Dar es Salaam Club, erstwhile preserve of a colonial administrative elite.[76] The clubs and some of the hotels of East Africa provided a venue for a new, exclusive, pattern of post-colonial drinking.

There was a brief period of contest around access at the time of independence; in Kenya, some clubs sought briefly to maintain racial barriers, but such restrictions could not long survive.[77] In Tanganyika, access to hotels became an issue immediately after independence. Famously, the proprietor of the Palm Beach Hotel asked a group of Africans to leave his premises; because, he said, they were not buying drinks. The group included the mayor of Dar es Salaam and Bibi Titi Muhammad, chair of the party women's organization. The manager was promptly deported, and the access of the political elite to

---

[69] Maliyamkono and Bagachwa, *The Second Economy in Tanzania*, 45; Uganda Government, *Uganda, Economic Conditions, 1985* (Kampala, 1985).

[70] *Daily Nation*, 8 Jan. 1972, 18. Jan. 1973.

[71] 'Imported Beer Ban Won't Affect Market', *Standard, Tanzania*, 7 Jan. 1971.

[72] Up by £655,340 to £2,290,393: 'It's Beer Cheer as Sales Rocket', *Daily Nation*, 29 Oct. 1971.

[73] 'Kenya Wine Agencies Limited in Kenya; State Trading Corporation in Tanzania', *Daily Nation*, 19 Jan. 1971; 'Wine Dealers Wind Up Business', *Standard, Tanzania*, 3 Jan. 1969.

[74] Int Nyoro19b, 4.

[75] Int Nyoro31a, 3; for price controls, see 'New Warning on Beer Prices', *Standard, Tanzania*, 18 Jan. 1971.

[76] 'Farewell to Envoy', *Nationalist*, 5 Jan. 1964.

[77] *Daily Nation*, 3 Jan. 1962.

hotels was secured.[78] A similar case occurred shortly afterwards at the Travellers' Hotel in Korogwe.[79] African public opinion across East Africa celebrated these public triumphs over racial exclusivity.[80] Having stormed the ramparts, the elite re-erected them; when a member of parliament questioned the right of another top Dar es Salaam hotel to exclude drinkers who were not wearing ties, he was told that 'it would be a disgrace if people were allowed to walk into hotels wearing vests'.[81] In Uganda, a group of party 'Youth Wingers' forced a night club in Jinja to close, accusing its manager of 'neo-colonialism'; the vice-president quickly denounced their action and the club reopened.[82] Clubs – and the more expensive hotels – came to play an important role in elite networking across East Africa; these were places of meetings and deals, and mere membership of them gave access to power and authority. In Kampala, the increasingly exclusive character of the first Obote government was neatly represented by the shift of the drinking focus of the leaders of the party – away from the White Nile Club in Katwe to the Uganda Club. In provincial towns, bars played this same role as the social focus of a select group: 'in a bar you would find doctors, whites, people of high calibre: the locals wouldn't drink there'.[83]

POPULAR DRINKING, POPULAR CULTURE

> The whole trouble with all this knowledge, is that it ends up at the off-licence.[84]

Post-colonial drinking was not a simple story of the rise of a post-colonial elite which assumed the role and pretensions of colonial rulers; nor of a simple economic alliance between a new elite and capital. Drinking could also reveal the contradictions of power in the post-colonial state. The ways in which bottled beer – and wine and spirits – were consumed played an important role in creating a new set of assumptions about power over well-being, which centred on development, and the related idea of nation-building. Drink was, of course, by no means the only discursive arena in which this notion was evoked; popular and official rhetoric became suffused with the idea of development. But drink's peculiar ability to serve as a focus for evoking and remaking assumptions of power was apparent again. While the economics of bottled beer revealed the importance of access to the state, and the exclusive practice of elite drinking was an essential element of

[78] *Daily Nation*, 17 Jan. 1962.

[79] *Daily Nation*, 18 and 20 Jan. 1962.

[80] Letter, Matovu, *Uganda Argus*, 27 Jan. 1962.

[81] 'Questions in the House', *Standard, Tanzania*, 17 Jan. 1968: appropriately, the question was asked by a member called A. Maskini ('Pauper')

[82] *Uganda Argus*, 'Closure of Club Hailed', 14 Jan. 1965 and 'Jinja Action Deplored', 19 Jan. 1965.

[83] Int Nyoro25b, 3.

[84] Comment made by a shoeshine man, watching graduates walking past: 'Boozers Delight in Drive-in Beer Shops', *Daily Nation*, 30 Dec. 1983.

patrimonialism, discourse on beer consistently linked modernity, health and prosperity; and provided an idea of power which could be used to criticize exclusivism and patrimonialism.

From the 1960s, advertising suggests how much bottled beer was linked to wealth and the lifestyle and pursuits of modernity; advertisements showed beer and a radio, a group of African golfers quenching their thirst.[85] Beer became an iconic product, used by other advertisers: one advertisement showed a 'proud' suited man demonstrating the beer-chilling capacity of his new refrigerator; a beer bottle stood conspicuously on the table in front of a man modelling trousers which kept their crease.[86] Such advertisements captured a world of things as wealth, and of technology: a group of drinkers sipped beer at the airport, with jets on the runway behind them, ready to fly.[87] Beer and other formal-sector liquors were 'refined drinks that supersede local liquor', as one report put it: 'The beer drinkers are on the increase, and so is beer-brewing. It is a race for progress. It reflects an increase in the income of the people and hence their purchasing power'.[88]

There was a marked change in the content of advertising in the 1970s. Women moved into the background, and the emphasis on partying and evening dress disappeared. KBL ran a series of advertisements which showed men working, and stressed 'nation building'; thus KBL emphasized that their drink was part of a world in which leisure was distinct from work. 'Building a strong nation demands hard work. After work, nation builders relax with a Tusker . . . Our national beer.'[89] The breweries had already been careful to argue that their kind of drink was entirely compatible with development and hard work: 'most of the beer drunk in Kenya [is] consumed by people who normally drink in moderation in their own leisure hours', they argued, claiming that beer was 'scarcely ever the cause of drunkenness or impaired faculties'.[90] In the early 1970s KBL produced what was to be their most enduring slogan, which again emphasized the particular compatibility of modern work demands and bottled beer: 'Beer is Best – After Work'.

A popular practice of drinking developed in the 1970s which in many ways reflected this focus on the male wage-earner as the centre of nation-building: the hard-working, beer-drinking hero of the post-colonial state. Many of these male drinkers drank in bars, rather than exclusive clubs or hotels. When the bars were too expensive they took their business to unlicensed beer bars, wholesalers or off-licences, known in Kenya as *masandukuni*, or 'boxes', from the upturned crates from which men would drink while keeping a wary eye out for police raids.[91] This was the drinking

[85] *Daily Nation*, 18 Jan. 1964 and 30 Jan. 1973.
[86] *Uganda Argus*, 9 Jan. 1962.
[87] *Standard, Tanzania*, 11 Jan. 1967.
[88] *Standard, Tanzania*, 5 Jan. 1973.
[89] *Daily Nation*, 6 Jan. 1970.
[90] *Daily Nation*, 12 Jan. 1967.
[91] 'Boozers Delight in Drive-in Beer Shops', *Daily Nation*, 30 Dec. 1983; 'Dar Council Rounds up Unlicensed Beer Traders', *Standard, Tanzania*, 8 Jan. 1971.

culture of the urban household, in which daily drinking practice asserted a model of authority dependent not on age but on wage; a world in which women were wives or barmaids. '[B] eer has become the drink of the working man (with money).'[92] Such drinking evoked the financial power of men in the household of the nation-builder. Men drank because they had money; women might only drink through their relationship with men, and 'decent women don't drink in bars'.[93] In official rhetoric, beer drinking was associated with the power of development; in practice, beer drinking was associated with a culture characterized by what Stichter has called 'a good deal of husband dominance in financial decision-making'.[94]

SUBVERSIVE DISCOURSES OF DRINK

[T]hose who shout the loudest about socialism are the very ones who are seen spending most extravagantly in bars.[95]

This process could rebound on itself. Exclusivism could be attacked through talking drink. When a group of men were thrown out of Lindi Club, in Tanzania, where they had gone because this was the only place in town which had a sure supply of beer, they argued the injustice of this exclusion; and hinted at the wider injustices of society.[96] More widely, the drinking of bottled beer – and, even more, of imported spirits – became central elements in popular outbursts against the new inequalities of post-colonial society. The story of the drunken big man who, having caused a traffic accident, ignored the police and stood swigging White Horse whisky from the bottle, was a classic of this kind of criticism.[97] Particularly in Tanzania, the fondness of the elite for imported spirits attracted comment from those who saw their behaviour as wasteful, and who mocked the rhetoric of the elite.[98] More humble officials too could be criticized for drinking at work in ways which obstructed development: for those faced by a bureaucracy which constantly frustrated those who had no insider knowledge, complaints about officials who drank beer and spirits at work neatly deployed the power of development in a critique of corruption and the exclusive nature of the post-colonial state.[99] Observing a group of administrators in a bar, a Ugandan man commented 'They will drink five bottles [of beer] each and stay here till three o'clock [pm]... They will then go back to their offices, tell people who have been waiting for them all day that they can come back in

---

[92] 'We Don't Come Here to Drink...', *Daily Nation*, 14 Jan. 1971.

[93] 'We Don't Come Here to Drink...', *Daily Nation*, 14 Jan. 1971.

[94] S. Stichter, 'The Middle-class Family in Kenya: Changes in Gender Relationships', in S. Stichter and J. Parpart (eds.), *Patriarchy and Class. African Women in the Home and the Workforce* (Boulder, CO, 1988), 177-203.

[95] Letter, George Ntambaro, *Standard, Tanzania*, 29 Jan. 1968.

[96] Letter, *Standard, Tanzania*, 19 Jan. 1973.

[97] Letter, Ngurey, 'Are There Tanzanians Who Are Above the Law?', *Standard, Tanzania*, 3 Jan. 1973.

[98] Letter, Ngila, *Standard, Tanzania*, 7 Jan. 1971.

[99] Letter, Kazoka, *Daily News*, 4 Jan. 1973.

the morning, and go off and drink somewhere else.'[100] After the overthrow of Obote, Amin characterized the corruption and exclusivity of Obote's regime in terms of drinking practice: 'Obote's mode of living was also anything but socialist. He heavily indulged in drink, smoking and women . . . This idle living was conducted at public expense'; later Amin made sneering reference to the ministers who used to 'drink and dance' with Obote at the Uganda Club.[101]

Drinking could argue the dangers of modernity too. The beer-drinking male wage-earner idealized by the advertisements might also appear as the drunken spendthrift whose neglect of wife and children threatened the stability of society. So one member of parliament suggested, in a vivid criticism of what he called the '*madaraka* people', those who had assumed wealth and status since independence: 'Some people leave their offices at 4.30 pm, they do not go home, they go straight to the bars, drink until the bars close at 11 pm, they then move on to the night clubs, drink until 2 am, and the wives and children at home have not seen daddy.' [102]

And in popular literature, the cheaply produced English and Swahili novels of the 1960s and 1970s, bottled-beer and other formal-sector drinks represented all the dangers to health and morality posed by the modern world – and particularly by the city. Meja Mwangi's predatory urbanites, the moral anomie of Mangua's characters (which attracted fierce criticism from students who deprecated what they saw as an idealization of drunkenness) and the hopeless sot in Maillu's *My Dear Bottle* were all aspects of this; so too were the fallen country girls of novels like *Anasa*.[103] All asserted the moral dangers of a world where bottled beer, and everything else, was available to any who had money. In popular discourse too, drinking exclusivity could underline a cautionary tale about the arrogance of those who assumed their status:

> Let me give you an example, we had a boy here but he died 10-15 years ago. That was a learnt man to the university level and he had a bachelor degree in education . . . he got his degree and went to one of the bars in the trading centre to show people how he had completed his studies. They were also pleased, saying that of all those they have seen who have been to Makerere that this the first they have seen. But we are on the topic alcohol, he was chased from duty . . . with alcohol, one who does not know how to drink it becomes foolish and wasted. That boy was buried in a coat which was left by his late father, he didn't even have a bed sheet to wrap him in. The reverend who conducted the ceremony asked 'Do you want your son to be buried like this?' We told

---

[100] D. Hills, *The White Pumpkin* (London, 1975), 77.

[101] 'The Revolution', *Uganda Argus*, 28 Jan. 1971 and 'Miria Can Go to Dar', *Uganda Argus*, 18 Feb. 1971.

[102] *Kenya National Assembly Debates*, Shikuku, 23 Sep. 1971, col. 481.

[103] M. Mwangi, *Going Down River Road* (London, 1976); C. Mangua, *Tail in the Mouth* (Nairobi, 1972); D. Maillu, *My Dear Bottle* (Nairobi, 1973); King'ala, *Anasa*. For criticism of Mangua and Maillu, see 'Dangerous Literature', *Daily News*, 14 Nov. 1976.

him, 'Since that child went to school he isolated himself from us. He has stayed with people, they drink together.'[104]

The state encouraged beer-drinking, and the bar provided economic and social space for the patrimonialism of the state; but beer also offered ways to criticize patrimonialism, and to question in a more fundamental way the role of development as the basis for wealth and health.

BEER IN THE VILLAGE

Nowadays people are modernized; they demand beer.[105]

Popular discourse contrasted town and village, bottled beer and traditional liquor. But bottled beer did move increasingly into the rural world from the 1960s. It was drunk by the emissaries which the developmental state despatched to rural areas – notably teachers, whose drinking habits set them apart from the rest of the rural populace.[106] But bottled beer also made its way into other drinking spaces. Given to elder men at funerals or weddings, or to seek forgiveness, bottled beer moved into patterns of non-commercial exchange which asserted the social dominance of elder men.[107] It was a movement which in one sense showed how different conceptual categories of alcohol could be elided. Yet there was ambiguity in this. Only those who had money could afford to seek the goodwill of elder men in this way, so only some received such offerings. Bottled beer differentiated and implied a special and individual access to the new power of money; it set off those elder men who were able to demand it as 'modernized', and therefore of especial influence and status.

And for most people, the public rhetoric and advertising around beer was a constant reminder of their exclusion – of how far their lives were from the idealized world of the nation-building beer-drinker. In everyday drinking, and in the weddings and funerals of most people – especially in rural areas – most of the drink given and consumed was not bottled beer. Drinks made in the informal economy, traditional and not so traditional, continued to dominate ritual as well as social drinking.

---

[104] Int Nyoro36a, 3.
[105] Int Nyoro4b, 3.
[106] Like the teacher in Ngugi, *Petals of Blood*, 8.
[107] Int Nyoro4c, 2; Nyoro29b, 12; Talle, *Women at a Loss*, 132, fn. 155. For a similar movement of beer into ritual space, see Colson and Scudder, *For Prayer and Profit*, 61-4.

9.1 *Independence drinking: 1960s beer advertisement* (photo reproduced courtesy of East African Breweries Limited)

9.2 *Nation-building drinking: 1970s beer advertisement* (photo reproduced courtesy of East African Breweries Limited)

Ten

Traditional liquor & development
c. 1960–90

Too many beerhalls will tend to hamper development.[1]

In 1966, the mayor of Nairobi announced that the council was turning one of its drinking-places into a public library.[2] A year earlier, a sisal estate beerhall in Tanzania had been transformed into an adult education centre. Rededicating the building, the regional commissioner 'cautioned against excessive drinking and instead urged for hard work for the success of the Five-Year Plan'.[3] Other councils closed beerhalls too, to 'reduce drinking activity to a minimum'.[4] There was a self-conscious symbolism to these acts which reveals at once one important strand of discourse on traditional liquor in the post-colonial state: there was a simple choice to be made, between tradition on the one hand and education and development on the other. Beerhall closures also highlighted the contrast between official attitudes to bottled beer on the one hand and traditional liquor on the other: while the regional commissioner was issuing his strictures on the dangers of excessive drinking, a minister made an approving visit to the expansion works under way at TBL.[5] When officials of state and party talked of the dangers of 'selfishness, intrigue, indolence and drunkenness', they evidently meant the kind of drunkenness that 'traditional liquor' produced.[6] Breweries officials insisted that bottled beer was for 'relaxing with' rather than 'getting drunk';[7] and newspaper leaders solemnly agreed that with bottled beer 'the primary aim is the one of refreshing as opposed to any idea of over-indulgence'.[8] Across the region, while bottled beer became part of the 'race for progress', traditional liquor came to serve as the antithesis of development, its consumption the mark of modernity's recusants and its

---

[1]   Bomett, in *Kenya National Assembly Debates*, 21 Oct. 1971, col. 1514.
[2]   *Daily Nation*, 17 Jan. 1966.
[3]   'Pombe Shop Converted', *Nationalist*, 22 Jan. 1965.
[4]   *Daily Nation*, 2 Jan. 1964.
[5]   'Babu Visits Brewery', *Nationalist*, 21 Jan. 1965.
[6]   'Intrigue, Alcohol, Enemies of Nation', *Nationalist*, 5 Jan. 1965.
[7]   'Beer is to Relax With...', *Daily Nation*, 9 Jan. 1971.
[8]   'Over-drinking', *Daily Nation*, 25 Jan. 1971.

sale subject to constant bans. Against such liquor were ranged the state, capital, the educated and the young.

Yet there is another more complex story here, too: about the ambiguities of state power and the ambivalence of popular and official attitudes to modernity. Very many people continued to straddle the gap between drinking-party and bar. As economic and discursive resource, alcohol appeared in often contradictory roles, used to evoke quite different ideas of power. This chapter and the next explore these contradictions, and seek to show how the period from 1960 to 1990 saw traditional liquor simultaneously demonized as the enemy of development and entrenched in its social and economic importance.

BACKWARD & DRUNKEN

> All Pombe shops in Morogoro district will be closed on all days except Saturdays and Sundays . . . The resolution, which takes immediate effect, is intended to give people more time to concentrate on work in their shambas.[9]

During the 1960s and early 1970s, traditional drink served as an occasional focus for a particular concern of the elite of the post-colonial states: the perceived idleness of a largely rural populace which it was feared might not work hard enough to 'bring about development.'[10] It was necessary, as one correspondent suggested, for people to 'sacrifice pombe' to solve 'national problems'.[11] District officials in Tanzania banned sales on or during any 'working day'.[12] Traditional liquor stood for the unhygienic world of the village – 'not very clean, but then nothing is very clean in these parts'[13] – and for a rhythm of work and time which was no longer suitable: 'villagers do not have arrangements for development and often squander their money on drinking parties'.[14] Officials sought to remake that rhythm by controlling drink. In Kenya, there was the same perception that rural people were 'heavy drinkers and light workers', and that it was popular fondness for traditional liquor which was 'hampering development' by perpetuating inappropriate work rhythms.[15] 'It was shameful for people to be hanging around beerhalls all day instead of doing something of use.'[16] Drinking was a failure on the part of the populace: 'excessive drinking, laziness and lack of co-operation'

[9] 'Pombe Shop Ruling', *Nationalist*, 8 Jan. 1966.
[10] 'Nyerere Calls for Laws to Make People Work', *Standard, Tanzania*, 31 Jan. 1968.
[11] Letter, Sankey, *Nationalist*, 31 Jan. 1966.
[12] 'Korogwe Ban on Pombe Sales', *Standard, Tanzania*, 25 Jan. 1968.
[13] Mangua, *Tail in the Mouth*, 190.
[14] 'Arusha to Get 12 More Ujamaa Villages', *Standard, Tanzania*, 18 Jan. 1970.
[15] 'Tembo Tipplers Outlawed', *Daily Nation*, 23 Jan. 1963.
[16] 'Hard Work Needed', *Daily Nation*, 19 Jan. 1970; 'Drinking Hampers Progress', *Daily Nation*, 13 Jan. 1969.

with government were all linked:[17] 'unless the people reduced their drinking they would remain poor for ever'.[18] In Kenya, as in Tanzania, the sale of traditional liquor was subject to much more rigorous restriction than was bottled beer.[19]

Even the long-standing official perception that crime was linked to drinking was drawn into the discursive differentiation of good bottled beer and bad traditional liquor: when the PC Kisumu decided that a crime wave was the result of 'excessive and uncontrolled drinking', he restricted the sale of traditional liquor – not bottled beer.[20] The national press supported him, asserting that crime was the work of those who sought money 'to enable them to satisfy the crav[ing] for pombe.'[21] The idea that traditional liquor lay at the root of popular 'idleness' and criminality dominated public rhetoric; concerns over the hygiene of these drinks, the topic of late-colonial discourse, played a much less prominent role.[22]

Yet the official hostility was not complete, for there was considerable ambivalence towards tradition. Heirs to the late-colonial legacy of a headlong enthusiasm for change, and a belief that it was the fight against 'poverty, ignorance and disease' which bestowed legitimacy, the elite of the independent states was simultaneously much influenced by a contradictory cultural nationalism which celebrated – even as it reified and reinvented – the pre-colonial past.[23] Officials of the post-colonial period frowned on backwardness, but they feared even more the disorderly ambition of youth and the uncontrolled sexuality of women.[24] Hence the enthusiasm for – and anxieties about control over – party Youth Wings, or the Green Guards of Tanzania.[25] Debates over appropriate clothing revealed the uncertainties of states which, while committed to modernity, feared its challenges to an order based on age and gender. The Tanzanian state tried to force Maasai into trousers and women out of mini-skirts.[26] The same ambivalence tempered official hostility to traditional liquor. Some politicians evoked traditional drinking as a desirable element of patriarchal authority;[27] Obote was even willing to claim status as an elder man by being photographed drinking millet beer through a straw (seated rather decorously on an armchair, of course).[28] Sentencing a young woman in Nairobi to three months in prison

---

[17] 'Nyanza PC Appeals', *Daily Nation*, 1 Jan. 1971; 'GPT First, Drink Last, Says DC', *Daily Nation* 19 Jan. 1970.

[18] *Daily Nation*, 15 Jan. 1971.

[19] In Kajiado, for example, *pombe* hours were reduced to 12-2 pm each day: *Daily Nation*, 20 Jan. 1971.

[20] 'Pombe Sale Restricted in Nyanza', *Daily Nation*, 18 Jan. 1971.

[21] Leader, 'Over-drinking', *Daily Nation*, 25 Jan. 1971.

[22] 'We Don't Come Here to Drink', *Daily Nation*, 14 Jan. 1977.

[23] Leader, 'Thanks to Kenya Culture', *Daily Nation*, 10 Jan. 1972.

[24] *Daily Nation*, 5 Jan. 1966.

[25] 'Green Guards', *Standard, Tanzania*, 2 Jan. 1969; 'What is Youth Wing for?' *Daily Nation*, 18 Jan. 1964.

[26] 'Girl Denies Indecency Charges', *Standard, Tanzania*, 28 Jan. 1971; *Daily Nation*, 23 Jan. 1968.

[27] Shikuku, *Kenya National Assembly Debates*, 30 Sep. 1971, col. 708.

[28] *Uganda Argus*, 26 Jan. 1966.

for being drunk and disorderly, a Nairobi magistrate similarly evoked a model of traditional drinking and proper patriarchy: 'Do you know according to Kikuyu custom a girl of your age is not allowed to drink liquor?'.[29]

While official ambivalence towards tradition restrained hostility towards traditional liquor, the selling and drinking of traditional liquor actually grew, facilitated by another of the contradictions of the post-colonial state: its commitment to regulations intended to promote development was vitiated by the multiple tiers of patrimonialism which actually constituted the state in operation. The trade in liquor was too lucrative to be bound effectively by law.

Controlling traditional alcohol, 1960–78

Central government is very concerned about the way the [traditional] liquor licensing laws are being ignored.[30]

In 1961, City Breweries ran a large advertisement which lamented 'dangerous tendencies with regard to the brewing of pombe' and the consequent 'loss of government revenue by way of excise duty and income tax.'[31] In 1963 the Brewers' Association stepped up this campaign against the producers whom they viewed as their real competitors, those who made and sold fermented brews, by presenting to the government a set of statistics on the legal and illegal sale of African-made liquor which stressed the loss of revenue consequent on this untaxed production. They gave figures for only certain parts of the country, but they suggested an annual revenue loss of over £1.6 million – a significant amount, at a time when total annual revenue from all sources was around £35 million – and they suggested (with a suspicious pretence of precision) a total monthly sale of 1,327,983 gallons of traditional liquor in these areas alone.[32] That was more than twice the amount of bottled beer sold across the whole country.

Despite the rapid growth in bottled beer sales after 1960, traditional liquor continued to dominate across the region. In per head terms, consumption of bottled beer (and of wines and bottled spirits) remained modest – even in Kenya, where the bottled beer industry was most successful. In 1978, a rough survey put Kenyan traditional liquor consumption at the equivalent of 24.1 million litres of absolute alcohol per year; as against bottled beer, wine and spirits consumption equivalent of 9 million litres of absolute alcohol.[33] In Uganda and Tanzania, where the supply of formal-sector drinks was far less reliable, the preponderance of traditional liquor was probably even greater. People were well aware of the idea that traditional

29 '"Dirty Behaviour" Leads to Prison', *Daily Nation*, 21 Jan. 1975. The next day a man was sentenced to ten days (or 80 shillings fine) for the same offence: *Daily Nation*, 22 Jan. 1975.
30 Ag. PC RVP to all DCs, 15 Jan. 1965, KNA DC KAJ 4/8/2.
31 *Daily Nation*, 13 Jan. 1961.
32 Figures with Brewers' Association Memorandum, in DC KAJ 4/8/2.
33 Nout, 'Aspects of the Manufacture and Consumption', 29.

drinking was the practice of those who had failed in the modern world: 'it is mainly drunk by people who don't have jobs.... [and] by people not working in offices. Failing to get something to do he goes and drinks'.[34] But most people did not have waged jobs; and while there were those who drank only bottled beer, wines or spirits, asserting in a very public way their wealth and status, the expense of these heavily taxed drinks meant that a far larger

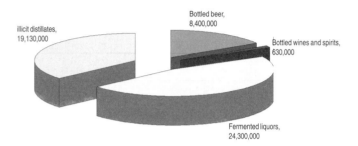

Figure 10.1 *Alcohol consumption in Kenya, 1978, in litres of absolute alcohol*

group of people would drink bottled beer – or bottled spirits – only on special occasions. One Ugandan man explained why he was going to the rural area for Christmas: 'When in the city you are tempted to drink costly beers, whereas in the village I can take malwa or any other local beer.'[35] Bottled beer and traditional liquor occupied distinct conceptual spaces, but the drinking population was not so clearly separated; people were aware that modernity demanded bottled beer, but they could not afford to support this ideal of drinking.

Demand of this magnitude supported a very active economy, which became an expanding area of local patronage politics. The formal licensing system continued to exist – indeed, it was elaborated – but immediately after independence local administrators, police and politicians all vied for the right to exercise patronage in this field, leading sometimes to open conflict. In 1964, '[p]olice were called in at one village where local councillors objected to attempts by chiefs to stop the casual sale of local beer'.[36] The contest is most clearly revealed by archival materials from Kenya. There, chiefs and district officers issued brewing permits which in theory permitted only the making of alcohol for customary purposes, but were widely understood to legalize sale.[37] In August 1963, for example, the chief at Ngong irked the police by issuing 37 such permits; some, rather improbably, for 'tea parties'.[38] Administrators higher up the hierarchy issued 'To Whom

[34] Int Nyoro23a, 3.

[35] 'Late Xmas Shopping Spree', *Uganda Argus*, 22 Dec. 1971.

[36] *Daily Nation*, 25 Jan. 1964.

[37] DO Loitokitok to Chiefs and Sub-chiefs, Kisonko, 20 Mar. 1965, KNA DC KAJ 4/8/2.

[38] Order, 9 May 1963 and Chiefs' and Sub-chiefs' meeting, 22 Aug. 1963, KNA DC NGO 1/18/30.

It May Concern' letters allowing individuals to sell liquor.[39] Councillors used their control of markets to open up space for their clients to sell liquor: 'There has been a tendency recently to grant more and more unnecessary beer clubs in the markets, the pressure usually being exerted by interested councillors.'[40] In Kenya, the constitutional uncertainty created by the brief experiment in federalism in 1964 heightened these conflicts, as police and administrators argued over control of traditional liquor licences.[41] In Uganda, the period immediately after independence saw a similar rush to authorize sales of traditional liquor, with calamitous results for local government revenues.[42] 'When we got independence, people made liquor freely', remembered one woman.[43]

By 1965, there was an attempt to reassert effective control of the sale of traditional liquor in Kenya, putting it in the hands of a local political and business elite in each district. In Kajiado, a new Liquor Licensing Board was constituted (distinct from the Licensing Court, which dealt with bottled beer and spirits) made up of the DC and four other men: 'a prominent businessman', 'an ex-Government school teacher and well-to-do rancher', a 'very influential Government chief' and the chairman of the local authority, which was now called Olkejuado County Council.[44] In Kenya, such district licensing boards ensured that traditional liquor was to be a space for private enterprise, not corporate provision: at the time of federalism in 1964, a policy of the exclusion of individual licences reminiscent of the late 1940s had been mentioned, but this was not pursued under the new constitution.[45] Indeed, the closure of estate and council beerhalls discussed at the beginning of this chapter may have different interpretations: while asserting a choice of education over inebriation, it also effectively opened up the sale of traditional liquor as a field of enterprise and patronage.

The boards were widely alleged to show considerable favouritism in the allocation of licences.[46] A woman who sought a licence thought it wise to submit with her application a letter from an assistant minister which pointed out that 'she is our Government and K[enya]A[frican]N[ational]U[nion] [the ruling party] supporter'. A man provided a letter from another powerful patron: 'I therefore as Chairman of KANU in District [*sic*] – though this is

[39] See the examples from DO Loitokitok and DO Ngong, 8 Oct. 1966 and 14 June 1967, KNA DC KAJ 4/8/2.
[40] Regional Govt Agent West Pokot to Civil Secretary, Rift Valley, 2 June 1964, KNA PC NKU 2/15/46.
[41] Regional Commissioner of Police to Civil Secretary, Rift Valley, 17 Dec. 1964 and Ag. PC to Provincial Police Officer, 28 Jan. 1965, KNA DC KAJ 4/8/2.
[42] Ministry for Regional Administration to Permanent Secretary, Ministry of Finance, Bunyoro Kingdom Government, 23 Oct. 1963, HDA FIN 4/64.
[43] Int Nyoro27b, 2.
[44] DC Kajiado to PC Rift Valley, 30 Sep. 1965, KNA DC KAJ 4/8/2.
[45] Ag. Civil Secretary, Rift Valley to Crown Counsel, 17 Mar. 1964, KNA PC NKU 2/15/46.
[46] *Kenya National Assembly Debates*, Kariuki, 23 Sep. 1971, cols. 456 and 459; Shikuku, 23 Sep. 1971, col. 477.

not political – would like to recommend him very strongly for a Native Beer [licence]'.[47] A man wishing to transfer his licence thought it useful to remind the board that 'I am a Government man, that is I am chair of Oloolaiser Local Council; Chairman of KANU; Chairman of Masai Stock Farmers; and Chairman of the Wheat Keekonyokie Farmers Co-operative Society'.[48] In 1967 the Kajiado board issued a licence to a chief, despite police protests that as a chief (and therefore not permitted to engage in private enterprise) he was ineligible, and had a previous conviction for illegal possession of traditional liquor.[49]

The police were on rather weak ground here, for they were complicit in the development of an extra-legal system of patronage which spread alongside the legal system managed by the licensing board. Keboi, tenant of the Kajiado beerhall, and other licensed sellers complained that their sales were reduced by the prevalence of unlicensed brewing, one focus for which was the police canteen in Kajiado town.[50] Chiefs as well as police were involved in this, through the established practice of issuing brewing permits for 'entertaining', dates and names on which were frequently changed to allow their reuse.[51] One Maasai woman who sold liquor at this time remembered that 'the chiefs helped us not to be caught'.[52] Such tolerance might reflect a pragmatic approach to the problems of exerting authority, rather than simple venality. Chiefs in Bunyoro, who did have the power to issue permits to brew and sell in return for a fee, actually took a similarly lenient approach to unlicensed brewing, to 'create friendship and good working relations',[53] and collection of permit revenue was lax indeed.[54] Similar tolerance seems to have prevailed elsewhere in Uganda, in parts of which the sale of traditional liquor was the second-largest source of income for men, after wages, in the 1960s.[55] The growth of unlicensed sale reflected the limitations of state power, as well as the workings of state patronage.

The legal restrictions on the issue of licences to women had all been removed by the time of independence, but evidence – fragmentary as it is – strongly suggests that the system of license issue favoured men.[56] Often,

---

[47] ?, Assistant Minister to DC Kajiado, 23 Oct. 1967 and Oloitiptip, Assistant Minister to Chair Liquor Licensing Board, 19 June 1968, KNA DC KAJ 4/25/2.

[48] Pulei to Oloolaiser Local Council and DC, 19 May 1967, KNA DC KAJ 4/8/2. He was also a relative of the chief.

[49] Officer Commanding Police Division, Kajiado to Chair, Liquor Licensing Board, 4 and 30 Dec. 1967, KNA DC KAJ 4/25/2.

[50] Keboi to Clerk, Olkejuado County Council, 12 May 1965; Kaurrai to DC Kajiado, 12 Sep. 1966, KNA DC KAJ 4/8/2.

[51] Chief Risa to OiC, Kajiado Police, 20 Sep. 1968; see also the copies of permits issued for 1967-9, KNA DC KAJ 4/23/9; Mrs Mary Nkogato to DC Kajiado, nd 1965, KNA DC KAJ 4/8/2.

[52] Int Maa15a, 1.

[53] Int Nyoro25b, 5.

[54] Financial Report for 1966, HDA FIN 28/2.

[55] J. Vincent, *African Elite. The Big Men of a Small Town* (London/New York, 1971), 204; Heald, *Controlling Anger*, 87.

[56] For Kampala, for example, see Obbo, *African Women*, 129-30.

these were men with some current or former role in local administration: a chief, a magistrate, a retired policeman.[57] This was a quite vast field of enterprise, though it is difficult to quantify. In Kenya, there were by 1978 more than 10,000 licensees selling traditional liquor; between 1963 and 1978 the number of licences in Central Province had grown from 317 to 2,072; at the coast from 50 to 467.[58] Mombasa town was the sole exception to this burgeoning of licences; there the municipality retained its primary role (if not a complete monopoly) in the sale of traditional liquor into the 1970s, despite political pressure from aspirant licensees.[59] Clearly, traditional beer licences were sought after; yet the prevalence of unlicensed sale meant that these were never a route to financial success in the way that bottled beer retailerships and distributorships could be. Petty patrimonialism and the realities of local administration undermined a policy of regulation and restriction.

FORMALIZATION: TAX & CHIBUKU

> Chibuku, your favourite traditional beer, is prepared from the best Tanzanian cereals in the most modern machinery and processes for very strict hygiene conditions to give you the promise of absolute purity.[60]

In Tanzania, an attempt was made to formalize and regulate the trade in traditional liquor in a more thorough way, building on practice in southern Africa, where the production of traditional grain beer had been undertaken on an industrial scale by large capitalist concerns.[61] Lonrho, the multinational company with extensive mining and other interests in Africa, had become involved in several such ventures, and in 1966 Lonrho went into partnership with Dar es Salaam City Council to found Darbrew, a company which was to produce a grain beer called Chibuku (a brand name drawn from Lonrho's Zambian operation) which was to be sold in a refurbished city council 'beer garden.'[62] The marketing of Chibuku played on the same themes as bottled beer: hygiene and modernity. 'Chibuku for Strength and Happiness' ran the text which accompanied a picture of well-dressed men and women enjoying the comfortable furniture of the beer garden.[63] Chibuku sales got off to a rather unsteady start, but by the 1980s they had

---

57 Ints Nyoro8c, 1; Nyoro12b, 2; Nya32b, 3-5.
58 Comparing the figures in the Brewers' Association circular with those given in Nout, 'Aspects of the Manufacture and Consumption', 26.
59 *Daily Nation*, 24 Jan. 1963 and 15 Jan. 1965; *Kenya National Assembly Debates*, Jahazi, 21 Oct. 1971, col. 1519.
60 Advertisement, *Daily News*, 3 Feb. 1977.
61 M. Rogerson and B. Tucker, 'Multinational Corporations, the State and Indigenous Beer Production in Central Africa', in C. Dixon *et al.* (eds.), *Multinational Corporations and the Third World* (London, 1986), 137-58.
62 The council held two-thirds of the equity and Lonrho one-third, and by 1969 Lonrho was considering a similar scheme in Tanga: 'Chibuku Firm Planned for Tanga', *Standard, Tanzania*, 4 Jan. 1969.
63 Advertisment, *Daily News*, 12 Jan. 1973.

settled down to just over 1 million litres a month, and they remained stagnant at this level thereafter.[64] Chibuku was not cheap enough to significantly undersell the unlicensed producers of palm wine and grain beer in Dar es Salaam; and here, as elsewhere, such unlicensed production was made possible by the myriad patronage relationships that developed around state power.

In Kenya, the government tried to turn traditional liquor into a source of revenue for central, rather than local government, partly in the context of debates over the desirability of doing away with direct taxes on the general populace, which were deeply unpopular and the collection of which proved extremely difficult.[65] In 1971 a new Traditional Liquor Act was passed, which sought to encourage the emergence of a small number of large sellers of such liquor. A licence fee of 1,000 shillings was introduced for anyone who wished to produce for sale, with a sliding scale of tax according to production – in effect an excise duty – on larger producers. According to the finance minister, the raising of revenue was 'the express purpose' of this act.[66] The act allowed small-scale producers to supply their brew to larger producers, who were allowed to retail; but made no provision for direct retailing by small-scale producers. The debates and misapprehensions which swirled around this legislation were as revealing as the terms of the act itself. Some politicians used this opportunity to condemn the elitism of those who consumed only imported liquor, and a few urged that the new law would put an impossible burden on small-scale producers who had no other way of making a living.[67] They turned the rhetoric of development to the defence of those who sold traditional liquor, arguing that such sales paid for the education of children.[68] Such criticisms had no effect on the legislation, which was passed with only minor amendments. Meanwhile, slightly confused press reports and the statements of some politicians had spread the impression that the legislation ended all restrictions on small-scale production and sale of informal-sector alcohol.[69] After a period of evident uncertainty over what the law actually said, the AG issued a statement reminding police and public that there were still legal restrictions on production of alcohol for sale, and that these would be enforced.[70] Meanwhile, some enterprising local administrators had begun to collect the new scales of licensing fees before they had the legal authority to do so.[71]

[64] Sales fell from 780,000 litres in the month of May 1969 to 570,000 litres in December 1970; *Standard, Tanzania*, 7 Jan. 1971, but within a few months they had improved: figures for later 1970s-1990s from *Statistical Abstracts* and Brian Davey, pers. comm.

[65] *Kenya National Assembly Debates*, Mwamzandi, 23 Sep. 1971, col. 448.

[66] *Kenya National Assembly Debates*, Kibaki, 14 Oct. 1971, col. 1302.

[67] *Kenya National Assembly Debates*, Mwamzandi and Wachira, 23 Sep. 1971, cols. 449-50.

[68] *Kenya National Assembly Debates*, Onyulo, 23 Sep. 1971, col. 461 and Marete, 21 Oct. 1971, col. 1511.

[69] 'Judgment Later in Liquor Case', and 'Repeal of Act Does Not Allow Illegal Brewing', *Daily Nation*, 12 and 24 Jan. 1972.

[70] 'Warning on Illegal Brewing', *Daily Nation*, 25 Jan. 1972.

[71] Cherono, *Kenya National Assembly Debates*, 23 Sep. 1971, col. 446.

The enforcement of this law was vitiated by the same factors which had affected the previous licensing system, and over the next few years the production of traditional liquor saw no significant concentration or enlargement of scale. In 1974 an industrial producer did start to manufacture a grain beer called Kibuku, but this proved even less successful than its Tanzanian counterpart.[72] Agents of the state undermined the agenda of the developmental state: from Cabinet ministers who owned rural clubs, to councillors who secured licences for their friends, to policemen who had sex with brewers instead of charging them. The vast bulk of production continued to be small-scale; in Kenya and Tanzania, state schemes for turning traditional liquor into a hygienic source of revenue were undermined by the state's role as a vast and complex patronage structure.

The informal economy of alcohol

. . . as we got into the 1970s, 1980s and 1990s the original logic of traditional liquor laws was lost, and the only logic left now was to make money for the chiefs and the assistant chiefs . . . This goes on to improve the personal economy of the chief. So the liquor laws continued merely as a pretext for obtaining bribes . . .[73]

The licensed sale of traditional liquor moved into the hands of men who had access to the formal machinery of licensing: friends and clients of the district administration in Kenya, and of local government in Tanzania and Uganda. The best connected dealt in bottled beer, but those who had licences and had the support of the administration in suppressing competition could earn handsomely from traditional liquor. In the 1960s *pombe* shops were among the 'best business enterprises in Meru',[74] and the sale of banana wine was one of the more common commercial enterprises of prosperous male farmers in Buganda in the late 1960s.[75] In the 1970s Omori found that the three men who owned bars in the trade centre which he studied, one of whom was a teacher, were among the wealthiest men in the area, and invested their profits in cattle, other businesses and land.[76] Women too earned from licensed sale, though on a lesser scale: in Rungwe, where women sold their beer through men who owned and ran clubs, the sale of beer was in the mid-1960s the principal source of cash for women who found money ever more necessary for daily existence.[77]

[72] Nout, 'Aspects of the Manufacture and Consumption', 12.
[73] Murungi, *Kenya National Assembly Debates*, 7 Oct. 1998, p. 1594.
[74] Puritt, 'Meru of Tanzania', 40.
[75] A. Richards, F. Sturrock and J. Forth, *Subsistence to Commercial Farming in Present-day Buganda* (Cambridge, 1973), 139-40, though this book merely mentions the activity, without discussing it.
[76] M. Omori, 'Social and Economic Utility of Omurmaba, the Chiga Sorghum Beer', *Senri Ethnological Studies*, 1 (1978), 89-104.
[77] H. Luning, *A Farm Economic Survey in Rungwe District* (Leiden, 1969), 33-4, 42-9, 74, 87.

It's due to the search for money. For now, money is available, that's why they buy and sell [traditional liquor]. And a long time ago they didn't know about money usage – there was only eating and dressing – different from now – they seriously need money to eat, to drink tea, to buy soap.[78]

The unlicensed sale of locally-made drink drew in a more diverse range of entrepreneurs. This was a large market indeed, though up to the late 1970s the legal market may have been larger, as Nout suggests of Kenya.[79] In 1970, Hake estimated that 8,000 of the 44,000 jobs in Nairobi's 'self-help city' were in brewing, and emphasized the extent of police corruption which allowed this.[80] A number of studies have emphasized the role of women in this illicit trade. Obbo's account of a Kampala suburb in the early 1970s suggested that the female dominance recorded by Southall and Gutkind 15 years before had not lessened. For women the production and sale of alcohol were the most active area of enterprise, and like the entrepreneurs of the 1950s those of the 1970s operated in a marginal area – not actually legal, but claiming a right to sell through association with (often male) licence holders.[81] In 1974 Nelson found 75 percent of women sampled in her field site in Nairobi were brewing for sale.[82]

Many rural women too made and sold drink illicitly; certainly many Nyoro women did so, and an increasing number of Maasai women – particularly those who were near to a trading centre of any size;[83] so too did many Nandi women, in western Kenya, where 'the beer industry seems to be the one profitable cash venture that was primarily controlled by women'.[84] More Nyoro women moved on from selling grain beer to selling banana wine, trodden by hired male labour from bananas which the women grew themselves.[85]

But illicit sale was not solely an area for female entrepreneurship, nor was it solely the refuge of the marginal. In eastern Uganda in the late 1960s, men who were prominent in their local communities sold – without licence – the beer their wives made, and kept the money for their own use.[86] In 1970 a Kenyan police inspector who was on extended leave found himself in court for running an unlicensed *pombe*-selling operation which had been going for eight months, evidently on a considerable scale.[87] Presumably

[78] Int Nya18a, 3.
[79] Nout, 'Aspects of the Manufacture and Consumption', 26-7, put the market for illicit fermented liquor at half the size of the legal market for fermented liquor (and therefore, at about the same size as the bottled-beer market).
[80] A. Hake, *African Metropolis. Nairobi's Self-help City* (London/Toronto, 1977), 115, 158, 184, 195.
[81] Obbo, *African Women*, 128-30; A. Southall and P. Gutkind, *Townsmen in the Making. Kampala and Its Suburbs* (Kampala, 1957), 60-1.
[82] Nelson, '"Women Must Help Each Other"', 80. Studies elsewhere in Africa have revealed a similarly important economic role for alcohol: see for example D. Curtis, 'Cash Brewing in a Rural Economy', *Botswana Notes and Records*, 5 (1973), 17-25.
[83] Int Nyoro5b, 4; Nyoro11b, 4, 6; Nyoro36b, 5; Maa21a, 1; Maa32b, 1.
[84] Oboler, *Women, Power and Economic Change*, 173.
[85] Int Nyoro12b, 2-3.
[86] Vincent, *African Elite*, 206.
[87] 'No Liquor Licence Man Fined', *Daily Nation*, 5 Jan. 1970.

the man had previously been protected from prosecution by his colleagues, and one can only speculate as to the circumstances which led to his downfall. Others enjoyed more enduring protection. In the 1980s events in Eldoret threw a bizarre and humorous light on the workings of patronage in illicit production: some wandering pigs came across a cache of concealed illicit liquor; having consumed it they careered drunkenly through the town. The chairman of the local branch of the ruling party called for police action – not against the illicit brewers, but against the owner of the destructive pigs.[88] Less well-connected men also sold illicitly. A man who worked as a chief in Hoima district in the late 1960s recalled that it was mostly men who made and sold banana wine without authority.[89] In Uganda the political and economic breakdown of the late 1970s led even some of the wage-earning employees of the state to turn to making and selling liquor to survive:

> I made liquor in the year of '79, during Amin's war. We spent most of the time making it. Because office work had stopped . . . They [buyers] would find us at home. We wouldn't walk on the roads, those were for soldiers at that time . . . offices had closed, the District Commissioner had fled, now who would demand a licence?[90]

Some clearly earned well from this, especially those whose connections with the state allowed them to escape paying any licence fees, and ensured the suppression of local competition. But for others, the profitability of this trade was profoundly compromised by official harassment. Corruption and favouritism allowed illicit manufacture and sale to exist, but they ensured the marginality of most of those involved, for they were in constant danger of arrest and fines if they fell out with their patrons, or when new policemen and administrators were posted to their area. A sudden crackdown could land dozens in court on a single day.[91] Urban women brewers were among those rounded up by a Tanzanian state that sought to expel from cities all who did not have recognized 'work'.[92] Magistrates sometimes dealt leniently with those charged,[93] perhaps persuaded by a popular rhetoric which insisted that sellers were pursuing an entirely developmental agenda: 'The villagers, men and women, were getting money from it [traditional liquor] for paying school fees for their children'; 'We have been able to send the children to school because of that money'.[94] But not all escaped so lightly: in 1969, 16,066 Kenyans were sentenced to periods of detention for liquor offences – almost half of the total number of detentions, and far above the figures for the colonial period.[95] Bribes, theft and unpaid debts were a

---

[88] 'Pig Owners May Be Prosecuted', *Daily Nation*, 1 Sep. 1989.

[89] Int Nyoro8c, 4.

[90] Int Nyoro25b, 5.

[91] 'A Spate of Fines', *Daily Nation*, 23 Jan. 1968.

[92] 'Loiterers Kicked out of Mbeya', *Nationalist*, 13 Jan. 1966; 'Dar Police Round Up Suspects', *Daily News*, 11 Jan. 1973.

[93] Some of the fines imposed in the late 1960s were lower than those inflicted by colonial courts in the 1950s: compare the 30 shillings fines mentioned in 'A Spate of Fines', *Daily Nation*, 23 Jan. 1968 with those recorded in the case register of Ngong court, KNA DC NGO 1/6/36.

[94] Ints Nya42a, 4; Nyoro24a, 2.

[95] Hake, *African Metropolis*, 205.

constant drain on the returns of those involved in the trade. Far from ensuring autonomy, liquor sale could reveal very starkly women's vulnerability to the state and their reliance on men as mediators of the contacts with state and money:

> We were caught one day, and it was not even mine [the liquor]. The calabash was found in the bush there, we were asked to name the owner, then we kept quiet. So we kept quiet, all of us. We slept in jail for one day, then the man came and released us, they charged an amount of money, they took 100/- per woman.[96]

Even women like those in Rungwe, whose beer was largely sold in licensed clubs, found that their inferior access to agencies of the state could make them vulnerable. There was a requirement for a brewing permit, under council by-laws; this and the occasional imposition of blanket bans on brewing meant that women were often technically in breach of the law, and had little recourse when the men to whom they supplied liquor for sale at the clubs simply refused to pay them. '[T]hey cheat you, and if you question them they give you a slap there and then.'[97] Men might point to women's beer sales as a source of female economic independence: 'A woman makes her beer to take to the club and get money. They do not belong to me [the husband], no!'[98] – but women had much less control over beer earnings than this suggests.

All this evidences the importance of alcohol in the informal economy; and offers a reminder that the informal economy was not an area of untrammeled free enterprise. It was full of relationships of hierarchy and dependence, many of which led back to the coercive and material resources of the state. The informal economy of liquor sale was an area of entrepreneurship for women and men who sought the means to live; but it was also a product of the way that the operation of the patrimonial state undercut attempts at regulation and formalization, and subverted the formal agenda of development.

Beyond the problems of debt, fines and extortion, another difficulty faced brewers: overproduction. In both urban and rural areas, many women and men were pushed to the sale of locally-made liquor by immediate circumstance or chronic poverty: 'One can have a crop failure on his farm, he will then make traditional liquor for people to come there and exchange farm produce for the liquor'; 'We make beer because of poverty'.[99] Widespread recourse to this technique meant that there was often an oversupply; as always, the extreme perishability of fermented drinks undermined the profitability of selling them: 'there was no profit in it, so many people had begun to make it'.[100] Such local oversupply could combine

---

[96] Int Maa21b, 1.
[97] Int Nya23b, 3.
[98] Int Nya27a, 2.
[99] *Kenya National Assembly Debates*, Osogo, 30 Sep. 1971, col. 715; Int Nya38b, 2.
[100] Int Maa21a, 2.

with legal difficulties to make the selling of illicit drink a marginal pursuit. Many women – and some young men – sought to improve their position not by selling drink, but by shunning it.

Tea-drinking progress

> We have lived a religious kind of life, there has been no misunderstanding, no quarrelling, no drinking alcohol.[101]

In 1949, the opening session of the first Rungwe council meeting had been celebrated in tea.[102] Tea, like bottled beer, was a symbolic consumption item of modernity, but it offered a quite different view of the demands of modernity and the responsibilities which power imposed. Tea had been an important element in the spiritual pharmacopeia of Christian evangelists – especially Protestants – and an index of respectability in the eyes of many administrators: advertising had associated tea with the lifestyle of African accumulators while beer had still been legally denied to them.[103] In 1946, one tea advertisement showed a man returning home in military uniform to be greeted by his wife and child: 'He has returned from work; let him have a cup of tea.'[104] After the Second World War, the social welfare centres which sprouted across Tanganyika had been seen as places for lectures, informed discussion – and tea-drinking.[105] An observer in Kenya in the 1950s had commented approvingly on the tea-drinking facilities enjoyed by the African elite of Mombasa, facilities subsidized, incidentally, from the profits of the beerhall where the rest of the African populace drank.[106] The consistent willingness of hostile Europeans to question the sobriety of African politicians presumably encouraged an overt preference for non-intoxicating drinks:[107] Kenyatta and his supporters publicly celebrated his election to Legislative Council in 1962 with another sober beverage of modernity – 'ice-cold Coca-Cola';[108] and – at least in their retrospective accounts – the emerging political elite preferred to stress the tea-kiosk, rather than the bar, as the central political rendezvous.[109]

After independence, this notion of tea-drinking propriety remained the essence of modernity for some. Alcohol, they argued, was more than unhygienic, or a cause of laziness – it was the root cause of evil at a personal

---

[101] Int Nyoro10a, 6.
[102] TNA 157 L5 5/1.
[103] See the advertisements in *Mambo Leo*, Apr., May 1946.
[104] *Mambo Leo*, Sep. 1946.
[105] See the photograph in *Mambo Leo*, July 1947. There was prolonged debate amongst European officials as to whether either beer or traditional liquor should be available in social welfare centres, and opinion was largely against this: see the contents of TNA 18/26/13; also Chairman, Christian Council of Kenya to CNC, 3 Jan. 1947, KNA MAA 2/5/165.
[106] Macmillan, *Introducing East Africa*, 168.
[107] Ag. PC Rift Valley to Secretary for Defence, 14 Sep. 1954, KNA MAA 2/5/212.
[108] *Daily Nation*, 13 Jan. 1962.
[109] E. Atieno-Odhiambo, 'The Formative Years, 1945-63', in B. Ogot and W. Ochieng' (eds.), *Decolonization and Independence in Kenya, 1940-1993* (London/Nairobi/Athens, OH, 1993), 25-47.

level. Members of Protestant churches, in particular, argued that alcohol was the path to demonic possession; and such churches, in the post-colonial period, came to claim a larger and larger proportion of the population. From the 1970s the activities of international evangelists, who derived much of their funding from the United States and who were mostly very hostile to alcohol, used their distinctive rhetoric of personal struggles with evil to encourage the notion that alcohol was a tool of the devil, who 'wants to be praised, so he creates problems'.[110] Alcohol of all kinds was banned from the weddings and funerals of these tea-drinkers.[111] Islam too continued to spread – in Tanzania and Uganda, in particular – and while many individual Muslims paid no routine regard to the prohibition on alcohol, this issue tended to come to the fore from the mid-1970s in active campaigns of Islamic proselytization, supported by money from the Middle East, so that Muslims, like evangelical Christians, tried to substitute tea for beer in ritual practice.[112]

Such tea-drinking modernity lent authority to some, for it gave them some access to the power of the state. The courts and the institutions of monotheistic religion and of the state – the *baraza* or public meeting, elected public bodies, the ruling political party, women's organizations – could offer sources of power to women and younger men, allowing them ways to argue their claims to wealth through evoking the developmental rhetoric of the state: as men are only too willing too assert: 'For now we are under the women. We are following the law of the government, that is why it has changed.'[113] For many women, assertion of such rights against the overwhelmingly male face of local authority might be difficult; and magistrates might tell women who came to court that they should use 'customary machinery' to settle disputes.[114] But for those who expressed in signal fashion their commitment to the ideal of development and modernity, access to the law might be easier. Debates over drink provided a basic way to express such commitment; drinking traditional liquor – and especially, drinking it to excess – was a sure way to earn the disapproval of officials at any level; shunning it, by contrast, commanded respect and could serve as the basis for an assault on elder men's drinking authority. Traditional liquor 'has hindered our progress', declared one literate rural man; and women denounced '[m]en who indulge in heavy drinking while women are raising funds for Harambee [self-help] projects'.[115] Drinking traditional liquor came to be a very visible acknowledgement of the continued power of elder men to affect the well-being of others; refusing such liquor made an equally visible refutation of that power, and a way of challenging the immediate authority of men by calling directly on the institutions of state power. Individual elder men might make similarly public gestures in refutation of the collective

[110] Int Maa32a, 2.
[111] Ints Nyoro22b, 3; Maa20b, 2; Nya41b, 3.
[112] Whyte, *Questioning Misfortune*, 94.
[113] Int Nya27a, 2.
[114] *Daily Nation*, 14 Jan. 1970.
[115] Letter, Kiiyuru, *Daily Nation*, 5 Jan. 1968; 'Women on Heavy Drinking', *Daily Nation*, 11 Jan. 1973.

drinking power of their elders: one attracted an approving official audience when he burned his drinking horn and shouted 'Take back your things, Mr Satan!'[116]

Drinkers and non-drinkers existed in profound tension; embodying some of the contradictions of post-colonial states which were committed to nation-building and development, yet consisting of complex hierarchies of patronage which encouraged division and nepotism and denied the majority any access to the state and the material rewards of development. In the 1970s, the complex evocations of power wrapped up in drinking discourse and practice encouraged a political rhetoric – and a popular climate – which led to even more restrictive policies on traditional liquor, most notably in Kenya, but in Tanzania and (briefly) Uganda too.

Banning the clubs

> Hundreds of Ngong residents yesterday said that they did not need beerhalls. [The DC] told them a nation of drunkards has no time for development.[117]

In Kenya, the later 1970s saw regular expressions of concern over the problem of backward rural drinkers: 'hardly any sign of development is seen in the village'.[118] The issue came to a head on the accession to power of Daniel arap Moi, after the death of the first president, Jomo Kenyatta, in 1978. Moi immediately launched a great campaign in support of a kind of national renewal, in which denunciations of drunkenness and avowals of support for the family played a major part.[119] Moi was a member of a non-conformist church, one of the tea-drinkers of the post-colonial world. His first pronouncements against drunkenness were unspecific, and served in effect as a criticism of beer-drinking as much as of traditional liquor: this rhetoric could be read as an assault on the corrupt networks of the state, and illustrated how unstable the apparent alliance between state and breweries might be. But Kenya Breweries, and many officials, insisted that the problem lay not in bars, but in beerhalls, where 'many people were idle all day long'. Responsible as ever, the chairman of KBL 'urged wananchi [citizens] not to engage in excessive drinking at the expense of nation building'.[120]

Soon the focus of the public campaign was on traditional liquor, not bottled beer or spirits. Moi directed that local people should be allowed to choose whether or not the legal sale of such liquor should be allowed to continue. In early 1979, often in emotive scenes at packed public meetings,

---

[116] 'Drama as Mzee Quits Drinking', *Daily Nation*, 18 Oct. 1989.

[117] 'Ban All Beer Halls', *Daily Nation*, 3 Jan. 1979.

[118] See for example, 'The Government should step in to stop excessive drinking', *Daily Nation*, 14 Mar. 1978.

[119] 'Populist Themes', *Weekly Review*, 12 Jan. 1979.

[120] 'Clampdown on Beerhalls', *Weekly Review*, 23 Feb. 1979; 'Easy on the Bottle, Says Beer Boss', *Daily Nation*, 16 Jan. 1979.

people across Kenya chose to close all traditional liquor clubs. 'Wananchi told District Commissioner J. Etemesi that beerhalls, which hindered development in the area in the past, must give way for development.'[121]

Again and again in these meetings, people expressed the opinion that 'those who spend their time drinking [*busaa*] are enemies of development' and that traditional liquor was the enemy of development and of 'the family', the social unit through which development must come.[122] 'Speakers noted that many people spent all their money and time in *busaa* clubs. Consequently they were unable to send their children to school and could not feed and clothe their families.'[123] Bottled beer was the drink of the modern male bread-winner; *busaa* was the drink of his antithesis, whose economic failure endangered the family. In Kajiado, the county council decided to close down its own beerhall, which had run on, in an increasingly dilapidated state, since Keboi's departure.[124] Like a number of other councils at the time, they returned to the theme of the early 1960s, and decided to turn the beerhall into an adult education centre – reminding everyone that the choice was between education and traditional drink.[125] In 1980 an amending act was passed which required the approval of a public meeting before any licence might be issued to sell traditional liquor in Kenya, and over the following years, public rhetoric reverted to the idea of traditional liquor as the cause of the failure of people to participate in development.[126] When debate turned to the drinking of bottled beer, Kenya Breweries again argued that their product was not intended to make people drunk: indeed, the managing director offered the surprising revelation that he himself was a teetotaller, and insisted that his company would not advise anyone to drink more than two bottles of beer in a day.[127]

In Uganda, an intensification of rhetoric on the subject of traditional liquor had been apparent in the early years of Amin's rule. Restrictions were placed on hours of drinking and denunciations made of those rural people whose 'laziness' threatened ambitious plans for doubled production.[128] In Hoima a 'Committee on Drunkenness' was created, which sought to control 'excessive drinking', but made it clear that this was not a problem of the elite of bottled-beer consumers: bars, it reported 'reflect business and economic growth' and should not be interfered with.[129] Drunkenness was a problem of rural drinkers of traditional drink, not of elite consumers of bottled beer: while the campaign against drinking during working time was in full swing, a newspaper photograph of officials enjoying a meal during a

---

[121] 'Council to Close All Beerhalls', *Daily Nation*, 4 Jan. 1979.
[122] 'Cut Down on Drink, Says DC'; 'Liquor Clubs to be Closed'; 'Liquor Boards build Beer Blockade', *Daily Nation*, 6 Dec. 1978, 7 Dec. 1978 and 15 Jan. 1979.
[123] 'All Nandi Busaa Clubs Closed Down', *Daily Nation*, 5 Jan. 1979.
[124] 'Pombe Halls', *Daily Nation*, 16 Jan. 1979.
[125] 'Populist Theme', *Weekly Review*, 12 Jan. 1979
[126] 'Arrest Brewers – DO', *Daily Nation*, 2 Jan. 1984.
[127] 'Banning of Off-licences', *Daily Nation*, 9 Jan. 1987.
[128] 'Okuda Orders Arrest of Offenders', *Voice of Uganda*, 2 July 1975.
[129] Minutes of Committee on Drunkenness, 7 Apr. 1972, loose in HDA.

visit to a coffee factory revealed a table groaning under the weight of beer bottles.[130] In Tanzania, the mid-1970s had seen traditional liquor assume a similar role, at the height of a policy of villagization which had moved from exhortation to an increasing degree of direct pressure. The drinking of traditional liquor was evidently considered to threaten the success of the villages; in 1974 one local official in Rungwe instructed that 'all Pombe in the village is forbidden . . . People will be permitted to make and drink pombe on Saturdays and Sundays only'.[131] This prohibition applied to 'customary' as well as commercial brewing and drinking: 'They stopped us from consuming liquor in the home.'[132] In 1976, the party branch in Rungwe decided that it would decide on a central basis which villages should have clubs; by 1977/8 almost all of the 70 licensed clubs in the district belonged to villages and were run as collective undertakings. These clubs were permitted to sell traditional liquor on only one day each week.[133]

The post-colonial state in East Africa had a close interest in the selling of bottled beer, and those who held office within the state were most likely to be consumers of bottled beer. But the identification of traditional liquor as a prime obstacle to development was not simply a consequence of the making of an alliance between capital and politicians. The extraordinary public enthusiasm for the closure of the beer clubs in Kenya, and the apparent willingness with which the majority in Tanzania greeted the changes of villagization, showed that the demonization of traditional liquor was more than the point of articulation of a narrow alliance. Debates on liquor evoked multiple ideas of power from which many believed they might construct authority. Haugerud has argued that these public meetings were part of the contested 'hazardous moral bargain' between public and state;[134] the state offered to ensure health and wealth, and the public therefore acknowledged the state's legitimacy. The terms of this bargain could be read in many ways. It stressed the value of education and the need for change; it offered women and younger men a means to evoke the power of the state in defence of their claims to health and wealth. Yet the 'family' in Kenya and the structures of collective community authority in the villages of Tanzania might also offer – to men who felt their position threatened by educated youngsters and the circulation of money – models of patriarchal authority which could contain the unruly ambitions of women and younger men. To all, the wave of public meetings and debates which swept Tanzania in 1977 and Kenya in 1978-9 offered – in different ways – an ideal of development where shared health and wealth would come from state patronage, from hospitals and schools, and not from tradition or the secretive power over well-being. People

[130] *Voice of Uganda*, 25 Nov. 1975.
[131] Katibu Kata (divisional secretary), Nkunga to 'all club owners', 14 Sep. 1974, Rungwe Archive, L3/2.
[132] Int Nya2c, 1; Nya1b, 2.
[133] List of licences; District Secretary Tanzania African National Union to all Divisional/Parish Secretaries, 16 Jan. 1976; Divisional Secretary Ikuti to District Development Director, nd Nov. 1976, Rungwe Archive, L3/2.
[134] Haugerud, *Culture of Politics*, 81.

sought to capture this power, to turn it to their use – through denouncing traditional liquor.

Denouncing this drinking, people still indulged in it. '[I]t is unfortunate that the same wananchi who publicly agreed to close the beerhalls have re-doubled their efforts to see that they drink as much as possible.'[135] Neither of the parties to the moral bargain could meet their obligations under it: the state could not provide health and wealth to all could not ensure that all could afford to buy bottled beer – nor could people change their lives in the ways demanded by the state. In February 1980 a letter to the newspaper in Kenya optimistically suggested that the closure of beerhalls 'has led to a great change in the health of the people and signs of rapid rural development are on the horizon – traditional drinking has been stamped out'.[136] But other correspondents had already suggested that the ban had done nothing to reduce the consumption of liquor, or to make people drink bottled beer.[137] After ten years of Moi's rule, public meetings still reverted to the same, unfulfilled and unfulfillable compact between state and public: 'President Daniel arap Moi yesterday banned, with immediate effect, the brewing and consumption of illicit liquor in the country . . . [he said] "We are sober people who are fully committed to nation building."'[138]

Commoditization, drinking practice & generational power

> . . . this local liquor is only for old men . . . the young people do not like it.[139]

Post-colonial public rhetoric asserted that problems with development were the result of the drunkenness of a recalcitrant populace. Seeking to acquire for themselves some of the authority that accrued from the power of development, ordinary people evoked these ideas in condemning traditional liquor, and talked of traditional liquor as a source of laziness: 'if you drink those ones [bottled beers] the next day you can wake up with sufficient energy, when you relax and eat, your energy goes back to normal. But those liquors of ours [traditional liquor], when you drink them, even the next day you cannot go to dig.'[140] Yet economic circumstance forced people to continue drinking and selling traditional liquor; and the weak and arbitrary nature of the state forced them into reliance on other notions of power. The contradiction between public rhetoric and drinking practice was matched by another, between popular practice and popular discourse. Most of the drinking of traditional liquor took place in commercial contexts which

---

[135] Letter, *Weekly Review*, 23 Mar. 1979.
[136] *Daily Nation*, 12 Feb. 1980.
[137] 'Brewing', *Daily Nation*, 31 Jan. 1979.
[138] 'I Won't Lead Drunkards', *Sunday Nation*, 11 June 1989.
[139] Int Maa21c, 1.
[140] Int Nya12b, 5.

evoked the power of money to overcome claims of privileged access to alcohol. Yet some drinking practice and discourse about ideal drinking could evoke quite different ideas of power: neither the bottled-beer drinking of the elite, nor the abstinence of the tea-drinkers, but the continued power of elder men over the well-being of their peers and subordinates.

During the 1960s and 1970s, the public practice of many of the rituals of social health declined even further, in the face of a complex alliance of state disapproval, the hostility of Christianity and the more evangelical forms of Islam. The colonial period had seen a substitution of water for alcohol in some rituals; the post-colonial period saw those rituals disappear from public view.[141] 'Nowadays they have stopped making offerings. They do not know how to make offerings, and if you tell them [to] they tell you, "OK, I am going to hospital".'[142] Men perceived that public performance of such rituals distanced them from the state, earning the disfavour of those politicians and civil servants who mediated access to coercive and patronage resources of the state. 'things have changed and things of "Tanzania" [ie the state] have overcome tradition. Some things are good but others we are not content with, because the sacrifices of the past are finished, and it is only religion that is remaining. The religious people forbid sacrifice. They say there is no sacrifice. You must not offer.'[143] And so they avoided such performance, in pursuit of their relationship with the state.

But the disappearance of public rituals of well-being, and the readiness with which most people turned to hospitals and clinics in time of illness, revealed only part of a continuing debate over well-being in which individuals pursued multiple strategies in response to multiple uncertainties.[144] In Maasai society, honey-wine and sugar-based liquor were still sometimes used publicly in rituals of blessing; and in societies where such overt use was avoided many took a pragmatic and inclusive approach to healing. In Bunyoro, when a Christian woman's ailing twins would not respond to baptism or hospital treatment, she turned to *embandwa*, and they were cured.[145] *Embandwa* disappeared from public practice, yet not from covert performance; and it apparently took on an increasingly patriarchal character from the 1940s, with senior men seeking to control lineage *embandwa* whose perquisites came to regularly include liquor.[146] People continued to understand, and talk about, illnesses which were beyond the capacity of hospitals to cure and required the invocation of the *embandwa*.[147] In Bunyoro and elsewhere, the curse of elder men continued to be feared, and a notion of witchcraft constantly informed people's ideas about health, occupying an ambivalent space between ideas of innate human power over the well-being of others and concepts of learned, esoteric power.[148] 'Even the sorcerer tells you

[141] Int Nya4c, 7; Nyoro33c, 3.
[142] Int Nya25b, 5.
[143] Int Nya32a, 4.
[144] Whyte, *Questioning Misfortune*, 224-32.
[145] Int Nyoro35c, 4.
[146] Ints Nyoro27b, 2-3; Nyoro29a, 5.
[147] Int Nyoro1c, 5.
[148] Int Nyoro11c, 2-3; Nyoro19c, 2.

that, "First quarrel with that one, that quarrelling can give me a way". Of giving you a herb [medicine] to kill him. When you haven't quarrelled with him he can't die.'[149] People still feared the anger and jealousy of others; and some of the ways in which they drank, and talked of drinking, still evoked the ideals of amity and openness amongst peers and deference to seniors. In particular, the rituals of marriage and death continued to involve transactions in alcohol which evoked particular ideas of power: for it was given to elder men, seeking their approval and goodwill. 'You can't go to tell an elder you want his girl with bare hands [ie, without a gift of drink], because it is not good. It is shameful to go barehanded.'[150] The giving and consuming of traditional liquor continued to evoke the importance of particular patterns of sociability, the idea that the goodwill and the anger of elder men was especially dangerous.[151] Alcohol could be bought and sold and yet remain a way of reproducing power and constructing authority.[152] Failure to provide a guest or relative or friend with the drink which showed respect and ensured goodwill was assumed to lead to dire consequences:

> In the past when we would see a friend we would have alcohol, but now even when a friend comes to visit there may be no alcohol. And in the past people had a healthy life, we would never get sickly, just like that, as we do these days. You will realize that among my mother's children there was none who ever went to hospital, but for our children, they are always sickly.[153]

While the selling of alcohol became the norm, and elder men were unwilling or unable – or both – to prevent this, they could turn this very pattern of commoditization to use in a discourse which resisted the wholesale vulgarization of traditional alcohol. Non-commercial drinking, like certain ritual uses of alcohol, became what Feierman has called 'drama remembered but not performed', an idea which continues to be discussed and evokes power – if in apparently increasingly contradictory ways.[154] Drinking practice had always differed from the idealizations of drinking discourse: the gulf between the two became even wider.

By the 1970s drinking events across most of East Africa had ceased to be the occasional practice at almost any household, and were largely focused on dedicated places of sale, whether these were licensed clubs or illegal drinking dens. Most drinkers were still men, and to some degree men sorted themselves into groups by generation within the drinking-place, with elders avoiding the direct drinking companionship of younger men. The existence of drinking groups, some with names, which bought and shared their drink

---

[149] Int Nyoro29c, 2.
[150] Int Maa35a, 2.
[151] Ints Nya2c, 1; Nya5c, 1-2; Nya16c, 4; Maa17b, 2; Nyoro 29c, 2.
[152] J. Willis, 'Enkurma Sikitoi: Commoditization, Drink and Power Among the Maasai', *IJAHS*, 32 (1999), 339-57.
[153] Int Nyoro1a, 3.
[154] Feierman, *Peasant Intellectuals*, 245-64.

together, was a feature of urban as well as rural drinking of fermented liquor.[155] Drinking continued to provide a central social activity for men, in particular: men met to talk and argue over drinks, and often they talked and argued in groups which reflected ideas of proper sociability, the reluctance to drink with strangers, and their combined fear of and reliance on their fellow drinkers. Many had a keen sense that drinking in public spaces, near to women and men of other generations, brought calamitous consequences of disease and disorder:

> In the past children and women did not drink, but now everybody just drinks, carelessly . . . this habit completely ruins life.[156]

> These days it is just foolishness, we drink carelessly . . . you share the container with a child. I drink with my grandchild, who can also receive that beer. That is why I am saying these ones have been spoiled . . . because it is not the proper way to drink.[157]

> . . . our fathers used to drink in their houses, and then they were not quarrelling. Those [drinkers] of these days are hurting one another, that is the way it has changed, because they are fighting there, young men, young girls and men too. For us, we used to drink inside our houses.[158]

In talking of drinking, people continued to construct an ideal of proper drinking as a distinct activity of men, socializing with other men of the same age; and to argue that deviations from this model brought illness and violence.[159] This continued to be an important way of talking about the dangerous consequences of young men or women attaining power through their possession of money.[160] Across East Africa, the way that people talked of drinking, and the way that they drank, evoked sharply contradictory ideas about power over health and wealth.

> Our children drink differently – you drink badly. It's different from the way our fathers drank those days. . . In the past it was hard to hear of diseases and deaths. It was hard to hear someone dead in the childhood days. That's why now fights have spread, things that are meaningless – even the government's. That's why nowadays these drinks have brought about diseases which we often hear about.[161]

---

[155] Heald notes the importance of these groups in Gisu drinking in the 1960s and the 1980s: *Controlling Anger*, 85, 231-33, 253. See also 'Meta Meta is the Busaa Guzzlers' Paradise', *Sunday Nation*, 28 Dec. 1986.

[156] Int Maa12a, 2.

[157] Int Nya35a, 3.

[158] Int Nya41a, 3.

[159] Ints Nya4b, 5 Nyoro21a, 7; Nyoro25a, 7.

[160] Ints Nyoro20a, 4; Nyoro29a, 3.

[161] Int Nya14b, 3.

Eleven

'Impure spirit'
Illicit distillation, health & power

> Somebody making *haragi* would carry [banana wine] to a hidden place, maybe four or five jerricans, and then start making it. And if the inspectors would find out they would come to you and destroy all your things; they would kick your bottles and break them. People had pipes made from the scrap of old cars, they knew how to make them. They would make three coils then they would fix these in a tin. The coils were for cooling the steam, they would put the coils in cold water, and there the steam would condense and *haragi* would come out, and they would put [the end of the pipe in a bottle] into which the distillate would drop. After the base they had put in the drum was finished they would open it and put in more, to make *haragi* for sale.[1]

Fermented informal-sector alcohol had become, in one strand of discourse, at least, the epitome of backwardness and resistance to change: traditional drink, in every way. But there was another kind of alcoholic beverage made in the informal-sector which came to occupy a quite different position in official rhetoric. If fermented drinks represented the dangers of the past, illicit distilled drinks served to encapsulate all that was threatening about the future: they were an impure form of modernity which threatened the health of society.

In popular discourse too these drinks were seen as different, and as essentially modern. But where official rhetoric cast illicit distillates as a danger, popular discourse identified them as power, a drink of modernity which was accessible and affordable for those denied bottled beer or wine or whisky. And, like fermented brews, they were an economic resource of growing importance in the post-colonial informal economy.

Gin & whisky:
the spirits of multi-racialism

In January 1955, the Legislative Council in Uganda passed, in a single day, a new Intoxicating Liquor Ordinance, which finally ended all forms of racial

---

[1]   Int Nyoro25a, 6.

discrimination in the sale and consumption of spirits, as well as beers. European members of the council were evidently the most enthusiastic supporters of the change. The CS announced that it removed a piece of discrimination 'which many of us feel should have gone years ago'. African members were more cautious about the change; one expressed concern over the difficulty of controlling drunkenness, and another, J. Bazarrabusa, said that the new law might 'let loose a ferocious beast'.[2] In the same year, similar laws were passed in Kenya and Tanganyika: legal racial restrictions on drinking had ended.

The debate in the Uganda Council was revealing, for the unravelling of these final restrictions was very much the result of European concerns over discrimination, rather than direct African political agitation. When the law was changed to allow Africans to drink beer in 1947, many officials were, like the governor of Kenya, 'unable to agree to the sale of spirits to Africans'.[3] But in the next few years, this resolve crumbled, eroded by an anxiety to secure the emergence of a group of African leaders who could be relied upon to support the agenda of controlled economic and political transformation which the postwar colonial state was busily elaborating. The European debate over spirits was part of an approach which identified political problems as essentially those of social discrimination, susceptible of resolution through a liberal spirit of colour-blind co-operation which would bring European officials together with Africans who were willing to accept their leadership and aspired to share their manners and the material trappings of their existence. This was what European discourse defined as 'multi-racialism',[4] the social and political vision which by the mid-1950s had crystallized briefly around the Capricorn Society, which offered an elitism of culture rather than colour and which, for a short period, captured the enthusiasm of many European 'unofficials' and a degree of discreet official support.[5] The first drinking manifestation of this kind of idea had been the United Kenya Club, founded in 1946, and with its own new premises under construction from 1952.[6] Erasto Mang'enya, one of those whom the late colonial state sought to co-opt, noted with some amusement the attempts of European officials to 'break down the racial barriers' by the distribution of drink at official receptions.[7]

The spirits ban impeded this drinking communion, though in Uganda some officials and bar owners evidently turned a blind eye to violation of the laws, at least by those who manifested the appropriate marks of civilization: 'an African may drink hard liquor in Uganda ... if he is sufficiently

---

[2] 'Liquor Bill Passed with General Support. "Discrimination" Gone', *Uganda Argus*, 14 Jan. 1955.

[3] Mitchell, Governor to SoS, 11 Feb. 1947, PRO CO 533/557/1.

[4] Chidzero, *Tanganyika and International Trusteeshi*, 20-2; C. Pratt, *The Critical Phase in Tanzania, 1945-1968. Nyerere and the Emergence of a Socialist Strategy* (Cambridge, 1976), 29-33; leader in *East African Standard*, 10 Mar. 1955.

[5] *Tanganyika Standard*, 27 Feb. 1954; Gunter, *Inside Africa*, 347.

[6] Nairobi African Affairs Report, 1946, 4, PRO CO533 558/7; Gunter, *Inside Africa*, 324.

[7] Mang'enya, *Discipline and Tears*, 221, 237.

respectably dressed to go into a bar and has the price of a gin or Scotch'.[8] Such tolerance to violations was not enough, however: a liberal American journalist touring East Africa in 1953 put the ban on African consumption of spirits at the top of his list of political problems, but there is little evidence of African political mobilization around this issue:[9] an element of sensitivity is apparent in retrospective accounts which identify the colour bar in hotels as an obstacle to respectable tea-drinking, rather than whisky-drinking, and one suspects that many Africans were – like Mang'enya – uncomfortably aware that acquiring the drinking habits of Europeans would distance them from 'the small man'.[10]

In Tanganyika, the government began in 1952 a scheme which granted named individuals the right to purchase and consume spirits (which, to the confusion of various officials, ran alongside but separate from the scheme of permits allowing individual Africans to sell bottled beer[11]). Those given such permits were to be 'persons of very reliable character vouched for by the DC and PC'.[12] The intention to create and cultivate an elite group was entirely overt, and it evidently put some of those so privileged in something of a quandary: in retrospect, Mang'enya deprecated the exclusivity of the system, but he and others evidently derived some enjoyment from using the privilege to discomfort the more openly racist among European bar and hotel owners.[13]

Co-option was the aim of the system, and when one PC suggested that one such permit be withdrawn because the holder had left his job with the Native Tobacco Board, the suggestion was quashed: it was noted that the man in question was politically active, but also that 'petty pinpricks of this nature' would only confirm any 'subversive leanings'.[14] A driver who applied was, on the other hand, refused a permit: the scheme was not aimed at those so far down the social scale.[15] Submitting an application for three men employed at his office to receive permits to drink spirits, one PC explained that 'All these Africans hold responsible positions and can be relied on to use the discretion looked for in any servant of Government in the consumption of such liquors.'[16] All applications had to be made through the district administration, and details of monthly income were required.

Between 1952 and 1954, 65 permits were apparently issued in Tanganyika: all were to men. Twenty-eight were given to employees of the central government (one of them a medical doctor); eight to chiefs and others who

[8] Gunter, *Inside Africa*, 417.
[9] Gunter, *Inside Africa*, 370, 406.
[10] Atieno-Odhiambo, 'The Formative Years, 1945-63', 33; Mang'enya, *Discipline and Tears*, 285.
[11] Member for Local Govt to PC Tanga, 8 Dec. 1952, TNA SMP 38758.
[12] Minute, Solicitor-General, 17 Jan. 1953, TNA SMP 20309.
[13] Mang'enya, *Discipline and Tears*, 221-3.
[14] PC Lake to Member for Local Govt, 20 Dec. 1952; Minute, ?, 3 Jan. 1953; Member for Local Govt to PC Lake, 7 Jan. 1953, TNA SMP 20309.
[15] Political Mbeya to Province, 2 May 1953, TNA 157 A2/25.
[16] PC Western to CS, 8 Jan. 1953, TNA SMP 20309.

worked in local administration; six to workers in co-operatives; five to entrepreneurs; and two to employees of private businesses. The employment of 16 was not recorded.[17] To be allowed to drink spirits was to have one's status as a member of this distinct group confirmed; and in European eyes, it brought this select group into desirable social intercourse with Europeans. Asking for approval for the permit of the medical doctor, a DC noted that the doctor 'finds the prohibition on the drinking of spirits a disadvantage socially'.[18]

The importance of socializing between Europeans and an African elite was also much on the mind of Andrew Cohen, who became governor of Uganda in 1951. Cohen came to Uganda from the Colonial Office in London, where he had been considered a high-flyer, and where he had already had cause to consider the implications of the racial restrictions on alcohol.[19] Because of his influence in London, and his belief that controls on alcohol were a barrier to effective political progress, Cohen dominated official debate on this issue for the next few years – though events actually ran rapidly beyond his control. The informal policy of tolerance to spirit-drinking was unevenly applied, and led to some embarrassing incidents with prominent Ugandan political leaders in Kampala hotels – and particularly, to difficulties with the *kabaka* of Buganda, who was young, recently returned from Cambridge and used to being able to drink whisky when he so chose.[20] Such incidents pushed Cohen into seeking a system of permits which would allow selected individuals to drink spirits. The Tanganyika permit system had been accepted without demur by the Colonial Office, but when Cohen proposed a similar system it was pointed out that this would violate Britain's international obligations under the Brussels Act of 1890, which had been restated by the Treaty of St Germain-en-Laye after the First World War.

Approval for the permit system was not forthcoming, though it was clear that there was no objection in principle.[21] Cohen became increasingly impatient; by 1953 he had decided that a permit system would no longer be enough, and that the law would have to be changed entirely.[22] After further delays, he (and other governors across Africa) were given permission to 'quietly disregard' the provisions of the Brussels and St Germain agreements; and all three East African territories passed new laws which did just that.[23]

[17] See the contents of TNA SMP 20309.
[18] DC Mbulu to CS, 13 Apr. 1953.
[19] See D. Apter, *The Political Kingdom in Uganda. A Study in Bureaucratic Nationalism* (London, 1997 (1st edn 1961)), 264-5, for Cohen's influential role in London.
[20] Memo, attached with Rogers (Colonial Office) to Simpson (Foreign Office), 19 May 1951, PRO CO 822/630.
[21] Rogers to Simpson, 19 May 1951, PRO CO 822/630.
[22] Cohen to Gorell-Barnes, 12 Feb. 1953, PRO CO 822/631.
[23] Secret Saving Telegram from SoS to Officers administering Kenya, Nigeria, Northern Rhodesia, Tanganyika, Nyasaland, Somalia, Uganda, Gambia, Gold Coast, Sierra Leone, 14 July 1953. This asked that publicity should be minimal and that introduction of legislation should await final approval: it is not clear when this final approval came, but presumably it was sometime in 1954.

The change produced most debate in Kenya, where a process of consultation with local administrators suggested that even 'the more advanced Africans could not necessarily be relied upon to consume spirits with moderation', and that some permit system should be operated.[24] Yet most officials considered this impracticable, and accepted that racial restrictions must be ended.[25]

Their haste in this matter was not due to any formal agitation by Africans on the issue; enquiry from one African member of the Legislative Council in Tanganyika suggested that there was a 'growing consciousness among educated Africans of racial discrimination practised in this matter',[26] and the 1954 Tanganyika government committee report worried about 'hatred and bitterness' caused by restrictions on social drinking,[27] but there was less letter-writing and petitioning on this subject than there had been over the restrictions on bottled beer. Exclusion from bars (which was due to exclusive policies by bar owners, not to the law), rather than denial of the right to buy spirits, exercised the minds of those Africans who were concerned about this issue at all.[28] It was African drinking practice, not political demands, which galvanized Cohen and his fellows.

'NUBIAN GIN': ILLICIT SPIRITS OF POWER

Before the 1930s, distillation was associated almost solely with the military, particularly with the 'Sudanese', the motley, multi-ethnic soldiery who were the backbone of early colonial armies in East Africa. Hence the sobriquet 'Nubian gin', long attached to illicit distillates in Kenya. In 1920, when the implications of the St Germain treaty were discussed, officials agreed that it was soldiers and ex-soldiers who would be affected by the enforcement of a legal ban on local distillation (which the treaty required, alongside the ban on importing spirits for African consumption).[29] Locally-distilled spirits were the drink of those who represented, most directly, the coercive power of the colonial state, whose service to the state made them quite distinct from the rest of the African populace. This was such a minor issue that in the early and mid-1930s, some European law officers were still rather hazy about what exactly distillation was.[30]

---

[24] Minute 1/54, Coast DCs' meeting, 22 Sep. 1954; OiC Nairobi to Secretary for Defence, 14 Sep. 1954, KNA MAA 2/5/212.

[25] Minute 1/54, Coast DCs' meeting, 22 Sep. 1954; PC Coast to Sec. for Defence, 28 Sep. 1954; Secretary for African Affairs to Sec. for Defence, 1 Dec. 1954, all in KNA MAA 2/5/212. It is not clear why the Secretary for Defence initiated this consultation process; there was clearly some uncertainty over who should deal with African drinking at this time. The legislation on the subject was finally passed under the supervision of the Asian Minister without Portfolio: Asst Sec. to Asian Minister without Portfolio to Legal Draftsman, 25 May 1955, KNA MAA 2/5/212.

[26] Colonial Office to Governor, Tanganyika Territory, 10 Aug. 1954, PRO CO 822/1069.

[27] Tanganyika Government, *Intoxicating Liquor Report*, 5.

[28] See for example Memorandum by 'Shinyanga Township Africans' to United Nations Organization, 20 Aug. 1948, PRO CO 691/201.

[29] Governor, Uganda to Governor, Kenya, 8 Nov. 1920; CS to all PCs, and Officer Commanding Bombo, 14 Feb. 1921 UNA A 46/1993.

[30] Crown Counsel to Director of Agriculture, 17 Apr. 1935, KNA AG 1/369.

Local distillation became more common during the 1930s, with illicit distillates as the drink of a distinct group of wage-earners and government employees: 'mission boys' joined soldiers as the drinkers of this powerful beverage, and in southern Tanganyika an administrator complained that he could not stop 'motor-car drivers, shop assistants employed by Indians and similar natives' from drinking a distillate from cashew fruit, which was potent indeed: '[t]wo small cupfuls are deemed sufficient to make a man pass into a state of coma'.[31] Increasingly disdainful of the fermented liquors which missionaries and many officials regarded as unhygienic, but legally – and financially – denied bottled beer and whisky, these men drank illicitly distilled spirits. They paid a premium to do so: in terms of absolute alcohol, distillates were, consistently, much more expensive than fermented liquor; this was not a cheap way to get drunk.[32] Particularly in Uganda, illicit spirits were associated with politically powerful Africans: haranguing the hierarchy of the Buganda kingdom in 1935, the PC accused them of setting a 'bad example' by their drinking: 'Here the Provincial Commissioner produced a gin bottle full of waragi and exhibited it all round, saying that he had been able to purchase it not very far away from the Lukiko [the seat of the Kingdom government].'[33]

From 1938, there was a detachment of police in Nairobi charged solely with the suppression of 'Nubian gin'; in less than four months in 1939 they secured 37 convictions.[34] In the 1940s there was increasing European concern over the drinking of illicit spirits – it was reported that soldiers were still particularly given to this, and that some were bartering their kit for Nubian gin[35] – and by the early 1950s, the illicit distillation of liquor was believed to have assumed enormous proportions, particularly in Uganda. From 1940, a succession of new laws were passed imposing higher penalties for the manufacture and possession of such spirits, called *moshi* or *konyagi* in Tanganyika and *waragi, haragi* or *enguli* in Uganda.[36] The new Kenyan legislation, in an attempt to make urban landlords police their tenants, allowed the prosecution of the owner of any premises on which a still was found, unless they could prove their ignorance.[37] In 1954, a committee of inquiry in Tanganyika recommended the formation of special police units to suppress illicit distillation.[38] At first, official rhetoric over this

---

[31] Municipal Native Affairs Officer, Nairobi to AG, 8 Oct. 1930, KNA MOH 1/74; Ag. PC Lindi to CS, 7 Oct. 1929, TNA SMP 12694, Vol. I.

[32] The calculations are complex and data rather scanty, but assuming distillates in the colonial period to be around 30 percent alcohol by volume, and fermented liquors to average 4 percent alcohol by volume, it would have cost around 18 shillings to buy a litre of absolute alcohol in the form of distillates, as against around 11 shillings a litre to buy it in the form of maize beer: price data from TNA SMP 3214, Vol. I; J. Leslie, *A Survey of Dar es Salaam* (London/New York/Nairobi, 1963), 251; KNA AG/401 and AG/404.

[33] 'Birthday of the Kabaka', *Uganda Herald*, 14 Aug. 1935.

[34] Minute, CNC, nd 1940, KNA MAA 7/378.

[35] Ag. Resident Magistrate (RM) Kisumu to Registrar, 10 Oct. 1944, KNA AP 1/1203.

[36] See for example the Bukoba Moshi Rules, 24 Oct. 1940, TNA SMP 12694, Vol. IV.

[37] Registrar to all Magistrates, 20 Dec. 1943, KNA AP 1/1203.

[38] Tanganyika Government, *Intoxicating Liquor Report*, 10.

drinking, like that around methylated spirits, concentrated on the idea that Africans, unused to their potency, would be driven violently insane by drinking them.[39] But by the end of the 1940s, the debate was implicitly linked to the model of drinking incorporation: whereas bottled, imported spirits could provide the communion for the racially-mixed rituals of modernity, illicit spirits threatened that communion by subverting the 'educated and cultured' Africans who should be drinking whisky with Europeans.[40] Beyond the control of state or tradition, they offered a kind of modernity which was not mediated by Europeans. The dangerous social and political consequences of this were emphasized in 1946 by the Kenya African Union when they called for the end of restrictions on African drinking of bottled beer: 'drunkenness among our people is increased daily due to the wrong kind of drinks they are forced by circumstances to take.'[41]

An inquiry in Uganda in 1950 – just before Cohen's arrival – had summed up the threat which illicit distillates posed: 'It is most disturbing to find that the younger and better educated Africans, who might be expected to be the leaders of the people, are the persons most addicted to this spirit.'[42] The assertion that illicit spirits were adulterated was central to these concerns – such spirits offered a poisoned form of modernity, which would destroy individual and social health, causing 'wasting, homicidal impulses and even death'.[43] Cohen himself wrote that 'the ban on the consumption of imported spirits by Africans has driven many people ... to the consumption of *waragi*.'[44] The ban on imported spirits encouraged illicit distillation – and illicit distillation threatened the vision of Europeans and Africans coming together over cocktails. By 1956, the disastrous social consequences of illicit distillation required no elaboration in official correspondence: 'I need not dilate on the evil effects of [illicit distillation] for they are too well known.'[45] The threat went beyond the possibilities of any system of permits, for illicit distillates were widely available, and the number of those potential leaders who might become addicted was considerable. The Officer in Charge of Nairobi reported that 'responsible African opinion is seriously perturbed' over the effects of Nubian gin; and 'responsible' Africans were the key to policy.[46] So some European officials came to believe that only by ending racial restrictions on the drinking of spirits could they deal with this menace to the health of society.[47]

[39] 'Illicit Traffic in Methylated Spirits', DC Nakuru, nd 1944, KNA PC NKU 3/15/1.

[40] Tanganyika Government, *Intoxicating Liquor Report*, 11.

[41] Kenya African Union Memorandum, 32, Oct. 1946, PRO CO 533/537/1.

[42] 'Report of the Committee of Inquiry into the Use of Jaggery', attached with Cohen to SoS, ? Sep. 1952, PRO CO 822/630.

[43] 'Report of the Committee of Inquiry Into the Use of Jaggery', attached with Cohen to SoS, ? Sep. 1952, PRO CO 822/630.

[44] Cohen to CO, ? Sep. 1952, PRO CO 822/630.

[45] PC Rift Valley to Asst Superintendent of Police Nakuru, 18 Feb. 1956, KNA PC NKU 3/15/1.

[46] OiC Nairobi to Secretary for Commerce, 19 Oct. 1955, KNA MAA 2/5/212.

[47] This idea had first been mooted by Tanganyika PCs in 1946: Minutes of PCs' Conference, 3-8 June 1946, Item 7b, PRO CO 691/199. At the time it seems to have been ignored.

Yet the change in the law in 1955 actually did nothing to reduce illicit distillation or anxiety over distilling. For the only legally available spirits were those which were imported and expensive. Cohen's scheme (like similar plans in the Gold Coast) had revolved around the local production of a cheap, legal spirit which could be sold to Africans and which would provide a useful stimulus to the local sugar-cane industry.[48] This would be a clean spirit, unlike the adulterated drinks of the illicit distillers.[49] It was a plan which instantly aroused the hostility of the government of Kenya Colony, which derived considerable revenue from imported spirits. The Uganda proposal was for an excise duty of around 4 shillings, so that a bottle of spirit would retail for 8 shillings; the Kenyan position was that a bottle should sell for 18 or 19 shillings.[50] This was not only a revenue issue, however; the debate over the price of liquor also reflected differing ideas over how large a group of Africans should be included in the spirits-drinking communion. An official in Kenya minuted his distaste for the idea of a 'gin-drinking working class' and suggested that 'the African should have freedom to drink spirits, but that . . . freedom should be limited by the usual [excise] duty, to those who by their superior standard of living may be considered able to afford it and likely to restrain their consumption'.[51] The government in Kenya effectively blocked Cohen's scheme, by ensuring that only a tiny minority of Africans could afford to drink legal spirits.[52]

DISTILLATES, POWER & THE RURAL ECONOMY

In 1955 the oil companies of Uganda began to complain that they were running short of the 44-gallon drums in which they sold their oil.[53] These were supposed to be returned when empty, but thousands were unaccounted for. The oil companies began to offer rewards for their return, and even to refuse to sell new drums unless old ones were returned – but the mysterious drum shortage continued.[54] Oil drums have various uses, but the timing of this shortage is suggestive; in the 1950s, techniques of distillation had begun to shift away from the use of the 4-gallon petrol tin, which had been popular since the 1930s, and towards the use of drums. At the same time, in Bunyoro at least, the sweet-potato base which had previously been used (especially by 'Nubi') for distillation was superseded by banana wine.[55] The linked changes were highly significant; marking an increase in the scale of production to supply a growing clientele who preferred modern distillates to traditional liquors:

[48] Cohen to CO, ? Sep. 1952; Administrator, East Africa High Commission to Under SoS, 9 May 1951, PRO CO 822/630.
[49] 'Sociological Aspects of Waragi Drinking', paper, anon, nd, circulated by Uganda Government, in KNA MAA 2/5/212.
[50] Record of meeting of 2 Dec. 1955, attached with Asian Minister Without Portfolio to Administrator, East Africa High Commission, 5 Dec. 1955, KNA MAA 2/5/212.
[51] Carey-Jones, Treasury, 8 Oct. 1955, KNA MAA 2/5/212.
[52] Minute, 26 Sep. 1955, PRO CO 822/1069.
[53] *Uganda Argus*, 4 Jan. 1955.
[54] *Uganda Argus*, 23 Jan. 1956.
[55] Int Nyoro17b, 3.

They left the system of potatoes, then they embarked on the production of alcohol from the local beer [meaning banana wine]. The juice from the bananas, the so-called sour bananas, together with the flour of sorghum, they mix and they ferment it for about 4 days, and from there the liquid is poured in. We had tins where kerosene was first sold. They put in the tins they cover them tightly, they would put a steam tube, boil and collect alcohol. But as the local industry developed, then they left the system of the tins, and moreover, by then, the white man discovered the system of using the jerricans. Directly intending to avoid, to abolish, the tin which was the main container for the people to brew this. But the people also likewise embarked on [the use of] these drums. Yes, people are always developmental, so nowadays alcohol is brewed by the use of drums.[56]

Where distillation was mostly carried out by women, this change was associated with another innovation; women found oil drums physically less easy to manipulate than did men, and women who had previously been distilling by themselves began to find men to work for them,[57] just as some women already used family labour or hired casuals to tread bananas for juice. This change in techniques was a slow one – many producers were still using petrol tins in the 1960s – but it did evidence the tendency of distillation to generate slightly more complex patterns of economic relationship than fermented brews.

The 1950s saw rapid growth in distillation across East Africa.[58] In 1950 the DC Bunyoro had reported that *waragi* drinking was not 'a social evil', and suggested that consumption of distillates was limited to 'detribalized Africans', and that it was made mostly by women around the towns.[59] The linkage of *waragi* and 'detribalization' was characteristic – distillates were a problem of those who were too modern – but otherwise the report was far from alarmist. Convictions for *waragi* offences had begun to rise steeply in 1949, however;[60] and by the early 1960s Bunyoro was one of 'large-scale pockets of production' identified by another official commission.[61]

There were two factors at work here. One was to do with supply. In Bunyoro, women played a much more prominent role in the organization and practice of distilling than they had done in the selling of banana wine, and it seems likely that the entry of more and more women into this business reflected women's attempts to find an area of entrepreneurship not affected by the gender-discriminatory legislation which had shut them out of the legal sale of fermented liquors.[62]

---

[56] Int Nyoro21a, 5 (this interview was conducted in English).
[57] Int Nyoro27b, 2.
[58] Tanganyika Government, *Intoxicating Liquor Report*, 9-10.
[59] DC Bunyoro to PC Eastern, 30 Oct. 1950, HDA NAF 9.
[60] Katikiro to DC, 6 Dec. 1950, HDA NAF 9; Bunyoro District Annual Report, 1950: loose in HDA.
[61] Babumba, *Report of the Spirituous Liquor Committee*, 4.
[62] Babumba, *Report of the Spirituous Liquor Committee*, 3-4 suggested that women dominated distillation in the 'north' (apparently including Bunyoro).

It was the old ladies who made it. Those are the ones I used to see make it. Like here there was my mother and the late Malitwe, there was also Catolina, those are the ones who made it. Those are the people who knew the problem of *haragi*, when the whites used to kick their bottles and break them. But once she would make it in a hidden place and come back, she would never agree that it was hers.[63]

Distilling and fermenting for sale without a licence were both illegal; but the technical differences between ferments and distillates meant, here as everywhere else, that distillates offered certain advantages: they could be made discreetly, far from official eyes, then stored for long periods for sale. However, distillation is a time-consuming process, and involves rather obvious equipment. The second factor leading to the great expansion in distilling, which began in the 1950s, was the degree of popular demand, much of it emanating from exactly those individuals who were supposed to enforce the laws against distillation. While many people – some of them policemen or chiefs – would know when and where distillation was taking place, they would do their best to conceal this knowledge from higher authority.[64]

The complex nature of popular attitudes to restrictions on the sale of fermented alcoholic beverages has already been discussed: how elder men's dislike of sale was mediated by their suspicion of chiefs and their awareness of the economic importance of such sales to individual households, and how between 1945 and 1955 elder men and the state reached a kind of compromise over the control of the sale of fermented liquors. No such accommodation was reached over distillates; even after 1955, there was no legal way for most Africans to buy spirits, simply because they could not afford imported whisky or gin. At the same time, the significance of European debates over African consumption of spirits had not been lost on the populace at large: spirits were intoxicants, but they were more than that, for the consumption of spirits gave drinkers membership of an elite – those who possessed money, and were close to the power of the state. Around Hoima, it was the 'government workers' who came to drink the spirits distilled by women.[65] The debates of the 1950s confirmed the idea established in the nineteenth century: spirits were power, and drinking them gave authority: 'chiefs, dignitaries and their friends' took to drinking *waragi*, and others sought to emulate them.[66] Yusto Kwezi, one of the Hoima club owners elevated to new respectability by the selective licensing policies of the 1950s, began his career surreptitiously trading as a *waragi* supplier.[67] It is striking

[63] Int Nyoro25a, 6.
[64] Southall, *Townsmen in the Making*, 25, 59-60, describes widespread collusion of chiefs and police in the sale of illicit spirits in Kampala. European officials in Tanganyika complained of similar widespread collusion in illicit distillation by those responsible for enforcing the law: Commissioner Police to all Officers-in-Charge of Police, 18 Nov. 1948, TNA SMP 13560, Vol. II.
[65] Int Nyoro25a, 6.
[66] Babumba, *Report of the Spirituous Liquor Committee*, 7, 8.
[67] Int Nyoro40b, 3.

that in colonial Tanganyika it was the area around Lake Victoria, where the most hierarchical political structures of the Territory lay, that illicit distillation was most prevalent.[68] In late-colonial Uganda the advertisements which dotted newspaper pages constantly reiterated – for the literate – this association of spirits (legal and illegal) and authority: 'Those who command, demand Queen Anne Scotch Whisky'.[69]

So it was that the DC Bunyoro complained in 1956 that whenever the police co-operated with chiefs in a search for *waragi*, none would be found: 'There is reason to believe that in some cases the chiefs have warned the makers of waragi'.[70] Controls on distillation were widely regarded as 'a colonial device to deny Africans a cheap spirit in order to encourage imports from overseas'.[71] The activities of illicit distillers were accommodated, even encouraged, by minor officials. 'If you lived under that chief, you would bribe him to let you distil. So when the patrol would come they would just pass you by.'[72] For some chiefs and policemen, this was an important source of income, as well as a drink of social power; they or their wives made and sold spirits, or they derived a steady flow of protection money from others who did so. 'We have no hesitation in reporting that the Waragi Prohibition Ordinance is responsible for much of the bribery and corruption in the country', reported the 1963 commission of inquiry in Uganda, suggesting that some chiefs were earning 2,000 shillings a month from this.[73]

Despite this, European officials and some police officers laid considerable emphasis on the importance of the ban, and tried to enforce it. The 1950s saw a steady rise in the number of prosecutions and imprisonments for illicit distilling, across the region.[74] Such efforts caused much individual hardship for distillers, but had no effect on the rapid growth of distilling. A woman arrested for distilling just outside Hoima went to prison for nine months; she went back to distilling after her release.[75] In 1956, a single police raid in Mbale town, in Uganda, seized 12 stills and resulted in the imprisonment of 40 people. Those convicted of manufacturing the spirit were sentenced to 15 months' hard labour.[76] In December 1957, a campaign of police raids across Uganda resulted in the seizure of 84 stills, and the recovery of 583 of the oil companies' missing drums, which were being used as fermenting tanks to produce the base for distillation.[77] In December 1958, police seized 29 stills along a 1-mile stretch of the road from Hoima to

[68]   Ag. PC Lake to CS, 12 July 1934; PC Lake to Chief Inspector of Labour, 10 Nov. 1938, TNA SMP 12694, Vol. III.
[69]   *Uganda Argus*, 22 Jan. 1958.
[70]   Gower, DC Bunyoro to Katikiro, 19 Feb. 1956, HDA NAF 9.
[71]   Babumba, *Report of the Spirituous Liquor Committee*, 4.
[72]   Int Nyoro38c, 4.
[73]   Southall, *Townsmen in the Making*, 192; Babumba, *Report of the Spirituous Liquor Committee*, 7.
[74]   From 320 in 1945 to 509 in 1951 and 835 in 1961: Babumba, *Report of the Spirituous Liquor Commitee*, Appendix IV.
[75]   Int Nyoro27b, 3.
[76]   '40 Sent to Gaol for Waragi Offences', *Uganda Argus*, 3 May 1956.
[77]   *Uganda Argus*, 11 Jan. 1958.

Kampala; their location, and the reported conviction of a taxi-driver for conveying *waragi*, suggest the increasing elaboration of a trade which brought distillates from rural stills to city consumers.[78]

Popular resentment against these raids was widespread. In January 1962 an attempt to arrest a Nubian-gin dealer in Chemelil, in western Kenya, led to a riot in which one man was shot dead.[79] European concerns about the effects of spirits on Africans had communicated themselves to some Africans who – like Bazarrabusa in the Legislative Council – feared the effects of the 'beast'.[80] But by the time of independence there was a widespread expectation that African governments would end the prohibition on small-scale distillation: an expectation which, bound up with the notion of spirits as a source of power, produced some striking new slang names for spirits in early 1960s Uganda: 'Minister', 'UPC' (the governing party), 'Apolo' (the middle name of prime minister Milton Obote).[81] It was an expectation which was, in different ways, to be disappointed by each of the East African governments.

The spirit of Uganda & the nature of the state

> . . . when the government found that it was practically impossible to charge for *haragi*, then it legalised it by saying that, now if you want to make *haragi*, come and have a licence, brew it then we shall find a market for it.[82]

The first distillery in East Africa to legally produce spirits for human consumption was established in Nairobi in early 1963, by the British company Gilbeys-Mathieson.[83] This produced gin from sugar-cane spirit but, while this gin cost a little less than imported whisky, it was far from the cheap clean spirit which some had seen as the answer to illicit distillation. The government of independent Kenya maintained the principle that had guided their colonial predecessors: distillates were a valuable source of revenue, and production of Nubian gin (or *chang'aa*, as it came increasingly to be called) should be repressed by policing: the clean spirit of modernity should only be supplied by industrial producers. 'Time and again people have said in your columns that Nubian gin must be legalized,' complained one letter writer, 'but the Government has decided to turn a deaf ear to this request.'[84]

[78] *Uganda Argus*, 10 Jan. 1959 and 24 Jan. 1958.
[79] *Daily Nation*, 8 Jan. 1962.
[80] 'Time Wasted', letter, *Uganda Argus*, 16 Jan. 1958.
[81] Babumba, *Report of the Spirituous Liquor Committee*, 9. There were similar popular expectations in Ghana: Akyeampong, 'What's in a Drink?'.
[82] Int Nyoro21b, 15.
[83] *Daily Nation*, 28 Jan. 1963.
[84] Letter, *Daily Nation*, 26 Jan. 1966.

In Uganda, popular expectations were even higher. Almost immediately upon independence the government appointed a committee of inquiry into the issue of illicit distillation. Meanwhile, enforcement of the ban on local distillation by small-scale producers seems to have ceased, as part of the general near-collapse of restrictions on drink manufacture and sale in the first year or two after independence through a mixture of corruption and popular defiance. 'When we got our independence . . . you are a chief, [but] I know you are a son of so-and-so, and moreover *waragi* is the chief source of income, probably, in your family; . . . you say "Please, why do you harass me whereas you are also interested in the same?"'[85] Newspaper reports of arrests ceased, and police action was restricted to the arrest of business-people (mostly Asian, it would seem) who supplied jaggery to small-scale distillers.[86]

Significantly, the committee of inquiry was headed by a doctor, Eriya Babumba, and included the Government Chemist – this was presented as an issue of individual and social health. The committee reported very quickly, and its decisions were evidently foreseen by some in government (since at least one of them was being implemented before the committee had finished its work). The report was a radical one: calling not simply for legalization of informal-sector distillation, but for a system which would license small-scale distillers to sell their produce to a central, industrial-scale, distillery which would redistil it, bottle it and sell it.[87] The report, which noted the economic importance of illicit distillation across Uganda, was couched in terms of health – individual and social. Borrowing whole phrases from the report of the early 1950s, it declared illicit spirits to be full of 'impurities', which caused 'inflammation of the nerves, lack of mental control leading to muscular weakness and wasting, and homicidal impulses', and led to 'social problems including the disruption of the family, encouragement of crime, laziness leading to unemployment and irregular attendance at work, and social instability'.[88] Like Cohen, Babumba identified this spirit as an affliction of modernity: 'Consumers include professionals, semi-professionals, chiefs, policemen, teachers, politicians and civil servants.' The provision of a 'cheap, wholesome spirit' was the only way to 'save our people from the dangers of *waragi*'.[89]

Babumba's report offered evidence of the health risks. Noting rather lamely that it could not be proved that anyone had actually died, the report nonetheless did produce one of the two reasonably systematic chemical analysis of illicit distillates which have been conducted in East Africa.[90] This revealed considerable fluctuations in ethanol content and the presence

---

[85] Int Nyoro21b, 15 (original interview in English).
[86] 'Charged with Bribing Police', *Uganda Argus*, 26 Jan. 1963.
[87] Babumba, *Report of the Spirituous Liquor Committee*, 20-1. Babumba stated that this system drew on practice in Ghana.
[88] Babumba, *Report of the Spirituous Liquor Committee*, 11, 17.
[89] Babumba, *Report of the Spirituous Liquor Committee*, 7,18,19.
[90] Babumba, *Report of the Spirituous Liquor Committee*, 11-12, and Appendix III. The other survey was that conducted by Nout in Kenya in the 1970s.

of various impurities, which he identified as the real danger, in particular methanol and furfural. However, comparative analyses of commercial whisky and brandy revealed similar furfural levels; and the methanol levels, while relatively high, were very far from the point where they would cause fatal poisoning. The analysis suggested – though Babumba did not stress this – that the real danger with illicit spirits was the same as that associated with legal spirits: that ethanol itself is poisonous, if taken in sufficient quantity.[91] But Babumba – like his colonial predecessors – was fascinated by the idea of illicit spirits as inherently impure.

The construction of the central distillery had begun before Babumba's report was complete, and at the beginning of 1965 new legislation – the Enguli Act, named for one of the many synonyms of local distillates – formally created a system of local boards which would license distillers to sell their produce to this distillery to be 'refined'.[92] The major shareholder in the distillery was the government, through the Uganda Development Corporation; Gilbeys-Mathieson also owned a share.[93] The product of the distillery was to be marketed as 'Uganda Waragi'. Popular practice came to maintain a new semantic distinction, between the product of small-scale distillers, known as *enguli*, *lira-lira*, or *haragi*, and the factory product, known as *waragi* and marketed with the slogan, 'the Spirit of Uganda'. Such was the spirit of the post-colonial state: in response to the popular demand for change, the government had produced a system predicated on the idea that the spirit of modernity had to be mediated through a centralizing, official structure which linked state and capital to produce a 'good, clean spirit'.[94] Rhetoric around the system, and the new spirit it created, constantly reverted to the idea of a mediated transformation from impure to pure. Even in deciding on the flavour of the product, samples of raw *enguli* were 'sent to London' so that 'a selection of flavours as near as possible to the original but without the harmful ingredients [c]ould be sent back.'[95]

The system thus created was, inevitably, a cumbersome and expensive one. Producers would bring raw spirit to local collection centres, from where it was taken by tanker to the distillery at Luzira, near Kampala. From the outset, it became a field for patronage. In Bunyoro, the local Enguli Board met, apparently for the second time, in October 1965. The board was all male, composed of district officials and local businessmen. Their first act was to raise their sitting allowance from 10 to 50 shillings per day, 'taking

[91] Babumba, *Report of the Spirituous Liquor Committee*, 11; the argument that the real problem was ethanol, not impurities, had already been made by the Kenya government in 1955, in arguing against the Ugandan proposals: Director of Medical Services to Secretary to Asian Minister Without Portfolio, 29 Dec. 1955, KNA MAA 2/5/212.

[92] Cap. 96, *Laws of Uganda*.

[93] The Uganda Development Corporation held 51 percent and Gilbeys-Mathieson 26 percent; the Development Finance Corporation of Uganda (a body partly owned by the Commonwealth Development Corporation) held the balance. For this and other information I am indebted to Mr Sentamu of Uganda Waragi.

[94] 'Waragi, Waragi', *Uganda Argus*, 14 Apr. 1965.

[95] 'Waragi on Sale in April', *Uganda Argus*, 19 Jan. 1965.

into account that most of the members of this Board are business men'. Then, considering a stack of 201 applications from men and women for licences, the board noted that it was only permitted to allocate a few more licences; and went on to award these to eight applicants, all male. The existing licensees mentioned at this meeting were also all male.[96] Babumba had stated that distilling was largely a women's occupation in Bunyoro, and oral testimony supports this:[97] it would seem that local networks of favour, operating along lines of gender, excluded most aspirant producers from the legal system – particularly women. Since the quota to be distributed was anyway very low – only 300 gallons per month for the whole of Bugisu, for example – it is perhaps unsurprising that in some areas few bothered even to apply for permits.[98]

There were other problems too. By late 1965 it was already clear that some licensees were not selling their *enguli* to the factory. Presumably they had already begun to employ what became a common technique: holding a licence as a cover for selling raw spirit direct to consumers.[99] There was a direct price incentive to do this; the factory offered 12 shillings a gallon for raw spirit at 50 percent ethanol by volume (with reductions for spirit below that strength). But *enguli* could be sold to consumers for 3-4 shillings a bottle, or 18-24 shillings a gallon;[100] there were many who were willing to buy raw spirit at 4 shillings, rather than refined spirit at 8 shillings, and so licensed distillers produced far above their quota level and sold the excess illegally.[101]

Once the Uganda Waragi system was in operation, well-publicized police raids on illicit distillers began again;[102] but production thrived as this continued to grow in importance as an area of patronage and source of additional income for police and administrators.[103] In 1971, a sub-county chief and magistrate in Bunyoro traded accusations over the illegal release of those accused of *enguli* offences.[104] In the same year an organization which claimed to represent 30,100 *enguli* distillers – by no means all, or even most, of whom can have been licensed – appealed for the Uganda Waragi factory to pay higher prices, an appeal which apparently went unanswered.[105] Management at the Uganda Waragi factory became increasingly erratic in the latter years of Idi Amin's presidency and during Obote's second period

[96] Minutes of meeting of Enguli Licensing Board, 6 Oct. 1965, HDA; and attachments.
[97] Babumba, *Report of the Spirituous Liquor Committee*, 3-4.
[98] 'Few Seek Enguli Licences', *Uganda Argus*, 9 Apr. 1965.
[99] Items 3/65 and 4/65, Minutes of meeting of Bunyoro Enguli Licensing Board, 6 Oct. 1965, HDA.
[100] A bottle being 26.666 fl. oz; price of *enguli* given in Babumba, *Report of the Spirituous Liquor Committee*, 10. This point is also made by Heald, *Controlling Anger*, 87-8.
[101] 'Enguli Excess Denied', *Uganda Argus*, 7 Feb. 1967.
[102] 'Women Sold Enguli Without Licence', and 'Enguli Licences', *Uganda Argus* 11 Jan. 1966 and 9 Feb. 1967.
[103] Obbo, *African Women*, 131.
[104] Kihika, Magistrate, Grade II to Administrative Secretary, Bunyoro, 20 Mar. 1971, HDA JUD/3.
[105] 'Enguli Producers' Memo', *Uganda Argus*, 12 Dec. 1971.

of rule, and the collection system became almost impossible to maintain. By 1986, when Yoweri Museveni took power, purchases of raw *enguli* were being made only around Kampala itself. In 1989 they ceased altogether. Meanwhile, spirits continued to be sought by those who aspired to the power of modernity, like the lapsed priest in Uganda who, when he could not find anyone to buy him bottled beer, carried his bottle of *enguli* concealed beneath a copy of Palgrave's *Golden Treasury*.[106] Years of military dominance and war steadily increased the demand for spirits in Uganda, where the arrest and prosecution of distillers became rare.[107] Soldiers evidently set much store by the notion of spirits as a kind of power, and by nature distillates lent themselves more easily to transport and consumption in the field. The nature of the state had steadily subverted control of this impure spirit of modernity.

In Tanzania, distilling was less common than in Uganda. Through the 1960s the government sought simply to suppress illicit distillation, which appears in newspaper reports as largely a phenomenon of urban areas: official rhetoric emphasized the health risks associated with *moshi*,[108] but low-ranking officials still wished to drink the liquor of modernity.[109] People continued to pay a premium for distillates, especially in rural areas: in 1965, a litre of absolute alcohol bought as distillates would cost around 20 shillings; bought as grain beer it would cost around 7 shillings.[110] Spirits were being made outside towns and brought in on public transport,[111] and newspaper reports suggest both men and women were selling *moshi* (or *gongo*, as some now called it); one of the men involved was described as a 'businessman.'[112] In a case against Hadija Omari, a woman *moshi* seller, the prosecutor remarked that 'the Government had enacted a law against "moshi" because it was injurious to health'. The magistrate noted that she was a divorcee with children, but sentenced her to two years in gaol, as 'no citizen should live or earn a living by breaking the law'.[113] Sentencing a man to six months for possession of *moshi*, another magistrate remarked that 'the Government is concerned about the an undesirable development of moshi.'[114] Development was the principal aim of the state – illicit distilling was an 'undesirable development' which was 'injurious to health'.

In January 1971 the Tanzania government decided to adopt the Ugandan model, establishing a distillery which would collect spirits from small-scale

---

[106] Hills, *White Pumpkin*, 76.

[107] There is a report of one crackdown in 1975: 'Swoop on Brewers', *Voice of Uganda*, 19 Aug. 1975.

[108] 'Death Ended Moshi Party', *Standard, Tanzania*, 27 Jan. 1968.

[109] 'TANU Expulsions', *Daily Nation*, 2 Jan. 1975.

[110] Calculating on the basis of prices given in Fukui, 'Alcoholic Drinks of the Iraqw' (5 shillings for 700cc of spirits; 50 pence for 1.8 litres of grain beer) and assuming spirits at 35 percent alcohol by volume and grain beer at 4 percent.

[111] '500/- Fines for Possessing Moshi Brew', *Standard, Tanzania*, 6 Jan. 1971.

[112] 'Dar Woman Fined for Having Moshi', *Standard, Tanzania*, 8 Jan. 1971; 'Moshi Jail Term Doubled on Appeal', *Standard, Tanzania*, 22 Jan. 1971; 'Three Deny Liquor Charges', *Daily News*, 12 Jan. 1973.

[113] 'Woman Had 29 Bottles of Moshi', *Standard, Tanzania*, 3 Jan. 1970.

[114] 'Seaman Who Had 27 Bottles of Moshi Jailed', *Standard, Tanzania*, 25 Jan. 1970.

producers and redistil it. The rhetoric was exactly that of the Babumba report: the new system would 'protect the public from the dangers of impure moshi', which contained 'poisonous' substances, owing to the poor 'hygiene conditions' under which it was manufactured. There was even an overlap in capital and personnel; the first manager of the new distillery came directly from the Uganda Waragi distillery, and Gilbeys-Mathieson were shareholders, along with their international rivals, International Distillers and Vintners, a prominent Tanzanian Asian and two Tanzanian government investment agencies. The new drink was called Konyagi.[115]

Though Tanzania was spared the political disruption which afflicted Uganda over the next 15 years, the Konyagi scheme suffered the same fate as Uganda Waragi. The system was cumbersome and expensive, and the state was unable to suppress illicit production and sale. The bottled product was too expensive for most, retailing at 33 shillings a bottle in 1976.[116] Licensed production was apparently limited to those rural distillers in coastal areas who produced *nipa*, a distillate from cashew fruit, and many producers continued to sell direct to consumers, by-passing the 'refining' process which was designed to render their product harmless to society.[117]

In Kenya no attempt was made to formalize small-scale distillation. The policy there remained one of outright suppression of a drink which was consistently represented as poisonous, 'a threat to the nation's health', as well as a cause of violence.[118] In 1965, a mob killed a policeman when a raid was made on distillers in western Kenya,[119] and in subsequent years there were repeated violent confrontations between state and distillers which served to emphasize the dangers of this uncontrolled spirit.[120] In Kenya, as in Uganda and Tanzania, illicit spirits were a form of power available to those who aspired to modernity but could not afford bottled beer: the armed forces were ready customers (and always game for a consequent fight with the police) and in Mombasa in the 1960s, illicit distillates were known as 'Lumumba for power', neatly running together ideas of drinking and political radicalism.[121] In Kenya, as in Tanzania and Uganda, control of spirits was undermined by the collusion of police and minor officials who drank illicit spirits and profited from their sale – like the police sergeant who 'wilfully removed' 18 bottles of spirits acquired as evidence against two

[115] 'Tanzania to Make Konyagi', *Standard, Tanzania*, 8 Jan. 1971.

[116] For a 50cl bottle, giving a cost of around 190 shillings per litre of absolute alcohol: *Daily News*, 14 and 15 Nov. 1976.

[117] For *nipa*, see *Daily News*, 5 Jan. 1973.

[118] 'What's Your Poison', *Daily Nation*, 21 Jan. 1977; 'Police Swoops', *Daily Nation*, 28 Jan. 1975; 'Dangers of Chang'aa', *Daily Nation*, 16 Jan. 1973.

[119] 'Policeman Killed', *Uganda Argus*, 13 Jan. 1965. For reports of various crackdowns, see 'A Spate of Fines', *Daily Nation*, 23 Jan. 1968; 'Warning on Chang'aa', *Daily Nation*, 9 Jan. 1971.

[120] 'Eight Held in Nairobi Incidents', *Daily Nation*, 30 Jan. 1968; 'Policeman Tells How He Was Attacked', *Daily Nation*, 7 Jan. 1972; 'Man Accused of Stoning Police', *Daily Nation*, 19 Jan. 1977.

[121] 'Warning on "Power" Drink', *Daily Nation*, 27 Jan. 1967; for military drinking see *Daily Nation*, 25 Jan. 1968 and 3 Jan. 1969.

distillers, or the Kisumu councillor caught by police (with whom he had a political dispute) with a gallon of *chang'aa*.[122] By the late 1970s, illicit distillation was common in all three East African countries – and in Uganda, it was very common indeed.

The economy of distillation

[The Magistrate] noted that chang'aa was one of the most money-making commodity [sic] but regretted that it unfortunately left scores of its consumers sick or dead.[123]

Distillates can be moved and stored and traded far more readily than ferments. Unsurprisingly, when compared with informal-sector ferments, spirits have encouraged more complex economic linkages and a tendency to more overtly commercialized labour relations within production. But the production of distillates generally remained small-scale. In many rural areas, distilling continued to be an auxiliary or adjunct activity, often run alongside the production of fermented beverages and used as a fall-back when a ferment went awry, or went too long unsold – distilling being a way to make good some of the loss involved.[124] Crucially, distillation freed sellers from the problems of localized over-supply; spirits could simply be kept, unsold, for another day; no doubt it was this which led some to consider this an 'exceptionally profitable' pursuit.[125] But production remained small-scale. Obbo's account of Kampala women distillers at the beginning of the 1970s suggested that some of these were operating on a large enough scale to employ male labourers, but it is not clear whether this went any further than the occasional use of casual workers to manipulate distilling drums.[126] The references to amounts of distillates involved in criminal cases consistently suggest a small scale of production, and small-scale retailing too: even a businessman dealing in *moshi* in Dar es Salaam had only 35 bottles on his premises, while a woman seller had only six.[127] After raids in Nairobi in January 1973, 18 people (13 and 5 women) were fined for possessing 47 gallons of *chang'aa* between them.[128]

It was in distribution and transport that money was to be made by those who could pass road blocks with impunity – sometimes by transporting *chang'aa* in ambulances with sirens wailing.[129] Impunity might be gained more simply by the well-connected: 'the big people you see today I am not

[122] *Daily Nation*, 17 Jan. 1966; 'Councillor on Gin Charge', *Daily Nation*, 22 Jan. and 24 Jan. 1969.
[123] 'Chang'aa Makers', *Daily Nation*, 4 Feb. 1980.
[124] Ints Nyoro1b, 2; Nyoro4b, 2; Journal, 10 Feb. 1997.
[125] Heald, *Controlling Anger*, 87-8, notes that this was Gisu opinion in the 1960s.
[126] Obbo, *African Women*, 131-2.
[127] 'Moshi Jail Term Doubled on Appeal', *Standard, Tanzania*, 22 Jan. 1971; 'Dar Woman Fined', *Standard, Tanzania*, 8 Jan. 1971.
[128] 'Chang'aa Offenders Fined', *Daily Nation*, 16 Jan. 1973.
[129] *Kenya National Assembly Debates*, Kariuki, 21 Oct. 1971, col. 1315.

afraid to say they depend on the cash from *haragi* for their education, for their standard of living, and the rest'.[130] But the patrimonial state was unpredictable in its operation. In 1974 a Kenyan businessman was arrested with 55 gallons of *chang'aa* in his car, on his way to Nairobi. He was evidently a regular trader, and it is unclear why he was caught on this occasion. He adduced the desire for development in his defence: 'Otieno told the magistrate in mitigation that he was going to sell chang'aa to enable him to get school fees for his children.' The magistrate was unimpressed. He confiscated the car and sent the man to prison for six months.[131] Others ran the roadblocks with less fear of arrest: in 1985 a Kenyan judge alleged that it was 'the rich' who promoted and backed the *chang'aa* trade.[132] The extended linkages of the distilling economy tended to create a series of additional points at which those who had access to the power of the state could extract income from the informal-sector of alcohol; it was they who could buy 'cars and matatus [taxis]' from their profits in the trade.[133] This was partly a story of women losing out to better-capitalized men, but it was also further evidence of the fundamental pattern of the post-colonial state: that those who have access to the manifold institutions of the state profit at the expense of those who do not. The informal economy of alcohol – distilled, as well as fermented – offered a constant subsidy to the lesser officials of the state.

BREWS & STILLS

In the colonial and early post-colonial periods, official rhetoric constantly reaffirmed the notion that spirits were different: that they were the drink of the urban, the wage-earners (if not the salaried), the educated. But from the later 1970s official rhetoric began to shift, and in the denunciations of drunkenness which became such a prominent part of public rhetoric from the end of the 1970s, distillates and informal fermented brews came to be increasingly blurred through the vague application of technical terms: distillates were referred to as brews, and stills described as breweries.[134] The stress which police and administration had once placed on the particular and especial dangers of distillation disappeared, and the rhetoric turned away from the issue of health to the general problem of drunkenness as a cause of laziness and a threat to the social institutions which underpinned development – notably 'the family'. In 1981, a magazine article contrasted *chang'aa* as containing 'a lot of unchecked and uncontrolled dangerous acid', with *busaa* (grain beer) which was merely 'unhygienically brewed'.[135] But a

---

[130] Int Nyoro21a, 7.
[131] 'Chang'aa Man', *Daily Nation*, 26 Jan. 1974.
[132] 'Alcoholism: Judge Blames the Rich', *Standard, Kenya*, 23 Apr. 1985.
[133] 'What's your poison?', *Daily Nation*, 21 Jan. 1977: the reference to the buying of cars is interestingly evocative of colonial complaints about the wealth of African liquor sellers: see chapter 5.
[134] 'Police Raid Breweries', *Daily Nation*, 25 Jan. 1979; 'Brewing…', *Daily Nation*, 31 Jan. 1979.
[135] 'Some Like It Hot!', *Drum (EA)*, Mar. 1981.

few years later journalism routinely lumped together traditional honey-wine, industrial Kibuku and *chang'aa* as elements of the drinking world of the marginal which destroyed homes and careers.[136] Warning against the drinking of *chang'aa*, an assistant chief declared that 'The Government . . . was determined to eradicate illicit liquor to enhance development and prevent their [sic] ruining individuals and families.'[137] A local magistrate in Tanzania assured me that the government treated illicit distillates so seriously because those who made them were 'saboteurs', the emotive term widely used in the 1980s of any activity which was perceived to harm national development.[138]

Popular discourse, however, continued to reproduce the idea that spirits were quite different from traditional ferments. They were power, and their consumption could by itself bring health.[139] The idea that these drinks were refined and modern, which had suffused official rhetoric for many years, continued to be reproduced in popular discourse.[140] In cities, distinct places of spirits drinking continued – like the '*chang'aa* dens' of Nairobi[141] – but spirits also began to be sold, discreetly, alongside other drinks in urban bars, and in smaller towns and rural areas illicit spirits made their way into the *ebirabo*, the *vilabu*, the *vikao* and into the more-or-less furtive gatherings where fermented brews were consumed in Kenya. Yet spirits remained different from fermented drinks. They were different in the unambiguously commercial intent of production; those who physically assisted in the distilling process might be rewarded with a drink, but generally distillers, men or women, did not retain a portion of their product to share with friends and neighbours.[142] And while – as with bottled beer – some elder men attempted to assert their authority over these drinks, by demanding that spirits be given as marriage gifts, distillates stayed largely remote from the ritual presentations of alcohol which continued to evoke elder men's authority.[143] 'This drinking of haragi ... is for your generation', one woman told myself and my research assistant.[144] In fact, many elder men did drink spirits, but such drinking continued to be an essentially individualistic activity, quite distinct from the sociability associated with the drinking of banana wine and millet beer. No drinking groups shared the price of a bottle of *enguli* or *chang'aa*. And, as appalled observers had noted in the 1970s, spirits drinking, much more than the drinking of ferments, mixed ages and sexes: 'Youths, some of them schoolboys and girls, are known to rub shoulders with elderly addicts . . . What more can one say, really?'[145]

[136] 'Feeling in a Different World for a Little Money', *Daily Nation*, 28 Aug. 1985.
[137] 'Keep Off Liquor, Pupils Warned', *Daily Nation*, 1 July 1985.
[138] Int Nya40a.
[139] 'Chang'aa Trade Booming at City Centre', *Sunday Times* [Kenya], 13 May 1984.
[140] Int Nyoro40b, 3.
[141] 'Chang'aa Trade Booming at City Centre', *Sunday Times* [Kenya], 13 May 1984.
[142] An exception is noted in Int Nyoro7c, 4.
[143] Int Nyoro7a, 4; see also Fukui, 'Alcoholic Drinks of the Iraqw', 141.
[144] Int Nyoro3b, 2.
[145] 'Dangers of Dhang'aa', *Daily Nation*, 16 Jan. 1973.

Drinking spirits, people drank power; distillates were the drink of people living uneasily between an unattainable modernity and the power over well-being exercised by jealous neighbours. Such drinking grew. By 1978, *chang'aa* was estimated to constitute more than one-third of the total alcohol intake in Kenya; twice as much as bottled beer and formal-sector spirits put together.[146] The ban on legal sales of fermented liquors in Kenya encouraged some sellers to switch to trade in the more easily concealed and stored *chang'aa*, and by the early 1990s a quarter of the women surveyed in one low-income area of Nairobi were selling *chang'aa*.[147] During the 1990s, the association of illicit spirits and power was to take on a new – and often grim – aspect.

---

[146] Partanen, *Sociability and Intoxication*, 47.

[147] D. Rodriguez-Torres, 'Lutte pour la vie et lutte pour la ville: Crise urbaine, politique urbaine et pauvreté à Nairobi' (PhD, Bordeaux I, 1994), 256.

Part Four

Drinking in the 1990s

> People in developing countries have not yet learned to live peacefully
> with alcohol, to fear its dangers and the consequences of abuse.[1]

In the 1980s, there was a brief spate of concern about alcohol as a 'problem'
in Africa and elsewhere in the developing world; a concern which in its
most naive expressions reverted to the infantilizing discourse of the late
nineteenth century, casting Africans as innocents in danger from the strong
drinks of more sophisticated societies.[2] In Kenya, there were newspaper
reports and seminars on this, but no major changes in popular rhetoric or
official policy.[3] But in the 1990s, when international temperance
organizations launched a new campaign in East Africa, their arguments
became drawn into vigorous public debates which revealed widespread
concern over drinking, and linked this drinking to an acute social crisis.[4]

The idea that moral crisis was manifested in – and propelled by – drinking
was not in itself novel; as has been argued, people had consistently turned
to alcohol as a discursive resource in arguments over proper behaviour and
authority. What was new in the 1990s was the intensity of these discourses,
in the context of rapid economic and political change which transformed
the nature and accessibility of power. Across East Africa, the machinery of
the state was in rapid decline, and inequality was growing. For the
accumulators, as well as for the excluded, such growing inequality at a time
when the state was increasingly weak created a profound challenge: the
state could neither guarantee well-being nor exercise coercive power – so

---

[1] Statement attributed to the Chair of the International Council on Alcohol and Addiction in
'Alcohol Consumption in Third World Alarming', *Daily Nation*, 18 Apr. 1986.

[2] G. Edwards, 'Drinking Problems: Putting the Third World on the Map', *Lancet*, no. 8139
(1979), 402-4.

[3] 'Seminar Starts', *Daily Nation*, 12 April 1985; 'Drinking Soars in the Third World', *Daily
Nation*, 1 May 1985.

[4] 'Alcohol Abuse Irks Bishop', *Daily Nation*, 9 April 1996; 'Leaders Want Government to Order
Bars Closed', Daily Nation, 3 Jan. 1997; 'The Bar Culture Sweeps the Land', *Daily Nation*, 4
April 1997; 'Lack of Education, Awareness, Leads to Alcoholism in Uganda', *East African*,
1-7 Feb. 1999.

241

where did authority lie, and who now judged proper behaviour? In widespread debates over the crisis of well-being and behaviour, alternative ideas of temperance played a central part. There was concern over how much people drank, and an implication – quite probably mistaken – that consumption was rising.[5] But even more, there was heightened concern over the way that people drank, and over what they drank: bottled beer, traditional liquors, illicit distillates and new kinds of drinks were all condemned by some and embraced by others in increasingly vocal and contradictory debates. These debates, and the sense of crisis they generated, reflected a striking commitment to a moral and economic diversification, pursued by accumulators and by those who sought, more simply, to survive.

[5] 'But Ugandans Have Not Always Been Such Heavy drinkers', *East African*, 2-29 June 1997.

Twelve

Beer wars & power drinks
State, capital & drinking well-being
1991–99

One wonders why we have to ban the traditional liquors and at the same time allow breweries ... to come into the country and take all our money.[1]

New-generation drinks

The tendency for the production – and even more so the distribution and transport – of illicit distillates to move to a slightly larger economic scale has already been noted, and a study of the *chang'aa* market in Nairobi in the early 1990s revealed a continuation of that trend.[2] In Uganda, while the production of distillates had remained small-scale, the trade in these became more and more overt in the 1990s. Prosecutions under the Enguli Act became infrequent – there were only 58 in the whole country in 1994.[3] Distilling had become the subject of joky comments rather than self-righteous fury in the press, and police in Kampala protested publicly at the loss of income when the officer in charge forbade the *enguli* trade in the police barracks.[4] In consequence of this relaxed official attitude, the 1990s saw the emergence in Uganda of a number of entrepreneurs who were buyers, not producers, and who bulked distillates in rural centres before selling them to other entrepreneurs who transported large quantities – hundreds of litres of spirits at a time – for sale in the cities or to war zones in the north or across the

---

[1] Karauri, *Kenya National Assembly Debates*, 14 Oct. 1998, 1704.

[2] D. Rodriguez-Torres, 'De l'informel à l'illégal. La production de Chang'aa à Nairobi', IFRA working paper, Nairobi, 1996.

[3] The *Statistical Abstract* gives prosecution figures under the Enguli Act as 91 in 1991, 88 in 1992, 69 in 1993 and 58 in 1994. There are no national figures for years since 1994: but in Hoima, court records show no prosecutions under the Enguli Act since 1993, when nine individuals were convicted in two prosecutions. Those convicted were four men and five women: none was over 30 years of age.

[4] 'Lira-lira Blast Rocks Nakawa' and 'Residents Cry Foul on Malwa Ban', *New Vision*, 7 and 9 May 1998.

border in Sudan or the Democratic Republic of Congo.[5] In Kenya, meanwhile, new circumstances led to the development of a new kind of production, which lay uneasily between formal and informal production: the 'new-generation' drinks, some of which came also to be known as 'power' drinks.[6]

These were a direct result of changing political and economic circumstances in Kenya, where international pressure – exercised through increasing restrictions on financial assistance packages for the government – had led to the introduction of multi-partyism and a prolonged economic downturn, exacerbated by wild spending by the government in the election year of 1992. Kenya Breweries had shown more enthusiasm than was strictly necessary for the transition to multi-partyism;[7] Matiba, former KBL director, had been a principal opposition candidate for the presidency. He did not win, and in the run-up to the 1992 elections, and afterwards, KBL found itself facing greatly increased taxes. The price of beer rose by 100 percent as a result of these taxes (and as a result also of the wild inflation which gripped the country in 1993).[8] And KBL was deprived of its political protection.

At this time, the Nairobi factory which made Kibuku – branded sorghum beer – started to produce a new drink, called Sorghum Sake, which was stronger and more stable than Kibuku and would seem to have been a sugar-based ferment, possibly fortified with additional alcohol. Although it was not 'in a state of continuing fermentation', as the law required, this was taxed as a traditional liquor at a rate very much lower than that paid by bottled beer. Sold in sealed plastic bottles, it was easy to transport and store, as well as cheap. Kibuku had never been popular, and Lonrho, the company which started the factory, had sold it after a few years to the Kuguru family, businesspeople and politicians from central Kenya. But this new drink was popular. For a drinking public who could no longer afford bottled beer but were reluctant to drink traditional liquor, Sorghum Sake was an attractive product. In the space of two years, sales of bottled beer fell by around 25 percent, a fall which KBL attributed largely to the popularity of drinks like Sorghum Sake.[9] Sorghum Sake was specifically marketed as a cheap substitute for beer, a drink compatible with modernity and development which could allow the drinker to drink, and still pay school fees for his children: 'Don't Drink Beer! Save for School Fees'.[10] Soon there was a plentiful supply of

[5] In a one-week survey of the trade in Hoima in 1998, wholesalers in the town were selling an average of 1,600 litres of spirit a day to dealers who transported the spirit elsewhere. At the wholesale price then prevalent, this was US$2,000 worth of spirits each day.

[6] For the identification of these as 'power' drinks, see 'On Matters of the Throat...', *Sunday Nation*, 6 Aug. 1998; Letter, Gichane, *Daily Nation*, 5 Sep. 1998; 'For Many Drinkers, There Are No Alternatives', *East African*, 31 Aug.–6 Sep. 1998.

[7] KBL produced a glossy publication, 'To the Future', comparing their own corporate re-structuring with the desirable political restructuring of the country and looking forward to a 'better atmosphere' under the multi-party system.

[8] 'Facts About the Kenya Beer Market': KBL advertisement in *Daily Nation*, 22 July 1997.

[9] 'Fighting Hard for Survival', *Weekly Review*, 16 Oct. 1998; pers. comm., Chris Odito.

[10] Sorghum Sake advert, *Daily Nation*, 18 Dec. 1996.

such drinks, in central Kenya at least, as others imitated the success of Sorghum Sake. By 1997 there were alleged to be around 40 factories producing these new-generation drinks, and the Kuguru group were planning major new investments.[11] It was an extraordinary and open burgeoning of an industry; and while Sorghum Sake was the product of a long-established factory, much of the rest of the industry was on the margins of legality. No attempt was made to control this growth, despite KBL's complaints; and KBL were reduced to conducting an advertising war and marketing a bottled beer which, by avoiding the use of malt, attracted a lower excise duty.[12] Yet the very lack of control which made the new-generation industry possible was soon to compromise it. Bottles and labels were used and re-used by an ever-growing body of apparently unregulated producers – from whom the makers of Sorghum Sake itself were careful to distance themselves[13] – who were working on a quite different scale from any of the informal producers of the 1970s and 1980s. One single producer was transporting 2,000 litres in one load.[14] Some of these producers took to flavouring and bottling industrial alcohol (diverted en route from the sugar refineries in western Kenya): the beverages made with this came to be known as power drinks, a tag which neatly expressed both the cultural role of spirits as a drink of power and the erstwhile role of this industrial alcohol as an additive to automobile fuel.[15] The production of beverage spirits from industrial alcohol was a long-established, if minor, part of the trade in East Africa;[16] but in Kenya in the mid-1990s it became widespread, with tragic results. There were a series of mass poisoning incidents, and a number of deaths.[17]

Accounts of these deaths suggest how much these power drinks had become the drink of those employed by the state, who had seen their real incomes fall sharply since the beginning of the 1990s. Among the 11 reported dead after one drinking bout were a Special Branch man, a teacher, a public health worker and an employee of the telecommunications corporation.[18] In September 1999 police raided a house in an upmarket estate in Nairobi, where a businessman had been distilling *chang'aa* and bottling it as a new-generation drink, presumably for the delectation of his upmarket neighbours

---

[11] 'High Tax Killing Brewing Industry', *Daily Nation*, 7 Jan. 1997; 'Brewery to put up Sh60m Bottling Plant', *Daily Nation*, 4 Jan. 1997.

[12] For the advertisement war, see for example the advertisement in the *Daily Nation*, 23 Sep. 1996; for the new beer, 'Citizen', see 'KBL First to Use Concept', *Daily Nation*, 12 Aug. 1997.

[13] See their advertisement in the *Daily Nation*, 23 Sep. 1996.

[14] 'Liquor Dealers Defy Ban', *Daily Nation*, 23 May 1998.

[15] 'How We Took the Lethal Brew', *Daily Nation*, 28 Aug. 1998.

[16] This technique was mentioned in the 1930s: Govt Analyst to Director of Medical Services, 29 Mar. 1932, KNA MOH 1/174.

[17] It is difficult to know how many deaths: extravagant figures were offered in the debate, but there is no reliable figure for the total: Michuki, *Kenya National Assembly Debates*, 1 July 1998, 947. For the actual composition of power drinks, see Michuki, *Kenya National Assembly Debates*, 1 July 1998, 947; 'How We Took the Lethal Brew', *Daily Nation*, 28 Aug. 1998.

[18] 'Eleven More Die After Taking Lethal Drink', *Daily Nation*, 22 Aug. 1998; 'For Many Drinkers, There Are No Choices', *East African*, 31 Aug. - 6 Sep. 1998.

who could no longer afford to buy beer all the time.[19] And, in a striking irony, bottled beer was becoming more widely advertised than ever, just as it was becoming less and less affordable for the servants of the state, its most assiduous devotees.

LIBERALIZING BEER

In September 1998, a new bottled-beer brewery was opened in Kenya by a new company. It was the first such entirely new venture in the region since the early 1960s. Shortly afterwards, another new company opened another new brewery, in Tanzania.[20] During the 1990s, the patterns of relationship between state and formal-sector alcohol which had been established since the 1960s were disrupted, and the effective monopoly held by breweries and distilleries which were either owned by the state, or in close alliance with elite members of the state, came to an end. The supply of beer improved dramatically in Uganda and Tanzania, and in both countries consumption of beer grew quickly – though not as rapidly as it had in the 1960s. It was not the teachers and civil servants who bought this beer, however; it was those employed by development agencies or men briefly enriched by the coffee boom of the mid-1990s, or other primary crop exports. In Kenya, meanwhile, economic difficulties and tax increases meant that beer consumption fell between 1992 and 1997; and KBL, which had so long flourished through its relationship with the state, found itself reduced to the position of a minor player in the contests of multinational capital.

At the beginning of the 1990s, TBL was moribund and the chronic shortage of bottled beer was a constant source of complaint among the elite. Economic liberalization brought in South African Breweries (SAB), the company which dominated the southern African beer market.[21] In 1993 SAB established with the government a 'joint venture' to run Tanzania Breweries. There were redundancies, and the new company rapidly disposed of the whole transport and distribution network which state control had created: bottled beer was to be moved and sold by private entrepreneurs.[22] In a few years, production and distribution were transformed. Bottled beer was in ready supply in all towns, and had even appeared in some village shops. TBL was paying dividends not only to SAB and the government, but also to private shareholders who had taken up a 10 percent stake in a public flotation.[23] TBL became a showcase of the success of liberalization; and seemed briefly likely to revive the brewery–state alliance of the 1960s, receiving a degree of fiscal protection and making much of its revenue

[19] 'Illegal Liquor Factory', *Daily Nation*, 9 Sep. 1999.
[20] 'SAB Open New Factory in Kenya', *East African*, 5-11 Oct. 1998; 'Kibo Expansion', *East African*, 10-16 Aug. 1998.
[21] Mager, 'The First Decade of European Beer', gives a good account of SAB's success.
[22] I am indebted to Wilfrid Mwingiza and Daniel Niemandt of TBL for information on all aspects of TBL's operations since 1993.
[23] 'Dar Shares Finally Get Investors', *East African*, 3-9 Aug. 1998

contributions to the government,[24] which totalled US$73 million in 1998.[25] In 1997, SAB expanded further, entering into a partnership with Nile Breweries in Uganda, a company which began brewing in the 1950s as part of the Madhvani investments in bottled beer, and which had come back into Madhvani's hands in the 1980s.[26] Again the venture was a success. Both these advances by SAB had serious consequences for KBL, since the Kenyan company had in the 1980s sold much of their beer in Tanzania, and they owned Uganda Breweries, Nile's rival. Then SAB came to an agreement with Njenga Karume, one of the Kenyan political-business elite who had prospered as a beer distributor since the 1960s; Karume and SAB would establish their own new brewery in Kenya.[27] This was the brewery which opened in 1998. Shortly afterwards, KBL and Karume came to be embroiled in a legal dispute over his distributorship, which KBL had cancelled, allegedly in consequence of his agreement with SAB.[28]

This was all far from the co-operative race for progress in 1960s brewing, when increasing production had been all that mattered; now these companies were in outright competition for a limited market. SAB and KBL became involved in complex legal disputes over tax regimes and brand names, while their rival distributors turned to violence against property and staff.[29] KBL sought to raise capital for new investments of its own; Guinness International took a large share of the company, and Guinness executives became increasingly involved in the running of the company.[30] KBL then established a new enterprise, in co-operation with a Tanzanian entrepreneur, to brew beer in Tanzania, which opened shortly after the SAB venture in Kenya. By 1998 there were competing major beer brewers in all three East African countries. The former close relationship between a single brewer and the state did not re-emerge, international capital dominated production, and all three East African governments allowed the importation of beer, as well as domestic competition. Meanwhile, a similar process of the increasing involvement of international capital was evident in the (very much smaller) formal spirits market. The Uganda Waragi factory in Uganda was taken over by International Distillers and Vintners (a member of the same international group as Guinness); the Konyagi factory in Tanzania became part of the SAB group.

---

[24] 'Back to Centralized Economy? We Shouldn't Even Think About It', *Guardian* [Tanzania], 30 Sep. 1997; 'Kenya Beer to Cost More Than SA's in Tanzania', 'Tanzania tax cuts likely', *East African*, 17-23 Feb. and 23-29 June 1997.

[25] 'Tanzania Breweries "Not Importing Malt from SA"', *East African*, 1-7 Mar. 1999.

[26] 'SAB Targets Ugandan Brewery', *Daily Nation*, 12 Aug. 1997; sometime later SAB bought out the Zambian brewing interests of Madhvani entirely: 'SA Beer Firm in New Deal', *East African*, 21-27 Dec. 1998.

[27] 'South African Breweries Seeks Foothold in Kenya', *East African*, 17-23 Feb. 1997.

[28] 'Karume Sues Beer Firm', *Daily Nation*, 5 July 1997.

[29] 'Brewers Entice Drinkers' and 'Beer Wars Spilling Over', *East African*, 16-22 Nov. 1998.

[30] It is not clear how intentional the Guinness role was; formally, it underwrote a share issue, which was undersubscribed, and so ended up with a reported 45 percent of the equity: 'KBL Half-yearly Profit up by 18 percent', *Daily Nation*, 17 Feb. 1998.

All these producers were more keenly aware than ever of the tax burden which they bore. They were scrambling for a market which was severely restricted by the price of bottled beer (and bottled spirits), and they complained constantly of this – even though taxes in Uganda and Tanzania were considerably below the extraordinary rates of the 1980s.[31] The goal now was not to persuade the bulk of the populace of the desirability of modern drinks, but rather to provide a beer that could compete with the cheap drinks of modernity – and particularly with illicit distillates and the new-generation drinks. There was no project of social transformation now, and the state was a burden rather than an ally.

Advertising increasingly suggested this change. The hard-working beer drinker of the 1970s disappeared. To an extent, breweries played on the idea of the nation in their advertising – particularly KBL, whose slogan came to be 'My country, my beer'.[32] But even more than this, 'strength' or 'power' – especially the strength or power of men – became the key terms:[33] Guinness resurrected an earlier slogan and made it the centrepiece of their marketing: 'Guinness. The Power'.[34] The average strength of bottled beers crept up, as formal-sector brewing companies competed with the power drinks of the illicit market.[35] Beer was to settle a 'man-size thirst',[36] and one brewery drew together the notions of the power derived from 'strong' drink and the financial power of the successful entrepreneur with their 'Chairman's Extra Strong Brew' brand. Bottled beer was the drink of the wealthy individual, and of men.

BANNING POWER DRINKS

Unable to compete with the new-generation drinks on price, the brewing companies – and in particular KBL – sought the assistance of the state, seizing on the poisoning incidents as a way of doing so. In July 1998, parliament in Kenya discussed a motion which called for the banning of the power drinks. The motion was brought by an opposition MP, and emphasized a constant point in opposition arguments: that corruption within the political elite meant that the state no longer had any legitimate claim to authority as the provider of health and wealth. Officials, it was argued 'must consider themselves as guilt [sic] for having allowed such dangerous drinks to be consumed by Kenyans for so long'.[37] The whole idea of a parliamentary motion on this subject offered a revealing glimpse into the workings of the

---

[31] 'Growth of Beer Industry "Hampered by High Taxes"', *Daily Nation*, 2 Mar. 1999; 'Nile Beer Seeks Tax Cut', *New Vision*, 12 May 1998; 'Uganda Breweries in Major Project to Boost Capacity', *East African*, 6-12 July 1998; 'Some Bitter Truths About Brewing in East Africa', *East African*, 22-28 Mar. 1998.

[32] See advertisements, *Daily Nation*, 16 Aug. and 3 Sep. 1997.

[33] See advertisements for Pilsner (*Daily Nation*, 22 May 1997); Citizen Special (*Daily Nation*, 16 Aug. 1997); Nile (*Monitor*, 9 May 1998).

[34] Advertisement, *Daily Nation*, 11 Aug. 1997.

[35] 'Uganda Brewers to Stop Producing "Weak" Beers', *East African*, 7-13 Sep. 1998.

[36] Advertisement, *Daily Nation*, 21 May 1997.

[37] Wamae, *Kenya National Assembly Debates*, 1 July 1998, 949; see also Muite and Kituyi, *ibid.*, 952-3, 960.

state in Kenya. Many of the new-generation brews were already clearly outside the law in terms of the tax they paid, or through violations of standards and packaging requirements, but no attempt had been made to enforce these laws. KBL, which supported the motion, evidently hoped that the publicity around the motion would force the state to act in defence of its claim to legitimacy as a guarantor of well-being. In this they were successful: the state – or rather, some within the state – were concerned about this legitimacy, for as soon as notice of the motion was given a concerted effort was made by administrators to suppress the new-generation drinks.[38]

The motion was passed in parliament, even though it was critical of the government.[39] It was carried through by a wave of popular concern which reflected widespread unease about the nature of proper drinking and societal well-being.[40] To an extent, such concern blurred power drinks with other kinds of informal and illicit alcoholic beverages:[41] 'traditional liquor, which makes people not work and makes children not go to school, should be banned', said one MP in the debate on the motion, adding that 'the intent which the Government of Kenya had in 1978 to ban traditional liquors because they had begun to hamper the development of the country must be maintained'.[42] In debates beyond parliament, too, new-generation drinks might be categorized with local brews which 'made most men economically and socially unproductive'[43] and threatened 'the family'.[44] There was anyway an intentional ambiguity in the wording of the motion, for it was intended to cover drinks produced by a wide range of informal enterprises which almost certainly varied widely in their ingredients and the circumstances of their production. At the same time, some MPs were anxious to aver that 'nobody is complaining about gin, brandy or beer';[45] and the mover of the motion was one of those men who had built a career of political and business success after acquiring a beer distributorship in the 1960s, and who therefore had a direct interest in suppressing illicit liquor.[46]

[38] See for example 'DC Bans Sale of Lethal Brews', *Daily Nation*, 13 May 1998.

[39] 'Motion on Lethal Brews Passed', *Daily Nation*, 2 July 1998.

[40] 'Brews Cause Alarm', *Sunday Standard*, 17 May 1998.

[41] See for example the list of producers and products in 'Cheap, Locally-made Brews: Who Produces What', *Daily Nation*, 27 May 1998; and the lists of drinks banned by local administrators in different places: 'DC Bans Sale of "Lethal" Brews' and 'Brew Dealers Arrested', *Daily Nation*, 13 and 19 May 1998.

[42] Kathangu, *Kenya National Assembly Debates*, 1 July 1998, 957-8. For the actual composition of power drinks, see Michuki, *Kenya National Assembly Debates*, 1 July 1998, 947; 'How We Took the Lethal Brew', *Daily Nation*, 28 Aug. 1998.

[43] 'Man Dies After Drinking Brew', *Daily Nation*, 19 May 1998.

[44] 'Cleric Acts Tough on Brews', *Daily Nation*, 31 Aug. 1998; 'Brews Cause Alarm', *Sunday Standard*, 17 May 1998; Michuki and Mwewa, *Kenya National Assembly Debates*, 1 July 1998, 959.

[45] Wamae, *Kenya National Assembly Debates*, 950.

[46] Keah and Michuki, *Kenya National Assembly Debates*, 1 July 1998, 954. The seconder of the motion was said to have a long-standing political rivalry with the Kuguru family, owners of the company which made Sorghum Sake: 'Legacy of Violent and Vicious Polls', *Daily Nation*, 9 Aug. 1997.

But the motion also revealed that public rhetoric and popular discourse were changing. The new-generation drinks were said to make men impotent, even incontinent.[47] 'Since my husband started taking the brew he is now useless. It is like sharing the bed with another woman', said one woman.[48] The power drinks of the modern world were reducing men to infants. In parliament, some emphasized that power drinks were not like other kinds of liquor, and called for the government to end the suppression of traditional fermented liquors 'which we have been drinking for centuries'.[49] Letters to the press and editorials made the same point: 'It is time the whole question of the traditional brews . . . was reassessed so that the positive values in them can be identified'; 'leaders should be calling for . . . the legalisation of cheap and safe traditional drink that ordinary people can afford'.[50] Some idealized the healthiness of bottled beer, and categorized power drinks with traditional drinks; but others identified power drinks with the dangers of modernity.

A few months later, parliament passed another motion, which explicitly called for the legalization of the trade in palm wine.[51] The ban on the trade in traditional liquor had been particularly resented at the coast, where palm wine was widely consumed, and this had offered one issue on which the political opposition (which was widely seen as rooted in other parts of the country) might manage to garner coastal support, so there was a particular element of political knockabout in the debate on the motion.[52] Some opposition parties had been making much of the petty oppression and extortion committed under the guise of enforcing the laws on traditional liquor;[53] government supporters in turn accused them of sabotaging development by encouraging such liquor: 'as a Government we have always stood firm on this question of traditional liquor. How can we run a nation whose people are only preoccupied with matters of drunkenness?'[54] They seized with glee on the apparent contradiction between the motion of July (which called for a ban on some illicit liquors) and this motion calling for legalization of other illicit liquors.[55] But this discursive homogenization of all illicit liquor was rejected by other MPs, who effectively broadened the debate from palm wine to cover all 'respected' traditional fermented liquors, 'which are not harmful and which our people have consumed for many generations'.[56] Thus they re-established in public political rhetoric the idea that traditional liquors were not only harmless but were part of a desirable social order which had come to be threatened by a modernity imposed by government regulation: 'in the absence of what people used to drink [they] rush for cheap dangerous

[47] Michuku, Ongeri and Muite, *Kenya National Assembly Debates*, 1 July 1998, 948, 951, 952.

[48] 'Cheap Brews Wreck Families', *Daily Nation*, 27 May 1998; 'Banned, But It's Business as Usual', *Daily Nation*, 27 May 1998.

[49] Keah, *Kenya National Assembly Debates*, 1 July 1998, 954.

[50] Leader, *Sunday Standard*, 17 May 1998; Letter, Gichane, *Daily Nation*, 5 Sep. 1998.

[51] 'Investors Being Sought to Start Wine Factories', *Daily Nation*, 4 Nov. 1998.

[52] Maitha, *Kenya National Assembly Debates*, 7 Oct. 1998, 1591.

[53] Murungi and Sunkuli, *Kenya National Assembly Debates*, 7 Oct. 1998, 1594.

[54] Sunkuli and Murungi, *Kenya National Assembly Debates*, 7 Oct. 1998, 1598, 1593.

[55] Sunkuli, *Kenya National Assembly Debates*, 7 Oct. 1998, 1598.

[56] Murungi, *Kenya National Assembly Debates*, 7 Oct. 1998, 1593; Kathangu, *ibid.*, 14 Oct. 1998, 1703.

brews and die in the process'.[57] John Michuki, the MP with a beer distributorship who had brought the July motion, announced that 'the traditional drinks that our people have been consuming since time immemorial were not harmful'; and he argued that it was not these drinks but the power alcohol that 'killed and made our people lazy'.[58] Tradition was healthy – modernity might not be. There was by no means complete unanimity on this return of traditional liquor to respectability: some sought to resurrect the theoretical division between cultural and sale use which had long been enshrined in law but had been largely ignored for more than a decade;[59] and one politician ingeniously sought to bring traditional liquor into the discursive world of time and waged labour which bottled beer had dominated, calling for the industrial development of 'indigenous' liquors and saying: 'We want people to drink palm wine – after work.'[60]

Such divisions revealed continuing debate over what proper drinking should be, in the context of post-colonial states whose coercive and patronage resources were very much diminished; and whose people were faced with a new and ambitious capitalism with its financial roots outside East Africa. There was by the later 1990s a widespread sense of vulnerability and uncertainty over how individuals and communities might seek health and wealth, which was revealed in the arguments over proper drinking. Public rhetoric, as well as private discourse and practice, had shifted: remarkably, more than one parliamentary contributor to the debate on palm wine characterized bottled beer not as the desirable drink of development, but as an alien and exploitative presence, and complained that: '[w]e have stopped the production of palm wine so that Kenya Breweries can continue to suck from us and entrap us.'[61]

Through the parliamentary notion and the public debate it stirred, officials were forced to act against the lethal brews, in defence of the idea that the state derived authority from its power to ensure health. Yet the state was too fractured to effectively suppress the new-generation drinks; newspaper reports revealed the continued sale of power drinks, and the continued role of servants of the state in this trade.[62] And the debate over these drinks had made very public the multiplicity of contradictory ideas of proper drinking, in which bottled beer was anathematized as often as it was idealized. The palpable sense of drinking crisis which gripped Kenya – and, to a lesser extent, Tanzania and Uganda – reflected an economic and moral diversification, which had become central to the survival and accumulation strategies of many people across East Africa.

---

[57] Karauri, *Kenya National Assembly Debates*, 14 Oct. 1998, 1705; Maitha, *ibid.*, 7 Oct. 1998, 1590, 1592.

[58] Michuki, *Kenya National Assembly Debates*, 14 Oct. 1998, 1701.

[59] Michuki, unsurprisingly, insisted that 'we are not saying that traditional drinks should be reintroduced in order for them to be marketed'; *Kenya National Assembly Debates*, 14 Oct. 1998, 1701.

[60] Raila, *Kenya National Assembly Debates*, 7 Oct. 1998, 1595-6.

[61] Mwakalu and Karauri, *Kenya National Assembly Debates*, 14 Oct. 1998, 1702, 1704.

[62] 'Brew: 29 Officers Arrested', *Daily Nation*, 28 Aug. 1998; 'Brew Impounded', *Daily Nation*, 10 Feb. 1999.

Thirteen

Crises of drinking & diversification
Wealth, poverty & the decline of the state

[The drunkenness] of nowadays is bad, because it is like madness, because – I think – a lot is drunk. Because of this 'development', this drunkenness came which wasn't there [previously].[1]

In 1990, the district headquarters at Tukuyu housed 30 officials. By 1999, only nine were left. The area commissioner was the only one with regular access to a vehicle, and the building's peeling walls and ramshackle furniture indicated the chronic shortage of funds; the part of the building which housed the district court was destroyed by fire in the early 1990s and had never been replaced. Across the region, the tide of state activity, which rose rapidly from the 1950s and peaked at around 1980, had ebbed away. For those in the higher levels of the system – the district commissioner and the heads of local councils – their position within the state still brought rewards. They might use the few remaining government vehicles to deal in foodstuffs; appropriate the taxes levied on those who extracted local natural resources; use their remaining influence on trade licensing bodies or on the legal system to extort bribes; and ensure that they were involved in business deals, such as land purchases, only on very advantageous terms. They could still impose themselves as gatekeepers, mediating relationships between the populace and representatives of foreign organizations (from medical workers to historical researchers) in ways which brought them benefit: the employment of a young relative, advice on how best to secure scholarships for their children to study abroad.

For those lower down the hierarchy of state institutions, there was more uncertainty. Wages were reduced by inflation, to the point where an assistant chief in Kajiado earned less (in wages, at least) than a gardener in Nairobi. The state offered few patronage resources – save those derived from aid projects – and only the most erratic coercive resources. When officials tried to organize a round-up of tax defaulters in Rungwe district, it was apparent that

[1] Int Maa3a, 3.

252

they simply could not do so – the brief enthusiasm of the volunteer militia on whom they relied soon petered out, and the exercise was abandoned. The services provided by the state had vanished. The schools, hospitals and clinics created in the 1960s and 1970s suffered from an almost hopeless shortage of resources; teachers, doctors and nurses were paid late, or not at all; there were no books and little medicine. All had turned to private enterprise; running private clinics or pharmacies, sometimes with pilfered goods; offering additional tuition or charging pupils for the supply at exorbitant rates of soap and toilet paper. The state had failed in its promise of development, and in popular discourse and in the press it was routinely vilified. The contrast with the expansive, self-confident state of the 1960s and 1970s was extraordinary. And as the state declined, contrasts between wealth and poverty intensified. Colonial and post-colonial states had been central to the creation in the twentieth century of new patterns of inequality which did not run solely along lines of age and gender; but these inequalities did not decline with the state. If anything, the increasingly exclusive and arbitrary nature of the state and the effects of globalization made these inequalities even more acute – particularly in Kenya.

In Kajiado, there had since the 1960s been an increasing inequality in the distribution of land, as a succession of land-use schemes led to the issuing of individual titles to land which encouraged people to establish single-family homes, limited the accessibility of water and grazing, and encouraged men – who hold titles to land – to sell part or all of their landholdings in response to the periodic crises of the pastoral economy, which became increasingly difficult to manage due to restrictions on movement.[2] As parts of land were sold, the maintenance of herds on the remainder of any individual's landholding became much harder.[3] In the late 1980s and 1990s, the concentration of land in the hands of a few accelerated dramatically in Kajiado, particularly in areas along the line of the main road, as individuals – many of them non-Maasai with positions of some seniority in government, who yet retained access to the patronage and protection of the state – bought up land, some of them with the intention of using it to go into the export horticulture business, the only really flourishing sector of the Kenya economy at the time. Plots were fenced off, and those who had cattle struggled to locate, and negotiate access to, grazing.

Such changes created a growing, impoverished body of Maasai, with few or no cattle, who congregated around towns and trade centres – Kajiado, Isenya, Bissil, Namanga, Sultan Hamud – in search of cash; and created too a profound sense of vulnerability and declining fortunes among the populace as a whole.[4] Change also created a small group of relatively prosperous

[2]   D. Campbell, 'Land as Ours, Land as Mine', in Spear and Waller (eds.), *Being Maasai*, 258-72; J. Galaty, "The Land is Yours": Social and Economic Factors in the Privatization, Sub-division and Sale of Maasai Ranches', *Nomadic Peoples*, 30 (1992), 26-40.
[3]   M. Kituyi, *Becoming Kenyans. Socio-economic Transformation of the Pastoral Maasai* (Nairobi, 1990), 11-12.
[4]   Kituyi, *Becoming Kenyans*, 156.

Maasai, who were accumulating land and fencing and building on it, and living lives which were remarkably and ostentatiously distinct from those around them. Yet the apparent distinctiveness of their clothes and housing might be misleading; they did not possess the resources to really transform their land, and actually relied in part on cattle-herding which involved them – like their poor neighbours – in co-operation and negotiation, and in the use of the labour of juniors as well as paid employees. Nor did they or the state possess the coercive resources to entirely safeguard their land and property (fences, after all, can always be cut). And such men felt as vulnerable as poor men did to insubordination by wives or daughters, against whose infidelities or desertions the state and the law offered no defence.[5] So such accumulators relied in part on their authority as senior men, and on the willingness of other senior men – fathers and husbands – to recognize the propriety of their claims to grazing, people and cattle: as Kituyi has observed, the Maasai accumulator 'has to husband local solidarity and nurture kin, family and local community ties. How he can do this while also accumulating surpluses is the challenge.'[6]

These inequalities and challenges to accumulators were not peculiar to the Maasai. In Rungwe, well-connected individuals might use their position to buy the use of land, and use the machinery of the state to ensure their access to this land for growing grain crops to supply a long-distance trade in foodstuffs. But the coercive machinery of the state could not prevent their crops being stolen, or guarantee to turn out and supervise labour to harvest. For these purposes, even a senior official would turn to local homestead heads, appealing to their authority as senior men, seeking their co-operation. As the state declined, accumulators relied increasingly – if only in particular circumstances – on the authority and support of senior men.

The informal economy & the remains of the state

In 1997, JM lived on the edge of Kajiado with her mother and daughter. She survived by selling sugar-based alcohol, *rorungana*. In 1997 it cost her KSh120 (about US$2) to make a jerrican of alcohol which, if all was sold and paid for, yielded Ksh500: an increase of Ksh380 (about US$6) on the cost of ingredients. Her clientele were men: elder men who made money from selling cattle, young men who earned money shovelling sand into the lorries of building contractors. But her house was close to a police station, and she was often visited by police who demanded bribes; and sometimes drink went unsold and was spoilt.[7]

A survey in Kajiado, Hoima and Rungwe/Kyela revealed a number of women in similar positions, living as heads of their households and selling

[5] Int Maa22c, 1.
[6] Kituyi, *Becoming Kenyans*, 185.
[7] Journal, 15 May 1997.

alcohol to maintain this position – but poor.[8] 'We make beer because of poverty.'[9] Men earned most cash, across the region: a few derived cash income from wages or pensions, or from formal, licensed, businesses, and others sold cash crops or livestock, but there was also a heavy reliance on informal sources of income – from activities which were unlicensed, untaxed and sometimes illegal.[10] Diversification has been the key to survival, and to a degree of accumulation for some; what the development economists call 'non-farm activities' ('NFA') are central to the rural household economy. In Rungwe/Kyela, cross-border smuggling offered a regular source of income; in Kajiado, petty trading brought in a little money, as it did in Bunyoro. In all three areas, however, the sale of locally-made alcohol was a major area of informal economic activity. While only a minority of households sold alcohol on a daily, or even weekly, basis, many (most, in Rungwe/Kyela and Bunyoro) derived occasional income from this.[11] In Kampala, brewing was the principal occupation of 10 percent of women surveyed in the 1990s.[12] In Bunyoro, this sale brought substantial amounts of money into the district, as much of the locally-made alcohol was in the form of spirits which were exported to other parts of Uganda, or to neighbouring countries. In Rungwe/Kyela and Kajiado the alcohol sold was consumed locally, and served largely to redistribute cash which comes into these areas through smuggling or through livestock sale.

More important for women than it is for men, making and selling alcohol was by no means a preserve of women; and men continued to use the (increasingly vestigial) powers of the state to establish a relatively advantageous position in the informal economy of drink. In Bunyoro, the local government rented out to individual entrepreneurs the right to collect the legally prescribed fees for brewing permits; all those involved were men, who tried to recoup the money they had paid (or promised to pay) through a mixture of bluster and pestering and vague threats to men and women who produced alcohol for sale.[13] Both these men and the brewers (and distillers) from whom they extracted payment were aware that police and higher officials would not enforce the law unless they were offered some inducement to do so; the art of collection lay in making this threat plausible. In Rungwe a similar delicate process of making plausible threats underlaid the activities of men who dominated the running of licensed urban clubs in Tukuyu, or who built their own structures in the designated village clubs

---

[8] Both Kituyi, *Becoming Kenyans*, 221, and Talle, *Women at a Loss*, 229, stress the marginal status of women who sell drink.

[9] Int Nya38b, 2.

[10] Tripp has emphasized the rapid growth in the informal economy in Tanzania since the mid-1980s: *Changing the Rules*, 108.

[11] See Appendix 4.

[12] S. Wallman, *Kampala Women Getting By. Wellbeing in the Time of AIDS* (London/Kampala/Athens, OH, 1996), 93.

[13] Journal, 10 and 12 Mar. 1998. I obtained a comprehensive list of those who held licences to collect permit money around Hoima in 1997-8: all were men. The fee paid by these men varied between around US$5 per month and US$70, the average being roughly US$13.

and charged women to sell beer in these structures:[14] such men had to make women brewers believe that the state might pursue and punish them if they sold their beer illegally outside the clubs.[15]

Local officials in Tanzania, in turn, relied on a kind of bluff in dealing with these club-owners, as they tried to force them to pay fees, ostensibly to the village governments who paid the licence fees to the council but in practice into the pockets of these officials.[16] And police, across the region, used their own kind of bluff; they could arrest those who distilled, or sold without a licence, and have them locked up; but might prefer to come to an accommodation which was less likely to attract the attention of superior officers: '[s]ome policemen virtually make a living out of the users and sellers of [illicit] brews'.[17] Everywhere, men used the remains of the power of the state to try to extract some immediate profit from the drinks trade. As they did so they relied on the popular presumption of their superior knowledge and access to the state to invent rules to fit local situations: so the beer-permit collectors of Bunyoro also collected brewing fees from distillers; Hoima council collected trade revenue from *enguli* wholesalers; police in Rungwe arrested people for drinking-hours violations; a Kenyan council officer issued a trade licence to a shop which sold only illicit liquor.[18] The state was in retreat, but it possessed sufficient coercive resources to give authority to those who could plausibly claim access to those resources.

The imposts of these men, and the ease with which people could enter this economy as producers, meant that at the end of the 1990s the economy of informal-alcohol production was still largely characterized by low returns and a proliferation of very small-scale producers. I met no producer who made more than 140 litres of fermented brew (the maximum capacity of an oil drum) at a time; and none who used anything other than basic equipment – oil drums, a plastic sheet, a metal frying pan, some tins – to make drink; or who hired labour – other than very occasional casual labour – in the production of alcohol. Such small-scale production and simple equipment meant that it was easy for people to enter this economy. Anna George ran away from her husband in 1981, at the age of 15, to live in Mbeya town with her sister, who made maize beer to sell. Her sister died in the early 1990s

---

[14] I did not come across any rural club buildings which were run by women. In Tukuyu town, a survey of the 15 clubs which operated there in December 1997 showed that in seven of these – including all the largest ones – the licensee was an individual man. In six others the licence was held by a women's group, though in three of those cases the actual premises belonged to an individual man. One licence – for the old beerhall – was held by the council; sellers in the other club refused to name the licensee. There were 23 bars in Tukuyu: in all of these except one (a staff bar run by the council) the licensee was a man. Of the premises, 14 were individually owned by men; the others were variously owned by the council or parastatals.

[15] Journal, 10 Feb. and 14 Dec. 1997.

[16] Journal, 16 Dec. 1997. There are 140 villages in Rungwe District, each with at least one club; and there are 15 clubs in Tukuyu town. But in the whole district only 17 licences had been paid for in the first quarter of 1997.

[17] 'Brews cause alarm', *Sunday Standard*, 17 May 1998.

[18] Journal, 12 Mar. 1998.

and she moved back to a village in Rungwe. She learned to make *mbege*, Chaga-style banana-beer, which has a small but consistent clientele. In 1997 she was selling two 20-litre jerricans of this a week; if all were paid for, she would have made about TSh1,200 (US$1.50) profit on each. She was typical of the smallest, most marginal producers;[19] as was Joyce Kaahwa, who was living with her two young children in the little shop she rented for USh5,000 (US$5) a month in a tiny trade centre outside Hoima. She made maize beer, about twice a month, making USh2,000 (US$2) on each jerrican she sold; from this she had to pay a fee to the collector of brewing permits, and also money to the parish chief, since she had no trade licence. She also retailed *enguli* made by others, selling about 40 litres each month, and – if all were paid for, and if she suffered no additional demands for bribes or fees – getting a return of about USh20,000 (US$20) on this.[20] The informal economy of alcohol was widespread, but the returns, for most of those involved, were very low, and as always, they constantly lost money when drinkers refused to pay.[21] 'On the side of brewing, it has no very great profit,' one woman told me, 'sometimes there are no customers and we drink it ourselves for food.'[22]

A survey suggested that those women who produced most often and most profitably were, in fact, those who did not rely on this as a sole source of income; those who were most able to diversify.[23] These were women who lived in long-term relationships with men, who could rely on those men to deal with authority or to help them buy ingredients or vessels for preparing drinks should they run out of capital, and who could support them in reclaiming debts.[24] And the reliance of these women on such support defined and limited their involvement in making alcohol for sale; this was a pursuit undertaken within a male-headed household economy, involving only family labour and producing income which was used to meet the cash costs of the woman and her children. Their ability to call on resources allowed them to sell alcohol profitably; yet it limited the autonomy they might derive from such sale. Perhaps the most significant kind of investment which took place in this was the spending of money on school fees, especially for sons; thus could women seek to secure their future well-being.

> If you would find the man is late in paying, then it was upon us to help so that it goes to the child who is in school. It was essential, it was essential that it should go for the child in school. They used to come out and we

[19] Journal, 10 Feb. 1997.
[20] Journal, 10 and 12 Mar. 1998.
[21] Int Maa6a, 2. Green has, however, recently argued that women brewers in modern Tanzania do derive reasobale profits from the trade: 'Trading on Inequality', 415.
[22] Int Maa12a, 1.
[23] Again, this contrasts with the findings of Green, who suggests that the most regular brewers are those who rely most completely on alcohol: 'Trading on Inequality', 416.
[24] A survey of brewing in Botswana in the late 1970s suggested that there too, while many of those who made alcohol to sell were poor, slightly more wealthy households were more likely to brew for sale: E. Roe, 'Who Brews Traditional Beer in Rural Botswana? A Review of the Literature and Policy Analysis', *Botswana Notes and Records*, 13 (1981), 45-53.

used to give out. We have been able to send the children to school because of that money, it did a lot of work.[25]

Men with other sources of income were similarly consistent participants in the selling of alcohol. In Rungwe, Job Kikonde and Luka Mwangosi both sold bamboo wine, which became increasingly popular there in the last three decades, and which they tapped from their own bamboos. They sold at home – both being respected men whom none would trouble with demands for a permit – and earned in the peak season as much as TSh800 (a little over US$1) from this. They also sold coffee and other crops.[26] Many men in Bunyoro make banana wine or *enguli* on a similar basis, as one of a range of activities which bring in a cash income. The only individuals whom I met who specialized profitably in selling alcohol were men who exploited particular relationships with the state to do so. One was the caretaker of a defunct government cocoa-drying station near Hoima. He had not been paid for more than two years when we met, but he had the run of the remaining buildings, including the canteen, and he made and sold a kind of banana wine whose fermentation is encouraged by the addition of tinned yeast: and he successfully refused to pay for any trade licence or brewing fee or any other impost, as he was running a 'government canteen'.[27] The other was a man in Sultan Hamud, a small market town on the edge of Kajiado district, who made and sold 'Miti ni dawa', sugar or honey-based alcoholic beverages which are flavoured with bark and herbs and are claimed to have medicinal properties. This man had secured a letter from the University of Nairobi offering a very brief chemical analysis of his product, and a trade licence which effectively protected him from police harassment; he employed others to work for him, and the shop was the second in what promised to be a 'chain'.[28] But these men were very much the exception. Across the region, production of informal-sector alcohol was mostly small-scale, pursued most successfully by those who used this as one of a variety of cash income sources, and who had access to land or livestock resources.

Drinking practice

During the 1990s the social basis of beer-drinking had shifted slightly, away from the state and its agents, but this remained very much the drink of an elite, consumed by a wider populace only on special occasions. One bottle of beer cost around US$1 across most of East Africa; a large amount for most people, and five times the price of informal-sector liquor. The consumption of alcohol remained dominated by informal and/or illicit liquors. And it seems likely that more and more of this was drunk in the form of illicit distillates or – in central Kenya – new-generation drinks: the prominence of distillates was one of the drinking changes of which people were most aware.[29]

[25] Int Nya42a, 4.
[26] Journal, 10 and 11 Feb. 1997.
[27] Journal, 12 Mar. 1998.
[28] Journal, 3 July 1997.
[29] Int Nyoro1a, 3.

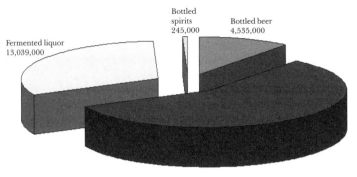

a. Uganda: 1998

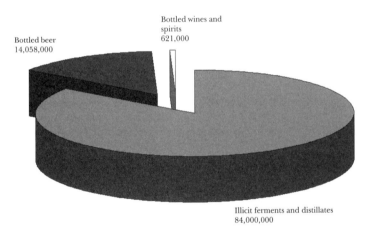

b. Kenya: 1994

The Uganda figures are based on extrapolation from survey figures and information on formal-sector production supplied by industry sources. The Kenya figures are based on a survey conducted by Kenya Breweries in 1994, and on figures for formal-sector consumption derived from the Statistical Abstracts.

Figure 13.1 *Estimated alcohol consumption in the 1990s, in litres of absolute alcohol*

13.1 *Ebikweete drinkers in Uganda, 1998*

These distilled and new-generation drinks continued to be involved in distinctive patterns of use: drunk individually, by customers who each bought their own tot in a little glass, or sipped furtively from a bottle when no one else was looking, in a secretive manner that did not only reflect fear of the police. In Uganda, perhaps in consequence of the official tolerance which permitted an increasingly open trade in distillates, the price of *enguli* fell relative to that of other kinds of liquor: for the first time there was a rough equality in terms of price per litre of absolute alcohol. But the drinking of *enguli* continued to be largely an individual, not a shared, activity – even where the same dealer was selling both. Rather than sharing the cost of spirits, people bought tiny amounts for themselves.

Table 13.1 *Approximate rural prices of alcoholic beverages, 1997-8, expressed in terms of US$ per litre of absolute alcohol*

	Bottled beer	Traditional liquor	Illicit distillates
Uganda	30	6.0	6
Tanzania	30	6.0	10
Kenya	30	7.5	17

Figures from journals. There can be considerable seasonal fluctuation in rural prices; urban prices for 'traditional' liquor are commonly up to 50% above rural prices.

13.2 *Haragi drinkers in Uganda, 1998*

And fermented liquors continued to be widely consumed; drunk at weddings and funerals by those who could not afford to provide bottled beer, and drunk every day in clubs and drinking dens, shared by groups of (mostly) men, who maintained the pattern of collective drinking and buying. Such was Wallman's observation of drinking in Kampala in the 1990s, as well as my own impression of rural drinking.[30] In the surveys of drinking in Kajiado, Hoima and Rungwe/Kyela, men, in fact, dominated drinking of all kinds; and even more, they dominated spending on drinking, for most of those women who did drink were having their drinks bought for them by male admirers. Young men drank as much as old men (except in Kajiado); but women drank very little.

There was not a complete divide between the beer drinkers, the drinkers of distillates and those who took fermented liquors – people straddled these distinctive drinking ideals, just as they straddled distinctive and in many ways contradictory ideas of authority and well-being. In the survey, many men expressed a preference for bottled beer; and those who usually drank banana wine or *komoni* might sometimes seek the strength of *enguli* or *gongo*. While there were those who would not stoop to drinking fermented liquor, those who routinely drank fermented liquor might aspire to bottled beer or distillates on occasion.

But not all did. Some feared the power of distillates, and identified new forms of drink as dangerous, destructive of individual and societal well-being:

---

[30]   Wallman, *Kampala Women Getting By*, 84-5.

now life is very hard and very complex. There is very great change in
the technology which is in use, from the drink in the past, to the drinks
of today. The drink in the past did not cause any harm because
knowledge was very little . . . Now they mix many drugs into the drinks.
That is why people are getting drunk so much, unlike the past. They
are putting many intoxicating things in the beer. That is why many
people are getting infected with very many diseases, many infectious
diseases which were not there in the past . . . That is why deaths are so
many now.[31]

Such drinkers insisted on their preference for fermented liquors, and
used drinking to construct an idealized picture of well-being and authority
based on co-operation and age-mate solidarity. Yet there were many drinkers
who, while talking of drinking in ways which insisted on the propriety of
non-commercial drinking, actually drank and dealt in drink in entirely
commercial contexts.

Meanwhile, in the marriages and funerals of members of evangelistic
and independent African churches, alcohol played no part; nor did it in
the lives of an increasing number of Muslims.[32] 'Those who know God say
they don't want beer in the weddings, they forbid . . . They know, and read
in the Bible, that a drunkard will not see the Kingdom of Heaven. That is
why people fear beer in the weddings.'[33] Such refusal to drink set the
abstainers aside from the social world occupied by their kin and neighbours:
'They say, "The Christian has separated himself".'[34] 'In many cases, the
parties of the Born Again are not enjoyed by other people,' said one man.[35]
Their abstinence challenged the acknowledgement of men's authority over
well-being which lay at the centre of rituals: 'without drink there is no
marriage ceremony', one man told me.[36] The Born Again had their own,
modern, liquor, which displaced tea: carbonated sweet drinks, or sodas,
are offered at weddings and funerals.[37] Soda drinking was largely for the
young and (while the real price of soda fell in the 1990s) the expense of
these drinks meant that only those who had a regular cash income could
afford to drink them. Soda drinking was a rather ostentatious display of
sobriety, a public way of distancing oneself from the sociable drinkers of
fermented liquor; and for the soda-drinkers traditional liquor was a twofold enemy, representative of the world of superstitious authority and of the
inner devil which tempts the individual to sin.[38] 'The beginning of sin is
alcohol. When you do not drink alcohol you know all what is good and bad,
but when drunk the good and bad all become bad.'[39]

[31] Int Nya34a, 1.
[32] Int Nya16b, 5; Nyoro8b, 4.
[33] Int Nya34a, 3.
[34] Int Nya33b, 3.
[35] Int Nyoro9b, 6.
[36] Int Nyoro29b, 13.
[37] Int Nyoro37b, 5.
[38] Int Nya31b, 3.
[39] Int Nya33b, 3.

Drinking crises

Nowadays things have changed money has been introduced in the past people would send liquor to their friends and friendship would begin with liquor. But nowadays there is money.[40]

In the early 1990s, informal-sector liquors could still be derided in Kenya as a 'waste of time' and their drinking as a 'national embarrassment';[41] and in the later 1990s a Tanzanian journalist could still assert that the country needed bottled beer 'produced scientifically' and could characterize the drinkers of informal-sector liquor as the enemies of development: 'They do not work, they do not contribute to nation-building.'[42] But as the debate around new-generation drinks and palm wine showed, there was an increasingly evident and widespread popular rhetoric which challenged this model of bottled beer as the ideal of drinking. Even before the events of 1998, some opposition politicians in Kenya had sought to challenge the whole linkage between traditional liquor and underdevelopment, calling for the legalization of distillation, for the end of the colonial restriction on the selling of fermented beverages.[43] Those with a flair for publicity took to public consumption of traditional liquor; two opposition MPs invaded urban bars to hand out *busaa*.[44]

These politicians argued the old point, that informal-sector liquor paid for education; but they also explicitly evoked the ideal of integrated drinking as they did this, conjuring up a world of orderly traditional drinking.[45] For a populace faced with the apparent failure of the state's promise of health and prosperity through development, the association of traditional drink with a world of traditional health and well-being was an attractive one, and drew alcohol into an argument which saw society as threatened by changes which had undermined traditional prosperity and well-being, and brought about a social disease manifest in illness and violence: 'Today's alcohol has made people sick and stupid and they have lost their morals.'[46] This idealization of traditional drinking wrapped youthful insubordination and unbridled female sexuality up with issues of well-being.[47] 'Long ago people used to drink and become happy, singing and dancing, but today people drink and fight, unlike the past.'[48] 'Many children do not like digging and instead go to drink beer. This has made people not to care about dying or working like we did because of beer. If you tell him [child] to work, he is

---

[40] Int Nyoro1a, 3.
[41] 'Any Case for Local Brews', *Daily Nation*, 3 June 1994; 'Shocking Disrespect for Time That Costs Plenty', *Daily Nation*, 17 Nov. 1995.
[42] 'Tax Reduction on Beer: We'll Drink to That', *East African*, 13-19 Apr. 1998.
[43] A motion brought in 1993 calling for an end to the prohibition had been defeated in parliament: 'Uproar as Godana Changes Ruling', *Kenya Times*, 4 Nov. 1993.
[44] 'Parents, Teachers in Beer-drinking Spree', *Daily Nation*, 14 July 1992; 'MPs Make Merry in Bar', *Standard* (Kenya), 10 Nov. 1997.
[45] 'Any Case for Local Brews', *Daily Nation*, 3 June 1994.
[46] Int Nyoro33a, 5.
[47] Int Nya8c, 2; Nya29a, 3; Nyoro7a, 6; Nyoro11b, 4.
[48] Int Maa9a, 2.

rude.'⁴⁹ '[T]his beer is drunk on the road-side, they just have little *vikao* [drinking-groups], there is not a [separate] place for the children, the woman, the school student – they are all together. As you can see, there are many prostitutes.'⁵⁰

> In the past they used to drink in clean and respectable conditions. Now it has come without respect. You can find a woman seated between the men, and then some undesirable things start to happen. They start using the marriage badly. In that way it has affected that respect. That is why young people of about eighteen years are drinking, together with their wives and their mothers. In that way that respect is not there like in the past. Now I'm blaming drinking. At the same time it has caused the breakage of many people's marriages, more than long ago... now there are so many things which are mixed up, and again diseases have increased more than long ago.⁵¹

There were multiple contradictions in this discursive condemnation of modern commercial drinking, and such contradictions allowed it to appeal to many individuals in the insecure circumstances of the 1990s. Accumulators drank bottled beer or 'power', but celebrated an idea of collective elders' power in the way they talked of drink. Many of those who called for an end to restrictions on traditional liquor simultaneously idealized traditional non-commercial drinking and supported the sale of such liquor; they condemned commercialization but supported entrepreneurship, for they relied on the sale of locally-made liquor for their survival. People acknowledged the economic realities which drove themselves and their fellows to sell drink: 'You would find somebody has children and has a wife, and he cannot take a whole jerrican and give it out freely rather than selling it at 25,000 shillings. So that he can get salt, books for the child and would remain with some for food.'⁵² Yet they deprecated the new tendency for people to bring fermented liquor to sell at funerals rather than presenting it out of respect to the bereaved.⁵³ Reliant on the sale of liquor, they yet had no sense that they prospered from it, and felt themselves vulnerable, neglected by the state and ill-served by the fickle power of money. They talked of new kinds of drink and drinking as destructive of well-being, and reproduced the idea that 'it is money that has brought problems' by undermining the sociability of non-commercial drinking and allowing the young to drink because 'they are the ones you find with a lot of money'.⁵⁴

Such drinking discourses constantly evoked and recreated the belief that elder men could directly affect the well-being of others. To defy an elder, to quarrel with a neighbour, to arouse the envy of one's fellows – all could lead to misfortune, whether through the innate power of elders, the outrage of

---

⁴⁹ Int Nya3b, 5.
⁵⁰ Int Nya36a, 3.
⁵¹ Int Nya40a, 1.
⁵² Int Nyoro16a, 4: Nyoro25b, 6.
⁵³ Int Nyoro6b, 6.
⁵⁴ Int Nyoro20a, 4; Nyoro29a, 5; Nyoro31a, 2; Nya11b, 4.

ancestral spirits or the malice of the living who seek the help of sorcerers: '[B]ecause of being better off than him, he can bewitch you so that you die and lose what you have.'[55] When in 1997 a young man in Tukuyu fell from his motorcycle and was killed, public speculation turned at once to his relationship with his father, whose authority the young man had just very publicly repudiated; some asserted that his death was, undoubtedly, a result of this defiance towards his father. The proper use of drink might have saved him: 'If I had been rude to my father, he could say, you have been cheeky to me, can you be cheeky to me? At once you start to suffer, for you are cursed. When you go to your father to repent, you must offer something. When you have given some money, he calls people . . . When he has made beer he calls people who can help him to remove the curse.'[56] People still assumed that the 'bad heart' or displeasure of elder men would cause them harm, and that well-being might be obtained through presenting alcohol to elders, or sharing it with one's fellow elders:[57] 'you take alcohol . . . then you will be blessed and you will recover'.[58] As the state became less and less effectual in local disputes, the authority derived from this became increasingly important. Those who had not retreated into the moral isolationism of evangelical religion feared the jealousy and ill-will of their neighbours. Such fear made accumulators all the more anxious to pursue the private drinking practices of power.

The rapid growth, and even more rapid decline, of the state had – has – led the people of East Africa to pursue strategies of diversification which are in many ways contradictory. They must seek to turn some relationships into purely commercial ones, while insisting that other relationships – sometimes, indeed, the same relationships – are governed by notions of propriety which derive from alternative notions of well-being. Men must insist on the ability of the written law to regulate transactions in land, while keeping such law out of their relationships with their daughters and wives. Women must try and exact cash from the friends and kin of their husbands in return for drink, yet evoke traditional claims on the resources of the household. All are suspended between multiple and contradictory ideas of authority and well-being. And all drink, and talk of drink, in their contradictory evocations of these ideas: bottled beer as a drink of development which few can afford; illicit distillates as a source of individual potency which shuns co-operation and risks poisoning; fermented liquors which are used to idealize co-operative gerontocracy yet must be made into commodities to prop up the fragile economy of the household.

The practice and discourse of drinking have always revealed the ambiguities of power. Now those ambiguities are greater than ever, and a profound unease over proper authority – a sense that the ability to manage health and wealth have been compromised by a modernity which has offered

---

[55] Int Nyoro9c, 2.
[56] Int Nya10b, 3-4.
[57] Int Maa5c, 2; Nyoro16c, 1.
[58] Int Maa17b, 1.

little in return – has found easy focus in the way people talk about modern drinking and idealize the past. 'Long ago', as one woman in Bunyoro told me, 'we used to drink for free, and peacefully.'[59]

[59] Int Nyoro15a, 4.

Appendices

I

European & Asian alcohol consumption
Kenya & Uganda,
1922–48

Figures are expressed in litres of absolute alcohol, assuming beer at 4 percent alcohol by volume and wine at 12 percent alcohol by volume (original spirits figures in proof gallons, so no assumption is necessary). Figures from *Blue Books*.

	Beer	Brandy	Gin	Whisky	Wine	Local beer	Total	Population
1922	10,600	17,208	10,474	95,282	10,263		143,827	
1923	11,265	21,053	16,888	97,543	14,423	N/A	161,171	
1924	18,563	28,737	20,915	115,199	19,820	N/A	203,234	52,403
1925	18,017	33,684	22,261	130,930	24,079	N/A	228,971	
1926	19,711	40,384	26,984	148,315	28,241	N/A	263,635	67,034
1927	20,847	32,288	26,364	146,539	27,410	N/A	253,448	
1928	27,937	38,430	27,766	154,718	26,347	N/A	275,198	
1929	29,977	38,467	31,741	154,463	27,070	N/A	281,718	
1930	30,539	29,646	26,716	139,438	20,887	N/A	247,226	89,863
1931	18,112	23,850	23,452	130,667	18,158	N/A	214,239	
1932	16,461	16,010	25,351	115,415	14,740	14,228	202,205	
1933	12,946	13,882	16,637	113,334	13,973	16,000	186,771	
1934	15,049	15,637	25,538	110,172	14,250	17,104	197,750	
1935	17,909	19,977	28,878	128,328	17,420	18,000	230,512	
1936	20,953	19,401	30,967	125,408	15,098	19,960	231,787	
1937	22,220	20,172	28,815	125,444	16,642	24,000	237,293	
1938	22,846	21,483	34,343	140,060	16,661	28,484	263,877	
1940	18,605	34,773	54,018	187,654	16,190	60,000	371,240	
1941	24,841	41,699	69,509	195,800	31,378	60,000	423,228	
1942	6,076	29,855	21,563	63,630	14,776	159,164	295,064	
1943	6,433	54,396	14,877	8,477	36,415	222,444	420,042	
1944	5,169	83,052	71,098	91,364	11,669	215,328	582,707	165,743
1945	9,524	119,896	63,862	77,621	17,815	219,552	508,269	
1946	8,615	82,469	41,019	117,450	37,851	215,328	502,732	173,707
1948	42,842	229,953	133,459	85,962	35,666	219,552	747,434	

II

Consumption of formal-sector alcohol in Kenya
1954–90

Expressed in litres of absolute alcohol.
Assuming beer at 4 percent alcohol by volume, wine at 12 percent alcohol by volume and spirits at 35 percent alcohol by volume.
Figures from East Africa High Commission Reports and *Statistical Abstracts*.

	Imported beer	Imported spirits	Imported wine	Local beer equ.	Local spirits	Total equ.	Population
1954	14,747	430,327	58,411	659,452		1,162,938	
1956	21,273	568,551	79,996	958,840		1,628,660	
1958	30,836	572,114	66,043	1,026,464		1,695,457	7,652,000
1960	21,167	522,921	93,468	998,064		1,635,620	8,115,000
1962	27,056	478,814	119,328	1,143,316		1,768,514	8,595,000
1964	36,348	288,782	73,278	1,335,844		1,734,252	9,365,000
1966	19,876	308,230	91,753	1,470,380		1,890,239	9,643,000
1968	24,394	369,622	93,165	1,759,928	57,666	2,304,775	10,209,000
1970	21,599	259,922	56,895	3,099,824	63,154	3,501,394	10,943,000
1972	8,920	274,750	86,160	4,082,360	117,852	4,570,042	12,067,000
1974	17,280	199,850	104,280	6,132,800	124,339	6,578,549	12,912,000
1976	4,520	237,650	108,480	6,616,080	124,893	7,091,623	13,847,000
1978	5,120	287,700	181,560	8,217,240	153,086	8,844,706	14,856,000
1980	7,440	227,500	148,440	9,307,400	196,293	9,887,073	16,667,000
1982	5,280	150,150	305,280	9,637,800	160,313	10,258,823	18,044,000
1984	2,040	43,050	69,360	9,199,760	228,602	9,542,812	
1986	800	94,850	91,440	10,209,400	276,698	10,673,188	
1988	560	100,800	118,440	12,578,240	416,107	13,214,147	
1990	920	32,200	93,120	13,007,760	248,878	13,382,878	21,443,636
1992	3,000	126,700	2,160,000	14,509,120	345,868	17,144,688	
1994	18,440	75,250	123,240	14,058,560	404,135	14,679,625	

III

Bottled-beer

production for local consumption
& excise revenue from beer

	KENYA		TANZANIA		UGANDA	
	Volume	Excise	Volume	Excise	Volume	Excise
1924	N/A	426	-	-	-	-
1926	N/A	1,115	-	-	-	-
1928	N/A	N/A	-	-	-	-
1930	N/A	N/A	-	-	-	-
1932	3,557	4,539	-	-	-	372
1934	4,276	5,158	N/A	-	-	662
1936	4,990	5,801	N/A	-	-	1,055
1938	7,121	7,674	1,965	2,000	-	1,894
1940	N/A	38,157	N/A	N/A	-	2,373
1942	39,791	59,603	N/A	N/A	-	7,010
1944	55,611	90,666	N/A	N/A	-	10,284
1946	53,832	116,914	N/A	35,417	-	14,872
1948	54,888	149,382	19,560	47,000	-	14,484
1950	78,048	N/A	27,054	85,000	6,409	31,126
1952	125,639	N/A	33,178	196,000	11,074	109,526
1954	164,863	N/A	22,841	259,000	16,638	148,821
1956	239,710	N/A	48,900	347,000	45,517	392,323
1958	256,616	N/A	44,331	347,000	65,415	420,908
1960	249,516	N/A	56,967	546,000	43,509	300,000
1962	285,829	N/A	75,273	832,000	67,992	743,293
1964	333,961	N/A	96,380	1,156,000	78,529	1,114,973
1966	367,595	N/A	188,160	1,495,000	120,408	1,357,090
1968	439,982	4,291,042	246,120	1,732,896	202,660	1,539,430
1970	774,956	5,838,041	311,940	2,503,798	277,670	2,063,637
1972	1,428,250	N/A	578,313	85,800,000	379,450	N/A
1974	1,576,330	11,116,000	658,867	N/A	N/A	N/A
1976	1,655,860	24,143,000	664,184	N/A	N/A	N/A
1978	1,991,100	15,617,000	814,580	N/A	N/A	N/A
1980	2,324,330	17,033,000	638,277	N/A	131,800	N/A
1982	2,337,360	17,555,000	641,887	N/A	97,871	N/A
1984	2,303,450	16,387,000	691,812	N/A	148,166	N/A
1986	2,926,330	20,180,000	651,782	N/A	70,354	N/A
1988	3,143,820	23,819,000	529,955	N/A	206,038	N/A
1990	3,311,140	20,686,000	450,441	N/A	194,210	N/A
1992	3,686,480	190,367,000	493,939	N/A	187,180	N/A
1994	3,025,010	284,696,000	523,502	N/A	308,220	N/A
1996	2,900,000	N/A	1,221,307	N/A	512,380	N/A

This table shows the amount of bottled beer produced for consumption within the territory in each country. It does not include beer produced for export. Volume figures are in hectolitres.

Excise figures are in £ (20 East African shillings) up to 1972. Thereafter the Kenya figures are in £Kenya (20 Kenyan shillings) for Kenya; shillings for Tanzania.

Figures are derived from *Blue Books*, East Africa High Commission Reports, *Statistical Abstracts* and *Reports on Trade and Industry*. Uganda derived a portion of the excise revenue from beer produced in Kenya from 1932 to 1948, under the customs agreement between the two territories.

IV

Modern drinking & production:
summary results of surveys

Small surveys by questionnaire were conducted in each research area in 1997-98. In each case, two sampling units were taken (villages in Uganda and Tanzania, sub-locations in Kenya), and approximately 10 percent of households were chosen by random ballot from each. The questionnaire was applied to all persons aged 16 and over currently living in the household. The questionnaire and full coded results may be seen at the ESRC data archive.

Kajiado district

The survey was conducted in the sub-location at Lenkisem, and at Sajiloni sub-location near Kajiado town. At Sajiloni, ten households were surveyed, containing 30 individuals; at Lenkisem five of the agglomerated settlements called *enkang* were surveyed. These contained 22 distinct households.

Overall, 89 persons were surveyed: 53 women and 36 men. There was a striking absence of young men, particularly at Lenkisem. Only nine individuals were unmarried (eight of them men), but 21were not living with a spouse, though they were married. Twenty of these were women, being six widows, seven women who had runaway or been abandoned, and seven women whose husbands were living elsewhere.

Nine individuals were in waged employ: one woman and eight of the men. The average wage was $48 per month; the woman earned $20 per month.

DRINKING
Thirty five of those surveyed considered themselves to be drinkers: 14 women and 21 men. The average age of the male drinkers was 45 years; that of the female drinkers 47.5 years. Altogether, these drinkers recalled 56 drinking episodes in the previous week; 48 recalled by men and eight by women.

Based on the estimates of consumption by men, they drank a total of

107.5 litres of honey-wine and sugar ferment and 11.5 litres of bottled beer; the women drank 24.5 litres of sugar ferment and 1litre of bottled beer.

Among the drinkers, 32 expressed a preference for particular types of drink. Eleven preferred bottled beer; 12 preferred honey-wine; eight preferred sugar ferment and one preferred chang'aa. There was a clear gender difference in preferences. Twenty men and 12 women expressed a preference; nine of the men and two of the women preferred bottled beer. Of those who preferred beer, only four said they were able to drink this 'usually'. The most commonly taken drinks were sugar-based ferments.

Thirty-three drinkers expressed a preference for a particular place of drink. Five (four men and one woman) preferred to drink in bars; 17 (six men and 11 women) preferred to drink at their own home; 11 (all men) preferred to drink at other people's homes.

Fifty-two characterized themselves as 'non-drinkers': 39 women and 13 men. Of the 14 who gave reasons for this, eight (two of them men) said it was because they were too young; four (one of them a man) said it was for religious reasons; and two (women) said that it was because of their sex.

MAKING

Fifty one individuals had made alcohol at some time; 40 of them women. Men had only made it for the purpose of gifts to others. Eighteen women had made alcohol to sell at some time in their lives. They were spread across 15 of the households surveyed. Five of them had made alcohol to sell in the last week; three in the previous week; three within the last six months; two in the last year; one in the last two years; and four more than two years ago.

Of the eight women who had made alcohol to sell in the last two weeks, all were living with a husband. The three who had made alcohol to sell at some time in the last six months were not living with a husband. Of those who had last made alcohol to sell more than six months ago, two were living with husbands and five were not.

Asked where they had obtained the money to buy ingredients for making alcohol to sell, 11 of these 18 women said that this came from their husbands (this included six of the eight women who had brewed in the last two weeks). One woman had provided her own ingredients; two had borrowed them from a shop-keeper; three had got them from kin; and one had obtained them from another source.

The average of the profits recalled by these women for their last batch of alcohol was US$3.50.

Rungwe/Kyela Districts

Twenty-five households were surveyed: ten in Ilenge village (Rungwe) and 15 in Ikolo village (Kyela). These households contained 77 individuals: 40 men and 37 women. Twenty-two of the men were married; seven were in polygynous marriages. Only one was not living with at least one wife. Thirty of the women were married, and only four of the married women were not living with their husband.

Three individuals (two men and one woman) were in waged employment; the woman (a teacher) earned much more than either of the men (US$94 per month).

DRINKING

Forty-three individuals described themselves as drinkers: 25 men and 18 women. The average age of male drinkers was 43 years; that of female drinkers 40 years. This group of drinkers recalled 123 drinking episodes in the previous week; 38 recalled by women and 85 by men. Based on the estimates of consumption given, the men drank a total of 195.5 litres of maize beer and 20.5 litres of millet beer during the week; and the women a total of 34.5 litres of maize beer and 1 litre of bottled beer. Men's total spending on drink for the week was US$43, based on their estimates; spending on drink by women was US$7.

Twelve of the male drinkers said they preferred bottled beer; nine preferred maize beer, four preferred millet beer. Of the female drinkers, ten preferred maize beer, five preferred bottled beer and one preferred bamboo wine. However, 20 of the male drinkers actually usually drank maize beer; three said they usually drank bottled beer; two said they usually drank millet beer. Of the women, 14 usually drank maize beer, one usually drank bottled beer, one usually drank bamboo wine. Of the male drinkers, 12 preferred to drink in *vilabu*, six at their own home, three in unlicensed groups and two at other people's homes. Of the women, 13 preferred to drink at their own home, one in *vilabu*, one in the homes of others and one in bars.

Of the 34 professed 'non-drinkers', five said they did not drink for reasons of health; six said they did not drink for religious reasons; one said he was too young.

MAKING

Twenty-eight individuals had made alcohol at some time in their lives; 26 women and two men. Twenty-four of the women had made beer to sell; no man in the sample had made any kind of drink to sell, but one had been involved in selling drink.

The 24 women who had made drink to sell were spread over 20 households. Five of these women were unmarried, one was a widow and one was not living with her husband. Of these women, only four had made drink to sell in the previous week (three of them married, one unmarried). One (unmarried) woman had made beer to sell in the previous week; five (three married, one unmarried, one separated) had made beer to sell within the last six months. None of the others had made alcohol to sell within the last year.

The average profit estimated from one batch of beer was US$6.50. Of the five women who had made alcohol to sell in the last two weeks, two had bought the ingredients themselves; the other three had received money from their husband or father to do so.

Bunyoro

The survey was conducted in the villages of Kitoba and Mpaija, ten households being chosen from each. These 20 households contained a total of 61 individuals aged 16 and over: 30 women and 31 men. Ten of the women were unmarried and two were widowed. Eleven men were not married; two were separated from their wives. Two of the men had more than one wife, but in each case they were living with only one wife. Six of these individuals were employed: four men and two women. The average monthly wage for the men was US$15; that for the women could not be determined.

Forty-six of these individuals described themselves as drinkers; 25 men and 21 women. The average age of the male drinkers was 38 years; that of the female drinkers 37 years. The replies of four of these seemed manifestly unreliable. The remainder recalled 67 drinking episodes in the previous week; 48 recalled by men and 19 recalled by women. Based on the estimates of consumption given, the men consumed a total of 9.5 litres of distillates, 11.25 litres of grain beer and 6.5 litres of bottled beer. The women consumed 1 litre of grain beer, 3.5 litres of pineapple-based drink, 8 litres of banana wine and 0.5 litre of bottled beer. The total spending of men on drink in the week was US$20, based on their estimations; that of women was US$17. There was one drinking episode among the men for which no useful estimate of consumption could be obtained.

Among the drinkers, 43 expressed a preference for a particular type of drink. Ten (six women and four men) preferred bottled beer; 11 (three women and eight men) preferred distillates; six (three men and three women) preferred banana wine and 16 (eight men and eight women) preferred grain beer. Nine (five women and four men) said they usually drank bottled beer; 11 (two women and nine men) usually drank distillates; six (four women and two men) usually drank banana wine; and 18 (nine women and nine men) usually drank grain beer.

Thirty-six expressed a preference for place of drinking. Twenty-three (13 women and 10 men) preferred to drink at home; three (one woman and two men) preferred to drink in bars; 11 (three women and eight men) preferred to drink in clubs and trade centres; one man preferred to drink in other people's homes. Twenty usually did drink at home (12 women and eight men); 20 (six women and 14 men) usually drank in clubs and trade centres; two drank elsewhere.

Fifteen individuals characterized themselves as non-drinkers: nine women and six men. Five of these (four women and one man) gave religion as the reason for this; one man said he was too young.

MAKING

Thirty-eight individuals had made alcohol at some time: 20 men and 18 women. Men and women were involved in distilling, making banana wine and making grain beer; though women predominated in the latter activity.

Forty-one individuals had been involved in selling alcohol. Three – all women – sold alcohol made by others; and two men had transported alcohol for sale. The other 36 (20 men and 16 women) made alcohol to sell. Of the male sellers, six were unmarried and three were widowed or separated; of the women, four were unmarried and two were widowed. Only three of the 20 households in the survey had not been involved in selling alcohol at some time.

Five individuals – two women (married) and three men (two married, one single) – had made alcohol in the previous week. Six individuals had made it in the last month: three women (all married) and three men (one married, one unmarried, one separated). It was not possible to determine the total earnings in the previous week. Distillates were clearly the most common product; and estimates of profit on one batch varied from US$2.50 to US$14.

V
Interview details

Translated transcripts of interviews are available from the ESRC data archive: search for study no. 4169 at http://biron.essex.ac.uk/cgi-bin/biron/

This list shows: **Interview identifier**
Name of informant
Place and date of interview
Size of file

Kajiado

Maa3a
Sitat ene Ololoso
Esonorwa, 21 May 1997
37 kb

Maa4a
Sintaro ene Olonkongoni
Oltepesi, 21 May 1997
39 kb

Maa5a
Titi
Lenkisem, 27 May 1997
30 kb

Maa5b
Titi
Lenkisem, 15 July 1997
26 kb

Maa5c
Titi
Lenkisem, 21 Dec. 1998
31 kb

Maa6a
Ndoyop
Lenkisem, 27 May 1997
31 kb

Maa6b
Ndoyop
Lenkisem, 16 July 1997
24 kb

Maa6c
Ndoyop
Lenkisem, 21 Dec. 1998
32 kb

Maa7a
Ole Sankaire
Kona Baridi, 4 June 1997
42 kb

Maa8a
Olkaponkoi ole Kipaika
Oltepesi, 4 June 1997
33 kb

Maa9a
Koisange Salaash
Lenkisem, 19 June 1997
27 kb

Maa9b
Koisange Salaash
Lenkisem, 29 April 1998
25 kb

Maa9c
Koisange Salaash
Lenkisem, 10 Dec. 1998
22 kb

Maa11a
NalepoEnkarr
Lenkisem, 19 June 1997
25 kb

Maa11b
Nalepo Enkarr,
Lenkisem, 30 April 1998
25 kb

Maa11c
Nalepo Enkarr
Lenkisem, 9 Dec. 1998
23 kb

Maa12a
Napuku Rereu
Isenya, 24 June 1997
25 kb

Maa12b
Napuku Rereu
Isenya, 29 Aug. 1997
25 kb

Maa12c
Napuku Rereu
Isenya, 19 Dec. 1998
25 kb

Maa13a
Mpaashie ole Mokotian
Isenya, 24 June 1997
29 kb

Maa13b
Mpaashie ole Mokotian
Isenya, 29 Aug. 1997
27 kb

Maa14a
Ole Naikoni
Engamata Sinoni, 25 June 1997
29 kb

Maa14b
Ole Naikoni
Engamata Sinoni, 29 Aug. 1997
25 kb

Maa15a
Taitiki Kijoolu
Bissel, 25 June 1997
25 kb

Maa15a
Taitiki Kijoolu
Bissel, 3 Sep. 1997
23 kb

Maa16a
Bernard Mwangi
Ngatataek, 25 June 1997
24 kb

Maa17a
Nailo ene Sinoni
Maili Tisa, 25 June 1997
24 kb

Maa17b
Nailo ene Sinoni
Maili Tisa, 17 July 1998
25 kb

Maa17c
Nailo ene Sinoni
Maili Tisa, 19 Dec. 1998
24 kb

Maa18a
Ole Sinoni
Maili Tisa, 25 June 1997
25 kb

Maa19a
Saani ole Kilempu
Maili Tisa, 25 June 1997
25 kb

Maa20a
Daudi Kanteri,
Mabatini, 26 June 1997
33 kb

Maa20b
Daudi Kanteri
Mabatini, 19 Dec. 1998
26 kb

Maa21a
Tatek Keton
Mabatini, 26 June 1997
26 kb

Maa21b
Tatek Keton
Mabatini, 8 Sep. 1997
22 kb

Maa21c
Tatek Keton
Mabatini, 19 Dec. 1998
27 kb

Maa22a
Namano ene Karionki
Lenkisem, 2 July 1997
30 kb

Maa22b
Namano ene Karionki
Mashuru Rd, 7 Dec. 1998
28 kb

Maa22c
Namano ene Karionki
Mashuru Rd, 20 Dec. 1998
28 kb

Maa23a
Naraya
Iloirero, 2 July 1997
25 kb

Maa23b
Naraya
Iloirero, 8 Dec. 1998
23 kb

Maa24a
Kupese Kisikon
Iloirero, 2 July 1997
26 kb

Maa24b
Kupese Kisikon
Iloirero, 20 Dec. 1998
25 kb

Maa25a
Nasianta Karat
Meshanani, 2 July 1997
25 kb

Maa26a
Milia Kilempu
Lenkisem, 2 July 1997
23 kb

Maa26b
Milia Kilempu
Lenkisem, 29 Apr. 1998
24 kb

Maa26c
Milia Kilempu
Lenkisem, 10 Dec. 1998
27 kb

Maa27a
Kitasho Kisaine
Makutano, 3 July 1997
22 kb

Maa27b
Kitasho Kisaine
Makutano, 7 Dec. 1998
27 kb

Maa27c
Kitasho Kisaine
Makutano, 20 Dec. 1998
26 kb

Maa28a
Kokoyia Ene Olobi
Enkirrikir, 9 July 1997
26 kb

Maa29a
Keramatisho ene Kardasi
Enkirrikir, 9 July 1997
26 kb

Maa29b
Keramatisho ene Kardasi
Enkirrikir, 12 Dec. 1998
26 kb

Maa30a
Kareiyia Ngurrishoi
Enkirrikir, 9 July 1997
27 kb

Maa30b
Kareiya Ngurrishoi
Enkirrikir, 12 Dec. 1998
22 kb

Maa31a
Mara ene Katampoi
Enkirrkir, 9 July 1997
31 kb

Maa32a
Julia Kelele
Olkinos, 10 July 1997
32 kb

Maa32b
Julia Kelele
Olkinos, 11 Dec. 1998
24 kb

Maa33a
Soitalel ene Dugume
Olkinos, 10 July 1997
29 kb

Maa34a
Leah ene Kitangus
Olkinos, 10 July 1997
24 kb

Maa34b
Leah ene Kitangus
Olkinos, 11 Dec. 1998
23kb

Maa35a
Ole Mooke
Olkinos, 10 July 1997
31 kb

Maa36a
Tepatet Salaash
Olkinos, 10 July 1997
31 kb

Maa36b
Tepatet Salaash
Olkinos, 12 Dec. 1998
28 kb

Maa37a
Sendui Kilempu
Lenkisem, 15 July 1997
27 kb

Maa37b
Sendui Kilempu
Lenkisem, 8 Dec. 1998
26 kb

Maa38a
Kipelil Melita
Lenkisem, 15 July 1997
31 kb

Maa38b
Kipelil Melita
Lenkisem, 8 Dec. 1998
27 kb

Maa39a
Nkoije Lankoi
Lenkisem, 9 Dec. 1998
27 kb

Maa39b
Nkoije Lankoi
Lenkisem, 21 Dec. 1998
28 kb

Maa40a
Ole Kosiyanka
Olooilalei, 9 Dec. 1998
30 kb

Maa40b
Ole Kosiyanka
Olooilalei, 21 Dec. 1998
31 kb

Bunyoro

Nyoro1a
Anastasia Tinkamanyire
Butale, 5 Feb. 1998
32 kb

Nyoro1b
Anastasia Tinkamanyire
Butale, 18 March 1998
34 kb

Nyoro1c
Anastasia Tinkamanyire
Butale,11 April 1998
45 kb

Nyoro2a
Christopher Byaleero
Butale, 5 Feb. 1998
42 kb

Nyoro2b
Christopher Byaleero
Butale, 18 March 1998
44 kb

Nyoro2c
Christopher Byaleero
Butale, 11 April 1998
61 kb

Nyoro3a
Adelaide Kajaja
Butale, 5 Feb. 1998
33 kb

Nyoro3b
Adelaide Kajaja
Butale, 18 March 1998
38kb

Nyoro4a
Peter Isingoma
Butale, 5 February 1998
38 kb

Nyoro4b
Peter Isingoma
Butale, 18 March 1998
31 kb

Nyoro4c
Peter Isingoma
Butale, 11 April 1998
39 kb

Nyoro5a
Yoniya Ruhirabake
Kasasa, 6 Feb. 1998
42 kb

Nyoro5b
Yoniya Ruhirabake
Kasasa, 19 March 1998
37 kb

Nyoro5c
Yoniya Ruhirabake
Kasasa, 21 April 1998
26 kb

Nyoro6a
Ernest Bandora
Kasasa, 6 Feb. 1998
35 kb

Nyoro6b
Ernest Bandora
Kasasa, 18 March 1998
44 kb

Nyoro6c
Ernest Bandora
Kasasa, 21 April 1998
26 kb

Nyoro7a
Janet Nyakahara
Kasasa, 6 Feb. 1998
39 kb

Nyoro7b
Janet Nyakahara
Kasasa, 19 March 1998
39 kb

Nyoro7c
Janet Nyakahara
Kasasa, 11 March 1998
34 kb

Nyoro8a
Yohana Tibahwerwa
Kasasa, 11 Feb. 1998
40 kb

Nyoro8b
Yohana Tibahwerwa
Kasasa, 19 March 1998
45 kb

Nyoro8c
Yohana Tibahwerwa
Kasasa, 11 March 1998
51 kb

Nyoro9a
Peter Kaheeru
Rukooge, 11 Feb. 1998
54 kb

Nyoro9b
Peter Kaheeru
Rukooge, 27 Feb. 1998
44 kb

Nyoro9c
Peter Kaheeru
Rukooge, 22 April 1998
39 kb

Nyoro10a
Yafesi Kyamiza
Kasingo, 14 Feb. 1998
33 kb

Nyoro10b
Yafesi Kyamiza
Kasingo, 21 March 1998
54 kb

Nyoro10c
Yafesi Kyamiza
Kasingo, 21 April 1998
41 kb

Nyoro11a
Gertrude Nyakamadi
Kasingo, 14 Feb. 1998
42 kb

Nyoro11b
Gertrude Nyakamadi
Kasingo, 21 March 1998
51 kb

Nyoro11c
Gertrude Nyakamadi
Kasingo, 21 April 1998
34 kb

Nyoro12a
Zebia Nyakoojo
Kasingo, 14 Feb. 1998
35 kb

Nyoro12b
Zebia Nyakoojo
Kasingo, 21 March 1998
37 kb

Nyoro13a
Jennifer Tibagwa
Kasingo, 14 Feb. 1998
40 kb

Nyoro13b
Jennifer Tibagwa
Kasingo, 27 Feb. 1998
36 kb

Nyoro14a
Peter Hairikata
Kasingo, 14 Feb. 1998
40 kb

Nyoro14b
Peter Hairikata
Kasingo, 27 Feb. 1998
39 kb

Nyoro15a
Milia Isoke
Mpaija, 18 Feb. 1998
37 kb

Nyoro15b
Milia Isoke
Mpaija, 4 April 1998
45 kb

Nyoro15c
Milia Isoke
Mpaija, 18 April 1998
42 kb

Nyoro16a
Mary Kabwongyera
Mpaija, 18 Feb. 1998
37 kb

Nyoro16b
Mary Kabwongyera
Mpaija, 4 April 1998
45 kb

Nyoro16c
Mary Kabwongyera
Mpaija, 22 April 1998
42 kb

Nyoro17b
Alexander Byarwanju
Kinogoozi, 4 April 1998
31 kb

Nyoro17c
Alexander Byarwanju
Kasingo, 19 April 1998
44 kb

Nyoro18a
Erina Bakyayaya
Mpaija, 18 Feb. 1998
39 kb

Nyoro18b
Erina Bakyayaya
Mpaija, 3 April 1998
45 kb

Nyoro19a
Richard Nyakatura
Mpaija, 18 Feb. 1998
43 kb

Nyoro19b
Richard Nyakatura
Mpaija, 3 April 1998
54 kb

Nyoro19c
Richard Nyakatura
Mpaija, 19 April 1998
40 kb

Nyoro20a
Suleman Kabagyo
Mpaija, 18 Feb. 1998
33 kb

Nyoro20b
Suleman Kabagyo
Mpaija, 21 April 1998
45 kb

Nyoro21a
Augustine Kiiza
Katasiiha, 19 Feb. 1998
58 kb

Nyoro21b
Augustine Kiiza
Katasiiha, 31 March 1998
110 kb

Nyoro22a
Kwebiiha Laurent
Katasiiha, 19 Feb. 1998
34 kb

Nyoro22b
Kwebiiha Laurent
Katasiiha, 31 March 1998
43 kb

Nyoro22c
Kwebiiha Laurent
Katasiiha, 20 April 1998
35 kb

Nyoro23a
Dolika Bagamba
Katasiiha, 19 Feb. 1998
35 kb

Nyoro23b
Dolika Bagamba
Katasiiha, 3 April 1998
42 kb

Nyoro23c
Dolika Bagamba
Katasiiha, 20 April 1998
38 kb

Nyoro24a
Mary Kahoyhoro
Katasiiha, 19 Feb. 1998
32 kb

Nyoro24b
Mary Kahoyhoro
Katasiiha, 3 April 1998
38 kb

Nyoro24c
Mary Kahoyhoro
Katasiiha, 20 April 1998
31 kb

Nyoro25a
Joseph Kiiza
Katasiiha, 19 Feb. 1998
67 kb

Nyoro25b
Joseph Kiiza
Katasiiha, 31 March 1998
48 kb

Nyoro25c
Joseph Kiiza
Katasiiha, 20 April 1998
40 kb

Nyoro26a
Natalia Kamugwabya
Katasiiha, 19 Feb. 1998
30 kb

Nyoro26b
Natalia Kamugwabya
Katasiiha, 31 March 1998
42 kb

Nyoro26c
Natalia Kamugwabya
Katasiiha, 20 April 1998
28 kb

Nyoro27a
Topista Mudondo
Kyesiga, 20 Feb. 1998
57kb

Nyoro27b
Topista Mudondo
Kyesiga, 31 March 1998
36 kb

Nyoro27c
Topista Mudondo
Kyesiga, 20 April 1998
36 kb

Nyoro28a
May Biferamunda
Kyesiga, 20 Feb. 1998
42 kb

Nyoro28b
May Biferamunda
Kyesiga, 20 Feb. 1998
48 kb

Nyoro29a
Joseph Baikaraine
Kyesiga, 20 Feb. 1998
45 kb

Nyoro29b
Joseph Baikaraine
Kyesiga, 30 March 1998
73 kb

Nyoro29c
Joseph Baikaraine
Kyesia, 20 April 1998
30 kb

Nyoro30a
Mary Lutgard Kacinca
Kyesiga, 20 Feb. 1998
38 kb

Nyoro30b
Mary Lutgard Kacinca
Kyesiga, 31 March 1998
39 kb

Nyoro31a
Paulo Barongo
Katasiiha, 20 Feb. 1998
30 kb

Nyoro31b
Paulo Barongo
Kyesiga, 30 March 1998
48 kb

Nyoro32a
Valeria Nyakahara
Kyesiga, 20 Feb. 1998
31 kb

Nyoro32b
Valeria Nyakahara
Kyesiga, 30 March 1998
42 kb

Nyoro33a
Erukana Rwakaikara
Omuryanja, 23 Feb. 1998
44 kb

Nyoro33b
Erukana Rwakaikara
Omuryanja, 1 April 1998
58 kb

Nyoro33c
Erukana Rwakaikara
Omuryanja, 18 April 1998
49 kb

Nyoro34a
Yurunimu Wandera,
Omuryanja, 23 Feb. 1998
34 kb

Nyoro34b
Yurunimu Wandera,
Omuryanja, 1 April 1998
69 kb

Nyoro34c
Yurunimu Wandera,
Omuryanja, 18 April 1998
45 kb

Nyoro35a
Sorsana Kiiza
Omuryanja, 23 Feb. 1998
40 kb

Nyoro35b
Sorsana Kiiza
Omuryanja, 1 April 1998
47 kb

Nyoro35c
Sorsana Kiiza
Omuryanja, 18 April 1998
64 kb

Nyoro36a
Rwangire Michael
Omuryanja, 23 Feb. 1998
38 kb

Nyoro36b
Rwangire Michael
Omuryanja, 3 April 1998
46 kb

Nyoro36c
Rwangire Michael
Omuryanja, 18 April 1998
52 kb

Nyoro37a
Nyensi Kaahwa
Omuryanja, 23 Feb. 1998
36 kb

Nyoro37b
Nyensi Kaahwa
Omuryanja, 3 April 1998
43 kb

Nyoro38a
Elizabeth Kanobe
Parajwooki, 25 Feb. 1998
59 kb

Nyoro38b
Elizabeth Kanobe
Parajwooki, 25 March 1998
50 kb

Nyoro38c
Elizabeth Kanobe
Parajwooki, 18 April 1998
52 kb

Nyoro39a
Yasoni Tibakunirwa
Parajwooki, 25 Feb. 1998
44 kb

Nyoro39b
Yasoni Tibakunirwa
Parajwooki, 25 March 1998
42 kb

Nyoro39c
Yasoni Tibakunirwa
Parajwooki, 18 April 1998
33 kb

Nyoro40a
Rafael Babyesiza
Parajwooki, 25 Feb. 1998
39 kb

Nyoro40b
Rafael Babyesiza
Parajwooki, 25 March 1998
41 kb

Nyoro41a
Cecilia Nzaireki
Parajwooki, 25 Feb. 1998
35 kb

Nyoro41b
Cecilia Nzaireki
Parajwooki, 25 March 1998
33 kb

Nyoro42a
Joseph Ndoleriire
Dwoli, 24 March 1998
34 kb

Nyoro43a
Rubenda Kassim
Hoima, 9 April 1998
56 kb

Rungwe/Kyela

Nya1a
Omari Mwamwaja
Lupando, 9 Feb. 1997
40 kb

Nya1b
Omari Mwamwaja
Lupando, 18 Nov. 1997
28 kb

Nya1c
Omari Mwamwaja
Lupando, 15 Dec. 1997
31 kb

Nya2a
Bope Tomasi
Lupando, 9 Feb. 1997
55 kb

Nya2b
Bope Tomasi
Lupando, 18 Nov. 1997
27 kb

Nya2c
Bope Tomasi
Lupando, 17 Dec. 1997
28 kb

Nya3a
Paul Samuel Mwandembwa
Mpuguso, 10 Feb. 1997
43kb

Nya3b
Paul Samuel Mwandembwa
Mpuguso, 19 Nov. 1997
47 kb

Nya3c
Paul Samuel Mwandembwa
Mpuguso, 18 Dec. 1997
52 kb

Nya4a
Job Kikondo
Ilundo, 11 Feb. 1997
39 kb

Nya4b
Job Kikondo
Ilundo, 15 Nov. 1997
48 kb

Nya4c
Job Kikondo
Ilundo, 22 Dec. 1997
64 kb

Nya5a
Dauti Pungo
Ilundo, 11 Feb. 1997
35 kb

Nya5b
Dauti Pungo
Ilundo, 26 Nov. 1997
31 kb

Nya5c
Dauti Pungo
Ilundo, 22 Dec. 1997
27 kb

Nya6a
Stemani Sanga
Isongore, 11 Feb. 1997
46 kb

Nya6b
Stemani Sanga
Isongore, 15 Nov. 1997
33 kb

Nya7a
Helena Mbilikile
Isongore, 11 Feb. 1997
39 kb

Nya7b
Helena Mbilikile
Isongore, 15 Nov. 1997
29 kb

Nya8a
James Mwaipyana Mukosyange
Ikolo, 12 Feb. 1997
42 kb

Nya8b
James Mwaipyana Mukosyange
Ikolo, 12 Feb. 1997
36 kb

Nya8c
James Mwaipyana Mukosyange
Ikolo, 28 Nov. 1997
38 kb

Nya9a
Belita Nkusa
Kingila, 12 Feb. 1997
23 kb

Nya9b
Belita Nkusa
Kingila, 29 Nov. 1997
30 kb

Nya10a
Andende Mwairunga
Kingila, 13 Feb. 1997
45 kb

Nya10b
Andende Mwairunga
Kingila, 29 Nov. 1997
37 kb

Nya11a
Jake Mwakibwiri
Masukulu, 14 Feb. 1997
44 kb

Nya11b
Jake Mwakibwiri
Masukulu, 20 Nov. 1997
36 kb

Nya12a
Jason Mwansyunguti
Masukulu, 14 Feb. 1997
47 kb

Nya12b
Jason Mwansyunguti
Masukulu, 20 Nov. 1997
39 kb

Nya13a
Katerina Ngosi
Masukulu, 14 Feb. 1997
34 kb

Nya13b
Katerina Ngosi
Masukulu, 20 Nov. 1997
27 kb

Nya14a
Isaac Mwakivinga
Ntandawala, 14 Feb. 1997
48 kb

Nya14b
Isaac Mwakivinga
Ntandawala, 14 Nov. 1997
42 kb

Nya14c
Isaac Mwakivinga
Ntandawala, 6 Dec. 1997
45 kb

Nya15a
Tuhobo Kirege
Ntandawala, 14 Nov. 1997
23 kb

Nya16a
Benson Mwakipagala
Mbambo, 15 Feb. 1997
41 kb

Nya16b
Benson Mwakipagala
Mbambo, 14 Nov. 1997
54 kb

Nya16c
Benson Mwakipagala
Mbambo, 6 Dec. 1997
91 kb

Nya17a
Hakimu Mwalyaje
Lugombo, 6 Oct. 1997
32 kb

Nya17b
Hakimu Mwalyaje
Lugombo, 30 Oct. 1997
34 kb

Nya17c
Hakimu Mwalyaje
Lugombo, 20 Dec. 1997
25 kb

Nya18a
Ngabagile Kivasyo
Lugombo, 6 Oct. 1997
37 kb

Nya18b
Ngabagile Kivasyo
Lugombo, 30 Oct. 1997
40 kb

Nya18c
Ngabagile Kivasyo
Lugombo, 20 Dec. 1997
28 kb

Nya19a
Grace Majid
Kandete, 6 Oct. 1997
36 kb

Nya19b
Grace Majid
Kandete, 22 Nov. 1997
38 kb

Nya19c
Grace Majid
Kandete, 19 Dec. 1997
42 kb

Nya20a
Kairi Mwakaje
Kandete, 6 Oct. 1997
40 kb

Nya20c
Kairi Mwakaje
Kandete, 19 Dec. 1997
24 kb

Nya21a
Singolile Mwakalobo
Ndembo, 9 Oct. 1997
18 kb

Nya21b
Singolile Mwakalobo
Ndembo, 22 Nov. 1997
27 kb

Nya21c
Singolile Mwakalobo
Ndembo, 4 Dec. 1997
37 kb

Nya22a
Amini Mwamlenga
Kanyelele, 9 Oct. 1997
21 kb

Nya22b
Amini Mwamelnga
Kanyelele, 4 Dec. 1997
27 kb

Nya23a
Retina Kayuni
Ikuti, 13 Oct. 1997
37 kb

Nya23b
Retina Kayuni
Ikuti, 8 Nov. 1997
32 kb

Nya23c
Retina Kayuni
Ikuti, 16 Dec. 1997
27 kb

Nya24a
Eliya Mwangono
Ikuti, 13 Oct. 1997
35 kb

Nya24b
Eliya Mwangono
Ikuti, 13 Nov. 1997
53 kb

Nya25a
Anyingisye Bukuku
Kyobo, 13 Oct. 1997
38 kb

Nya25b
Anyingisye Bukuku
Kyobo, 3 Nov. 1997
40 kb

Nya26a
Nikomitika Ngemela
Kyobo, 13 Oct. 1997
30 kb

Nya26b
Nikomitika Ngemela
Kyobo, 3 Nov. 1997
34 kb

Nya26c
Nikomitika Ngemela
Kyobo, 16 Dec. 1997
25 kb

Nya27a
Pambialo Kanama
Mpuga, 16 Oct. 1997
30 kb

Nya27b
Pambialo Kanama
Mpuga, 25 Nov. 1997
37 kb

Nya28a
Jenny Ngamilo
Mpuga, 16 Oct. 1997
29 kb

Nya28b
Jenny Ngamilo
Mpuga, 25 Nov. 1997
29 kb

Nya29a
Hasani Mwakasege
Bugoba, 16 Oct. 1997
33kb

Nya30a
Nabwike Kalabaja
Bugoba, 16 Oct. 1997
36 kb

Nya31a
Hannah Kabonga
Tukyu, 18 Oct. 1997
46 kb

Nya31b
Hannah Kabonga
Tukuyu, 27 Nov. 1997
44 kb

Nya32a
Albert Weston Mwaipungu
Tukuyu, 18 Oct. 1997
36 kb

Nya32b
Albert Weston Mwaipungu
Tukuyu, 26 Nov. 1997
61 kb

Nya33a
Christine Kamwera
Tukuyu, 20 Oct. 1997
46 kb

Nya33b
Christine Kamwera
Tukuyu, 20 Dec. 1997
33 kb

Nya34a
Jason Jacob Mwakibete
Tukuyu, 20 Oct. 1997
37 kb

Nya35a
Patrick Kapambile
Bujesi, 24 Oct. 1997
34 kb

Nya36a
Blaki Mwakanjala
Mpunguti, 29 Oct. 1997
33 kb

Nya36b
Blaki Mwakanjala
Mpunguti, 28 Nov. 1997
33 kb

Nya37a
Hans Mwampaja
Mpunguti, 29 Oct. 1997
33 kb
Nya37b
Hans Mwampaja
Mpunguti, 28 Nov. 1997
36 kb

Nya38a
Eva Kyando
Itunge, 30 Oct. 1997
35 kb

Nya38b
Eva Kyando
Itunge, 29 Nov. 1997
27 kb

Nya39a
Amani Mwambhabhala
Itunge, 30 Oct. 1997
33 kb

Nya39b
Amani Mwambhabhala
Itunge, 29 Nov. 1997
36 kb

Nya40a
Mwambagi
Kiwira, 6 Nov. 1997
31 kb

Nya41a
Nikusubira Kyage
Ilenge, 15 Nov. 1997
32 kb

Nya41b
Nikusubira Kyage
Ilenge, 20 Dec. 1997
24 kb

Nya42a
Lusubilo Kipesile
Ntandawala, 6 Dec. 1997
36 kb

Nya42b
Lusubilo Kipesile
Ntandawala, 20 Dec. 1997
32 kb

Bibliography

Acuda, S.W., 1985, 'International Review Series: Alcohol and Alcohol Problem Research. East Africa', *British Journal of Addiction*, 80: 121-6.

Aguilar, M., 1998, 'Gerontocratic, Aesthetic and Political Models of Age', in M. Aguilar (ed.), *The Politics of Age and Gerontocracy*, Trenton, NJ/Asmara, 3-39.

Aguilar, M. (ed.), 1998, *The Politics of Age and Gerontocracy in Africa*, Trenton, NJ/Asmara.

Akyeampong, E., 1998, *Drink, Power and Cultural Change. A Social History of Alcohol in Ghana, c. 1800 to Recent Times*, Portsmouth, NH/Oxford.

Akyeampong, E., 1996, 'What's in a Drink? Class Struggle, Popular Culture, and the Politics of *Akpeteshie* (Local Gin) in Ghana, 1930-67', *JAH*, 37: 215-36.

Ambler, C., 1987, 'Alcohol and Disorder in Precolonial Africa', Boston University African Studies Centre, Working Paper No. 126.

Ambler, C., 1988, *Kenyan Communities in the Age of Imperialism. The Central Region in the Late Nineteenth Century*, New Haven, CT/London.

Ambler, C., 1990, 'Alcohol, Racial Segregation and Popular Politics in Northern Rhodesia', *JAH*, 31: 295-313.

Ambler, C., 'Drunks, Brewers and Chiefs: Alcohol Regulation in Colonial Kenya, 1900-39', in Barrows and Room (eds), *Drinking: Behavior and Belief in Modern History*, 165-83.

Ambler, C. and J. Crush, 'Alcohol in Southern African Labor History', in Crush and Ambler (eds), *Liquor and Labor in Southern Africa*, 1-55.

Anderson, D. and D. Johnson (eds.), 1995, *Revealing Prophets. Prophecy in East African History*, London/Nairobi/Kampala/Athens, OH.

Appadurai, A., 1986, 'Commodities and the Politics of Value', in A. Appadurai (ed.), *The Social Life of Things. Commodities in Cultural Perspective*, 3-63, Cambridge.

Apter, D. 1997, *The Political Kingdom in Uganda. A Study in Bureaucratic Nationalism*, London.

Arens, W. and I. Karp, 1989, 'Introduction', in W. Arens and I. Karp (eds) *Creativity of Power. Cosmology and Action in African Societies*, Washington, DC/London, xi-xxix.

Ashe, R.P. 1970 (1st ed. 1889) *Two Kings of Uganda, or Life by the Shores of Victorian Nyanza*, London.

Atieno-Odhiambo, E., 1995, 'The Formative Years, 1945-63', in B. Ogot and W. Ochieng' (eds), *Decolonization and Independence in Kenya, 1940-1993*, London/Nairobi/Athens, OH, 25-47.

Babumba, E., 1963, *Report of the Spirituous Liquor Committee*, Entebbe.

Bache, E., 1934, *The Youngest Lion. Early Farming Days in Kenya*, London.

Baker, E.C., 1931, 'Memorandum on the Social Conditions of Dar es Salaam', in African Studies Centre Library, Cambridge.

Baker, S., 1962 (1st edn 1867), *The Albert N'yanza. Great Basin of the Nile and Explorations of the Nile Sources* (2 vols), London.

Baker, S., 1895 (1st edn 1874), *Ismailia. A Narrative of the Expedition to Central Africa for the Suppression of the Slave Trade*, London/New York.

Barrows, S. 'Parliaments of the People: The Political Culture of Cafés in the Early Third Republic', in Barrows and Room, *Drink: Behavior and Belief*, 87-97.

Barrows, S. and R. Room (eds), 1991, *Drinking: Behavior and Belief in Modern Society*, Berkeley, CA/Los Angeles, LA/London.

Barrows, S. and R. Room, 'Introduction', in Barrows and Room (eds), *Drinking: Behavior and Belief*, 1-28.

Bibliography

Beattie, J., 1960, *Bunyoro. An African Kingdom* (New York/Chicago, IL/San Francisco, CA/Toronto/London.

Beattie, J., 1969, 'Spirit Mediumship in Bunyoro', in J. Beattie and J. Middleton, *Spirit Mediumship and Society in Africa*, London, 159-70.

Beattie, J., 1971, *The Nyoro State*, Oxford.

Beckman, V., 1988, *Alcohol. Another Trap for Africa*, Orebro.

Beidelman, T., 1971, *The Kaguru: a Matrilineal People of East Africa*, New York/Chicago, IL/San Francisco, CA.

Berger, I. 'Fertility as Power: Spirit Mediums, Priestesses and the Pre-Colonial State in Inter-Lacustrine East Africa', in Anderson and Johnson, *Revealing Prophets*, 65-82.

Berman, B., 'Bureaucracy and Incumbent Violence. Colonial Administration and the Origins of the "Mau Mau" Emergency', in Berman and Lonsdale, *Unhappy Valley*, II, 227-64.

Berman, B. and J. Lonsdale, 1992, *Unhappy Valley. Conflict in Kenya and Africa* (2 vols), London/Nairobi/Athens, OH.

Bradford, H., '"We Women Will Show Them": Beer Protests in the Natal Countryside, 1929', in Crush and Ambler, *Liquor and Labour in Southern Africa*, 208-34.

Bravman, B., 1998, *Making Ethnic Ways. Communities and Their Transformations in Taita, Kenya, 1800-1950*, Portsmouth, NH/Nairobi/Oxford.

Brennan, T., 'Social Drinking in Old Regime Paris', in Barrows and Room, *Drink: Behavior and Belief*, 61-86.

Brown, G. and A. Hutt, 1936, *Anthropology in Action*, London.

Bourdieu, P., 1977, *Outline of a Theory of Practice*, Cambridge.

Buell, R. L., 1926, *The Native Problem in Africa* (2 vols), New York.

Burton, R. F., 1961 (1st edn 1860), *The Lake Regions of Central Africa* (2 vols), New York.

Cagnolo, C., 1933, *The Akikuyu: Their Customs, Tradition and Folklore*, Nyeri.

Callaghy, T., 1987, 'The State as Lame Leviathan: the Patrimonial Administrative State in Africa' in Z. Ergas (ed.), *The African State in Transition*, London, 87-116.

Cameron, V.L., 1885 (1st edn 1876), *Across Africa*, London.

Campbell, D., 'Land as Ours, Land as Mine', in Spear and Waller (eds.), *Being Maasai*, 258-72.

Carlson, R. G., 1989, 'Haya Worldview and Ethos: An Ethnography of Alcohol Production and Consumption in Bukoba, Tanzania' (PhD, Illinois at Urbana-Champaign).

Carton, B., '"The New Generation . . . Jeer at Me, Saying We are All Equal Now": Impotent African Patriarchs, Unruly African Sons in Colonial South Africa', in Aguilar, *The Politics of Age and Gerontocracy*, 31-64.

Casati, G., 1891, *Ten Years in Equatoria and the Return with Emin Pasha* (trans. J. Clay), London.

Chabal, P., and J.-P. Daloz, 1999, *Africa Works. Disorder as Political Instrument* (Oxford/Bloomington, IN.

Chanler, W., 1891, *Through Jungle and Desert. Travels in Eastern Africa*, London.

Charsley, S.R., 1969, *The Princes of Nyakyusa*, Nairobi.

Chazan, N., P. Lewis, R. Mortimer, D. Rothchild and S. Stedman, 1999 (3rd edn), *Politics and Society in Contemporary Africa*, Boulder, CO.

Chidzero, B., 1961, *Tanganyika and International Trusteeship*, Oxford.

Clark, P., 1983, *The English Alehouse: A Social History, 1200-1830*, London/New York.

Collis, M., 1972, 'Cancer of the Oesophagus and Alcoholic Drinks in East Africa', *Lancet*, 7797: 441.

Colson, E. and T. Scudder, 1988, *For Prayer and Profit: The Ritual, Economic and Social Importance of Beer in the Gwembe District, Zambia, 1950-82*, Stanford, CA.

Colvile, H., 1895, *The Land of the Nile Springs. Being Chiefly an Account of How We Fought Kabarega*, London/New York.

Comaroff, J. and J. (eds), 1993, *Modernity and Its Malcontents: Ritual and Power in Post-colonial Africa*, Chicago, IL/London.

Corran, H. S., 1975, *A History of Brewing*, Newton Abbot.

Bibliography

Crush, J. and C. Ambler (eds), 1992, *Liquor and Labor in Southern Africa* (Athens, OH/ Pietermaritzburg.

Culwick, A. and G. Culwick, 1935, *Ubena of the Rivers*, London.

Curtis, D.,1973, 'Cash Brewing in a Rural Economy', *Botswana Notes and Records*, 5.

Curto, J., 1989, 'Alcohol in Africa: A Preliminary Compilation of the Post-1875 Literature', *Current Bibliography on African Affairs*, 21: 3-31.

Dawson, J., 1933, 'Account of the Engapata Ceremony' and ' Milk-drinking Ceremony' (typescript in British Institute in Eastern Africa Library), Nairobi.

Ddirar, H., 1976, 'The Art and Science of Merissa Fermentation', *Sudan Notes and Records*, 57: 115-29.

Dennis, P., 'The Role of the Drunk in an Oaxacan Village', in Marshall, *Beliefs, Behaviors and Alcoholic Beverages*, 54-64.

Douglas, M. (ed.), 1987, *Constructive Drinking: Perspectives on Drink from Anthropology*, Cambridge.

Dreyfus, P. 'Effects of Alcohol on the Nervous System', in Gastineau *et al.*, *Fermented Food Beverages*, 341-57.

Driberg, J., 1923, *The Lango. A Nilotic Tribe of Uganda*, London.

Dunbar, A.R., 1965, 'Mutala Survey of Bujenje (Kisonga), Bunyoro', *Uganda Journal*, 29: 61-74.

Dundas, C., 1924, *Kilimanjaro and Its People*, London.

Dundas, C., 1955, *African Crossroads*, London.

Edwards, G., 1979, 'Drinking Problems: Putting the Third World on the Map', *Lancet*, 8139: 402-4.

Elton, J.F., 1968 (1st edn 1879), *Travels and Researches Among the Lakes and Mountains of Eastern and Central Africa*, London.

Emerson, H., 1934, *Alcohol. Its Effects on Man*, New York/London.

Engels, F., 1958, *The Condition of the Working Class in England* (trans. W. Henderson and W. Chalmer), Oxford.

Ewing, J., B. Rouse and E. Pellizzari, 1974, 'Alcohol Sensitivity and Ethnic Background', *American Journal of Psychiatry*, 206-10.

Fabian, J., 2000, *Out of Our Minds: Reason and Madness in the Exploration of Central Africa*, Berkeley, CA/Los Angeles, LA/London.

Farson, N., 1953 (1st edn 1949), *Last Chance in Africa*, London.

Feierman, S., 1990, *Peasant Intellectuals. Anthropology and History in Tanzania*, Madison, WI.

Fisher, R.B., 1911, *Twilight Tales of the Black Baganda*, London.

Foran, W.R., 1936, *A Cuckoo in Kenya. The Reminiscences of a Pioneer Police Officer in British East Africa*, London.

Ford, P. and G. Ford, 1951, *Breviate of Parliamentary Papers, 1917-1939*, Oxford.

Fotheringham, L., 1891, *Adventures in Nyasaland*, London.

Fox, D. Storrs, 1930, 'Further Notes on the Masai of Kenya Colony', *Journal of the Anthropological Institute*, 60: 447-65.

Fukui, K., 1970, 'Alcoholic Drinks of the Iraqw. Brewing Methods and Social Functions', *Kyoto University African Studies*, 5: 125-48.

Fulleborn, F., 1906, *Das Deutsche Njassa- und Ruwuma-Gebiet*, Berlin.

Galaty, J., 1979, 'Pollution and Pastoral Antipraxis: the Issue of Maasai Inequality', *American Ethnologist*, 6 (4): 803-16.

Galaty, J., 1992, '"The Land is Yours": Social and Economic Factors in the Privatization, Sub-division and Sale of Maasai Ranches', *Nomadic Peoples*, 30: 26-40.

Gastineau, C., W. Darby and T. Turner (eds.), 1979, *Fermented Food Beverages in Nutrition*, New York/San Francisco, CA/London.

Ghalioungui, P., 1979, 'Fermented Beverages in Antiquity', in C. Gastineau, W. Darby and P. Turner (eds.), *Fermented Food Beverages in Nutrition*, 4-18.

Giddens, A., 1979, *Central Problems in Social Theory*, London.

Glassman, J., 1995, *Feasts and Riot: Revelry, Rebellion and Popular Consciousness on the Swahili Coast, 1856-1885*, London/Athens, OH/Nairobi.

Bibliography

Golding, J., 1987, *Colonialism: the Golden Years*, Ashford.

Grant, J., 1864, *A Walk Across Africa, or Domestic Scenes from My Nile Journal*, London.

Great Britain, 1898, *British Foreign and State Papers, Vol. 84, 1891-92*, London.

Great Britain, 1899, *British Foreign and State Papers, Vol. 86, 1893-94*, London.

Great Britain, 1901, *British Foreign and State Papers, Vol. 89, 1896-97*, London.

Great Britain, 1905, *British and Foreign State Papers, Vol. 95, 1902*, London.

Green, M., 1999, 'Trading on Inequality: Gender and the Drinks Trade in Southern Tanzania', *Africa*, 69: 404-23.

Greenberg, L.A., 1953, 'Alcohol in the Body', *Scientific American*, 189: 86-90.

Gross, M. (ed.), 1977, *Alcoholic Intoxication and Withdrawal*, Vols IIIa, IIIb, New York/London.

Gunter, J., 1957 (1st edn 1955), *Inside Africa*, London.

Guthrie, M., 1971, *Comparative Bantu* (4 vols), Farnborough.

Gutkind, P., 1963, *The Royal Capital of Buganda. A Study of Internal Conflict and External Ambiguity*, The Hague.

Guyer, J., 1981, 'Household and Community in African Studies', *African Studies Review*, 24: 87-137.

Hake, A., 1977, *African Metropolis. Nairobi's Self-help City*, London/Toronto.

Harris, G., 1978, *Casting Out Anger. Religion among the Taita of Kenya*, Cambridge.

Harrison, B., 1971, *Drink and the Victorians: The Temperance Question in England, 1815-72*, London.

Harwood, A., 1974, 'Beer Drinking and Famine in a Safwa Village: A Case of Adaptation in a Time of Crisis', *Proceedings of the East African Institute of Social Research Conference*.

Hattersley, C., 1908, *The Baganda at Home*, London.

la Hausse, P., 'Drink and Cultural Innovation: the Origins of the Beer Hall in South Africa, 1903-16', in Crush and Ambler (eds.), *Liquor and Labor in Southern Africa*, 78-114.

Haugerud, A., 1995, *The Culture of Politics in Modern Kenya*, Cambridge.

Heald, S., 1989, *Controlling Anger. The Sociology of Gisu Violence*, Manchester/New York.

Hemedi 'l Ajjemy, A. bin, 1962, *Habari za Wakilindi*, Nairobi.

Herbert, E., *Iron, Gender and Power: Rituals of Transformation in African Societies*, Bloomington, IN.

Herlehy, T., 1984, 'Ties That Bind: Palm Wine and Blood Brotherhood at the Kenya Coast During the Nineteenth Century', *IJAHS*, 17: 285-308.

Hills, D., 1975, *The White Pumpkin*, London.

Hinde, S. L. and H. Hinde, 1901, *The Last of the Masai*, London.

Hobley, C., 1910, *Ethnology of the Akamba and other East African Tribes*, Cambridge.

Hohnel, L., 1968 (1st edn 1891), *Discovery of Lakes Rudolf and Stefanie. A Narrative of Count Samuel Teleki's Exploring and Hunting Expedition in Eastern Equatorial Africa in 1887 and 1888* (2 vols), London.

Hollis, A.C., 1970 (1st edn 1905), *The Masai. Their Language and Folklore*, Westport, CT.

Horsley, V. and M. Sturge, 1907, *Alcohol and the Human Body*, London.

Horton, D., 1943, 'The Functions of Alcohol in Primitive Societies: A Cross-Cultural Study', *Quarterly Journal of Studies on Alcohol*, 4: 199-320.

Hull, J. G. and C. F. Bond, 1986, 'Social and Behavioral Consequences of Alcohol Consumption and Expectancy: A Meta-Analysis', *Psychological Bulletin*, 99: 347-60.

Hutchinson, B., 'Alcohol as a Contributing Factor in Social Disorganization: The South African Bantu in the Nineteenth Century', in Marshall (ed.) B*eliefs, Behaviors and Alcoholic Beverages*, 328-41.

Huxley, E., 1935, *White Man's Country. Lord Delamere and the Making of Kenya* (2 vols), London.

Iliffe, J., 1979, *A Modern History of Tanganyika*, Cambridge.

Jackson, F., 1930, *Early Days in East Africa*, London.

James, W., 1972, 'Beer, Morality and Social Relations Among the Uduk', *Sudan Society*, 5: 17-27.

Jellinek, E., 1977, 'The Symbolism of Drinking: A Cultural-historical Approach', *Journal of Studies on Alcohol*, 38: 849-66.

Johnston, H., 1911, 'Alcohol in Africa', *The Nineteenth Century and After*, (Sep.) 476-94.

Johnston, H., 1986, *The Kilima-Njaro Expedition*, London.

Karp, I., 1980, 'Beer Drinking and Social Experience in an African Society: An Essay in Formal Sociology', in I. Karp and C. Bird (eds.), *Explorations in African Systems of Thought*, 83-115, Bloomington, IN.

Keddie, J and W. Cleghorn, 1979, *Brewing in Developing Countries*, Edinburgh.

Kerr-Cross, D., 1890, 'Geographical Notes on the Country Between Lakes Nyassa, Rukwa and Tanganyika', *Scottish Geographical Magazine*, VI: 281-93.

King, K., 1996, *Jua Kali Kenya: Change and Development in an Informal Economy, 1970-95*, London/Nairobi/Athens, OH.

King'ala, Y., 1984, *Anasa*, Nairobi.

Kituyi, M., 1990, *Becoming Kenyans. Socio-economic Transformation of the Pastoral Maasai*, Nairobi.

Kjekshus, H., 1977, *Ecology Control and Economic Development in East African History: the Case of Tanganyika, 1850-1950*, Nairobi/Ibadan/Lusaka.

Klausner, S., 1964, 'Sacred and Profane Meanings of Blood and Alcohol', *Journal of Social Psychology*, 64: 27-43.

Kollman, P., 1899 , *The Victoria Nyanza* (trans. H. Nesbitt), London.

Kopytoff, I., 1987, 'The Internal African Frontier', in I. Kopytoff (ed.), *The African Frontier. The Reproduction of Traditional African Societies*, Bloomington, IN, 3-84.

Krapf, J.L., 1860, *Travels, Researches and Missionary Labours During an Eighteen Years' Residence in Eastern Africa*, London.

Kratz, C., 1994, *Affecting Performance. Meaning, Movement and Experience in Okiek Women's Initiation*, Washington, DC.

Landau, P., 1995, *Realm of the Word. Language, Gender, and Christianity in a Southern African Kingdom*, Portsmouth, NH/London.

Last, J., 1887, 'A Visit to the Masai People Living Beyond the Borders of the Nguru Country', *Proceedings of the Royal Geographical Society*, ns, V: 517-43.

Laswai, H., A. Wendelin, N. Kitabatake and T. Mosha, 1997, 'The Under-exploited Indigenous Alcoholic Beverages of Tanzania: Production, Consumption and Quality of the Undocumented "Denge"', *African Study Monographs*, 18: 29-44.

Leakey, L.S.B., 1930, 'Some Notes on the Masai of Kenya Colony', *Journal of the Anthropological Institute*, 60: 185-209.

Leakey, L.S.B., 1977, *The Southern Kikuyu before 1903* (3 vols), London.

Leslie, J., 1963, *A Survey of Dar es Salaam*, London/New York/Nairobi.

Lindblom, G., 1920, *The Akamba in British East Africa. An Ethnological Monograph*, Uppsala.

Lloyd, A., 1907, *Uganda to Khartoum. Life and Adventure on the Upper Nile*, London/ Glasgow.

Lonsdale, J., 'The Conquest State of Kenya, 1895-1905', in Berman and Lonsdale, *Unhappy Valley*, vol. 1, 13-44.

Lugard, F. D., 1968 (1st edn 1893), *The Rise of Our East African Empire* (2 vols), London, 1968.

Lugard, F. D., 1897, 'The Liquor Traffic in Africa', *The Nineteenth Century*, 42: 766-84.

Lugard, F. D., 1926 (1st edn 1923), *The Dual Mandate in British Tropical Africa*, Edinburgh/London.

Luning, H., 1969, *A Farm Economic Survey in Rungwe District*, Leiden.

Macandrew, C. and R. Edgerton, 1970 (1st edn 1969), *Drunken Comportment: A Social Explanation*, London/Accra/Lagos.

Mackenzie, D., 1925, *The Spirit-Ridden Konde*, London.

Macmillan, M., 1955 (1st edn 1952) *Introducing East Africa*, London.

McCall, M., 1996, 'Rural Brewing, Exclusion and Development Policy-making', *Gender and Development*, 4: 29-38.

Bibliography

McClure, H.R., 'Memorandum on the Masai' and 'District Records for the Guidance of the Officer Administrating the Masai Southern Reserve' (copy in British Institute in Eastern Africa Library, Nairobi).

McGregor Ross, W., 1968 (1st edn 1927), *Kenya from Within. A Short Political History*, London.

McKenny, M., 1973, 'The Social Structure of the Nyakyusa: A Re-evaluation', *Africa*, 43: 91-107.

Madsen, W. and C. Madsen, 'The Cultural Structure of Mexican Drinking Behavior', in Marshall (ed.), *Beliefs, Behaviors and Alcoholic Beverages*, 38-54.

Mager, A., 1999, 'The First Decade of "European Beer" in Apartheid South Africa: the State, the Brewers and the Drinking Public, 1962-72', *Journal of African History*, 40: 367-88.

Maillu, D., 1973, *My Dear Bottle*, Nairobi.

Mair, L., 1934, *An African People in the Twentieth Century*, London.

Maliyamkono, T. and M. Bagachwa, 1990, *The Second Economy in Tanzania*, London/ Athens, OH/Nairobi/Dar es Salaam.

Mandelbaum, D.,1965, 'Alcohol and Culture', *Current Anthropology*, 6: 281-93.

Mang'enya, E., 1984, *Discipline and Tears. Reminiscences of an African Civil Servant on Colonial Tanganyika*, Dar es Salaam.

Mangua, C., 1972, *Tail in the Mouth*, Nairobi.

Marshall, M. (ed.), 1979, *Beliefs, Behaviors and Alcoholic Beverages. A Cross-cultural Survey*, Ann Arbor, MI.

Mathias, P., 1959, *The Brewing Industry in England, 1700-1830*, Cambridge.

Mbilinyi, M., '"This is an Unforgettable Business": Colonial State Intervention in Urban Tanzania', in Parpart and Staudt (eds.), *Women and the State in Africa*, 111-29.

Meillassoux, C., 1981, *Maidens, Meal and Money. Capitalism and the Domestic Economy*, Cambridge.

Meinertzhagen, R., 1957, *Kenya Diary, 1902-1906*, London/Edinburgh.

Merker, M., 1910, 'The Masai' (translation for private circulation of *Die Masai. Ethnographische Monographie eines ostafrikanische Semitenvolkes*), Berlin.

Meyer, T., 1993, *Wa-Konde. Maisha, Mila na Desturi za Wanyakyusa*, Mbeya.

Middleton, J., 1960, *Lugbara Religion. Ritual and Authority among an African People*, London.

Miers, S., 1967, 'The Brussels Conference of 1889-90', in W. Gifford and P. Lewis (eds.), *Britain and Germany in Africa. Imperial Rivalry and Colonial Rule*, London/ New Haven, CT, 83-118.

Miers, S., 1975, *Britain and the Ending of the Slave Trade*, London.

Miller, N. and R. Yeager, 1994, *Kenya: The Quest for Prosperity*, Boulder, CO/San Francisco, CA/ Oxford.

Mitchell, P., 1954, *African Afterthoughts*, London.

Mosha, D., J. Wangabo and G. Mhinzi, 1996, 'African Traditional Brews: How Safe are They?' *Food Chemistry*, 57: 205-9.

Morgan, P., 'Alcohol, Disinhibition and Domination: A Conceptual Analysis', in Room and Collins, *Alcohol and Disinhibition*, 405-20.

Mwangi, M., 1976, *Going Down River Road*, London.

Mwesigye, P. and T. Okurut, 1995, 'A Survey of the Production and Consumption of Traditional Alcoholic Beverages in Uganda', *Process Biochemistry*, 30: 497-501.

Nabudere, D., 1980, *Imperialism and Revolution in Uganda*, London/Dar es Salaam.

Nelson, N., 1982, '"Women Must Help Each Other": The Operation of Personal Networks Among Buzaa Brewers in Mathare Valley, Kenya', in P. Caplan and J. Bujra (eds), *Women United, Women Divided*, Bloomington, IN, 77-98.

New, C., 1971 (1st edn 1873), *Life, Wanderings and Labours in Eastern Africa*, London.

Ngokwey, N., 'Varieties of palm wine among the Lele of Kasai', in Douglas, *Constructive Drinking*, 113-21.

Ngugi wa Thiong'o, 1975, *Petals of Blood*, London.

Nikander, P., *et al.*, 1991, 'Ingredients and Contaminants of Traditional Alcoholic Beverages in Tanzania', *Transactions of the Royal Society of Tropical Hygiene and Medicine*, 85: 133-5.

Nsimbi, M.B., 1956, 'Village Life and Customs in Buganda', *Uganda Journal*, 20: 27-36.

Nout, M.J.R., 1981, 'Aspects of the Manufacture and Consumption of Kenyan Traditional Fermented Beverages' (PhD dissertation), Wageningen.

Obbo, C., 1980, *African Women. Their Struggle for Economic Independence*, London.

Oboler, R., 1985, *Women, Power and Economic Change. The Nandi of Kenya*, Stanford, CA.

Omori, M., 1978, 'Social and Economic Utility of *omuramba*: The Chiga Sorghum Beer', *Senri Ethnological Studies*, 1: 89-104.

Pan, L., 1975, *Alcohol in Colonial Africa,* Uppsala.

Parker, E. and E. Noble, 'Drinking Practices and Cognitive Functioning', in Gross, *Alcoholic Intoxication and Withdrawal*, vol. IIIb, 377-88.

Parkin, D., 1972, *Palms, Wine and Witnesses: Public Spirit and Private Gain in an African Community*, London.

Parpart, J. and K. Staudt (eds), 1989, *Women and the State in Africa*, Boulder, CO.

Parpart, J. and K. Staudt, 'Women and the State in Africa', in Parpart and Staudt (eds.), *Women and the State in Africa*, 1-19.

Partanen, J., 'Towards a Theory of Intoxication', in Room and Collins (eds), *Alcohol and Disinhibition*, 324-6.

Partanen, J., 1991, *Sociability and Intoxication: Alcohol and Drinking in Kenya, Africa, and the Modern World*, Helsinki.

Peristiany, J., 1939, *Social Institutions of the Kipsigis,* London.

Platt, B. S., 1955, 'Some Traditional Alcoholic Beverages and Their Importance in Indigenous African Communities', *Proceedings of the Nutritionists Society*, 14: 115-24.

Platt, B. S., 1964, 'Biological Ennoblement: Improvement of the Nutritive Value of Foods and Dietary Regimens by Biological Agencies', *Food Technology*, 18: 662-70.

Pratt, C., 1976, *The Critical Phase in Tanzania, 1945-1968. Nyerere and the Emergence of a Socialist Strategy*, Cambridge.

Puritt, P., 1971, 'The Meru of Tanzania: a Study of Their Social and Political Organization', (PhD), University of Illinois at Urbana-Champaign.

Purvis, J.B., 1909, *Through Uganda to Mount Elgon*, London.

Rekdal, O., 1996, 'Money, Milk and Sorghum Beer: Change and Continuity among the Iraqw of Tanzania', *Africa*, 66: 367-85.

Richards, A., F. Sturrock and J. Forth, 1973, *Subsistence to Commercial Farming in Present-day Buganda*, Cambridge.

Robbins, M., 'Problem Drinking and the Integration of Alcohol in Rural Buganda', in Marshall (ed.), *Beliefs, Behaviors and Alcoholic Beverages*, 362-74.

Robertson, C., 1997, *Trouble Showed the Way: Women, Men and Trade in the Nairobi Area, 1890-1990*, Bloomington, IN.

Rodriguez-Torres, D., 1994, 'Lutte pour la vie et lutte pour la ville: Crise urbaine, politique urbaine et pauvreté à Nairobi' (PhD), Bordeaux I.

Rodriguez-Torres, D., 1996, 'De l'informel à l'illégal. La production de Chang'aa à Nairobi (IFRA working paper), Nairobi.

Rodwell, E., n.d., *Sixty Years of Kenya Breweries*, Nairobi.

Roe, E., 1981, 'Who Brews Traditional Beer in Rural Botswana? A Review of the Literature and Policy Analysis', *Botswana Notes and Records*, 13: 45-53.

Rogerson, M. and B. Tucker, 1986, 'Multinational Corporations, the State and Indigenous Beer Production in Central Africa', in C. Dixon *et al.* (eds), *Multinational Corporations and the Third World*, London, 137-58.

Room, R. and G. Collins (eds), 1983, *Alcohol and Disinhibition: Nature and Meaning of the Link*, Rockville, MD.

Room, R., 1984, 'Alcohol and Ethnography: a Case of Problem Deflation?', *Current Anthropology*, 25: 169-80.

Roscoe, J., 1966 (1st edn 1915), *The Northern Bantu. An Account of Some Central African Tribes of the Uganda Protectorate*, London.

Roscoe, J., 1923, *The Bakitara, or Banyoro*, Cambridge.

Roscoe, J., 1924, *The Bagesu and Other Tribes of the Uganda Protectorate*, Cambridge.

Ruhumbika, G., 1968, *Village in Uhuru*, London.

Sangree, W., 1966, *Age, Prayer and Politics in Tiriki, Kenya*, London/New York/Nairobi.

Schoenbrun, D., 1998, *A Green Place, A Good Place. Agrarian Change, Gender and Social Identity in the Great Lakes Region to the 15th Century*, Portsmouth, NH/Oxford.

Schweinfurth, G., 1888, *Emin Pasha in Central Africa* (trans. R. Felkin), London.

Scott, J., 1990, *Domination and the Arts of Resistance: Hidden Transcripts*, New Haven, CT/London.

Sournia, J.-C., 1990, *A History of Alcoholism* (trans. N. Handley and G. Stanton), Oxford.

Southall, A. and P. Gutkind, 1957, *Townsmen in the Making. Kampala and its Suburbs*, Kampala.

Speke, J.H., 1967 (1st edn 1864), *What Led to the Discovery of the Source of the Nile*, London.

Speke, J.H., 1969 (1st edn 1863), *Journal of the Discovery of the Source of the Nile*, London.

Spencer, P., 1988, Maasai of Matapato. A Study of the Rituals of Rebellion, Manchester.

Spring, J. and D. Buss, 1977, 'Three Centuries of Alcohol in the British Diet', *Nature*, 270: 567-72.

Stanley, H.M., 1874, *How I Found Livingstone. Travels, Adventures and Discoveries in Central Africa*, London.

Stanley, H.M., 1988 (1st edn 1879), *Through the Dark Continent: Or, the Sources of the Nile Around the Great Lakes of Equatorial Africa and Down the Livingstone River to the Atlantic Ocean* (2 vols), New York.

Stanley, H.M., 1890, *In Darkest Africa, or the Quest, rescue and retreat of Emin, Governor of Equatoria* (2 vols), New York.

Steinhart, E., 1977, *Conflict and Collaboration: The Kingdoms of Western Uganda, 1890-1907*, Princeton, NJ.

Steinhart, E., 1979, 'The Kingdoms of the March: Speculations on Social and Political Change', in J. Webster (ed.), *Chronology, Migration and Drought in Interlacustrine Africa*, London.

Steinkraus, K., 1979, 'Nutritionally Significant Indigenous Foods Involving an Alcoholic Fermentation'; in Gastineau *et al*, *Fermented Food Beverages*, 36-57.

Stichter, S., 1988, 'The Middle-class Family in Kenya: Changes in Gender Relationships', in S. Stichter and J. Parpart (eds), *Patriarchy and Class. African Women in the Home and the Workforce*, Boulder, CO, 177-203.

Strange, N., 1934, *Kenya Today*, London.

Sutton, J., 1993, 'The Antecedents of the Interlacustrine Kingdoms', *JAH*, 34: 33-64.

Swainson, N., 1980, *The Development of Corporate Capitalism in Kenya, 1918-1977*, London.

Talle, A., 1988, *Women at a Loss: Changes in Maasai Pastoralism and Their Effects on Gender Relations*, Stockholm.

Tanganyika Provincial Commissioners, 1931, *Reports on Native Administration for 1930*, Dar es Salaam.

Tanganyika Provincial Commissioners, 1954, *Reports on Native Administration for 1930: Intoxicating Liquor Report*, Dar es Salaam.

Tantala, R., 1989, 'The Early History of Kitara in Western Uganda: Process Models of Religious and Political Change' (PhD), University of Wisconsin at Madison.

Taylor, J. and S. Joustra, 1996, 'Sorghum Beer Technology' (2 vols), University of Pretoria/CSIR.

Thomson, J., 1968 (1st edn 1881), *To the Central African Lakes and Back: the narrative of the Royal Geographical Society's East Central African Expedition, 1878-80* (2 vols), London.

Thomson, J., 1968 (1st edn 1885), *Through Masailand. A Journey of Exploration Among the Snowclad Volcanic Mountains and Strange Tribes of Eastern Equatorial Africa*, London.

Tignor, R. , 1972, 'The Maasai Warriors: Pattern Maintenance and Violence in Colonial Kenya', *JAH*, 13: 271-90.

Todhunter, E., 'A Historical Perspective on Fermentation Biochemistry and Nutrition', in Gastineau *et al.*, *Fermented Food Beverages*, 83-97.

Bibliography

Tripp, A., 1997, *Changing the Rules. The Politics of Liberalization and the Informal Economy in Tanzania*, Berkeley, CA/Los Angeles, CA/London.

Vincent, J., 1971, *African Elite. The Big Men of a Small Town*, London/New York.

Waller, R., 1985, 'Economic and Social Relations in the Central Rift Valley: The Maa-speakers and their Neighbours in the Nineteenth Century', in B. Ogot (ed.), *Kenya in the Nineteenth Century*, Nairobi, 83-151.

Waller, R., 'Kidongoi's Kin. Prophecy and Power in Maasailand', in Anderson and Johnson (eds.), *Revealing Prophets*, 28-64.

Wallgren, H. and H. Barry, 1970, *Actions of Alcohol* (2 vols), Amsterdam/London/New York.

Wallman, S., 1996, *Kampala Women Getting By. Wellbeing in the Time of AIDS*, London/Kampala/Athens, OH.

Walsh, M., 1985, 'Village, State and Traditional Authority in Usangu', in R. Abrahams (ed.), *Villages, Villagers and the State in Modern Tanzania*, Cambridge, 135-67.

Weeks, C., 1929, *Alcohol and Human Life*, London.

West, M., 1992, '"Equal Rights for All Civilized Men": Elite Africans and the Quest for European Liquor in Colonial Zimbabwe, 1924-65'. *International Review of Social History*, 37: 376-97.

West, M., 1997, 'Liquor and Libido: "Joint Drinking" and the Politics of Sexual Control in Colonial Zimbabwe, 1920s-1950s', *Journal of Social History*, 31: 645-67.

Weule, K., 1909, *Native Life in East Africa* (trans. A. Werner), London.

White, L., 1990, *The Comforts of Home. Prostitution in Colonial Nairobi*, Chicago,IL/London.

Whyte, S., 1997, *Questioning Misfortune. The Pragmatics of Uncertainty in Eastern Uganda*, Cambridge.

Willis, J., 1999, 'Enkurma Sikitoi: Commoditization, Drink and Power Among the Maasai', *IJAHS*, 32: 339-57.

Wilson, G., 1938, 'An Introduction to Nyakyusa Society', *Bantu Studies*, 10.

Wilson, M., 1963 (1st edn 1951), *Good Company. A Study of Nyakyusa Age-Villages*, Boston, MA.

Wilson, M., 1957, *Rituals of Kinship Among the Nyakyusa*, London/New York/Toronto.

Wilson, M., 1959, *Communal Rituals of the Nyakyusa*, London/New York/Toronto.

Wilson, M., 1977, *For Men and Elders. Changes in the Relations of Generations and of Men and Women among the Nyakyusa and Ngonde*, London.

Wood, S. and J. Mansfield, 'Ethanol and Disinhibition: Physiological and Behavioral Links', in Room and Collins, *Alcohol and Disinhibition*, 4-23.

Wright, M., 1972, 'Nyakyusa Cults and Politics in the Later Nineteenth Century', in T. Ranger and I. Kimambo (eds), *The Historical Study of Religion in Africa*, London, 153-70.

Wright, M., 1993, *Strategies of Slaves and Women. Life-Stories from East/Central Africa*, New York/London.

Wrigley, C., 1996, *Kingship and State. The Buganda Dynasty*, Cambridge.

Ylikahri, R. and K. Eriksson, 1985, 'Physiological and Medical Problems Associated with Excessive Alcohol Intake', in G. Birch and M. Lindley, *Alcoholic Beverages*, Barking and New York, 183-200.

Index